FROM MAIN STREET TO MALL

AMERICAN BUSINESS, POLITICS, AND SOCIETY

Series editors: Andrew Wender Cohen, Pamela Walker Laird, Mark H. Rose, and Elizabeth Tandy Shermer

Books in the series American Business, Politics, and Society explore the relationships over time between governmental institutions and the creation and performance of markets, firms, and industries large and small. The central theme of this series is that politics, law, and public policy—understood broadly to embrace not only lawmaking but also the structuring presence of governmental institutions—has been fundamental to the evolution of American business from the colonial era to the present. The series aims to explore, in particular, developments that have enduring consequences.

A complete list of books in the series is available from the publisher.

FROM MAIN STREET TO MALL

THE RISE AND FALL
OF THE AMERICAN DEPARTMENT STORE

VICKI HOWARD

PENN

UNIVERSITY OF PENNSYLVANIA PRESS

PHILADELPHIA

Published by
University of Pennsylvania Press
Philadelphia, Pennsylvania 19104-4112
www.upenn.edu/pennpress

Printed in the United States of America
on acid-free paper

10 9 8 7 6 5 4 3 2 1

A catalogue record for this book is available from the
Library of Congress
ISBN 978-0-8122-4728-2

In memory of David A. Howard, 1938–2011

CONTENTS

INTRODUCTION

I N 1947, crowds of Houston shoppers stood on Main Street outside Foley's new downtown flagship department store, waiting for the doors to open. With its buff-colored windowless facade rising high above show-window canopies that ran around the entire perimeter, the building must have seemed the pinnacle of modernity, marking Houston's place in the postwar national scene and signaling a commitment to downtown commerce and the future. Considered "revolutionary" and "radical" by contemporary observers, the six-and-a-half-story building (later expanded to ten) took up an entire city block and featured air conditioning to fight the southern humidity, a five-floor garage with store access by tunnel to attract suburban shoppers, and rapid-moving escalators for the seven million transactions it expected the first year. Today, almost seventy years later, much has changed. The building—which became a Macy's in 2006—was recently shuttered and demolished, its owners opting to put up office towers instead of trying to resuscitate downtown Houston as a shopping destination.[1]

Although not one of the early "palaces of consumption" that came to define mass retailing in major urban centers in the late nineteenth century, Foley's had a trajectory that was fairly representative of the life of an American department store. Originating as a small-town Texas dry goods operation in 1900, the store passed out of the Foley brothers' hands to another family in 1917 and by the next decade was the largest department store in Houston, its new Main Street building offering some of the same amenities available in major urban centers like New York or Chicago. Shopping at Foley's, with its beauty salon, restaurant, and auditorium for special events or community meetings, could be "an all-day affair" in the 1920s and

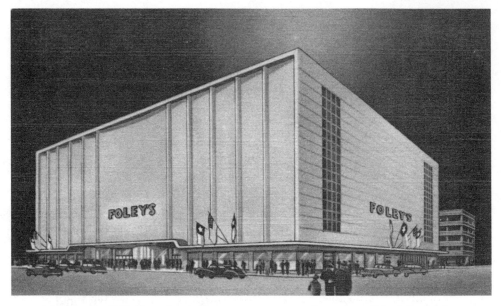

FIGURE 1. In 1947, like other department stores across the country, Foley's invested in downtown, building a modern new outlet at Main and Lamar in Houston's central business district. Author's collection. Courtesy of Lake County (Ill.) Discovery Museum, Curt Teich Postcard Archives.

1930s. Continued investment in downtown Houston after World War II put the store at the center of social activity and political change brought about by the civil rights movement. As a major commercial institution, Foley's was part of the vital fabric of this growing southern city. While other Houston stores relocated to malls beyond the I-610 beltway, Foley's flagship remained, even as the firm also ventured out into the surrounding suburbs in the early 1960s and across Texas in following decades.[2]

In 1947, Foley's was still a downtown store and a much-beloved local institution, yet like many other traditional or conventional department stores at the time, it was no longer independent. Two years earlier, Federated Department Stores had acquired it as part of an aggressive postwar expansion campaign led by the holding company's president, Fred Lazarus Jr. Foley's new building was the product of Lazarus's national vision, one still characterized by a commitment to downtown. More broadly, it was also a product of postwar corporate expansion, a force that would quickly take such institutions out of the cities and into the suburbs.[3] Despite some past variations specific to the South and to Houston, Foley's was following a national trend.

In many ways, the rise and fall of Foley's is the story of the creation and transformation of the American department store industry. By World War I, a national department store industry was in place, consisting of individual merchants, department store executives, and their trade organizations. These figures shaped the cultural meaning of the department store and helped determine its economic trajectory. They also made decisions that refashioned downtowns, transforming their geography and affecting their vitality and symbolic resonance.[4] They benefited from and helped drive urban growth from the late nineteenth through the early twentieth century, then took part in the major decentralization movements after World War II. By embracing postwar urban renewal, suburban branch expansion, and shopping center development at the same time as they encouraged automobility, leaders of the department store industry undermined the economic prosperity of downtown.[5] Their decisions remade the commercial landscape, facilitating suburban sprawl for better or for worse.

With the post–World War II expansion of massive holding companies and department store chains, region no longer mattered much. Massive mergers in the 1980s resulted in the loss of local nameplates across the country, in small towns, provincial cities, and even in major urban centers like New York and Chicago. After the 2005 megamerger of Federated and May Department Stores, Foley's and many others, such as Marshall Field's, Hecht's, Strawbridge's, and Filene's were rebranded as Macy's and ceased to exist as local or regional nameplates. The experience of department store shopping became the same pretty much everywhere. Lost stores like Foley's became the subject of local nostalgia. Former shoppers remembered the Texas firm fondly, reviling the new, standardized Macy's that took its place. "Foley's was more than a department store to Houston," claimed a recent local historical society exhibition titled "Foley's Department Store: Houston's Community Partner 1900–2005."[6]

After a long good-bye lasting well into the postwar period, American department stores eventually parted ways with downtown. A few cities have successfully maintained their vital historic central business districts, most notably world-class cities such as San Francisco or New York, where a few traditional department stores like Nordstrom's, Bloomingdale's, Saks Fifth

Avenue, and Macy's still hold court. Small-town Main Streets continue to engage in trade and serve local residents, but without the traditional department stores that had long served as anchors for their business districts. Some downtowns have survived the loss of their independent department stores and department store chains, having reinvented themselves as leisure centers for certain portions of their populations. Many cities have re-created downtown in a lucrative nostalgic guise through "festival market-places" such as Faneuil Hall in Boston, Baltimore's Harborplace, Milwau-kee's Grand Avenue, and San Francisco's Ghirardelli Square. Department stores, however, do not have a place in these reinvented marketplaces, focused as they are upon tourism and leisure pursuits. Traditional depart-ment stores have even disappeared from urban malls, as in the case of Philadelphia's Gallery at Market East, which opened to great success in 1977 and initially attracted such solid anchors as Strawbridge & Clothier, Gimbels, and the chain J. C. Penney. All are now gone from this struggling urban mall, replaced by discount big-box stores like Kmart.[7] Downtown Philadelphia's Market Street, once a leading shopping district and home to the famous Wanamaker's, Lit Brothers, and many others, boasts only a single traditional department store—the national chain Macy's.

For the most part, in the early twenty-first century, shopping does not mean going downtown to peruse the wares of these luxurious, multistoried palaces of consumption. Instead, in metropolitan and nonmetropolitan areas alike, it means driving (or shopping on the Internet—e-commerce sales in 2011 were $194 billion, or 4.7 percent of total sales; quarterly e-commerce reports in 2013 ranged from 5.5 to 6 percent of total sales). For a majority of the population, wants and needs are satisfied by a trip to a neighborhood or community shopping center or the nearest regional shopping center anchored by a discount department store chain. "Power centers" pull together several big-box stores, like Target or Costco, and "category killers" like Home Depot or OfficeMax, so called because of their ability to do in smaller specialty stores selling their line of merchandise.[8] And Wal-Mart, for many years now the nation's largest retailer, has become a mainstay for most shoppers in rural, suburban, and, increasingly, urban areas.[9] Although a discount department store in name, Wal-Mart has come to be understood as the antithesis of a department store—a no-frills mass distributor of low-priced and low-quality general merchandise that achieved its success by driving out small businesses and traditional retailers through cutthroat competition and sometimes illegal means. Beginning in the late 1980s, with the introduction of Wal-Mart supercenters—hypermarkets that included a full-service supermarket—shoppers could fulfill all their needs, from food, pharmaceuticals, and clothing to garden supplies, furniture, and hardware, all under one roof, something once claimed only by the traditional department store. Today, department stores are no longer on the cutting edge of retail, nor are they major players in the lives of cities or even suburban commercial developments, as are these newer retail formats.

Although they have been called "dinosaurs" for many decades and their death has been predicted by different camps over the years, department stores have only recently gathered attention as historic or nostalgic artifacts. Since the origin of the department store in the nineteenth century, its meaning and place in American society has changed over time, once inspiring fear and antipathy, then fascination, and finally nostalgia. Such shifts have been evident in popular culture, as department stores wove their way into fiction, newspapers and magazines, film, and cartoons. Today, the local department store looms large in the popular imagination. The reaction to the closure of Foley's and subsequent loss of its downtown flagship store in Houston reveals nostalgia for local institutions, for the role these firms played in the larger community, and for the downtown of memory. As is often the case with nostalgia, however, memory tells us more about contemporary concerns than about the past. Historic nameplates associated with independent firms, the loss of which generated widespread nostalgia, were often long-standing members of either massive holding companies or department store groups, as we shall see.

Department stores have attracted much attention outside the world of academic history. Store closures have resulted in a veritable industry for nostalgic accounts of local institutions, attractively produced with many photographs of store interiors and exteriors, window displays, and signage, as well as fondly remembered landmarks, store brands, and special services or traditions associated with holidays. In addition, since the beginning of the department store industry, marketing or retail scholars have published countless articles on store performance. Such accounts have portrayed changes in the industry in cyclical terms, with retail firms running a natural course of development. Whether part of a life cycle or part of the "wheel of retailing," these descriptive models focus on the inner workings of the business and on the role of competition, separate from larger historical forces that are considered here.[10] This book breaks with that perspective and is ultimately concerned with different questions, namely the role of government, business, and consumers in the success and failure of an industry and a particular way of shopping. Here, department stores are considered as social as well as economic institutions.

In the past, historical work on the American department store has focused on the fashionable, large urban department stores of Philadelphia, New York, and Chicago, stores such as Wanamaker's, Macy's, and Marshall Field's.[11] According to this perspective, nineteenth-century department stores were harbingers of the rise of a national commercial society. They introduced spectacles of light, color, music, and imagination, becoming symbols of a new consumer ethic based on spending, not the rural values of thrift and saving. Emphasizing the rise of the big, urban retailer, most of these histories end either before or just as branch stores and shopping malls began their serious challenge to central business districts in the early post-war period.[12] More glamorous, better documented, and seemingly of greater cultural significance, the metropolitan department store has right-fully attracted serious attention from historians. But it is important to include nonmetropolitan mass retailers in the narrative of the decline of the local department store.[13] Doing so not only creates a more complete picture of an industry but the result also challenges the time frame or peri-odization of so-called retail revolutions. By putting the decline of tradi-tional emporia, large and small, in the context of the rise of discounters and category killers in more recent decades, this book also hopes to give a more complete account of the trajectory of the industry as a whole. Bring-ing in the smaller department stores found outside of major urban centers suggests that change happened more slowly and in a messier way than once thought. Rather than a "retail revolution," as it has been characterized, the rise of the department store, the process of consolidation, and the demise of "the local store" took place in a gradual and uneven fashion across met-ropolitan areas and small towns.[14]

Most people probably have a general understanding of why these com-mercial enterprises are now gone. The rise and fall of different retail forms, like the mom-and-pop shop or the local department store, is widely seen as a natural progression, for good or for bad. More formally, this retail revolution has been attributed to the "creative destruction" of capitalism, in which older forms are superseded by new, following the inexorable logic of the market. Just as mom-and-pop stores battled department stores in the late nineteenth century, department stores faced Wal-Mart at the end of the twentieth century. The recent rising tide of nostalgia, however, raises the question of responsibility. Popular explanations point to suburban shopping malls, blame Wal-Mart, and tie the loss of local stores to a broader decline of American cities and their grand public spaces.[15] These explanations are not wrong, but they leave out an important element—the state.

The decline of local department stores was tied to the actions (and inaction) of federal, state, and local policy makers, regulators, jurists, legislators, and lobbyists. Broad structural changes in the United States economy of course shaped the evolution of department stores from the beginning. Post–Civil War industrial expansion aided the rise of mass retailing. Corporate consolidation in the middle decades of the twentieth century transformed the department store industry. Since the 1970s, faith in the logic of the market has left an indelible mark. Judging from the outpouring of nostalgia for lost downtown stores and Main Street institutions in recent decades, many believe the changes—whatever their cause—have been for the worse. A Wal-Mart world, many contend, is a poor substitution for the vibrant local commerce of the past. In his 1992 autobiography, *Made in America*, even Wal-Mart founder Sam Walton felt compelled to counter charges that his chain had destroyed small-town America, a milieu out of which he had risen: "What happened was absolutely a necessary and inevitable evolution in retailing, as inevitable as the replacement of the buggy by the car and the disappearance of the buggy whip makers. The small stores were just destined to disappear, at least in the numbers that once existed, because the whole thing is driven by customers, who are free to choose where they shop."[16]

Walton's words aside, transformations in retailing were never inevitable but rather were contingent, dependent on diverse historical actors and the changing frameworks within which they operated. Consumer demand played a role in these changes, as Walton asserted, but so did policy makers, legislators, and jurists, as well as the broader retail industry and its many lobbyists. All the pieces for a discount world were in fact in place by the early 1960s, but it was not until the 1970s, with the rise of neoliberalism, that these pieces were able to come together. The subsequent death of the department store fits into this larger process characterized by privatization, deregulation, and decline of social provisioning. According to critic David Harvey, neoliberal thinking held that social good was best served by "liberating individual entrepreneurial freedoms and skills within an institutional framework characterized by strong private property rights, free markets,

and free trade." The federal government's role was to uphold that framework, keeping its interventions to a minimum. The neoliberal political and
economic practices that were the product of that thinking led to unprecedented income inequalities and immense concentration of corporate
power. Over the past thirty years, a select few amassed immense fortunes,
even controlling entire sectors as in the case of retail and the Walton family.
Neoliberalism, and the bargain consumers made with its practices, made
the Waltons the richest family in the United States, worth $93 billion in
2013.[17]

The rise of the discount industry after World War II and the subsequent
death of the traditional department store at the end of the century went
hand in hand. After strenuous opposition to these "bootleg" merchants,
the department store industry came to terms with discounters by the early
1960s, just as the new industry began to overtake it. In response to competition from discounters, department stores began to embrace their methods.
As inflation soared in the early 1970s and the economy fizzled, however,
traditional retailers struggled to keep up with their stripped down, low-cost
competitors. Deregulation aided the spread of discounting with the passage
of the Consumer Goods Pricing Act in 1975, which unshackled the industry
from pricing legislation that had protected traditional retailers and manufacturers. By the 1980s, weak antitrust enforcement and lack of industry
oversight allowed for massive consolidation in the department store industry. Financially unsound mergers resulted in the bankruptcy and closure of
many historic firms with long traditions in their local communities. In this
context, discount department stores like Wal-Mart, which could claim to
sell everything under the sun under one roof as had the great nineteenth-
century palaces of consumption, were able to flourish. Nostalgic out-
pourings for the lost local department store did nothing to challenge this.

CHAPTER 1

The Palace of Consumption

Such stores as the Silks and Dress Goods, the Laces and Suits,
the Groceries and Horse Goods . . . set thrifty buyers on the jump.
A dozen other places in the store are just as active. We mean that
before long there shall not be a dull corner in the building. Be a little
patient.
    —Manly M. Gillam, Advertisement for Hilton, Hughes &
    Company, 1895

THE massive, ornate "palaces of consumption" of the late nineteenth
century were in some ways the Wal-Marts of their era. Their founding
families—with such names as Wanamaker, Straus (successors to Rowland
Macy's retail legacy), Gimbel, Filene, Hutzler, and Bamberger—joined
forces with the wealthiest in the nation. Their mode of buying and selling
challenged traditional forms of distribution, generating opposition and
cries of monopoly from manufacturers and single-line merchants at the
end of the nineteenth century.[1] Shoppers, however, saw no threat. Like
today's Wal-Mart customers, they flocked through the doors to find everything under one roof at prices that undercut specialty stores. Innovations
in advertising, merchandising, and display beckoned. Unlike Wal-Mart,
however, the elegant doors of places like Marshall Field's in Chicago were
a portal to luxurious amenities and services. Also unlike Wal-Mart, these
palaces of consumption were local institutions. Their founding families
were deeply involved in the social and economic goings-on of their home

cities; their names came to adorn college buildings, streets, and philanthropic foundations. Moreover, the appearance of big urban department
stores did not obliterate Main Streets and Market Streets across the country
but instead enlivened them. Where the big merchants built their multistoried stone and brick emporia, central business districts appeared. Streetcar
lines were laid and city thoroughfares grew crowded with foot traffic and
vehicles.[2] When merchants moved within the city, retail districts followed.
Such stores in fact helped create downtown, making it *the* place to be.

The introduction and expansion of this urban institution spanned the
second half of the nineteenth century and corresponded with the great economic and social transformations of urbanization, industrialization, and
immigration. The mass distribution counterpart to mass production,
department stores facilitated the rise of a consumer society in major urban
centers. By 1908, advertisers were heralding the department store as "the
greatest channel for distribution of merchandise today."[3] Retail transformations initiated in cities like New York, Philadelphia, and Chicago spread
across the country as "progressive" merchants in smaller cities and towns
also came to admire the department store's ability to lower the costs of
distribution. Older trade practices, however, hung on in these smaller communities. Even in big cities, the economic effect of large emporia was
limited—nothing on the scale of mass retailing today. With few exceptions,
these early departmentalized emporia were single-unit independents that
could not command a national or even a regional market, except perhaps
in their wholesale divisions. Most retail trade in the nation still took place
in financially precarious mom-and-pop businesses and in the general stores
that continued to serve rural areas.[4] The department store, however, had
been invented.

Origins

Department stores were the first mass retailers, but they were not the first
mass distributors. As the speed, regularity, and dependability of transportation and communication improved in the second half of the nineteenth
century, wholesalers became the first to use the modern multiunit enterprise to market goods on a mass scale. Well-financed wholesalers began to
dominate the dry goods, drug, grocery, and hardware trade. By 1870, full-
line, full-service wholesalers who owned their inventory replaced the commission agents or jobbers who had previously handled distribution for a

fee without purchasing goods from the manufacturers. Wholesalers like Butler Brothers catered specifically to the new mass retailers, though some department stores preferred to buy directly from manufacturers in order to avoid the added cost of a middleman. Some became wholesalers themselves in order to cut out a link in the distribution chain. No matter which path they took, department stores moved toward tightening their hold on the supply of goods, cutting off the power of traditional wholesalers. Not surprisingly, with the emergence of different forms of mass retailing, such as mail order and department stores, the market share of wholesalers fell off after the early 1880s.[5]

Out of this context, the New York wholesaler/retailer A. T. Stewart developed a new system of merchandising that eventually transformed the way goods were bought, sold, and even manufactured. Beginning with a small shop in the 1820s, the Irish-born wholesaler-retailer built his famous white "marble palace" in 1846, a massive four-story Anglo-Italianate dry goods emporium on lower Broadway. Business flourished, and in 1862 Stewart spent $2.75 million of his fortune building "The Greatest Store in the World." At Broadway and Tenth, this "iron palace" became a major attraction in New York with its imposing cast-iron facade painted to look like marble, hundreds of plate-glass windows, a grand staircase, central rotunda, and domed skylight. More than just an architectural wonder filled with beautiful things to admire and buy, A. T. Stewart's introduced many of the features and policies that would become standard in all big department stores by the end of the nineteenth century.[6]

Stewart helped establish three major principles of modern selling—the one-price system, rapid stock turn, and departmentalized organization of goods. A set price eliminated the tradition of haggling, an age-old practice that required skill on the part of the seller and surveillance on the part of the owner. The one-price system was key to growth, allowing merchants to hire inexperienced clerks and cut labor costs. Good stock turn was also crucial as it represented the store's ability to free up its capital to reinvest in more merchandise. Calculated as the number of times the store's inventory turned over in a year (was sold), stock turn became a much-studied figure by modern, progressive merchants as the department store field matured in the early twentieth century. Other early innovations during this period included a purpose-built, multifloored building in a central location; a free entrance policy, meaning customers could browse at will; customer services such as merchandise return, delivery, restrooms, parcel wrapping, and

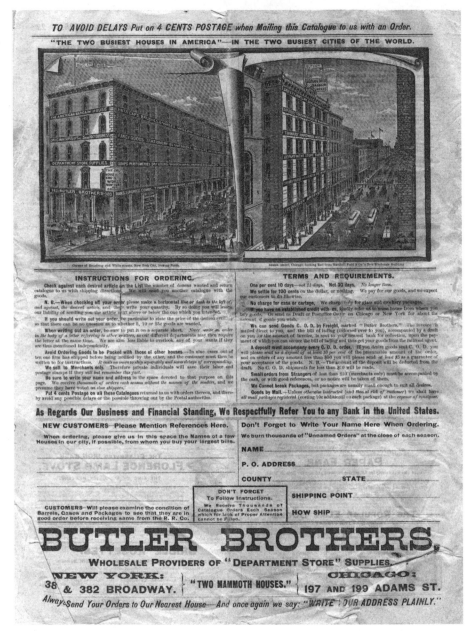

FIGURE 2. A prominent full-line wholesaler, Butler Brothers supplied department stores across the country. Advertising Ephemera Collection, #A0673, Emergence of Advertising in America On-line Collection, John W. Hartman Center for Sales, Advertising & Marketing History, Duke University David M. Rubenstein Rare Book & Manuscript Library.

checking; low markup; cash selling or short credit terms; large sales volume; centralization of nonselling functions; and stock clearance through bargain sales.[7]

Departmentalization became the defining feature of this new form of distribution, something that clearly distinguished it both from the jumble of the general store and from the narrowness of the specialty shop. Keeping voluminous accounts, the new type of retailer tracked profits and losses by departments—administrative units organized around the different lines of goods. Departmentalization also aided growth, permitting expansion on a scale not attainable by the general merchant. It allowed merchants to keep separate accounts for different kinds of stock and provided the statistics for dropping unprofitable goods and departments, as well as ineffective employees. Later, with the rise of ready-to-wear, merchants faced increased pressure to departmentalize, as new lines required differing sales appeals and distinct display and sales areas.[8]

Stewart's departmentalization, however, was limited largely to dry goods, which were extremely popular in the age of home and custom production. Standard dry goods included muslins, calicoes, silks and satins, black goods for mourning, velvets, worsted goods, and laces, as well as embroidery and edging, linings, and notions—such things as needles, thread, and dressmakers' tape.[9] Dry goods emporia like A. T. Stewart's and dry goods departments in major department stores also sold plush carpets and rugs, soft velvet chairs and couches, furniture covers, table scarves, curtains, draperies, and swags for shelves, mantels, and doorways. Women were the main consumers of these lines, and A. T. Stewart was one of the first merchants to make special appeals to them to ensure their patronage. Around these goods, he created a new kind of shopping environment for the female market, one that big-city department stores developed even further by the late nineteenth century. He and other dry goods merchants supplied the socially important cascades of fabric necessary to create a fashionable, middle-class parlor and woman's dress in the Victorian era. Dressmaking and millinery departments, with craftswomen on staff, catered to middle-class women by the 1910s in major big-city stores like Macy's, Gimbels, Filene's, and Jordan Marsh. A woman planning her wardrobe and decorating her home shopped from an amazing array of imported and American factory-produced textiles at Stewart's palace and even at smaller dry goods shops. While an emerging ready-to-wear industry supplied these emporia with such things as boys' clothing, cloaks, and ladies' underwear, sales of ready-to-wear clothing in department stores would not outpace fabric sales until 1920.[10]

Modern selling, as it took place in the many departments under Stewart's roof, was tied to the innovative policy of free access. Stewart's dry goods emporium became a new kind of place in the city where white middle-class women could stop in to relax, browse without buying, and socialize. By the mid-1890s, department stores were a major source of urban leisure for these women (and employment for others), a phenomenon that generated humor in the press with accounts of "the bread-winning end of the family" having their dinner hour delayed as their wives did their Christmas shopping and being "gently persuaded into putting out a little more money." Stewart put amenities in place that actually encouraged such previously frowned-on behavior. For example, he was the first in New York to introduce revolving stools in front of counters, a feature that allegedly drew women shoppers from miles around just to rest their weary feet on shopping trips. Staffed by saleswomen and frequented largely by women shoppers, department stores would eventually become known as an "Adamless Eden," a haven of sorts for middle-class women in the city, though not, perhaps, for the women who served them. As it was later remembered, Stewart's iron palace served as "a great women's club and was the place for hundreds of appointments each day for women who desired to see each other."[11]

While A. T. Stewart was one of the better-known innovators of the department store form, other important figures joined him in this early rough-and-tumble period of mass retailing and wholesaling. H. B. Claflin was his main competitor. In 1864, Claflin was reported to have (likely grossly exaggerated) sales of $72 million. Although less prominent than Stewart, his dry goods wholesale business, then organized as Claflin, Mellin and Co., outsold Stewart's better-known wholesale-retail firm. The two men's tremendous success came in part out of their shared willingness to pursue self-interest ruthlessly. Stewart gained his position as the third richest man in the country, following William B. Astor and Cornelius Vanderbilt, through his merchandising genius but also through a calculating, hardnosed approach to credit, and strict control over a labor force that eventually reached two thousand. One anonymous merchant in 1877 described Stewart as "one of the meanest merchants that ever lived." Unlike Stewart, however, self-interest was not a part of Claflin's public persona.[12] Upon Claflin's death in 1885, a memorial piece in the *New York Times* praised the merchant, contrasting his personality and policies with that of his famous contemporary. As portrayed in the press, Claflin was much loved by his contemporaries and was believed to have given many dry goods men across the country their start by providing training as well as capital. He was also believed by contemporaries to be liberal with the merchants who were his customers, giving larger credit and longer time than Stewart. Described as having a benevolent face and being "free from all airs, from all selfishness," he was well known at the time for his trusting disposition and generosity, which also got him into trouble with hucksters. Press accounts, however, reveal a different assessment of the merchant's character not visible in the laudatory piece published after his death. In 1870, for example, Claflin's firm was investigated for selling shoddy blankets and other items at inflated prices to a jail to supply prisoners. At one point, he was also indicted for smuggling silk. After decades of double-dealing, scandal, and close encounters with the law, his firm was incorporated in 1890 and the business was carried on by Horace Claflin's son John.[13]

Although both Claflin and Stewart were major figures in the history of nineteenth-century distribution, they never saw their businesses become full-fledged department stores. The innovation of chain organization, however, gave Claflin's original firm greater longevity. By the turn of the twentieth century, H. B. Claflin's was a multiunit, centrally owned operation, though it was not standardized in the manner of the tea and coffee chains of the time. Lacking the tight organizational structure, management supervision, and accounting control methods of later chains, Claflin's was more subject to the personalities and idiosyncrasies of its proprietors as well as to the vagaries of the market. Personal troubles continued to follow the firm. Claflin's partner, for example, died of a chloroform overdose while being treated for a morphine addiction. Eventually, H. B. Claflin's overextended itself and collapsed, but it was reorganized to become one of the first department store chains in 1916, the Associated Dry Goods Corporation.[14]

As the strange story of H. B. Claflin's suggests, the path toward the big department store chains of our era was not straightforward, nor was it populated only by success. The end to A. T. Stewart's story supports this as well. Within two decades after his death in 1876, Stewart's massive fortune was drained and his international merchandising organization run into the ground by the two executors of his estate, his legal advisor Henry Hilton and his business partner William Libbey, both of whom took advantage of the third executor, Stewart's widow. Hilton and Libbey reorganized the firm with themselves as partners and ran the dry goods emporium under its original name. In 1882, their partnership was liquidated after six years of inept management, poor judgment, and several scandals involving Henry Hilton's exclusion of prominent Jews from a hotel he owned, a feminist protest against his reneging on a promised philanthropic gift of a working women's hotel, and his inaction after the theft of A. T. Stewart's corpse from his crypt. Over the next fourteen years, Henry Hilton put Stewart's fortune into two more reincarnations of the original company, E. J. Denning & Co., followed by Hilton, Hughes & Co., both which drew on the good name of their more famous predecessor by always including the phrase "Successors to A. T. Stewart & Co." below their name in advertisements and catalogs.[15]

Although A. T. Stewart was a department store pioneer in many ways, his influence should not be overstated. The rise to mass retailing did not occur quickly or cleanly. Pushcart vendors and peddlers still cried their wares in front of the Irish merchant's imposing iron palace; single-line specialty shops and general stores offering book credit continued to battle for his customers; and some New York City dry goods stores still employed the "closed door" system, which prevented browsing at one's leisure. Stewart himself held on to older methods of trade to some degree. Ultimately he was a transitional figure, never embracing many of the innovations that were commonplace by the last decades of the 1800s. Stewart did not engage in aggressive, specialized advertising and promotions or employ window displays, as most department stores would by the end of the nineteenth century. Nor did he use loss leaders, items duplicitously advertised for sale at or below cost to pull shoppers into the store, as was sometimes done. And importantly, the firm did not sell hard lines like furniture, which signaled the transition from dry goods to department store.[16]

Close successors, however, like Hilton, Hughes & Co., made the full transition to the modern department store. Occupying the Stewart store building on Broadway and Fourth, Hilton, Hughes & Co. undertook several innovations in merchandising and advertising. It offered the same luxurious shopping experience as had the original dry goods emporium but added more lines, becoming in effect a true department store rather than simply a departmentalized dry goods emporium like Stewart's. Financed by A. T. Stewart's executor, Henry Hilton, its sole proprietor became Hilton's youngest and favored son, Albert B. Hilton, who sought to make the store a leader in the New York dry goods market.[17]

ALPHABETICAL LIST of DEPARTMENTS

Art Goods,	Basement
Awnings,	Main Floor
Baby Carriages,	Basement
Bedding, Mattresses, etc.,	Main Floor
Blankets and Quilts,	Basement
Books	"
Boys' Clothing,	1st Floor
Calicoes and Wash Fabrics,	Basement
Carpets, Oil Cloths, etc.,	2d Floor
Children's Clothing,	1st "
Chinaware and Crockery,	Basement
Cloaks and Suits,	1st Floor
Clocks,	Basement
Cloths and Men's Suitings,	Main Floor
Corsets,	1st "
Curtains,	Main "
Cutlery,	Basement
Dress Goods,	Main Floor
" " (Popular)	" "
Dresses (Ready-made),	1st "
Dressmaking,	4th "
Embroideries,	Main "
Flannels,	" "
Furs,	1st "
Furniture,	1st "
" (Bedroom),	2d "
Gentlemen's Furnishing,	Main "
Glassware,	Basement
Gloves (Ladies' and Children's),	Main Floor
" (Gentlemen's)	" "
Hardware,	Basement
Hosiery and Underwear,	Main Floor
House Furnishing,	Basement
Infants' Apparel,	1st Floor
Japanese Goods,	Basement
Jewelry,	Main Floor
Knit Goods,	1st Floor
Laces,	Main "
Ladies' Collars and Cuffs,	" "
" Handkerchiefs,	" "
" Hosiery and Underwear,	" "
" Muslin Underwear,	1st "
" Suits and Cloaks,	1st "
Lamps,	Basement
Leather Goods,	"
" " (small articles),	Main Floor
Linens,	" "
Linings,	" "
Millinery, trimmed,	1st "
" untrimmed,	Main "
Misses' Suits and Cloaks,	1st "
Mourning Goods,	Main "
Muslins (Domestics),	Basement
" (Fine and Dotted,	Main Floor
Notions,	" "
Perfumery, Toilet Articles,	" "
Parquet Flooring,	2d "
Pictures and Frames,	Basement
Ready-made Garments,	1st Floor
Ribbons,	Main "
Shawls,	1st "
Shoes,	Main "
Silks,	" "
Silverware,	Basement
Sporting Goods,	"
Stationery,	Main Floor
Suits and Cloaks,	1st "
Tinware,	Basement
Toys,	"
Trimmings,	Main Floor
Trunks and Valises,	Basement
Umbrellas and Parasols,	Main Floor
Underwear and Hosiery,	" "
Upholstery,	" "
Velvets and Plushes,	" "
Window Shades,	" "
Wooden and Willow Ware,	Basement
Worsteds and Yarns,	Main Floor
Wrappers and Tea Gowns,	1st "

FIGURE 3. Hilton, Hughes & Co. made the leap from dry goods emporium to department store, carrying everything from baby carriages, blankets, and books to shoes, silks, and silverware. Hilton, Hughes & Co., *A Visit to Hilton, Hughes & Co., Broadway, New York: Leaves from an Artist's Sketch Book* (New York: Giles Company, lith., ca. 1895). Baker Old Class Collection, Baker Library, Harvard Business School.

Surviving illustrations of Hilton, Hughes & Co. allow a more detailed imagining of the selling space than the (also now lost) A. T. Stewart's. Free entry, a marker of the department store form, was likely the policy at Hilton, Hughes & Co. An artist's depiction of shoppers in different departments in the early 1890s shows women fingering wares and talking to salesclerks, but it also depicts them in nonpurchasing activities (Figure 4). Well-dressed women in small groups or pairs linger on staircases; a mother and small daughter look over a third-floor banister at the busy scene in the open atrium below. On the main floor was the staple of its business— general dry goods. The large, well-lit, open space under the rotunda on the main floor set a luxurious stage for women to browse the vast counters housing the silk, velvet, glove, and ribbon departments. The ground floor was a prime space for what would later be understood as impulse buying and was stocked with goods appealing to female shoppers. This level also housed the shoe department, jewelry and small wares, and gentlemen's furnishings. Up the stairs on the first floor were the dress and cloak salesrooms and workrooms, as well as an expansive furniture department with model room displays. Carpets were spread out on the second floor. The dressmaking department, with its well-appointed trimmed millinery department, was tucked away on the fourth floor. Here also, perhaps, were the fur department and boys' clothing. House furnishings, the books and pictures department, and toys occupied the basement. In all, the store occupied twenty-five acres of floor room, which meant that visitors were never "inconveniently crowded," according to one celebratory press account.[18]

Hilton, Hughes & Co. vividly demonstrates the scope of operations in the late nineteenth-century department store. The store building housed many other kinds of work spaces and facilities other than sales floors. At Hilton, Hughes & Co., as was likely the case at its predecessor, the basement was home to the delivery department and stables; the blacksmith shop, wagon repair, and harness manufacturing was nearby on West Tenth. Manufacturing took place on the fifth floor, the location of such things as the upholstery department. A. T. Stewart's iron palace had lacked some of the amenities that were becoming commonplace in major department stores. As it had under Stewart's management, Albert Hilton's store continued to offer only basic toilet facilities. Two writing desks for customers stood by the cashiers' desks in the center of the main floor. While there was no indication that Hilton, Hughes & Co. had expanded these meager offerings to match the lavish facilities at stores like Wanamaker's, in 1894 Hilton

VIEW FROM GRAND STAIRWAY BEHIND OFFICES AND WAITING-ROOM—Main Floor

FIGURE 4. The successor to A. T. Stewart in New York City, Hilton, Hughes & Co. was a true "palace of consumption." Hilton, Hughes & Co., *A Visit to Hilton, Hughes & Co., Broadway, New York: Leaves from an Artist's Sketch Book* (New York: Giles Company, lith., ca. 1895). Baker Old Class Collection, Baker Library, Harvard Business School.

refitted the building with "commodious" rooms for women to try on garments. Expensive alterations to the physical plant, which likely contributed to the firm's financial shakiness, were also undertaken then, including a $100,000 electric light plant in the store's basement.[19]

Hilton, Hughes & Co. also took advantage of new developments in advertising in the late nineteenth century. After initial resistance, it pursued advertising talent trained at one of the most prominent department stores of this early period, hiring Manly M. Gillam away from Wanamaker's in 1894. Gillam was reportedly an "expert advertising manager" of long experience. A Civil War veteran who had been severely wounded, Gillam first did secretarial work then was a newspaper editor in Boston and Philadelphia. Between 1886 and 1894 he was a highly paid advertising manager at Wanamaker's, where he likely helped bring about a much-heralded improvement in newspaper advertising there.[20] Experts like Gillam used advertising not only to move goods but also to shape the reputation of their firm.

As Gillam had done in Philadelphia, he transformed Hilton, Hughes & Co. advertising to court the popular market. Before Gillam, the press portrayed the successor to A. T. Stewart as one of the "best stores" that sold goods for "the indwelling of American kings" and costumes "suitable for the women who [were] to adorn such rooms." The New York retailer certainly sought an elite clientele able to afford $450 evening gowns from Worth or to furnish their homes with the Louis XVI and Empire-style furniture displayed in the store's fourth-floor model drawing rooms.[21] At the same time, however, ads between 1892 and 1893 signaled the store's difficulties and its desperate attempt to increase its stock turn rate, with appeals such as "bargains in 1,800 Ladies' Swiss Ribbed Balbriggan Combination Suits," which were manufacturers' seconds, and "immense reductions in this season's latest importations." Before Gillam took charge, Hilton, Hughes & Co. ads were straightforward, unembellished accounts that prominently featured the name of the store, its address, followed by a list of goods sold and their price. New ads by Gillam omitted introductory material about the store, instead launching into a catchy narrative. One from 1895 headlined "Almost Like Monday—was yesterday. Not quite so many people, but just as surprised." The innovative ad copy that followed presented the goods on sale as part of a story, with prices embedded in text.[22] Clearly geared for a lower middle-class and working-class market, Gillam's ads were colloquial, chatty, even ungrammatical, and full of colorful phrases.

Under Gillam's influence, window displays at Hilton, Hughes & Co. also reflected recent innovations in promotion. The store had been known for covering its windows with blue-curtains. But bargain appeals and popularized editorial material were certainly at odds with the image of an elite store that did not engage in window displays. Late in 1894 the store changed its outmoded practice. The much-heralded opening of window displays at Hilton, Hughes & Co. brought the emporium more in line with the department store idea, which sought to encourage consumption through spectacle and easy access to a wide range of goods all under one roof. Gillam brought a central feature of the modern department store to the firm, using light and extravagant display of goods to sell merchandise and promote the store as a palace of consumption. Windows across the entire store front from Ninth to Tenth Streets were lit at night with over one thousand incandescent bulbs, attracting large crowds of passersby as well as the attention of streetcar riders. Window-shopping was still a recent enough invention, perfected by big-city department stores with their extensive plate-glass windows and electric lights. An article titled "An Opening of Much Interest" captured the novelty of this museum-like display, noting that "from the sidewalk one may look as long he wishes on goods that represent the workshops of all countries." The packed displays of carved, imported furniture; brass, copper, and iron household goods; and "endless variety of fashions and makes" of women's and children's shoes were cornucopia-like in their abundance.[23]

The success of these big urban stores must have inspired many across the country. A variety of paths in fact led to mass retailing in the late nineteenth century. Some merchants started in wholesaling, serving as middlemen between manufacturers and small retailers, while others grew out of specialty stores by adding dry goods to their lines of merchandise. Many others got their start as peddlers and traveling salesmen. Prominent merchants in the department store field, such as Lazarus Straus, Louis Kirstein, Adam Gimbel, Nathan Snellenburg, and Morris Rich as well as lesser-known figures began by selling on the road. Jewish immigrant Louis Pizitz in Birmingham, Alabama, began as an itinerant peddler.[24] And in upstate New York, Frank H. Bresee began peddling his wares in 1882 while still in his teens, selling notions on foot along Otsego County's roads, a path that ultimately led him to open the Oneonta Department Store in 1899. Many department stores started as small dry goods shops or apparel shops and added new lines of merchandise until they became mass retailers that sold everything imaginable under one roof. The now monolithic Macy's grew this way, expanding from a small retail clothing or dry goods shop founded in 1858 to become a department store before 1870. Bloomingdale's and Brooklyn's Abraham & Straus became full-line department stores by the late 1870s and mid-1880s, respectively. Others like Marshall Field made their names as dry goods wholesalers before entering the retail business.[25]

Marshall Field made his fortune building on the innovations of those before him but also by breaking with traditional retail practices. His entrance into the department store arena was in essence a move toward vertical integration, an innovation that tightened control over the entire manufacturing and distribution process and allowed firms to grow bigger than ever before. In an era when shoppers were accustomed to visiting small shops or larger specialty merchants offering a single line of merchandise, such as jewelry or stationery, the breadth of wares offered by Field's must have been dazzling. Size gave the firm many advantages, allowing it to command helpful discounts from manufacturers who rewarded cash buying and large-volume customers. Field and his partners were able eventually to bypass jobbers and purchase goods directly from individual manufacturers, eliminating wholesalers' markup. Large-volume purchasers received exclusive distribution rights with manufacturers as well, which gave their goods greater distinction. Vertical integration into manufacturing also helped. Early in-house specialty workshops produced such things as cloaks, suspenders, and fur coats for both retail and wholesale divisions. In later decades, the firm began producing cotton textiles through its manufacturing arm Fieldcrest Mills. All of this reduced distribution costs by ensuring quick delivery and replacement of stocks manufactured by the firm and speeding up inventory turnover. Integration between the wholesale and retail divisions permitted the firm to follow consumer tastes more closely, aided by the traveling salesmen in the wholesale division who traveled across the country to promote its product lines. As a result of these factors, stock turn increased from 4.6 in 1885 to 5.4 in 1905 for retail on average, meaning the firm sold its entire inventory almost five and a half times a year by the early twentieth century; inventory turnover for retail dry goods alone was even higher.[26]

But Marshall Field's innovation in vertical integration might not have been as successful as it was without the management skills of Harry Gordon Selfridge. In less than ten years, Selfridge worked his way up from a Field's stock boy (1879) to general manager of the retail division (1887). Under the future London department store magnate's hand, the Chicago firm experimented with merchandising, finding new ways to appeal to shoppers that went beyond that seen at A. T. Stewart's. While Marshall Field resisted, Selfridge transformed the firm into a department store. After the 1890s, department store managers turned their focus from buying to selling. Selfridge believed in advertising and rapidly increased spending on newspaper advertising, running larger ads more frequently. Expenditures on advertising increased sixfold between 1880 and 1902. The store began to broaden its appeal, seeking middle- and working-class shoppers. To this end, Selfridge introduced a new basement "bargain center" in the mid-1880s, a controversial move that was advertised as a response to the "growing demand for lower priced goods." In spite of, or perhaps because of the store's continued upscale image, the basement salesroom was wildly successful, with sales topping $3 million by 1900, accounting for nearly a quarter of the store's retail total. Thousands of shoppers flocked the basement center during its first week to purchase "Specially Attractive Bargains!" in hosiery, gloves, handkerchiefs, ribbons, embroideries, underwear, housekeeping linens, cloaks, shawls, dress goods, white goods, and cheaper silks.[27]

Increasingly, stores like Marshall Field's sought to keep patrons on the premises with a range of services, amenities, and luxury that would boggle the mind of today's consumer used to purely functional shopping spaces and self-service. Their buildings were attractions in and of themselves—technological wonders for their time. Between 1850 and 1890, big-city department stores adopted all the latest in urban construction, using "iron, steel, and reinforced concrete construction as well as elevators, electric lights, forced-air ventilation, telephones, pneumatic tubes, and modern plumbing and heating systems." Technological advances allowed for new conveniences. Strawbridge & Clothier installed the first elevator in 1865, while electric lighting came to Macy's and Wanamaker's in 1878. Marshall Field's was the first in the Windy City to introduce modern technology on a large scale. It was the first big store in Chicago to use electric globes (1882) and to install a central switchboard with telephone lines in every department (1883). By the time of the Chicago's World's Fair in 1893, Self-ridge could boast that it was "an exposition in itself," with twenty-three elevators, twelve entrances, revolving doors, one hundred different departments, and three thousand employees selling Belgian laces, French lingerie, hosiery, and hats, Irish linens, and ornaments and glass from Bohemia. Even so, the new replaced the old as Marshall Field razed older store buildings and erected a twelve-story palace on State Street in 1902, which would be added to over the next ten years. With more than one million square feet of floor space, it offered customers restaurants, reading rooms, a nursery, an infirmary, and luxurious lavatories.[28]

Nineteenth-century department stores also offered free delivery services. Before it became a department store, the dry goods emporium of Hills, McLean & Haskins in Binghamton, New York, used "bundle boys" to deliver purchases on foot or by handcart, sometimes to the outskirts of town. Sending packages home was meant to help customers continue shopping unimpeded. While specialty stores might also offer free delivery, this was a more important service for the department store, with its wider range of offerings and its policy of free access, which encouraged browsing and impulse buying. To expand delivery within a city, nineteenth-century retailers relied on horse and wagons. Smaller firms did not necessarily own these but instead rented outfits and drivers to provide the service. Between 1880 and 1915, big urban retailers established a far-reaching free delivery system. Some department stores used the service to entice small-town shoppers to make a trip into the city to do their shopping. By the first decade of new century, big stores were introducing motorized delivery. Wanamaker's in Philadelphia and New York employed over six hundred horses and sixty-seven motor trucks in 1911, delivering approximately eighty-four thousand packages daily in the holiday season. Other alternatives, such as the electric truck introduced by Strawbridge & Clothier in Philadelphia in 1912, were featured in advertisements as a sign of the merchant's modernity. At the same time, the Electric Vehicle Association waged a campaign against traditional modes of delivery, warning merchants "to guard against the heavy losses on horse-flesh during hot weather" by deploying efficient, economical electric trucks (Figure 5).[29] By the 1920s, motorized vehicles were replacing wagon deliveries, though some stores still used horse-drawn wagons.

These many innovations were intended to spur mass consumption, something that was really only possible among middle- and upper-class markets. Most working-class women lacked the leisure for browsing, spending their time instead earning wages or doing household chores at home. Working-class women were able to afford department-store purchases only occasionally. As the field expanded, this changed. Major cities increasingly offered a range of department store types that made appeals to specific markets. In Chicago, Marshall Field's had established itself as a luxury department store, having a reputation for serving presidents like Grover Cleveland or, more frequently, their wives, including Mary Todd Lincoln and Ida McKinley. Its bargain basement, however, broadened the store's appeal. And neighboring emporia like Carson Pirie Scott and Schlesinger & Mayer served a solidly middle-class market. Working- and lower-middle-class shoppers had their own stores with the Beehive, the Boston Store, and the Fair. In Baltimore, "popular price" cash-only department stores like Bernheimer Brothers actively sought this market with circus-like in-store entertainments and bold advertisements some called "undignified."[30] By the turn of the century, a broader range of department stores catering to wider swathes of the buying public had appeared.

FIGURE 5. Free delivery was a department store tradition throughout the early twentieth century. Retailers made the transition to motorized delivery in the teens, perhaps in response to an industry-wide campaign against horse-drawn delivery that highlighted the drawbacks of wagons. *Dry Goods Economist* (August 24, 1912), 10. New York State Library, Albany.

The Rise of the Provincial Department Store

Urged on by the department store trade press, retailers in the provinces set out to follow in the footsteps of big urban emporia. By the early twentieth century, their innovations in merchandising, display, and promotion had spread more widely. Santa found his way to places like Galbraith's Cash Store in Hattiesburg (1903) and to a department store in Aberdeen (1916), drawing great crowds of Mississippians. Dry goods firms like Herpolsheimer's, Gold & Company, and Miller & Paine brought modern retailing to outposts like Lincoln, Nebraska; the Dannenberg Company did the same for Macon, Georgia. More modest than the big-city palaces of consumption, these emporia were typically family-owned single outlets, but they were sources of pride for communities outside major retail centers in the early twentieth century and helped put provincial cities on the map. In the words of William McLean Sr. on the occasion of the fortieth anniversary of his firm in 1921, "We are looking forward. We shall not be content until we shall have given Binghamton the best store in Southern New York."[31]

FIGURE 6. First a dry goods shop in 1881 with eight employees and 1,200 square feet of floor, by its fortieth anniversary Hills-McLean & Williams had grown into a modern department store with 100,000 square feet and 283 employees in Binghamton, New York. Photo 592, "View of Building on Court Street," McLean's Department Store; "A Story of Forty Years." McLean's Department Store Collection. Broome County Historical Society, Local History & Genealogy Center, Binghamton, New York.

Although department stores spread across the country with boosterish fervor, ownership remained limited to white men who had access to capital and markets. Unlike other areas of entrepreneurship where African Americans could reach black consumers and thrive, the department store field was almost impossible to enter. Black shoppers continued to face discrimination in white-owned and operated department stores, receiving service under protest from white salesclerks or being prohibited from trying on clothes as Jim Crow customs and regulations spread through the South.[32]

In cities with sizable African American populations that could support a black-owned department store, some modest black-owned emporia began to appear at the turn of the century, albeit in very small numbers. For example, the Samuel W. Trice & Company billed itself as a department store—"the only store of its kind in Chicago"—in the *Colored People's Blue Book and Business Directory* of 1905. Trice's department store sold the typical range of lines, including dry goods, men's and women's clothing, shoes, umbrellas, canes, gloves, linens, suitcases, and notions, but also advertised more specialized items that signaled the occupations available to black Chicagoans at the turn of the century: waiter's jackets, aprons, and overalls. The store also sold telescopes, perhaps appealing to amateur stargazers. Trice's business, for which shares could be bought from the firm's secretary for ten dollars, was unusual, even in a city the size of Chicago, but the idea itself of a black-owned department store was gaining popularity at the turn of the twentieth century as the black self-help and "buy black" movement spread.[33] Most of the enterprises were short-lived and left no records, except for brief announcements of opening plans in the press. One significant black-owned department store, however, was founded in Richmond, Virginia, in 1905 by twenty African American women who were members of the mutual benefit society the Independent Order of St. Luke. The St. Luke Emporium employed fifteen salesclerks to start and offered low prices to the black community. Facing opposition from white merchants and a Retail Dealers' Association, who protested to New York City wholesalers that they were being undercut by the black-owned department store, the St. Luke Emporium folded after seven years.[34]

During this period of expansion, traditional small-scale forms of distribution hung on. General or country stores still served rural and small-town markets. Characteristically dark, odorous places lined with shelving and cluttered with piles of merchandise, they crowded their floors with bulk goods in barrels, bins, and kegs, rather than following a departmentalized organization. Larger businesses might have a second story that housed surplus stock or served as a salesroom for rugs and other large items. Every purchase required assistance from a clerk, who was aided by only a few mechanical devices. The storekeeper often kept his books on the store floor, where he seated himself on a stool at a high desk on a small, wire-enclosed platform. The general store was also a social space for men, with farmers gathering around the much-remembered potbellied stove in a circle of chairs or sitting on a bench near the front door.[35]

While by definition the department store was a significant break with general or country stores, in practice there was overlap in the provinces between the two retail modes. While many small-town and provincial merchants modernized their operations in the early twentieth century, others continued to evoke the cracker barrel even as they called themselves department stores. The physical plant of even the grandest of these provincial operations never achieved the level of luxury and scale of retailers like Marshall Field's or Wanamaker's. Census data confirms the persistence of traditional trade practices. At the date of the first distribution census in 1929, the department store classification included departmentalized emporia with relatively modest sales.[36] Reflecting the conservative nature of their field, some kept their "dry goods" appellation even after they transformed themselves into full-fledged department stores. Even very modest one-level Main Street emporia—like Stewart's in Delhi, New York—were considered department stores by their proprietors and local communities.[37]

Small-town merchants, moreover, sometimes embraced both traditional and "progressive" trade practices. When Frank Bresee opened the Oneonta Department Store, for example, his plate-glass storefront had much in common with the typical general store. First, small-town department stores like his were quite modest in size. Bresee's opened with seven departments and six salespeople. A list of fixtures from a turn-of-the-century ledger allows one to visualize the store's original interior. The furnishings, valued at just under $70, bring to mind a general store without self-service, consisting entirely of a pump and tank, a coffee mill, scales, a tobacco cutter, a chimney holder (glass chimneys for gas lamps), an umbrella stand, and a stepladder, probably for clerks to reach the goods that would have been piled high on shelves. Customers would ask for items, which would be brought out from a drawer or taken down from the wall for them to inspect before purchase.[38] Small-town or frontier department stores also maintained noncash relationships with some customers as had general stores. One Ed. D. Hirshey is noted in a turn-of-the-century ledger as having been given "credit by work" by Bresee at his Oneonta Department Store. The practice of trading work for goods was distinctly not "progressive" in a modern retailing sense as it created record-keeping difficulties in terms of accounting for labor costs. As late as 1905, Bresee engaged in other atavistic trade practices that progressive merchants should have shunned: one customer appeared to be paying portions of his bill with large amounts of butter. Similar practices took place at the Fair Store in Pipestone, Minnesota, which accepted butter and eggs as payment in the early teens. Jacome's Department Store in Tucson, Arizona, accepted payment in corn, wood, watermelons, and frijoles from Mexican and Indian customers at the turn of the twentieth century.[39]

These merchants also held on to one of the key traditional retailing practices eschewed by large urban department stores—credit. In the first decade of the twentieth century, many of Bresee's customers used open-book credit to buy such things as chocolate, coffee, cloth, hats, collars, and boots. Extant store ledgers detail customers' purchases, amounts owed, and payments made. Bresee did not start his business on a cash-only basis probably in response to the many cash-strapped farmers that traded in Oneonta. In other regions where capital was scarce, such as the South and the West, small department stores had a history of extending this kind of credit to customers in the late nineteenth and early twentieth centuries. By 1905 it appears as though Bresee was trying to change this reliance on credit and become a cash-only business. Local newspaper ads attempted to educate customers about the practice, as if the firm faced opposition in its desire to become cash only. Folksy ads made strong arguments for the "Power Behind the Throne—CASH." Paying cash gave the customer "independence" and the feeling that "you owe no man, that what you eat is yours, that what you wear is yours." It allowed merchants to charge lower prices and saved customers money in the long run, granting them "independence in old age."[40] Such simple, personal language perhaps was an attempt not to offend rural customers but to persuade them to accept a more "modern" arrangement.

By the early twentieth century, a fledgling department store industry and a national trade association were urging "progressive" merchants to move away from open-book credit. In Oneonta, New York, the campaign for cash was over by 1910, suggesting that perhaps Frank Bresee had finally succeeded in shifting his rural and small-town customers to modern department store procedure. In fact, small-town stores like Bresee's were about to become part of a growing network of department stores across the country, linked by a national trade press, annual conventions in New York City, and a growing professional identity tied to institutions of higher learning. Across the country, department stores big and small were still local institutions serving local markets, but no longer were they isolated from new directions in the field. Which direction merchants and their new industry followed is the subject of the next chapter.

CHAPTER 2

Creating an Industry

Great stores are an absolute necessity in the transaction of the
enormous commerce of this day and age. They are a necessary
link in the great commercial chain.
    —*Dry Goods Economist*, 1899

AS department stores and other mass retailers grew in size and number in the last two decades of the nineteenth century, they drew
criticism from small merchants and their allies. Anti–department store
sentiment fit into larger fears of big business and the power of monopoly
emerging during this period of growing economic concentration. Able to
offer lower prices because they bought and sold in volume, followed strict
cash-only policies, and used cost-accounting procedures, department stores
were perceived to have an unfair advantage over the traditional small shop,
a type of enterprise that, unlike the department store, could be owned and
operated by merchants of limited means or restricted access to capital.
Moreover, the variety of goods that department stores gathered under one
roof challenged traditional trade divisions and offered strong competition
for single-line firms.[1] And finally, their command over pricing encroached
upon the traditional prerogatives of manufacturers, who, with the help of
Progressive Era reformers and small-merchant allies, would seek judicial
and legislative solutions to price-cutting. As the deflation of the late nineteenth century was replaced by an inflationary regime in the early twentieth
century, mass retailers' lower prices became more attractive to wage earners

struggling with a rising cost of living (up 31 percent between 1897 and 1916).[2]

A national department store industry emerged out of these battles. Around World War I, independent department store merchants and their trade associations began to forge a professional identity that promoted chain organization and privileged "bigness"—two things that would eventually contribute to the demise of the local department store. Through their state and national trade associations, department store merchants formed a modern identity that actively engaged government policy, identifying and seeking to shape political and economic issues that affected their pricing strategies and costs. Efficient business organization, innovative merchandising, and good management were important to success, but legislative and regulatory environments also determined which types of firms would prosper and which would fail. While the path to our discount world was neither linear nor inevitable, its roots can in part be found in the close ties forged between this emerging department store industry and government policies in the early twentieth century.

Early Opposition to Department Stores

In the boom and bust economy of the 1880s and 1890s, "store wars" broke out between department stores, small merchants, and manufacturers.[3] Department stores had cut into the trade of specialty retailers in urban, industrial markets. Smaller single-line merchants were unable to keep up with the velocity of department stores' stock turn, which allowed mass retailers to accept lower margins and sell at lower prices, all the while making higher profits. The wholesale jobbers who had traditionally acted as middlemen between manufacturers and specialty retailers were hurt in the process. Department stores had almost completely eliminated their services. Between the 1880s and the end of the 1890s, the number of dry goods wholesale jobbers plummeted.[4]

The conflict enmeshed entire cities. In Chicago, small retailers banded together with skilled and unskilled workers, women reformers, labor leaders, and real estate men who had interests in land at the city's margins, outside of the downtown business districts dominated by big retailers. Marshall Field's had prospered through the economic crisis of 1893, the year of the World's Columbian Exposition, even as hundreds of firms went bankrupt. This probably helped a rough coalition raise public opinion against

FIGURE 7. Marshall Field's was a true "palace of consumption." Completed in 1907, the year after Marshall Field died leaving a fortune estimated at $100 million ($1.9 billion in 2001), this Chicago institution was the world's largest store, a symbol of the economic and cultural power of the new mass retailers. Author's collection.

big stores and push politicians to favor restrictions against them. Chicago's mayor and city council took actions against their big department stores, denying their applications for expansion and imposing a graduated scale of license fees on merchants who sold more than a single line of goods.[5]

Opposition spread across entire industries. During the 1880s and 1890s, small merchants and manufacturers across the country used industry-wide agreements to challenge big retailers. Small retailers in a variety of trades had organized to fight their version of "the octopus," lobbying legislators to pass anti–department store laws to protect, in the words of some New York grocers in 1897, the "little man" from "the all-devouring monsters." Local trade associations exerted pressure on their suppliers. Acting through their trade associations, for example, groups representing booksellers launched boycotts against manufacturers who sold to department stores. In 1898, a Chicago druggists association asked patent medicine manufacturers to stop selling to local department stores that were price-cutting their products, arguing that they could not compete. Such efforts, however, could backfire. Some department stores responded by integrating vertically into production. In 1881, for example, when a Morris chair maker under pressure from a Philadelphia furniture trade association refused to sell to Wanamaker's, the big retailer began manufacturing its own.[6]

Industry-wide agreements in turn caused a dilemma for manufacturers, who were put in a difficult position, torn between the traditional specialty outlets for their goods and the promise of higher volume through department stores. The jewelry industry was a case in point. Jewelers saw big stores like Macy's and A. T. Stewart's as "a serious menace to their existence." Large manufacturers sided with specialty jewelers in an attempt to protect their reputation from the "bargain-counter atmosphere" of department stores. Retail jewelers, who had been the principal outlet for silverware and electroplate goods, also made their position known. Local jewelry dealers in Philadelphia, for example, threatened to stop buying from Reed & Barton when a representative for the manufacturer took a large silver order from a department store in the city.[7]

The anti–department store movement advanced to the state legislative level by the end of the 1890s. Unlike a century later, legislators were persuaded to try to rein in mass retailers. Punitive bills reflected the powerful influence of small merchants and their allies. A bill in Maryland, for example, called for a separate license of up to $500 for every different line of goods carried. The Massachusetts legislature considered a similar bill that imposed a personal tax and special taxes for different lines of goods. Opponents of these proposed laws tried to turn popular support for traditional modes of trade in their favor. In 1897 in Minnesota, for example, opponents of the Theden Occupation Tax bill, which was aimed at department stores like the Golden Rule, argued it "would work severely on country stores, some of which carried twenty-eight lines of goods under the classification proposed."[8] Retailers fought back. Even smaller department stores, which still could have fifteen or more separate departments, voiced the deepest concern about the way these proposed taxes were structured. Through the main trade press publication, the *Dry Goods Economist*, department store merchants expressed their fear and outrage, condemning each "hostile law" and celebrating its defeat. In response to a hostile Missouri law in 1899, the trade press linked department stores to progress and

modernity, stating it "would be as easy to transact the retail business of today with the old-fashioned stores as it would be to transact the transportation business with pack mules and oxen."[9]

The anti–department store movement lost steam around 1900. One
manager argued in an address on retail methods in 1913 that the late
nineteenth-century "crusade against department stores" failed when it was
shown that "department stores were conducting business on the same principles as the cross roads store, except on an enlarged scale and with increased facilities."[10] In the teens, the department store industry made
connections between itself and the "crossroads store of yesterday," but such
comparisons were more likely about justifying their trade practices and
healing divisions after the store wars than about any real similarities.[11]

Small-town merchants were engaged in another battle at the same
time—with the national mail-order firms of Sears, Roebuck, and Company
and Montgomery Ward. While both of these would become major
twentieth-century department store chains, at this point they had no retail
outlets but sold a vast variety of goods through their popular illustrated
catalogs. Such mail-order firms cut costs in ways the small-town merchant
could not, buying in bulk, eliminating the middleman, and reaching a
national audience through their catalogs. Reforms in mail delivery were a
potential threat to Main Street department stores as well as traditional small
merchants. Department stores, independent merchants, and the jobbers
and traveling salesmen who supplied them resisted legislation benefiting
catalog houses like Sears. Opposition to Rural Free Delivery (1896) and
parcel post (1913) was strong in small towns and rural areas. Department
stores in smaller cities that drew on a surrounding rural market also
endorsed mail-order tax bills and pushed their local commercial clubs to
do the same. While anti–mail order crusades took place in small towns and
provincial cities, in big urban centers like Philadelphia and Chicago it was
the department store that was condemned as a "colossus of trade" at the
turn of the twentieth century.[12]

Opponents also criticized department stores' pricing practices. Manufacturers had long demanded that department stores sell merchandise at
suggested retail prices. By 1908, Macy's carried merchandise that was
intended to be sold at prices fixed by a wide range of reputable manufacturers, including Arrow Collars, Community Silver, Bissell Carpet Sweepers,
Gillette Razors, and Eastman Kodak.[13] With its low-price focus, however,
Macy's found itself continuously in the courts. The first major challenge to

department store pricing came from book publishers, who sought to maintain the retail price levels of their products. In 1901, publishers began their fight against price-cutting by department stores, signing an agreement to punish book manufacturers and shut out mass retailers who did not sell at a suggested retail price determined by the industry. A few department stores signed the agreement, but some publishers could not resist the profits of volume selling and undercut the book industry agreement. The department store trade press ridiculed this campaign against them, suggesting that "publishers were suffering from an enlarged cranium on account of the plethoric profits they have enjoyed."[14]

Contention over Macy's book-selling operation resulted in important Supreme Court cases ruling in favor of department stores. The first began in 1901 when one publisher, the Bobbs-Merrill Company, sued Macy's for selling one of its copyrighted novels, *The Castaway*, for eleven cents below the suggested price of one dollar. The Supreme Court rendered a judgment in favor of Macy's in 1908, arguing that as the department store had purchased its books from a wholesaler and not directly from the manufacturer, the copyright holders did not have the right to set prices in subsequent sales.[15] In 1913, a related Supreme Court case between Macy's and the American Publishers' Association affirmed that publishers and booksellers violated the Sherman Act and acted in restraint of trade when they combined in an effort to maintain prices on copyrighted books. The department store trade press followed this judicial wrangling over copyright, making clear to its readership that federal policies and the courts would be no barrier to price-cutting at this time.[16] Judicial efforts to determine a suggested retail price along industry lines had failed. In this early period in the industry's history, retailers were given the power to cut prices, a power that would eventually cut both ways—to the detriment of the local department store.

Just as the courts ruled in their favor against the power of manufacturers, so too did department stores come out on top in the "store wars" with specialty merchants and their allies. State legislatures across the country sided with department stores, turning back proposed laws. And where anti–department store laws had passed, state supreme courts found them unconstitutional. Big stores also received major support from a 1901 Federal Industrial Commission in Washington, D.C. The Industrial Commission, formed by Congress in 1898 to study trusts, praised big merchants for their role in creating "a nation of large consumers," arguing that they "had 'materially widened the field for specialty stores' and they 'must be located in the trade centers of our cities.' "[17] As reflected in the words of the Federal Industrial Commission's report, the department store had become a central urban institution by the turn of the century. Again and again in the coming century, policy promoted mass distribution and with it, mass consumption and a national consumer society.

Department Store Merchants, the Government, and the Rise of an Industry

While ultimately unsuccessful, local and state-level challenges were not without effect. Anti–department store efforts prompted the industry to forge its own professional identity. Prior to the store wars or the early pricing challenges by manufacturers, department stores could not be said to be part of an industry in the sense that they still lacked a national organization that could isolate the issues that were important to their profitability and lobby on their behalf. Significantly, after forty years of coalescing into a recognizable type of firm, coming out of dry goods emporia, specialty stores, and wholesaling, the name *department store* became current in the 1890s during the era of the store wars.[18]

Around the turn of the century, publications defining the field as a whole began to appear.[19] Until this time, as a group they did not share a coherent identity except as "merchants." Small and large independent dry goods retailers and wholesalers, and emergent and well-established department stores shared some interests but diverged on others. Reflecting this, the trade press published articles and ran ads for a relatively heterogeneous audience made up of store founders and their descendants, as well as top store management, including buyers, store controllers and accountants, heads of personnel, display managers, and advertising executives. The central field of dry goods retailing, moreover, was in transition as many retailers added new lines to become fledgling department stores. Even the major trade publication for these merchants, the *Dry Goods Economist*, would not receive a name change that reflected its audience until 1938, when it became the *Department Store Economist*, a fact that also signaled what was shaping up to be a fairly slow-moving, conservative industry. Subtitled "The Buyer's Paper" from 1889 to1902—reflecting the peak of buyers' power and influence in department store organizations during this period—its articles and trade ads centered on issues of interest to independent retailers, both dry goods wholesalers and retailers and the increasingly important department store. By the 1920s, even small-town department store owners were receiving several trade papers, which they shared with department heads and other employees.[20]

In the late 1890s, the trade press provided this heterogeneous group with a voice in the conflict over regulation and taxation. In its pages, prominent retailers began pondering the role of their institution in modern society and began to forge their industry's professional identity. The small-merchant campaign against the department store, for example, raised the consciousness of executives like Lawrence M. Jones, president of the Jones Dry Goods Company in Kansas City, Missouri. In 1899, Jones detailed the "prominent achievements" of big retailers in a local publication and in the national trade press. His firm had originated as a dry goods or single-line store, but by the turn of the century it was a full-fledged department store selling wallpaper, paints, draperies, "gents'" furnishings, perfume, notions, underwear, hosiery, corsets, coats, hats, furniture, and carpeting. The firm's success resulted in plans for a large, purpose-built building in 1900, something that might have been put in jeopardy if the Missouri anti–department store law held.[21] Expressing outrage at the Missouri law in 1899, Jones wrote that it was "unjust, un-American and revolutionary," the ideas behind it having "never found lodgment anywhere except in the diseased brain of a political quack." Department stores, he argued, made significant contributions to society, benefiting both consumers and workers. They eliminated haggling or the two-price system, paid good wages, reduced the hours of labor, and offered tremendous opportunity for women, both as potential employees and as shoppers. Their advertising even democratized the newspaper, in his words making "the cheap paper possible."[22]

More than just a self-interested backlash, Lawrence Jones's impassioned account provides insight into the mind-set of early department store merchants. Members in the industry felt besieged, not only by the small merchants seeking legislative solutions to competition but also by the Progressive reformers who had recently turned their attention to the plight of department store women employees and working conditions in big stores. Jones's account of his industry clearly sought to paper over areas that were increasingly under scrutiny as the laissez faire Gilded Age gave way to the more regulated Progressive Era. At the same time, though, he appropriated some of the era's antitrust sentiment and tried to turn it into a defense of big stores. Inverting the usual argument, he contended that it was because of economies of scale that department stores represented "one of the strongest forces in the competitive system" and that they were able to wage "warfare against all combinations, monopolies and trusts which have for their object the raising of the prices of merchandise." Writing from the provinces, Jones saw the department store as "progress," a modern form of mass distribution required by the new era of mass production and linked to the welfare of the nation.[23]

After their fight against anti–department store legislation, mass retailers took the next step in the creation of a nationwide department store industry with the formation of the National Retail Dry Goods Association (NRDGA) in 1911. Like department stores themselves, however, a national organization also challenged traditional divisions in the marketplace. Dry goods and department store merchants initially encountered resistance when they tried to form a national trade association, perhaps because local and other professional ties weighed more strongly among retailers. Other related trade associations defined along narrower occupational lines had been in existence for about a decade. For example, the Buyers' Association was founded in 1897 as a wholesalers' group. In 1900 it was transformed into a retailers' group and acted as an important link between department stores until the NRDGA came on the scene. Retailers also supported city-or statewide trade associations, reflecting their powerful local orientation during this period. Merchants typically belonged to other business groups, such as the Chamber of Commerce and state-level trade associations. The first steps toward a national group took place at one of these—the Connecticut Retail Dry Goods Association. And even after the emergence of a national association, local groups like the Retail Dry Goods Association of San Francisco and the trade association for Los Angeles continued their work. After a slow initial start, when the NRDGA held its first annual convention at the Hotel Astor in New York in 1912, membership had grown to 273 firms across thirty-seven states.[24]

While the group was a national organization, it remained provincial before World War I. Conventions were always held in the Big Apple—the center of retailing for the nation. But major urban centers like New York City, Philadelphia, and Chicago—cities where the first major department stores emerged—were consistently underrepresented in meeting leadership. Leading trustees came from smaller communities, including Salem, Massachusetts; Schenectady, New York; and Lancaster, Pennsylvania. Reflecting the local nature of retailing as a whole during this period, membership in

FIGURE 8. Annual meetings of the National Retail Dry Goods Association shaped the agenda of a nascent department store industry. In 1913, at their second convention, over two hundred members gathered to hear speakers on taxes, freight rates, and tariff rates. Songs and humorous speeches at the annual banquet likely also helped form members' professional identity. At the banquet, for example, guest of honor, U.S. Senator Gore of Oklahoma, quipped that it was fitting that he address a group of dry goods men, coming, as he did, from a dry state. *Dry Goods Economist* 67 (February 8, 1913), 27. New York State Library, Albany.

the NRDGA consisted largely of independent department stores well into the era of the chain department store.[25] The trade association attracted firms like Rudge & Guenzel in Lincoln, Nebraska, at the time a small store with fifteen departments consisting mostly of apparel, dry goods, household furnishings, hardware, and furniture. When Rudge & Guenzel joined the NRDGA in 1912, it paid only fifteen dollars per year for its membership. (Membership fees were probably determined on a sliding scale linked to the store's yearly sales.) Leading department stores were conspicuously absent. John Wanamaker, for example, refused to join, though he maintained that he supported the venture. Similarly, R. H. Macy & Co. was not a member in the early years, although Percy S. Straus, one of the sons of Macy's owner, Isidor Straus (who died when the Titanic sank in 1912), was a convention banquet speaker at the Hotel Knickerbocker in New York

City. By the 1920s, the organization had full regional representation, with vice presidents elected from all regions in the country, a structure in place through the middle of the century.[26]

The NRDGA was part of a trade association movement that began in the mid-nineteenth century and rose to importance during the Progressive Era. With the rise of corporations and the development of wider markets, business required greater regularity, continuity, and stability. To further these ends, loose combinations developed in different industries along product line or according to function (such as wholesaling or retailing). These trade associations gathered statistics about markets, shared information, lobbied, and in some cases, even coordinated production and prices in their industry. The NRDGA was formed in part out of the growing need for standardized data. According to a Willoughby, Ohio, retailer in a 1913 address given to the Association of Women's Wear Manufacturers in his state, "efficiency" was "the new slogan." Retail trade associations thus fostered modernization, working on behalf of mass retailers and chains to further "bigness."[27]

World War I helped solidify retailers' sense of themselves as a distinct industry. Wartime agencies pushed merchants to articulate their own interests and concerns as a group. The War Industries Board, for example, sought cooperation from manufacturing and distribution sectors of the economy, working through their professional groups or trade associations. Department store leaders met to discuss what shape their cooperation might take. The industry's annual meeting in February 1918 at the Hotel Astor in New York City was designated "the War Convention" and attracted strong attendance. The organization prepared merchants to accept the inevitability of " 'governmental interference' in business" and encouraged members to work closely with governmental agencies to cooperate with the war effort.[28]

The experience of World War I pushed merchants toward greater rationalization of their methods. With the Federal Income Tax Law and rise in tax rates during World War I, for example, stores were forced to improve their expense accounting. Growing reliance on new experts in the field furthered professionalization of the industry. Harvard's Bureau of Business Research became more influential within the department store industry in part as a result of these wartime changes. After the war, department stores began cooperating with the Bureau of Business Research at Harvard in ways that helped standardize the industry and improve their operations. The

NRDGA began to work closely with Harvard business school faculty, funding some of the bureau's research. Under the prominent leadership of NRDGA president Lew Hahn (who in 1939 was behind the successful campaign to move the date of Thanksgiving to accommodate more Christmas shopping), the industry began to adopt newly popular scientific management techniques to eliminate wasteful practices and plan store expansion.[29] This process, however, was slow, and scientific management continued to be a mantra of trade experts after World War I.[30] Problems to do with wartime inflation and the ruinous postwar deflation of 1920–21 further spurred such reform efforts in the department store industry.[31]

Mass retailers developed stronger ties with the federal government as they cooperated to counter wartime inflation and potential food shortages. The war greatly accelerated the inflationary trends that had plagued consumers since the turn of the century. Rising food prices in particular generated protests in cities across the country. Once war was declared on April 6, 1917, President Woodrow Wilson "launched a sustained campaign against inflation," pushing for passage of the Lever Food Control Act, which "forbade hoarding, speculating on, monopolizing, or manipulating the nation's food and fuel supply." At first, the NRDGA was an active supporter of the Lever Act and its agency, the Food Administration. In the early twentieth century, many department stores still had grocery departments and would have had an interest in the issue. Remembering their participation twenty years later, the NRDGA noted that at the time, many retailers accepted "local or state responsibility for the forward progress of this work." As head of the agency in charge of conservation, Herbert Hoover enlisted voluntary support from ordinary housewives as well as trade groups, manufacturers, and retailers. Department stores and chain stores played a role in the agency's campaign to conserve food, collecting housewives' signatures on pledge cards and distributing information about meatless meals, wheatless meals, and meals of leftovers. Major mass retailers cooperated with the conservation movement, using their power and influence to spread the word to smaller merchants. As Meg Jacobs has shown, they "supported Hoover's philosophy of eliminating waste and increasing efficiency, because they saw themselves as the vanguard of modern distribution" in opposition to mom-and-pop stores and their high prices. For example, B. Altman department store owner and president, Michael Friedsam, became New York State's quartermaster general and retail merchant representative. Colonel Friedsam assisted the food conservation campaign, coordinating the distribution of twenty-five window display posters. Similarly, Edward Filene, his prominent manager Louis Kirstein, and Julius Rosenwald of Sears all played a role in supporting Hoover's efforts.[32]

There were limits to this cooperation, however. Always eager to turn to the federal government to protect their interests or further their own goals, many members of the department store industry rejected government oversight when legislation favored consumers or undermined their power. After the war, when the government extended the power of the Lever Act into peacetime, and with retailers accused of price gouging, department store merchants rebelled, their national association spearheading a lawsuit that would find the act unconstitutional. According to Lew Hahn, speaking for the national trade association, retailers were "to be organized for their own protection" against proposed amendments to the Lever Act as well as other "stupid legislative experimentation."[33]

In some ways, the department store industry benefited from its cooperation with the wartime state. The NRDGA was given a leadership role. Establishing a War Advisory Committee consisting of executives from Saks & Co., the J. L. Hudson Co., Maison Blanche, Scruggs, Vandervoort & Barney, and the Bailey Co., the merchant group sought to eliminate waste in the industry. Eliminating waste meant paring back some of the costly services that customers had come to expect of department stores, such as free delivery and returns, and cash on delivery. One large store, for example, increased the percentage of packages carried by customers from 40 to 70 percent. After the war, merchants' associations sought to continue these cost-saving measures, but for the most part they failed. Department stores continued to cater to demanding customers, and costs continued to mount.[34]

While a central concern of the NRDGA was the professionalization of dry goods merchants and department stores, the organization set its sights on bigger things, seeking to shape the business climate at large. A broad question that engaged retailers during this period was the relationship between government and the market. As we have seen, small merchants in the 1880s and 1890s pushed for anti–department store legislation; in the early twentieth century, opposition to price-cutting by big retailers reached the highest court. All of this, however, did not mean that the dispute over the role of federal policy in fostering competition was over. New avenues of debate opened up in the teens. Through its annual convention, which was covered extensively in the *Dry Goods Economist* and also in separate publications, the national trade group debated and established consensus on key political, economic, and social issues that affected retail trade. In between the fraternal dinner engagements, speeches by sympathetic senators and presidents, and the camaraderie created by singing popular songs and receiving convention souvenirs like silver key chains, members pounded out a platform on issues that affected their profitability, such as free trade and interest rates. In the reform-oriented climate of the teens, the NRDGA thus worked to strengthen the ties between local businesses and the government.[35]

Two issues taken up by the NRDGA that required merchants to redefine their relationship with government were resale price maintenance (fair trade laws) and the minimum wage for women. The first was connected to the antitrust movement of the Progressive Era. During the early twentieth century, groups with vastly different perspectives—consumers, small business owners, and corporations—campaigned for new antitrust legislation. Two measures were passed in 1914 as a compromise between these very different groups—the Clayton Act and its companion bill, the Federal Trade Commission Act. The Clayton Act amended the Sherman Act, giving a more detailed definition of restraint of trade. It declared unfair methods of competition illegal and empowered the Federal Trade Commission (FTC), created in 1914, not only to determine which practices were unfair but to order violators to cease and desist. If the FTC followed the impulse of its most prominent supporter, the "people's lawyer" Louis D. Brandeis, it had the potential to be a strong tool for small merchants in their fight against mass retailers.[36]

Brandeis saw resale price maintenance (RPM) legislation as a means of protecting smaller traditional stores from large modern retailers. RPM agreements between manufacturers and retailers established a minimum resale price for the (fair-traded) goods covered under their terms. Without price protections offered by such legislation, large-scale retailers would be able to cut prices and undersell smaller merchants, who were burdened by higher costs and were unable to follow suit. Department stores, in Brandeis's testimony before the congressional committee considering the price-fixing bill he had drafted, were only able to undersell smaller competitors because they bought in bulk and benefited from quantity discounts. Without protections, he believed, competition would be damaged and there would be the potential for social and economic harm.[37]

In spite of the FTC's close ties with Brandeis, however, it and the courts would ultimately work on behalf of mass retailers, ruling against RPM during this period. Opponents of RPM saw it as anticompetitive and called it price-fixing. The Supreme Court started the controversy earlier in 1911, when it ruled in a patent-medicine case that price-fixing was illegal under the Sherman Act and under common law. *Dr. Miles Medical Co. v. John D. Park & Sons Co.*, a case involving the sale of trademarked elixir and a contested requirement that jobbers and retailers sign a contract stating they would not undersell the firm's fixed price, killed retail price maintenance for manufacturers using jobbers. The FTC followed in this mode, to the benefit of department stores and big retailers in general. An "exemplar of cooperation between business and government," as historian William Leach has shown, the FTC was an example of "new institutional relationships" that aided the rise of large-scale business.[38]

Big retailers in the mid-teens, of course, could not know what future lay in store, but they nevertheless realized that the ability to cut prices was central to their survival and that the fair trade movement was a major threat. By 1914, nineteen states had passed legislation prohibiting price-cutting. Single-line dealers like grocery, drug, and hardware stores provided the backbone behind the first national resale price maintenance bill, the Stevens bill in 1914.[39] Introduced in opposition to the *Miles* case and intended to circumvent the ruling that price-fixing contracts were in restraint of trade, the Stevens bill sought to give manufacturers the right to restrict the resale price of any article—patented, trademarked, or otherwise—as long as no monopoly resulted from the privilege. Designed to protect small retailers, it also demanded the removal of such advantages as the "cash discount and quantity price" enjoyed by highly capitalized volume buyers like department stores. Manufacturers, it was widely argued, would also benefit, since price-cutting competition allegedly made distributors loath to carry their goods if they would not command a profit. The manufacturer Cheney Brothers, for example, saw its Boston retail market dry up when merchants refused to stock its silks after a price war involving the brand. As it went forward, the Stevens bill drew wide support from specialty retailers and merchants' associations, with manufacturers providing some financing.[40]

Mass retailers, however, were nearly a united front on this issue, opposing the bill. Macy's, Wanamaker's and Marshall Field's were "all known as avowed enemies of trade-marked advertised merchandise" who "refuse to handle such goods just as long as they possibly can," according to the advertising trade journal *Printers' Ink* in 1915.[41] There were a few exceptions, such as B. Altman & Co. and Bloomingdale Bros. in New York,

Shepard-Norwell & Co. of Boston, and the Shepard Co. of Providence, which supported price controls. Percy S. Straus of R. H. Macy & Co. spoke out against the Stevens bill. Macy's was well known at the time as a low-price retailer able to undersell its competitors. Manufacturers who spoke out in favor of fair-traded goods, like William H. Ingersoll of "watch fame," argued that only large department stores (like Macy's) were against the Stevens bill, but this was not the case. The progressive trade organ *Dry Goods Economist* surveyed its subscribers in moderate and small centers across the county and found that the "great majority" opposed the Stevens bill. In smaller centers, where department stores were likely to be modestly sized, 78 polled were in favor of the Stevens bill and 208 against it.[42] The trade press likely played a role in shaping the views of modest department store and dry goods merchants, influencing them to adopt the position taken by big stores like Macy's, but sentiment for small dealers in their communities may also have swayed some to support the bill. Small department store and dry goods proprietors and others affected by the bill could read detailed trade press reports on House Committee hearings and follow the arguments of its main advocates—Brandeis, the National Pharmaceutical Association, and the American Fair Trade League, an organization controlled by manufacturers of advertised brand-name products.[43]

As the Stevens bill provoked countless discussions in the trade press, at the annual convention of the NRDGA, and at Chamber of Commerce meetings across the country in 1915, the department store industry connected with Washington to a greater degree than ever before. The debate over prices brought many political, social, and economic tensions to the surface and helped articulate the outlines of the industry's modern identity. On a broad ideological level, supporters drew on President Wilson's New Freedom program, arguing that the government should protect small independent businessmen against competition from large monopolies. Manufacturers, for example, claimed that price-fixing was necessary to protect small merchants from the "distribution trust." In Brandeis's summary, price maintenance was to the benefit of manufacturer, dealer, and consumer. Supporters of such legislation drew upon gendered notions of the consumer, emphasizing its positive effects for women. Some argued that standardized prices protected consumers, particular irrational women shoppers, from the chaos and mistaken purchases created by bargain hunting. Others argued that the policy was not in the public's interest. Retailers against resale price maintenance also used women shoppers to make their point, noting the negative effect it would have on housewives "of limited means" who needed to economize.[44]

While retailers made a range of arguments in their campaign against price maintenance laws, the trade press overwhelmingly emphasized the modern needs of business that were ill served by what it characterized as a backward-looking agenda. Press rhetoric painted the small merchants and manufacturers as disconnected from market demands. Again and again, the trade press emphasized that the Stevens bill would reduce competition between merchants and would injure "business efficiency." Pointing out the variability of fashion, opponents argued that the loss of the ability to cut prices on stocks that would not move would be "disastrous" from "a business point of view." Price reductions were necessary because of the variability of "public taste": "Every line of goods, like every dog, has its day; and frequently the end of the day comes, like a thief in the night, without warning, finding retailers all over the country with stocks which refuse to move at the original price."[45] Regional variations in the ability or willingness to pay a particular price, they argued, made uniform prices impossible: "The demand for Cheney's Shower-Proof foulards may be good in Los Angeles at 85 cents a yard, but in Marysville or Truckee there may be no buyers at that price." Without control over prices, consumers and merchants would be forced back in time to a less efficient era dominated by mass manufacturers and traveling salesman. And finally, some, like the owner of T. W. Marse & Co. in Taylor, Texas, opposed the Stevens bill because it was "contrary to American progress," which he felt was based on free markets. Ultimately, opponents of the Stevens bill won—it went down to defeat in 1915.[46]

Sentiment against fair trade, however, continued to grow in the 1920s. When the Federal Trade Commission polled consumers in 1929 on whether they favored or opposed legalizing resale price maintenance contracts between manufacturers and retailers, with the exception of manufacturers all occupation groups came out in majority against such legislation. Department stores themselves came out 78 percent opposed to RPM, with chain stores following close behind at 71 percent. Not surprisingly, the federal study showed that independents, such as druggists, grocers, jewelers, stationers, and hardware stores, overwhelmingly supported RPM legislation, while independent dry goods stores were more evenly split. An early 1930s survey of members of the American Economic Association found the vast majority opposed it.[47]

Although big merchants for the most part came together as a united front against resale price maintenance through their trade press and national organization in the early twentieth century, the industry as a whole was not uniformly against all types of government regulation. Through the Progressive Era issue of a minimum wage for women, the department store industry would further work out its relationship with government—and, as we shall see, with female consumers. Protective legislation for women had strong support during this period. In 1908, the Supreme Court upheld the constitutionality of limits on the hours women could work in the landmark case *Muller v. Oregon*. Gender-specific minimum wage laws also began appearing, spreading through the states until 1923, when the Supreme Court overturned them on the basis of freedom of contract.[48]

Retailers' political opposition to government regulation and their focus on cost cutting made the department store trade press a likely opponent of minimum wage legislation, but in the early years of the debate, the *Dry Goods Economist* and some in the NRDGA in fact offered their support, making typical progressive arguments for a stronger state. The *Dry Goods Economist* suggested in 1913 that while "business men are proverbially averse to Governmental dictation of their affairs . . . it is essential, however, to recognize the fact that Governmental 'interference' as some term it, is a real development of the present day, and one that cannot be averted." Modern retailers were those who worked with "their Government, State or National, for a higher citizenship, to foster the future of this nation . . . to ascertain the causes which tend to the debasement of the individual, and to remedy, if not remove these causes." Retailers in all regions of the country jumped ahead of their states, as in the case of B. H. Gladding Dry Goods Co. in Providence, which began paying female employees a weekly minimum wage of eight dollars, or Hannah & Lay Mercantile Co. in Traverse City, Michigan, which set the minimum for women at seven dollars a week. A spokesman for Marshall Field & Co. testified before the Illinois minimum wage hearings, however, that the "increased cost to the merchant would be passed on to the public."[49]

Having put its finger in the wind, the trade press decided, albeit reluctantly, to support Progressive Era trends toward a greater regulatory state by supporting a minimum wage for women. The industry's position on minimum wage was certainly influenced by the fact that it was a mass-consumption industry with an interest in increasing purchasing power overall. Such was the case with the prominent Boston retailer and author

Edward A. Filene, who advocated industrial democracy and supported the minimum wage for women.[50] But it was the fact that it was a minimum wage for women that allowed merchants to unite, more or less, behind the issue. Dry goods and department stores were among the largest employers of women, by their own recognition, making the trend toward protective laws "a matter of intense interest to every retailer throughout the country." The number of saleswomen jumped from under eight thousand in 1880 to over fifty-eight thousand in 1890 as department stores grew and as they increasingly accepted women behind the counter. To a much smaller degree, women also participated in management. Some firms had significant percentages of women buyers. At Macy's, a relative of R. H. Macy's named Margaret Getchell rose from cashier to the position of general superintendent in the 1860s, retiring from the store in 1870 after the birth of her first child. At Macy's, women were also hired as floorwalkers, general supervisors, and buyers. By 1918, 42 percent of Macy's buying staff was female. As we have seen, women were also the stores' best customers. As such, women had the potential to push retailers in different directions. Ultimately, Mrs. Consumer, as she would come to be called in the 1920s, played a stronger role. One 1913 trade press report on the minimum wage movement leaned on readers to understand the implications for the industry: "Consumers throughout the country, and especially *women*—who form the *bulk* of the dry goods retailer's customers—will unquestionably take this matter up in one way or another. . . . From purely selfish motives, then, the retailer can look with equanimity on the minimum wage movement. He can even afford to *boost it*. For it is in his interest to stand before his community as broadminded, progressive and philanthropic."[51]

Merchants bent their thinking on the relationship between business and government policy in part to conciliate middle-class white women shoppers who were their most important market and who were increasingly influenced by prominent women reformers and consumer organizations. By the early twentieth century, reformers like Louise de Koven Bowen of the Juvenile Protective Association of Chicago, Mary Van Kleek of the Russell Sage Foundation, and the Vice Commission study of the effect of low wages on women had cast a dark shadow on department stores. Various accounts of appalling conditions for female department store workers spurred affluent women to found the National Consumers' League in the 1890s, which took on big-city department stores as their first main adversary. The National

Consumers' League published "white lists" of fair employers who voluntar-
ily adhered to certain standards. Historian Landon Storrs has argued that
the white lists, along with the "white label" tactic directed at factories, were
unsuccessful in changing employer practices but useful for "recruiting
middle-class women and educating them on labor issues and the workings
of state government."[52] The department store industry, however, did sit up
and take notice in the early teens when faced with a phalanx of vice commission reports, reformer publications, and legislative campaigns.

The NRDGA turned to the National Civic Federation, a policy reform
organization of corporate business leaders, trade union leaders, and reformers, for help in countering the most damaging charge that department
stores' low wages and immoral contacts pushed saleswomen into prostitu-
tion. The Welfare Department of the National Civic Federation conducted
a study of department store employment, compiling data from nineteen
firms employing thirty-three thousand workers, twenty-two thousand of
whom were women. Its 1913 report was largely complimentary and was
rejected by policy reformers, who labeled it a "whitewash." All of this combined to damage the reputations of department store managers, saleswomen, and the stores themselves as places of employment. Accused of
exploiting young girls and women through such things as forced overtime,
no sick pay, vice-inducing low wages, discipline and fines, and punitive
physical conditions in their stores, department store merchants had to work
double-time to reclaim the faith of women customers who shopped with
the latest "white list" in hand.[53]

Alongside their cautious support of state minimum wage laws for
women, individual stores and the industry itself promoted voluntary programs of reform. The industry stepped up calls for training programs and
welfare work, which, alongside its support for a minimum wage for women,
would "give retailing professional standing" and go about "setting the trade
right with the public," according to one trade account. Store executives
responded to external pressures from customers and social reformers, as
well as from financial pressures within the store, by coming up with new
policies that emphasized the importance of salespeople to the image of the
store and the success of the business. Training was increasingly understood
as a means to a larger end. After discussing the need for educating salespeople in the 1890s, in-store training programs began to emerge, first in
Filene's in Boston in 1902. By the late 1920s, full-scale training programs

were found in most stores, small and large, and universities had begun to offer their own retailing programs, of course with the major financial support of local merchants. The NRDGA supported training schools as well, the most prominent of which was the Boston school of salesmanship founded by Mrs. Lucinda Wyman Prince, who was the Educational Director of the NRDGA between 1915 and her death in 1935.[54]

More comfortable with voluntary action than with government-mandated change like minimum wage laws, throughout the 1920s merchants supported store policies that reflected business's turn to "welfare capitalism" during this period. Adopting such things as "pleasant lunch rooms and sanitary locker rooms," they intended, according to the trade association, "to improve the lot of employes [sic]" and develop closer relations between them and their employer. Such welfare benefits had social costs, giving "management's heavy hand" greater opportunity to control workers, as historian Susan Porter Benson has suggested. In the South, such benefits were segregated along racial lines. At Thalhimer's and Miller & Rhoads in Richmond, Virginia, for example, black and white workers joined different employee associations, attended dual banquets and company picnics, and used separate employee restrooms and lunchrooms. Motives were sometimes paternalistic, as in the case of store owner C. H. Rudge in Lincoln, Nebraska, who left money in his will for the "benefit of needy employees and ex-employees," money likely used to start an employees' relief fund in the early 1920s. Some benefits were certainly a way to supplement employee incomes without the fixed cost of a payroll raise. Mandel Bros. in Chicago, for example, introduced a commissary department that sold groceries to employees at cost, even delivering free of charge by its own wagons. In the prosperous decade, benefits that could placate workers, reduce the notoriously high turnover rates in the industry, and help avoid unionization likely seemed a reasonable operating expense. Such benefits could also easily be taken away during times of economic hardship.[55]

During this period, the government in fact worked on behalf of business. Looking back on the period 1920–1933, the NRDGA celebrated "a wonderful legislative record" and its success in fighting bills that were "inimical to retail interests." Significantly for department stores, federal agencies sought to modernize distribution during this decade in ways that helped the rise of big business. FTC reports, for example, provided merchants with much-valued information about business conditions.[56] More broadly, a pro-business decade saw the rise of a stronger Department of Commerce, which under Secretary Herbert Hoover's leadership held numerous conferences on retailing, gathered statistics, and produced numerous studies of trade conditions. With the help of the trade press and professional associations, this federally funded information was widely disseminated, helping retailers evaluate their operations, plan for the future, and become more competitive.

In 1924, Hoover initiated the first Census of Distribution, something that would be a boon for the burgeoning department store industry. According to William Leach, it was "one of the most rewarding boons to business ever proposed by any government." Retailing experts at the time, like Columbia University marketing professor Paul H. Nystrom, considered it long overdue, especially given the fact that retailing was the third largest occupation in the United States by 1920. Such a census, Nystrom believed, provided retailers with the statistics they needed to counter criticism from producers and consumers that there were too many stores and that retailers made too much profit. It also provided merchants with figures on business conditions that would allow them to "check their individual operations against the general trends." Efforts to get it going slowly coalesced, first with a sample distribution census of eleven representative cities; then, with the help of the prominent merchants Herbert Tilly of Strawbridge & Clothier and Edward Filene of Boston, the census was approved by Congress in 1929.[57]

The new distribution census had the potential to modernize smaller independent businesses, but statistics and market reports were more likely to aid larger firms. Department stores with the buying staff and capital to take advantage of such information would be better positioned to follow trends than mom-and-pop stores. While the Department of Commerce took special interest in the plight of small merchants, issuing reports on their status, it also helped big retailers become more efficient and profitable, which likely aided their rise to power. Even more directly, new federal policies aided the rise of big business. Large department store merchants credited such things as proposed new tax policies for the "good business conditions" that had led to a "banner year" in 1925.[58] Supported by a pro-corporate federal government, the reputation and influence of the department store industry reached a new height in the 1920s, even as cracks appeared in its foundation.

CHAPTER 3

Modernizing Main Street

A swarm of chain stores is pressing hard upon the small
independent retailer, who had things far more his own way
in the nineties.
    —Robert and Helen Lynd, *Middletown*, 1929

CULTURALLY and geographically dominant in cities and towns
across the country, department stores nevertheless saw their share
of the consumer dollar decline in the 1920s. Shoppers had already begun
to drive out of town in their Model T Fords in search of low prices or better
selections. New consumption habits shifted spending to other areas not
served by traditional department stores. And the rise of chain stores during
the decade also cut into profits. In response, department stores searched
for new ways to cater to Mrs. Consumer, returning to costly levels of service
and amenity and intensifying modernization efforts. Merchants modernized unevenly across metropolitan and nonmetropolitan areas but by the
end of the decade the difference between the big-city department store and
the Main Street emporium had narrowed.

A new national department store industry was behind many of these
changes. As competition from the chain stores mounted, many in the
industry believed they had two choices—to beat chains at their own game
or to join them. Nervous about their declining power but in awe of the
wonders of chain organization, major retailers and small-town merchants
alike began to model themselves on chains, creating their own large-scale

buying groups or hiring the services of a buying organization and forming figure exchange groups to share market information. Others turned to consolidation, establishing powerful department store groups and holding companies as a solution to increased competition from chains. In spite of this, most firms remained under local management, retaining their unique identity and luxurious atmosphere even as they increasingly enjoyed the benefits of bigness. Overall, however, the industry did not undergo wholesale transformation, even in the face of changing markets and new competition.

The federal government played an indirect role in the industry's modernization efforts and its adoption of chain methods in the 1920s. Department stores benefited from the decade's pro-business political climate, as did many other industries. While big business met opposition from the anti-chain movement, no federal policy contained it. In this context, the department store industry, still largely composed of independents, missed the opportunity to fight monopoly and "bigness."

The Department Store as a Cultural Institution in the 1920s

Traditional department stores had emerged from the Progressive Era as prominent local institutions. The massive stone buildings merchants erected to house expanding operations became landmarks; the streets where they located grew into fashionable downtown centers; their store name or logo branded their city or part of the country, contributing to its unique identity. Even smaller department stores played a part. While they did not build palaces of consumption or amass wealth of robber-baron proportions, the founders of small-town and smaller provincial city stores exerted comparable influence over the social and economic life of their community. They were well-to-do men in their business communities, founding merchants' organizations, providing leadership for local chambers of commerce, and exerting power over banks, real estate development, politics, and local institutions such as schools, colleges, and churches.[1]

By the 1920s, they had come to stand for the might of American capitalism and the democracy of goods, concentrated and most physically apparent in the booming cities of New York, Philadelphia, Boston, and Chicago, but also in the boosterism of provincial cities and towns. Many had at least one of these growing concerns—a solid Main Street enterprise that sold seemingly everything one needed under one roof for fixed, low prices. Their presence on Main Street was strong in the 1920s, with one mid-decade count listing 2,000 "real department stores" while another estimated the total at 4,500. By yet another count, their numbers had reached 4,962 by 1927. In any case, traditional department stores still dominated their retail category in 1929.[2] Census figures likely even undercounted their overall presence, omitting from the category the many small-town departmental- ized dry goods emporia or general merchandise shops serving rural markets that may have identified with the department store field. Even the black community in Chicago saw "the realization of one of its most cherished dreams," according to the city's main black newspaper, with the opening of the multistoried, eighty- to ninety-square-foot South Center Department Store on Forty-Seventh Street in 1928. Although part of a white-owned development and headed by a well-known Jewish merchant, the South Cen- ter Department Store was the only such concern to hire blacks in top man- agement and in sales, even employing a black store doctor and a black law firm to handle its business.[3]

Widely embraced by an expanding consumer market, the local depart- ment store began to appear in popular culture in a more positive light during this decade. In turn-of-the century fiction, film, and social commen- tary, the American department store had been a morally ambiguous public space that ensnared women through tempting window displays and luxuri- ous settings. Moralists condemned them for arousing envy and spurring vice or even criminal behavior. Well-to-do women rubbed shoulders with poorer shoppers, who were then made aware of their lack of finery and lower status, as in Theodore Dreiser's novel *Sister Carrie*. The 1905 Edwin S. Porter film *The Kleptomaniac* exposed female temptation, addressing the well-known phenomenon of middle-class shoplifters in the Victorian department store. They were the subject of comedy in film, with depictions of women out of control in their search for bargains. Perhaps the first example of this type of department store comedy was a Buster Brown film in 1904 showing crowds of crazed women elbowing each other at a counter manned by a harassed-looking dry goods clerk trying to clean up his department.[4] By the 1920s, the moral ambiguity of this commercial world receded in popular culture. Sex, social mobility, and department stores now went together, as saleswomen married men of higher class they met at work. In films like *It* (1927) and *Our Blushing Brides* (1930), these employers of women offered romance, glamour, and a social space for the assertion,

FIGURE 9. The South Center Department Store opened in 1928 on the corner of Forty-Seventh Street and South Parkway in Chicago as part of a development that included the Regal Theatre, the Savoy Ballroom, and several national retail chains like Walgreens. Promotional material by developers Harry M. and Louis Englestein lauded the department store's "up-to-the-minute stock and equipment," boasting it would "attract customers—both white and colored—from all sections of Chicago and suburbs." Lake County (Ill.) Discovery Museum, Curt Teich Postcard Archives; "A City of 300,000 Offers Its Business to You!" Chicago, IL, South Central Dept. Store A118873 A119976 (production file), Illinois Digital Archives.

albeit limited, of female power. Representations changed to reflect a new acceptance of consumerism. According to one banker speaking at the annual convention of the National Retail Dry Goods Association (NRDGA) in 1926, "The department store might be considered the greatest single factor in raising the American standard of living to where it is today, the highest in the world."[5]

Some social critics saw them in a different light, however. While they were still local institutions, by the 1920s department stores symbolized the increasing standardization of life in modern consumer society. Mass retailers made mass consumption of mass-produced goods possible. Some intellectuals in the 1920s were disturbed by this economic transformation.

Samuel Strauss, a journalist and political philosopher, condemned what he termed "consumptionism," a new mentality that supported unending, escalating mass production and its corollary, mass consumption, seeing it as a threat to democratic culture and political life. For some, standardization in store organization and operation had gone too far by the late 1920s. One prominent consumer advocate and advertising expert lumped department stores with chains, criticizing both for their "machine-like 'soulless' and one-sided efficiency" and "mechanical point of view of customers."[6] Fiction writers who condemned their era's new acceptance of consumerism used the department store in their fiction as a way to satirize crass materialism, middlebrow culture, and the stultifying nature of consumer society for women in particular. From the comparison of a department store with the unnamed, generic State University where George F. Babbitt received his "education," both of which turned out "standard ware," to depictions of the wasteful, ignorance-inducing habit of daily department store shopping for women, authors like Sinclair Lewis and Booth Tarkington used these emporia as a metaphor for what was wrong with provincial America in the prosperous decade.[7] Most, however, embraced what department stores had to offer.

Modernization in the Department Store Industry

Given the confident consumerist mode of the decade, it is not surprising that retailers across the country felt the moment was right for expansion. Department store executives undertook an aggressive construction campaign to build bigger stores or modernize older structures in the 1920s. The rise of finance capitalism during this period presented new avenues of growth for department store merchants. Since the beginning of the department store era, merchants financed additional stores or expansions by reinvesting net profits. In the early 1920s, however, stores began to finance growth through mortgage bond issues of up to $1 million. The success that department stores had in weathering the depression of 1921, moreover, had helped develop public interest in their potential as an investment possibility. As stocks were increasingly seen as a lucrative investment by more and more people, their issuance allowed stores to generate large sums. According to historian Richard Longstreth, department stores "no longer had to grow according to business achievements alone; they could expand on business projections."[8]

Smaller firms and major big-city department stores alike pursued capital improvements. Unlike capital improvement programs of later decades, these reflected a commitment to downtown and the city itself. The George Innes Dry Goods Co. in downtown Wichita, Kansas, for example, expanded into a multifloored building that housed a basement cafeteria, a soda fountain, luggage department, book department, beauty parlor, barber shop, and gift department. In Philadelphia, Gimbel Bros. opened an $8 million, twelve-story addition to its Philadelphia store in 1927, an event much heralded in the trade press, which lauded its classic exterior design, with huge Corinthian columns, and its grand, open first-floor arcade with an embellished, vaulted ceiling and crystal and bronze overhead lamps. Leading firms erected nearly fifty buildings during the decade, a number that equaled and perhaps surpassed those put up in the ten years before the war. Not only did they stay downtown, but for the most part new emporia did not break with their surroundings as would later department store architecture. Instead they simply sought to eliminate the mazelike appearance of nineteenth-century buildings that had grown in piecemeal fashion over the decades.[9]

Merchants addressed nineteenth-century store interiors that seemed outmoded by the modern decade. With "floor-through" construction, they filled in and covered up the open courts in their buildings, those grand public spaces popularized by the nineteenth-century palace of consumption. In 1927, for example, the large rotunda in the 1901 Hahne & Company building in Newark, which opened the main floor to the roof, was filled in on every floor, adding thirty thousand square feet of selling space. This new construction format emphasized efficiency over luxury. By allowing selling departments to spread upward, it also made transportation within the store more important. Escalators became increasingly common during this period as traditional elevators did not permit customers to move in a continuous flow. In addition to creating bottlenecks, elevators had to be staffed. The trade press promoted escalators as a solution, claiming that a single one could move as many people in an hour as six elevators—as many as forty in one account.

Some of the earliest escalators were in New York's Siegel-Cooper and Simpson, Crawford, and Simpson in 1902. Wanamaker's and Bamberger's, a Newark, New Jersey, institution, installed theirs by 1912. After World War I, escalator systems increasingly penetrated all selling floors even in smaller city stores, with larger buildings installing several pairs in different areas of

FIGURE 10. The main manufacturer of vertical transportation for department stores was the Otis Elevator Company. "Walking stair-cases," which appeared in big urban stores in the first two decades of the twentieth century, usually connected only the lower two floors. A popular modernization, escalators spread to the provinces in the 1920s. Scranton Dry Goods Company installed theirs in 1924. *Dry Goods Economist* (January 22, 1927), equipment section cover. New York State Library, Albany.

the store. When Gimbel Bros. in Philadelphia built its lavish twelve-story addition in 1927, it included two sets of up-and-down escalators along with a bank of seventeen elevators in the center of the building, with other elevators in each corner. Multifloored massive store buildings created another problem—stale air. Refrigerated cooling became a popular store modernization in the 1920s, but no department store was fully air-conditioned before World War II.[10]

The technologies introduced by late nineteenth-century big retailers spread to smaller firms and to the provinces by the early twentieth century. Pneumatic tubes and National cash registers replaced traveling rope systems like the Lamson system, which sent a whirring, clicking basket contraption that sped along wires overhead, occasionally derailing in the process. In the 1920s, stores like McLean's in Binghamton saw the need to update their cash carrier system of elevated tracks and hollow wooden balls containing receipts and change. Over the first half of the twentieth century, department stores in Syracuse, Rochester, Cleveland, Cincinnati, and Grand

Rapids, Michigan, modernized these systems. Even in the South, when the Belk department store remodeled one of its North Carolina stores in 1927 it replaced its Lamson cash carrier system—a modernization in and of itself—with pneumatic tubes. By the 1920s, such modernizations were an everyday part of life in towns and provincial cities across the country.[11]

New building materials also allowed lesser stores to mimic the luxuriousness of a Wanamaker's or Marshall Field's. Instead of marble flooring, for example, a mineral composition called Marbleloid was used in institutional or public buildings since at least the midteens and on railroad coaches perhaps earlier. The Marbleloid Company, founded in 1899, eventually produced flooring used in department stores. According to a 1927 Marbleloid ad, its "Travertine Terrazzo" possessed "the artistic appearance and light reflecting qualities of the imported travertine marble" and gave "the 'class' of Italian travertine without its cost, duty and transportation." Composed of plastic magnesia and travertine marble chips, it replicated travertine marble but was installed easily as a cement. The advertisement, likely intended for merchants updating old store interiors, lauded the material's ability to be installed quickly over uneven flooring without long disruption. Although it was a low-cost material, it was adopted by large eastern department stores. Some stores, like Newark's Hahne & Company, replaced their old wooden flooring with the material, giving their interior a modern, updated appearance that would have appealed to customers then.[12]

Retailers of the 1920s viewed advertising as integral to modernization. Newspaper advertising had been central to department stores since the early days of the industry. Even when other businesses resisted such expenditures, department stores were sold on its importance, advertising so heavily that they have been credited with the democracy of newsprint. Newspaper advertisements made certain that the names of local firms were on the breakfast tables of households across the country, like the department store ads read by Sinclair Lewis's fictional Mrs. Babbitt every day. Categorized as an operating expense, an advertising budget was generally understood to be an indispensable part of a progressive business, allowing a firm to plan ways to get rid of excess inventory and make room for new merchandise. The need for high-volume sales and high stock turn (the number of times stock was sold and replaced each year) justified such expenditure. National investment in advertising grew from $30 million in 1880 to $600 million by 1910. As advertising gained in status as a method for creating new needs and raising the standard of living, American businesses quadrupled what they spent between 1909 and 1929. By 1928, U.S. businesses spent $2 billion on advertising.[13]

Beginning in the 1920s, radio offered an unprecedented way for department stores to reach customers. Department store trade publications and the NRDGA first addressed radio in 1922, encouraging stores to start their own stations as a way to stimulate the sale of radio receivers. As set sales increased, department stores began to purchase expensive radio equipment and install their own stations. By early 1923, at least twenty-nine department store radio stations were in operation.[14] Early department store radio programming was not segmented according to different audience types, nor did it have the professional, commercial gloss of later programming. For example, on a single day, Gimbels' station WIP in Philadelphia offered a mix of program listings, including a talk on planting trees, a livestock report from the Department of Agriculture, a hotel orchestra and dance music, a selection of songs and "dinner music," and a talk by an insurance company. Radio sponsors typically produced their own programs in the 1920s, with some help from station personnel, as in "'Once upon a Time' by the Employees of R. H. Macy and Co., Inc." In Philadelphia, stores devoted their Sunday airtime to religion, with organ recitals and sermons courtesy of Wanamaker's WOO, Gimbels' WIP, or Strawbridge & Clothier's WFI. One Philadelphia store, Lit Brothers, did not broadcast religious programs, offering instead such musical selections as the overture from *The Marriage of Figaro*.[15]

As in print advertising and on the radio, department stores developed merchandising tactics and services that tied them closely to the everyday practices of modern life, practices increasingly influenced by national trends. Merchandising had long played into seasons, holidays, and rites of passage. By the 1920s, however, a broader range of department stores followed even more elaborate merchandising calendars, targeting June brides, high school graduates, and holiday shoppers. Even small-town department and dry goods stores and emporia in provincial cities began following these calendars, paying increased attention to their window displays and advertising and promotional campaigns. Marshall Field's in Chicago introduced the first department store wedding gift registry and wedding secretary service in 1924. Soon after, smaller communities began to see the customer services typical of big urban centers in their stores. For example, by 1929 more than half of both large and small stores in one study influenced wedding gift customs by creating gift suggestion services. Consumers in the provinces certainly experienced more elaborate commercial spectacles. Just as major retailers had made themselves part of tradition, as with New York's annual Macy's Thanksgiving Day parade in 1924, less well-known firms in the provinces also grabbed publicity from commercializing the noncommercial, as in the wedding publicity stunt held in 1925 at the Louis Pizitz department store in Birmingham, Alabama, to honor a store anniversary.[16]

Despite these close ties to a national commercial culture, these emporia remained local institutions in many ways. As historian Sarah Elvins has demonstrated in her study of retailing in western New York State, regional variation persisted through the 1920s and 1930s in terms of the availability of goods and the merchants who supplied them. According to Elvins, while the hinterland did borrow from the metropolis, small-town and small-city residents and merchants "took pride in their local institutions and their ability to put a local spin on national trends and innovations."[17] In the 1920s, department stores in particular were still local institutions whose management, store image, and of course employees and customers were tied to a specific and limited geography. As such, they participated in community events or regional traditions and supported organizations connected to their specific locale.

Stores still reflected regional characteristics in the 1920s. In Bellingham, Washington, for example, local department stores like J. B. Wahl's took part in the area's Tulip Festival Parade. In Lincoln, Nebraska, the founders of the Rudge & Guenzel department store promoted their broader rural markets in a variety of ways, from serving on the State Board of Agriculture to sponsoring trophies at the Nebraska Crop Growers Association's annual corn show. State identity was also an important part of their firm's image. Charles H. Rudge (an Ohioan) and Carl J. Guenzel (a Nebraska City native) helped to plan the fiftieth anniversary of Nebraska's admission to the Union. Such civic engagement was typical of founders of independent department stores. Usually the business and social leaders of their community, whose descendants became local power elites, department store executives took part in highly localized philanthropy, spreading donations among the YMCA, Boy Scouts, Jewish charities, and church groups.[18] The local traditions they perpetuated, however, were not always benign. Department stores like Abraham & Straus in Brooklyn staged a minstrel show in 1926, reflecting the popularity of racist blackface entertainment. While likely offending potential black customers, the event attracted "a magnificent mob," in the trade press account's unfortunate choice of words.[19] As these examples demonstrate, the local could also be exclusionary and divisive.

The Rise of Chains

Throughout the twenties, chain stores increasingly challenged all forms of trade, but to what degree they did so was not fully clear at the time. Although retailing appeared only briefly in *Middletown*, the landmark 1929 study of life in Muncie, Indiana, the book captured the tension between older modes of trade and the new forms of distribution. Its authors, sociologists Robert and Helen Lynd, observed a quickening of pace and "a swarm of chains," yet they did not cry revolution. Instead, they noted that "retail selling remains much the same kind of thing that it was a generation ago." Specialized shops selling menswear, women's wear, gifts, leather goods, and electrical goods, they wrote, were displacing "the Busy Bee Bazaar and the Temple of Economy on Main Street." In other words, chains and specialty stores selling fashion goods and higher priced consumer durables were taking the place of the low-price general merchandise store on Main Street. Observing the same phenomenon nationwide, however, experts in the retail field were more definitive in their interpretation of the transformation brought about by chain distribution. Speaking to a likely somber audience of Harvard business school alumni in 1931, the retailing pioneer Malcolm P. McNair outlined the "distributive revolution" that had given birth to large-scale retailing in the 1920s. McNair's 1931 speech highlighted three contemporary trends within this revolution that he (rightly) believed would shape the future: the rise of chain stores, the application of scientific methods in retailing, and the breakdown of recognized channels of distribution between the manufacturer, wholesaler, and retailer. All of these, in his view, had laid "small-scale shopkeeping" to rest.[20]

Although the rise of chains was labeled a "distributive revolution" by the retail expert McNair, the Lynds were right to emphasize continuity. Simply put, big retailers did not completely replace older forms of trade in the 1920s. In 1923, according to one estimate, department stores took 16 percent of total retail trade while chain stores received 8 percent, mail order 4 percent, and company stores 4 percent, with all other retail shops, including general stores and single-line firms, taking 68 percent of total sales for that year. Country or general stores, for example, were common in the South and typical in places like northeastern Maine, northern Vermont, and New Hampshire. By the first distribution census in 1929, general stores were still hanging on, though sales had surely declined with the rise of national chains mid-decade. Under "general merchandise" along with variety stores (five-and-dimes), as an overall category they gathered 18.7 percent of total retail sales. General stores contributed 7.9 percent to that general merchandise sales total.[21] From the forward-looking urban perspective of a Harvard professor of marketing, these figures meant that the era of the cracker barrel was over.

Chains, though, were not new to the 1920s. They first appeared in the late 1850s in the United States in the grocery trade, with the Great Atlantic and Pacific Tea Company (A&P). By the early twentieth century, chain organization had spread to other categories. Cheap retail chains like Woolworths, Kresge, and W. T. Grant became a ubiquitous feature of Main Streets across the country. And by 1929, the A&P grocery chain dominated its market as the world's largest retail business with more than seventeen thousand stores and annual sales of more than $750 million. Retail chains reached a mass market by the end of the decade. In Chicago, chain stores even made inroads on the strong loyalties of ethnic shoppers who had previously purchased goods from neighborhood stores owned by compatriots. African Americans in Chicago shopped at them as well, appreciating their fair prices and willingness, in the face of boycotts, to hire blacks.[22] As early as 1925, the industry as a whole even gained its own trade press with the founding of the long-lived magazine, *Chain Store Age*, a sign that chain organization had surely arrived.[23]

The department store chain was a creation of the 1920s. With their cash-only policies, department stores chains (and mail order) represented a significant break with the traditional open-book credit of the company stores and country stores that had dominated distribution in the South, the West, and rural areas in general. Department stores numbered among the four leading kinds of chain store operations in small towns, joining variety stores, dry goods and apparel emporia, and automobile accessory outlets. While only a few department store chains dominated the category, the number of units skyrocketed over this decade.[24] The earliest of these department store chains was J. C. Penney, which opened its first store in 1902. Initially located in county seats to serve farmers and small-town customers, they dealt largely in staple rather than fashion goods. By 1920, medium-sized cities like Fort Worth, Texas, had their own downtown outlets. Benefiting from large-scale buying and centralization combined with local decision making, the chain was able to grow rapidly from 297 outlets in 1920 to more than 1,000 in 1928. With total sales of more than $91 million in 1925, J. C. Penney was the largest chain of small department stores. At the same time, mail-order giant Montgomery Ward expanded into retail, transforming itself into a department store chain. Montgomery Ward remained committed to mail order, however, moving into sites like the defunct Chevrolet assembly plant in Fort Worth, which allowed it to expand its local mail-order operation and operate a small retail store in the same location. Sears, which eventually became a retail giant, started in 1895 as a mail-order business and began selling over the counter in 1925. Its first retail outlets were located downtown in cities with populations of at least one hundred thousand. By the late 1920s, J. C. Penney, Montgomery Ward, and Sears had competition from smaller chains in the provincial markets, where chains flourished. In the South, chains like Belk department stores, the Perkins stores, and the Efird Department Stores expanded. In Mississippi alone, twelve out of the state's fifty department stores belonged to national chains in 1929.[25]

The chains' proliferation in the 1920s certainly worried small or single-line merchants, but the situation was more complex for department store merchants, who did not clearly or consistently view them as a threat. Some department store lines were certainly adversely affected. Departments that overlapped with the offerings of five-and-dime and variety chains suffered. Department stores, for example, lost sales of hosiery, notions, cosmetics, shoes, and lingerie.[26] As a rule, moreover, most single-unit department stores simply could not command the economies of scale available to multiunit retailers. Size provided many advantages. First, chain stores were able to reduce the cost of individual transactions or units sold. They did this by centralizing management and standardizing management practices, implementing buying systems or pools, centralizing warehousing, standardizing national advertising, and, eventually, bringing in electronic data processing. Their massive size gave them the power to force vendors to compete for their business with discounts and allowances. Multiple store operations, moreover, spread the cost of various marketing strategies across many outlets. Chains benefited from lowered costs of securing capital, first choice of location, and lower rental costs. Higher profits could fund further investment, allowing these enterprises to grow even larger.[27]

Many in the 1920s viewed chains as impersonal entities, managed from afar, with no stake in their home community. Unlike multiunit chain operations, independent department stores were run by the founding family, who often owned the vast majority of the store's assets and had a personal interest in the firm. Their owners knew their neighbors' buying habits intimately and were sometimes even of the same ethnic background, as in the case of Goldblatt's Department Store in 1920s Chicago. Sons of a Jewish grocer, the Goldblatt brothers catered to their ethnic, working-class neighborhood with long hours, cheap prices, and a marketplace atmosphere of bargain tables piled high with goods for customers to handle. Independent merchants who fought the chains vehemently during this period drew such distinctions.[28]

Chains countered their competitors and critics by making their own appeal to localism. J. C. Penney ran national ad campaigns touting its status as a " 'local store' as any other." Chain headquarters, for example, encouraged store management to get involved in local affairs and charities and become community leaders like their independent counterparts. Even big mergers of local stores that might have been objectionable prompted the holding company to make local appeals.[29] When Rudge & Guenzel merged in 1928 with Hahn Department Stores, Inc., for example, the firm continued to promote its identity as a "Lincoln store for Lincoln and all Nebraska." The Hahn Department Store group certainly was aware of the hatred generated by chain stores and sought to keep Rudge & Guenzel's customers' loyal patronage by such ads, which emphasized continuity with the past. Management would stay the same, and the firm's individuality would remain unchanged, their ads argued. There would be the added benefit of lower prices, however, because of the "vast resources" provided by the organization and the prestige of belonging to the modern-looking group of stores in the ad's illustration. After a merger, stores typically emphasized the length of their operation and their connection to local institutions. Rudge & Guenzel did so in the University of Nebraska's yearbook, *The Cornhusker*, in a 1938 ad that noted "your university founded in 1869" and "your favorite department store founded in 1886." After the merger, the store continued celebrating its local identity by marking its forty-third anniversary with an elaborate lighting ceremony for a forty-pound candle in a store window.[30]

Despite the rise of chains in the 1920s, the department store industry's independent status was still very strong. Most department stores were independents of small to moderate size. Even when the bar for being considered a chain was quite low—in 1929 two outlets made one a chain according to the Federal Trade Commission, four or more according to the Bureau of the Census—most department stores were not chains. Most were family-run, single-outlet operations. As the census classified them, moreover, their sales could be quite modest. The census accepted relatively small departmentalized emporia as department stores. Stores with annual sales under $100,000 in 1929 were counted, though in 1933, census classifications of the minimum sales for inclusion in the category shifted higher and those smallest department stores were shifted into the general merchandise store category.[31] Of the 581 firms studied by the Bureau of Business Research at Harvard University, in 1926 more than half had less than a half million in sales. The smallest of these had less than $250,000 in annual sales. In the study, however, eighteen firms had a sales volume of over $10 million. The largest of these firms were powerful economic forces in their home city and regional markets. By 1925, a small number of big metropolitan independent department stores were in the $50 million range, the highest category provided for a retail firm operating a single unit. The same year, one department store with units in three cities did over $102 million in business.[32]

Aided by their new professional identity as modern merchants and part of a national department store industry, many began to view their chains as a source of new ideas. In small towns and provincial cities, chains pushed the independent department store merchant to modernize in the 1920s. On Main Streets across the country, independents observed national grocery and general retailing chains engaged in self-service and cash-only pricing. Competition pushed them to counter by improving product lines, stressing service, and expanding credit options. Contact between chain store managers and independent merchants sometimes resulted in direct adoption of chain methods.[33] By the late 1920s, the department store trade press heralded chain efficiencies and pointed out that they made lower prices for consumers possible. One trade writer saw a decline in anti-chain sentiment, arguing that "the rapid concentration of business in all lines, to our mind, is one of the most important and significant trends in modern business, and it is particularly worth noting that public opinion has completely reversed its attitude with regard to such consolidations." Looking over more than a half decade of consolidation and the adoption of chain methods like group buying, independents felt optimistic about their place in the distribution chain. One 1927 editorial in the *Dry Goods Economist* boasted (perhaps hopefully) that the independent merchant was not "doomed."[34]

Chain competition was cutting into their overall share of retail trade, however. Looking back over this period, it is clear that rising expenses and declining profits had become a problem for the department store field. By the end of the decade, overall department store sales accounted for 14–15 percent of total retail trade, while chain store sales were pushing 20 percent, having passed department stores in total volume in 1928. The three largest components of store expenses, or the cost of doing business, were payroll, real estate costs, and advertising. As department stores offered more service and amenity, as they competed with each other through more advertising and expanded their facilities, and as labor costs rose, all these expenses increased. Advertising, which was 2 percent of net sales in 1920, rose to around 3 percent in the mid-twenties, then moved slowly to 3.5 percent of net sales by 1930. Other expenses, like payroll, climbed from 13.9 percent of net sales in 1920 to 16.8 percent in 1929.[35]

Merchants and industry experts grew concerned by the end of the decade by a related issue—rising gross margins. These important figures were determined by subtracting the merchandise cost from the retail price and were typically expressed as a percentage of net sales. In the early decades of the department store field, when markups were low and volume high in relation to expenses, gross margins were as low as 20 percent by one account. The low gross margins and low expenses of this formative period, however, were no longer possible in the competitive context of the early twentieth century. Although cumulative figures for early periods are sparse, one reputable account suggests that department store gross margins had risen to around 30 percent by 1914.[36] By 1929, they were 33.5 percent. Many department stores had shifted away from low-margin staple goods to items that carried higher gross margins, such as fashion goods and home furnishings. Moreover, high gross margins in a sense were paying for the many free services and amenities offered consumers. Higher gross margins could offset expenses like free delivery and credit, as well as advertising. But falling profits in the late 1920s called the relationship between high gross margins and rising expenses into question. Significantly, by the end of the decade the department store industry was not faring as well as other sectors of the economy, such as manufacturing.[37]

It frustrated those in the business that just as consumption expanded overall and the economy appeared to be steaming along in some sectors, the department store was becoming a less economically dominant institution. Looking back over the decade of the 1920s, University of Pennsylvania marketing professor Frank Hypps used a variety of colorful metaphors to capture the inflexibility and inefficiency of traditional department stores, describing them as barnacle-encrusted ships and oversized elephants. Writing from the point of view of the Depression, his evaluation that the "department store stopped growing as a national institution" between 1920 and 1929 perhaps overstated the decline of this still influential and important form of distribution. Still, at the time, industry experts, trade organizations, and independent department store owners expressed concern about chain competition and declining market share.[38]

In the late 1920s, some merchants turned to merger as a solution to the flagging profits that plagued the industry during this period of rising operating costs, chain competition, and changing consumer habits. In 1928, Lew Hahn, a director of the NRDGA, organized one of one of the biggest department store holding companies, Hahn Department Stores. The deal at first included twenty-two prominent stores from coast to coast—including the modest Rudge & Guenzel department store in Lincoln, Nebraska. One year later it had twenty-nine under its control and did approximately $115 million in annual sales combined. Stores included Boston's Jordan Marsh, St. Paul's Golden Rule, and Seattle's Bon Marche. In the South, Hahn's consolidation included Meyer's Company of Greensboro and Goettinger Company, Inc., of Dallas. Celebrated as "another industrial star in the making" by the press in cities where his group took over local stores, Lew Hahn and his chain gained national prominence. The chain was indeed massive, capitalized at $60 million.[39]

The biggest deal in the industry to date was the creation of the holding company Federated Department Stores in 1929. Federated emerged out of the Retail Research Association (RRA), which held its first meeting in New York City, initially inviting representatives from eighteen other stores, including the J. L. Hudson Company, the Dayton Company, the Emporium, and the Joseph Horne Company. Renamed the Associated Merchandising Corporation (AMC) in 1918, the RRA provided Federated with already established instruments for group buying and the transmission of basic data among member stores.[40] The merger was put together by retailer-turned-investment banker Paul Mazur, and Louis Kirstein and Lincoln Filene of Filene's, Fred Lazarus Jr. of F. & R. Lazarus in Columbus, Ohio, and executives from Abraham & Straus of Brooklyn. The holding company was made up of wholly owned, geographically dispersed, locally managed firms, each of which maintained its own identity and consumer base. The merger meant some loss of managerial independence, however, which led Edward Filene to oppose the deal. Expecting that his ongoing employee cooperative plans and radical reforms would be squashed at his Boston store, which they were, Edward split with his brother Lincoln over the issue. He lost control of Filene's in 1928, and the two never spoke again.[41]

By mid-1929, after the conflict had settled and pieces of the Federated Department Stores were falling into place, another apparent wave of merger mania led the banker and retail expert Louis Kirstein to write to Lincoln Filene that in New York everyone seemed to be buying everybody else out. May Department Stores (perhaps the first department store holding company, formed in 1910), Macy's, and the Hahn chain all wanted to take over Bloomingdale's; the Straus brothers of Macy's were pursuing Bamberger's, a member of the Associated Merchandising Corporation. The consolidations that took place during this period, however, should not be overstated. For example, in Malcolm McNair and Eleanor May's comprehensive performance analysis of department stores, which was based on the Harvard reports, few companies operated more than one store in 1929.[42]

Mergers forced some changes in long-standing department store practice. Generally, the mergers that took place during this period in the department store industry did not increase coordination in the way seen among chain retailers and thus did not lead to the same competitive efficiencies. Whereas department store chains featured centralized policies and management, department store groups allowed individual units to continue operating largely under their own management. They could follow their own policies, though some experienced control from the central organization. Stores that consolidated did engage in group buying but not at all to the extent employed by chain stores. By one 1930 account, consolidations of department stores led to less than 10 percent of total volume purchased centrally by the group. For some who had merged in the early twentieth century, consolidation did not deliver the expected benefits. While City Stores and May prospered, Gimbels and Hahn were less successful. National also experienced losses. Disagreements emerged in the department store industry over the benefits or dangers of consolidation, with no consensus on the issue by the decade's end.[43]

Department stores struggled with one of the key strategies of chain organization—centralized buying. Part of a conservative industry, many held on to their tradition of decentralized buying. Resistance to pooling resources and engaging in large-scale central buying had to do with the customary internal organization of department stores and the division of labor. Major urban stores had well over one hundred departments, each headed by a buyer who was responsible for both buying and selling and whose performance was judged by departmental profits. Buyers typically received a percentage of increased net sales in their departments, in addition to their salary.[44] In their procurement role, buyers dealt with manufacturers and their sales representatives and were responsible for pricing decisions. They also hired and managed their sales force. They gained intimate knowledge of the goods they sold as well as customers' response to them. Buying and selling were bundled together because of the need for this dual knowledge of supply and demand. Replacing this system of decentralized buying with the centralized purchasing favored by chains or large merged companies went against owners' belief in the value of the knowledge buyers had about consumer taste, buyers that they themselves had often trained. In addition, as department stores increased their emphasis on fashionable goods over staple goods in their competition with chain stores, they furthered their attachment to decentralized buying.[45] Staple goods were standardized and changed little over time, meaning they could be purchased safely by a central office removed from the local tastes of individual markets. But only highly trained and skillful buyers could predict the tastes for such things as rising hemlines and cloche hats.

Without too much change to their traditional mode of operation, department stores moved in the direction of centralization by joining figure exchange groups. These voluntary groups emerged as a way for independents to keep abreast of changes in the market and new ways of doing things. With the rise of chains they took on new importance, providing independents with some of the benefits of larger firms. Members shared information about markets and operations with noncompeting stores within a region or designated area. The earliest example dated to 1916 and operated only citywide. This group, unnamed in the source though likely the Retail Research Association (RRA), shared figures on operating expenses and profits for different departments and was held up by a National Retail Dry Goods Association executive as an example of a shift in the "department store field" away from "speculation" toward "scientific analysis." The RRA (which became the buying office AMC, then gave rise to Federated in 1929), had been organized by Lincoln Filene and his fellow merchant Louis Kirstein, allegedly as a means for Lincoln's older brother Edward to experiment with his cooperative ideas (before their split). The RRA studied problems of store operation and merchandising and worked toward a uniform system of record keeping. A means of competing with chains, such figure exchange groups may have gone far to professionalize independents. However, they could do only so much. As voluntary organizations dependent on the sharing of information, they were not perfect tools as members often struggled to overcome traditions of secrecy.[46]

Cooperative buying groups emerged at the same time as another way for independents to gain the advantages of size. One form that narrowed the distance between the local department store and the chain was the associated buying organization, an entity "financed and controlled by a limited group of stores" and intended to serve them rather than make a profit. Like figure exchange groups, these organizations provided information about market conditions and facilitated the exchange of ideas and operating experiences, but their main advantage was the savings created by large-scale buying of merchandise, a savings that could be passed on to consumers in the form of lower prices. Associated buying organizations also conducted research for the mutual benefit of member stores. Groups produced various studies geared toward improving operating efficiency and also worked to standardize accounting procedures to enable comparisons between stores.[47]

New York City, the retail/wholesale center of the country and leader in stylish goods, was home to the two largest cooperative buying offices. One of the first, if not the first, cooperative buying office was founded in 1900 by Frederick Atkins in New York City's Union Square. Atkins began working at the age of thirteen as a stock boy and general handy boy for one dollar a week in 1874, and by the late 1930s his firm represented thirty department stores in the United States and abroad. Flagship stores in the group included local institutions like the Halle Bros. Co. in Cleveland, Woodward & Lothrop in Washington, D.C., and the City of Paris in San Francisco. At the time of his death in 1946 member clients controlled the firm.[48] Another early example of a cooperative buying group was the Associated Merchandising Corporation (AMC) of New York City, which grew out of the success of the Retail Research Association. Unlike the RRA, which was essentially a figure exchange group that allowed smaller organizations to benefit from shared information about larger markets, the AMC was created to pool buying power of member stores and help them compete against the massive buying power of chains like Sears. Bullock's, Strawbridge & Clothier, Hutzler Brothers, and A. Harris & Company were just some of the prestigious independent firms in the group. By 1927, the AMC consisted of seventeen stores in cities across the country engaged in group buying with a central office in New York City. Together they purchased $40 million worth of merchandise from the United States and Europe.[49]

Outside of New York, regional buying organizations emerged, serving small- to moderate-sized firms by the late 1920s. Through them, Main Street independents grew closer to chains. In the Midwest, the buying organization Central States Department Stores pulled in the business of stores like Zahn Dry Goods Co. of Racine, Wisconsin. Members supported the expenses of the organization, formerly known as Mid-West Stores, through a membership fee and annual dues paid on a sliding scale proportional to sales. In 1928, the annual dues for Zahn's were $1,650, which reflected its net annual sales between $1.1 and $1.2 million. The buying organization included annual dues for stores with net annual sales under $500,000 on its lower end, going only up to $2 million on its upper range, which commanded annual dues of $2,850. The smallest department store would likely not find the annual dues of $600 too burdensome. Thus, even small-town department stores or modest city outlets could benefit from centralized purchasing and the expertise on markets offered by such offices. "Combined buying power" even became a selling tool, a standard feature of institutional advertisements as stores promoted their ability "to effect economies that are passed on to their millions of friends and patrons."[50]

By the 1920s, smaller department stores could also gain some of the economic advantages of cooperative buying by engaging the services of an independent buying office. In one account, some small-town merchants in the 1920s continued to prefer to purchase directly from jobbers and manufacturers, resisting the efforts of buying associations. But others modernized. In 1926, for example, the Oneonta Department Store affiliated with the buying organization of Alfred Fantl in New York City. The move gave Frank H. Bresee's small-town store the advantages provided by a group with an annual purchasing power of $150 million to $500 million and a staff of fifty expert buyers. Firms like Fantl's were private businesses engaged in the work for a profit, unlike the associated buying organizations financed and controlled by groups of stores. The success of these firms depended on their ability to combine orders from different stores to create quantity purchasing. They were not cooperative in the way that associated buying organizations like AMC were. Stores using the service were not related in any way and not obligated to exchange figures. While weaker than associated buying groups, they were nonetheless more efficient than the store's own buying office in the market, which was usually under the control of the store's general merchandise manager. Such store buying offices, which were typically in New York City, could simply be a place for buyers to use as their headquarters or a more elaborate affair, such an office with a permanent buyer and staff of assistants. And finally, a buying agency was another option. The buying agent served as a commission agent for the manufacturer and did not represent any group of stores.[51]

Advantages came not only from increased buying power but also from the closeness of these organizations to the pulse of fashion. Alfred Fantl, for example, reported on what retailers were buying, noting such things as "growing demand" for "mannish tailored coats of white flannel selling for $25" and softness in the market for "plain white goods, such as Swiss organdie, lawn, batiste and broadcloth." Store trends in "larger cities" were particularly noted, such as the "increased call" for "the vagabond hat of antelope felt in neutral shades for street wear." This type of on-the-ground information was available in Fantl's brief reports in the trade press, but subscribers to his service would have had even more access to shifts in styles, something that could provide a competitive edge to a small-town retailer trying to access big-city consumer trends.[52]

Fighting for Mrs. Consumer

As department store merchants were finding out, consumers had changed since the Great War—in ways that did not necessarily work to their advantage. Many had more to spend, but they were spending that income differently than before. The average income for all families in 1925 by one estimate was $2,000 a year, up from $1,434.94 in 1919. In small towns, middle-class households purchased a wide array of electrical appliances, from washing machines to vacuum cleaners to curling irons. Pianos, phonographs, and radios graced many homes. Services, however, rather than these consumer goods sold by department stores, took a greater portion of income as people spent money on telephone service, electricity, beauty shops, medical treatment, education, and leisure activities. Expenditure on consumer durables leaped forward by 75 percent, but this category included automobiles, the sale of which indirectly benefited only those department stores engaged in tire sales and auto accessories (Macy's sold goggles, dusters, and running board baggage trunks, for example). Many factors, moreover, influenced where someone chose to purchase consumer goods. In some cities, department stores led in per capita sales, but popular consumer durables could come from a variety of establishments. Chains of specialty shops selling women's ready-to-wear clothing and accessories, like Grayson-Robinson in California, were expanding rapidly. According to advertising expert Christine Frederick, author of the best-selling 1929 book *Selling Mrs. Consumer*, women had "deserted department stores" and were instead patronizing these specialty shops for their service.[53]

Consumers also demanded greater availability of credit in the 1920s. This demand for credit, however, conflicted with standing practice in the department store field. A. T. Stewart, the mail order firms Sears and Roebuck and Montgomery Ward, and Macy's had been well known for their cash-only policies. As consumer credit grew increasingly popular, some in the field pushed back. Trade journals published correctives on the practice, condemning the massive consumer debt it generated as well as its costs. The administration of credit needed extra bookkeeping, merchants knew. It required expenditure on monthly statements, collection correspondence, billing machines, office supplies, and the salary of credit managers. The cost of return-goods privileges and delivery services was higher in credit stores. Most significantly, credit policies led to bad debt losses. And finally, credit accounts often took a long time to settle. People chose to pay their food bills more quickly than they settled with their local department store.[54]

In spite of these costs, the department store industry acceded to consumers and pushed for credit modernization among its members. Advocates for credit saw several advantages. Some, like department store chain founder W. T. Grant, had a change of heart and began advocating credit as a way for shoppers to increase their purchasing power (and thus increase sales volume). Spurred by the post–World War I depression, a wide range of retailers moved into installment selling, including the mail-order firm Montgomery Ward. By the 1920s, department store chains led in the practice. Even conventional department stores like Wanamaker's began to introduce financing plans. Such financing lay behind the rise in sales of expensive consumer goods such as radios, vacuum cleaners, fine jewelry, and refrigerators, items the ordinary shopper would have been unable to afford on a cash-only basis. Installment plans and other forms of credit were very successful, leading to the expansion of consumer debt from about 4–6 percent of income between 1900 and 1920 to about 10 percent of income in the 1920s. The annual volume of retail installment credit itself rose from just over a half-billion dollars in 1910 to around $7 billion in

1929. Some who offered it found that almost half their business was sold on credit terms by the 1920s.[55]

As with credit modernization, competition also led more department stores to offer costly services and amenities. In the prosperity decade, an even wider range of department stores found more ways to cater to Mrs. Consumer. Stores in provincial cities began offering tearooms and restaurants, public lending libraries, luxurious restrooms, beauty salons, and the professional services of interior decorators. Big city stores also expanded their customer offerings. In Boston, Shepard's introduced an elaborate playroom where mothers could drop off their children while they shopped. The trade press recognized that these types of free services for customers took up valuable selling space, but retailers saw them as a justifiable cost that brought in charge accounts and kept all of the customer's business in the store. Baby shops in the 1920s, like those introduced by Joslin's Dry Goods Company in Denver, offered the services of a nurse, with free advice, weekly weigh-ins for the baby, and wicker rocking chairs for customers to sit in while viewing merchandise for their nursery. Other emporia sought the loyalty of club women through fashion events and teas, even going so far as to take their advice on styles and prices for use in newspaper advertisements. During this period, department stores also innovated ways to reach male shoppers, opening radio, motor accessories, and sporting goods departments specifically to cater to their needs. Women, however, as the purchasing agents for their households, remained their primary market.[56]

Retailers began to pay more attention to women's increasing demand for stylish goods and specific fashions, making it a part of their buying plans in the prosperous decade. According to contemporary accounts, fashion became increasingly important to consumers, and thus to the department store industry, in the 1920s. Department stores had been style leaders in big cities through fashion shows, fashion lectures, and monthly publications like Marshall Field's *Fashions of the Hour*. Fine American department stores had long imported the latest designs or had copies made of Parisian styles. Wealthy clientele were admitted to special showrooms or luxurious "French rooms." In the 1920s, however, the industry saw increased potential in the provinces for fashion goods. Small-city firms maintained an active buying force that consulted women customers before making numerous purchasing trips to New York City. Buyers in small-town stores were

FIGURE 11. During the teens, the Emery, Bird, Thayer Company, Missouri's largest department store, published a series of photographic postcards featuring store interiors and exteriors. A uniformed maid handed them out to customers in the store's writing room. Missouri Valley Special Collections, Kansas City Public Library, Kansas City, Missouri.

admonished to do more than just stock up on merchandise but to study their clients' needs and train their clerks on fashion trends. New systems of stock control emerged to help them stay attuned to buying patterns.[57]

Department stores, however, did not simply follow consumer demand. Management urged salesclerks to shape or control the desires of their customers. At Macy's in the 1920s, for example, the goal of selling stock in hand took precedence over a customer's individual taste. One Parisian-trained milliner recalled feeling pressure from the male floorwalker to make a sale rather than prevent an unfortunate customer from purchasing an extremely unflattering hat. According to sociologist Frances Donovan, who did department store fieldwork in the 1920s, some buyers instructed salesclerks "to try to educate customers, to improve their taste in dress." Donovan observed that this effort at education often failed, as customers had their own notions of taste. Employees sought to shape consumers' minds more broadly by actively promoting an ethic of spending. Merchandise managers urged buyers and salesclerks to sell the modern idea of style itself and not emphasize "old-fashioned" things like " 'staple dresses' or 'durable coats' or suits with 'wearing qualities.' "[58] Urging women to buy particular items of apparel was nothing new, of course, but the context of ready-to-wear fashion was.

Ready-to-wear women's apparel was fully ensconced in department stores by the 1920s. Ready-to-wear clothing for women had become more widely available in the years before World War I as looser, simpler styles in women's fashions spread, decreasing the demand for individually fitted clothing. Factory-produced clothing, however, often required alterations, which department stores provided at minimal cost or even free of charge. Even with altering, these garments were much less expensive than the custom creations of dressmakers. Dry goods became less important as a wider variety of ready-made clothes became available. As early as 1911, brides who wanted a formal wedding could purchase a ready-to-wear white bridal gown from a department store. Even elite women, who had traditionally had their clothes custom made, sought out ready-made fashions. When Margaret Oliver married in 1914 at St. Stephen's Church in New York City, she wrote her friend about the wedding costume she purchased: a "lovely three piece taupe poplin (from Lord & Taylor—the only suitable thing they had)" and a veil that was "coral color faced with taupe." She wrote "they all have proud French labels so I pretend I think they saw Paris." Prestigious department stores would have helped legitimize ready-made fashionable clothing for discriminating shoppers. The high-end New York City department store Bergdorf Goodman introduced its women's ready-to-wear department in 1923, signaling broad consumer acceptance.[59]

Fashion was an important selling tool, but department stores also relied on price appeal. Retailers of the 1920s were far less reluctant to emphasize low price than their forebears were. Increased demand for fashionable, yet modestly priced apparel in the 1920s pushed department stores across the economic spectrum to engage in price-conscious promotions. In that decade, even bastions of the carriage trade like Marshall Field's had introduced such items as the fifteen-dollar stylish ready-made dress.[60] Retailers now had to work to reconcile their tradition of service and amenities with shoppers' demand for low prices, and the wealth of goods promised by mass production.

While the first consumer-buying preference surveys addressing the role of price in decision making would not appear until the early 1930s, other evidence suggests price was increasingly becoming an issue for department store customers. Low prices were the main attraction of mail-order firms, according to one market study of middle-class small-town women shoppers in the 1920s. In response, large urban department stores added mail-order divisions during this period. These allowed them to compete with specialized mail-order houses as well as reach rural consumers. Others offered promotional sales like "Dollar Days" to attract the crowds. Some experts, however, interpreted the retail scene differently. With a confidence she would surely later regret, Christine Frederick sold the optimistic message to her trade readers in 1929 that more generous family budgets meant that "we are now definitely less interested in 'bargains,' 'price comparisons,' 'cut-prices,' and lower grade qualities."[61]

Shoppers' expectations changed during the period in part because of their increased mobility, though contemporaries were mostly unclear about the direction they were heading. Early in the century, small-town merchants feared the competition of "larger city stores" and the mail-order house and sought ways to "keep trade at home." Trains had long transported shoppers to larger destinations. Such an excursion might be necessary to find clothing for special occasions, especially for elite women like Mamie McFaddin, who traveled from her home in Beaumont to Dallas in 1919 to have a wedding gown made and spent several long days shopping for her trousseau at the luxurious new department store Neiman Marcus. Improved transportation likely hurt small-town merchants more than those in larger cities, which had the potential to draw shoppers in from wider markets. With the rise of automobile ownership, merchants in the 1920s were increasingly concerned that their customers would drive to larger trade centers where stores with higher volumes of trade could offer fresher merchandise or better assortments. These concerns were justified, as sales per capita in city department stores were higher than in the stores' metropolitan areas, reflecting not only the concentration of population but "the trend toward larger centers for certain types of shopping."[62] Good roads and railroad schedules encouraged out-of-town shopping, but according to one 1926 study, in the "most progressive towns," dealers kept the majority of their local business. Fashionable goods like shoes, dresses, hats, and coats were the items most often purchased by women in larger trade centers. Not surprisingly, small items, such as ten-cent-store items, groceries, drugs, and

FIGURE 12. Ohioan Isaac Herbst opened a dry goods store in Fargo, North Dakota, in 1891, and by 1900 it had become the Herbst Department Store. Popular merchandising events like Dollar Day, shown here in 1922, spread to department stores in smaller communities during the prosperity decade. Institute for Regional Studies, North Dakota State University, Fargo (rs001408).

toilet preparations, were rarely purchased there. Other types of goods were also rarely bought out of town, including appliances, automobiles and auto accessories, and Christmas gifts. Anything to do with children—their clothes and toys—was bought largely in town.[63]

Another issue connected with the automobile was parking. One prominent downtown merchant believed the situation was so bad that if changes were not made, "within 15 years, there will be no down-town shopping districts of any importance." Unclear on the direction the automobile was taking them, however, department stores responded in a variety of ways. By the middle of the decade, some considered offering free parking for customers. Sears was a pioneer in this area in the 1920s, offering off-street parking in an era when street parking was the norm. Independent down-town department stores, on the other hand, lagged behind and were already suffering the consequences. Adding parking was one option for the down-town merchant. Moving was another. During this period, some specialty stores opened branch outlets in outlying areas in response to downtown congestion. Outlying areas increasingly attracted chain store development in the 1920s, pulling trade away from central business districts where real estate was more expensive.[64]

Automobiles expanded retailers' reach beyond their local markets, justi-fying a turn to regional advertising and marketing. Stores in larger cities tried to use automobility to their advantage, sending out catalogs to reach shoppers in their region. In the 1926 study of Kansas and Missouri women, a range of city stores sent their catalogs to 120 potential out-of-town cus-tomers. Of these firms, department stores were the largest single group to mail either sales sheets or catalogs to distant markets. Women in the study received such sales material mostly from Kansas City department stores but also from department stores in Lincoln, Omaha, Nebraska City, Chicago, and St. Louis. Perhaps reflecting the success of this sales material, the study found that women preferred Kansas City department stores for their fash-ionable purchases, shopping at Peck's, John Taylor's, Jones's, and the Emery, Bird, Thayer department store. Specialty shoe, jewelry, music, furni-ture, and drug stores, a few miscellaneous shops, and specialty dealers in women's and men's clothing attracted the rest of out-of-town patronage.[65]

With the exception of catalogs and sales sheets mailed within a regional market, department stores confined their appeals to their local markets. Department stores did not try to reach consumers by advertising in the growing national media, even though evidence suggested that women shop-pers were increasingly influenced by it. National magazines in particular had begun to compete with newspapers for small-town women's attention. In the Kansas City region in 1926, for example, 63 percent of women paid more attention to magazine advertising than newspaper ads, 24 percent focused more on ads in newspapers, and 13 percent were equally interested in both. Yet department stores remained local newspaper advertisers for the most part. Newspaper advertising underlined, rather than erased, local identities for most of this period. In New England mill towns, for example, some local department stores sought customers from a variety of ethnic groups through foreign-language advertising in Hungarian, Portuguese,

French, and Italian newspapers. In was only by the late 1920s that department stores began to drop foreign-language ads, not because they no longer wanted customers from these ethnic groups but because they believed they could reach them through mainstream English newspapers.[66]

Department stores also had to contend with the fact that shoppers increasingly preferred the brand-name goods featured in national advertising campaigns. One middle-class small-town shopper answered a marketing study question about the influence of advertising on everyday buying this way: "I should say advertising does influence my buying. Practically everything I buy is nationally advertised. Cantilever shoes, Berkey and Gay furniture, Imperial tables, Hughes' electric range." Other women revealed a similarly positive attitude toward advertising, something that must have pleased the advertising company, which had produced the study to convince businesses of the need for its services. In various ways, many expressed their lack of confidence in unadvertised products and their belief that nationally advertised brands were "safer." Some women in the study expressed their view that "price is the important thing" they look for in advertisements. Only one, however, the authors were careful to point out, "expressed the conviction that advertised products cost more," a low number that surely reflected the pro-advertising bias of the study.[67]

By the end of the decade, department stores were still working out their relationship with national brands. Department stores had long eschewed nationally advertised brands, given their narrower margin of profit compared to unbranded or private label goods. The rising trend toward nationally advertised brand-name goods challenged department stores' traditional reliance on private label brands. Each department store carried its own private label for most lines. Both traditional and chain department stores introduced long-standing popular private brands in the 1920s. For example, Marshall Field's began manufacturing Frango Mints on its premises in 1929, making them a local staple in Chicago. And Sears introduced its Kenmore brand in 1927 with a wringer washing machine that would reach a national market through its catalog. Whether local or national in reach, private brands like these competed with nationally advertised goods. In the past, department stores had come into conflict with manufacturers that established minimum resale prices for their brands. Their interests now also came into conflict with advertisers, whose voice had grown more powerful in the 1920s. Advertising experts criticized department stores' reliance on private brands. Christine Frederick revealed her connections to *Printers' Ink*

and *Ladies' Home Journal* when she came down strongly against department stores that vied with manufacturers of national brand goods for "consumer prestige." Distributors who packed their own brands, she argued,
mixed their functions in a confusing way when they went into manufacturing and wholesaling and were not able to produce the same quality or
provide the same service as a manufacturer who focused his energies on the
production of a single line of goods. Macy's private brand of canned peas,
she strongly asserted, might be a good price but was of inconsistent quality,
unlike national brands of the same foodstuff.[68]

Most department stores left the prosperity decade as they had entered
it—as local institutions committed to their private brands and local newspaper and radio advertising. By the end of the 1920s, department stores still
had a professional identity based on the independent merchant, but cracks
in the industry threatened to change this. The decade had been one of great
growth. The emergence of finance capitalism, which led many merchants
to incorporate, facilitated modernization and expansion.[69] New consumer
habits had cut into department stores' share of the retail market. Shoppers
had more to spend but also a wider range of consumer goods and retail
outlets from which to choose. The spread of automobile ownership allowed
consumers to hop in their cars and drive away to larger or different trade
centers. Shiny chain stores like W. T. Grant, A&P, and the famous five-and-
dime Woolworths lined Main Streets across the country, attracting budget-
conscious shoppers. By the end of the decade, such chain operations had
become a new and more powerful purveyor of bigness that galvanized
smaller merchants into a more effective oppositional movement than the
goliath department store had two decades prior.[70]

In response to these challenges, department store executives of the
1920s went down a path that brought their industry closer to Wal-Mart.
Individual merchants reacted to declining market share and chain competition not by joining the anti-chain movement gathering steam near the end
of the decade, as they might have, but by choosing to become more like the
competition. Department store expansion and modernization came in part
in response to these outside pressures. Prominent merchants, department
store trade associations, and the national trade press urged independent
members to reform along the lines of chains, extolling their efficiencies.

The industry could not do this on its own, however. A supportive federal government was a necessary, if not sufficient, condition for the restruc-
turing of the department store field that began at the end of the decade,

when some of the first big mergers took place. As individual merchants and their trade associations professionalized and modernized, they strengthened their ties to the federal government in ways that would continue to foster bigness in the coming years. While the 1920s did not see a retail revolution among department stores, the decade was a turning point for the industry—a definitive moment when Main Street merchants shifted toward consolidation and chain organization, aided by a pro-business state and by increasingly price-conscious consumers.[71]

CHAPTER 4

A New Deal for Department Stores

With headquarters in Washington, Retail Lobbyist Sherrill is expected to bring unity out of the babel. "We merchants," said Merchant (Louis) Kirstein with feeling, "dealing directly with more than 100,000,000 customers, would like to be consulted about national and economic problems. That will be the job of the American Retail Federation, and I believe that Mr. Sherrill will see that it is done."
—*Time,* 1935

THE economic hardship of the 1930s shook the foundation of the department store industry, pushing retailers to reexamine their relationship with consumers. Department stores had traditionally catered to women with lavish services; higher-priced, quality merchandise; and amenities at a downtown location. But purchasing power declined drastically in the face of widespread unemployment, failed banks, disastrous deflation, and an overarching loss of confidence in business leaders and the economy. The Consumer Price Index fell 2.6 percent in 1930, an additional 9 percent the following year, and by 1933 it stood at 18 percent below what it had been the year of the stock market crash. As shoppers became more price conscious, department stores had to explore other ways to compete with lower-price retailers for customers' dwindling purchasing power. With profits declining and customers seemingly poised to abandon them, department stores sought to increase control over their markets and intensified their professionalization and modernization efforts. Individual firms stepped up advertising, introduced a range of creative merchandising ploys, modernized their facilities, and promoted their local image. They tried all things: stronger price appeals, strengthening their role as civic institutions serving local interests, studying their markets and making preliminary adaptations to suburbanization and the automobile, challenging long-standing free customer services, and standardizing operations and slashing payroll to address rising store expenses. Some sought to redefine themselves as low-price department stores. With high fixed capital expenses, high labor costs, and a tradition of customer service and luxurious amenities, however, they could only narrow the gap between themselves and low-price retailers. At root a conservative industry, they remained committed to high advertising expenditure and their downtown locations, two things that had served them well since the nineteenth century but had begun to erode their competitiveness.[1]

Rather than fighting the low-price model and supporting the push for state and federal anti-chain policies during this period, the department store industry sided with chains, even though they challenged their traditions of luxury and service. In the face of government support for small business and independent retailers, the department store industry unified over its opposition to fair trade (Miller-Tydings Act) and restrictions on large-scale buying (Robinson-Patman Act). Mass retailers became more organized in their opposition, creating a powerful new national federation of chain and independent department store retailers to lobby on behalf of their shared interests. At the same time, the New Deal and World War II pushed the retail industry to cooperate with the federal government in unprecedented ways. A massive decline in consumer purchasing power and the deflationary trends of the 1930s led government-averse merchants to cooperate with the National Recovery Administration (NRA) for a short time. This negotiation, however, also aided the department store industry's reorientation toward chains and "bigness." When prosperity returned with the coming of World War II, the department store industry was dedicated to bigness and empowered to meet the challenges and changing markets of wartime and beyond.

Shopping in the 1930s

While department stores cut back free services and amenities during the Depression, they largely upheld their image as bastions of luxury. Well-established, big-city firms in fashionable retail districts continued to supply costly goods and lavish service to those for whom money was no object. Such elite customers raised the reputation of the shopping districts they patronized and contributed to the traditional department store's luxurious image, even in a decade of personal hardship and economic crisis. One such prominent Gilded Age district had been New York's Ladies' Mile, the former home to such venerable stores as Siegel-Cooper & Company, Stern Brothers, Lord & Taylor, Arnold Constable & Company, and B. Altman & Co., before they all moved uptown.[2]

By the 1930s, it was Fifth Avenue that attracted such customers as the wife of former New York governor Al Smith. A loyal charge account customer at B. Altman & Co., Catherine A. Smith (Dunn) left a record of extravagant purchases and personal services spanning the crash of 1929 and the early years of the next decade. As the wife of a public figure, with five children and numerous young grandchildren, Mrs. Smith's consumer needs (or wants) were vast. While living at the Hotel Biltmore in New York in December 1928 after her husband's unsuccessful presidential run against Herbert Hoover, she ended the year owing B. Altman $17,641.58. Moving to a Fifth Avenue residence, Mrs. Smith turned to her favorite department store for linens, towels, and furniture. Along with her extensive Altman's wardrobe of suits, dresses, negligees, hats, gloves, shoes, scarves, ribbons, hose, jewelry, and furs, her total charges amounted to just over $10,000 between March and December 1930.[3]

This politician's wife's charge record documented her expensive tastes and love of clothes, but it also signaled how local department stores at the time could still connect with diverse aspects of their customers' social lives. The purchase of a rosary for $5.50 at B. Altman's serves as a reminder of one of the reasons her husband's presidential campaign failed. Her shopping record also revealed her to be the matriarch of a large extended family. One day's shopping on December 17, 1931, supplied Mrs. Smith with a circus set, two pistol sets, a tractor, ferry boat, fire engine, doll, blackboard, and a host of other toys, all likely Christmas gifts for her grandchildren. B. Altman's also helped make her life easier, providing convenient services under one roof, with a full-time staff that gave advice on decorating apartments and houses. The New York City store monogrammed her towels, hemmed her clothing purchases, and provided labor to hang new draperies. Several of the services her favorite store provided were likely for goods not even purchased there. She turned to them for fur storage for her numerous wraps and coats, jewelry repair work, and dressmaker services for alterations. In these ways, department stores sought middle-class and elite shoppers not through price appeal but through their reputation as a fashionable emporium that provided quality goods and a high level of service.[4]

Mrs. Al Smith was not a typical shopper in any time period, of course. In the early Depression her charge account stood in stark contrast to the experience of most people, who would have had little to spend at department stores or any other retail establishment. A yearly income of $2,500 put one's household in the top tenth percentile and allowed a comfortable standard of living, but over half of families survived on $500 to $1,500 a year, an income that precluded shopping for much of anything besides bare necessities.[5] With about a quarter of the workforce out of a job, expenditure on personal consumption declined in the United States from $79,000 million in 1929 to a low of $46,400 million in 1933, climbing slowly back up to $71,900 million in 1940. Banks had failed at a rate of around five hundred per year in the flush times of the 1920s. In 1930, closures rose to well over a thousand. Business failures reached a record of 26,355 by the end of 1930, and gross national product dropped 12.6 percent from the year before. Farm prices collapsed after the stock market crash. Farms and homes across the country went into foreclosure.[6]

In this context, many shoppers were simply unable to pay their bills. Bad-debt losses were a continual problem in the department store industry, but during the Depression they escalated, reflecting hard economic times but also the spread of credit. Most stores had charge-account customers, and some small-town or rural department stores still employed book credit, despite industry exhortations against the practice. Installment plans also flourished. Even Macy's, a late holdout, offered its first store-sponsored credit plan by 1939, allowing everything to be sold on installment except wines and liquors. Independent department stores faced particularly high credit losses and were unable to spread those losses across an organization. The Higbee Company, a prominent Cleveland institution founded in 1860, for example, had a net loss through bad debts in 1934 of $181,212 against a sales volume of $10,730,241, while the net losses of eight Associated Dry Goods Corporation stores in 1933 were just $248,293. Small family-run department stores in rural communities were particularly challenged and had to pull payments out of their cash-strapped customers a dollar at a time.[7]

Department stores addressed bad debt in a variety of ways, depending on their size and clientele. In 1930, people living in communities of less

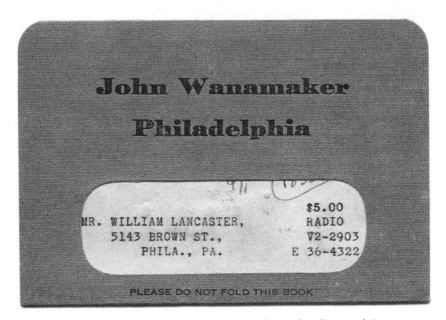

FIGURE 13. Through department stores, consumers' use of credit spread. In
Philadelphia during the Great Depression, Wanamaker customers purchased
expensive goods like radios "on time," keeping track of their payments in booklets
like these. Author's collection.

than ten thousand made up just over half the total population, which meant
that local retailers had more opportunity to engage in face-to-face negotiations with their clientele over bad debts. Independent stores engaged in
creative accounting and made personal accommodations. Collection agents
for department stores in small communities like Filer, Idaho, for example,
accepted payment in kind. One customer, Joe Starrie, was not on the collections list for the Falk Mercantile Company in Idaho but came forward and
"admitted he owed us for a sack of flour and offered me a sack of red beans
for the bill." The collection agent, who was known in Filer for "being a
very zealous person in his collections," wrote the following account: "I sold
the beans for 2.00 and his sack of flour was 1.98."[8] Local retailers like Falk's,
which had expanded in 1929 to buy stores in more than half a dozen small
communities in Idaho, worked with their newly acquired hard-up clientele.
When Hardy Hopkins got his first job in months through the New Deal's
Civil Works program, for example, Falk's returned his repossessed washer

after ten-dollar payments were worked out. Personal information on customers, however, was also used to deny credit. A retailer's knowledge of customers' employment through the New Deal could sink their credit rating. Customers employed by the Works Progress Administration (WPA), for example, were routinely denied credit and were not allowed to open charge accounts. WPA workers below the executive or foreman class were especially regarded as a "very poor credit risk by most stores." One credit manager from the Roos Bros. store in Oakland provided his fellow merchants with "an easy 'out' for declining WPA accounts," suggesting that customers be told that regulations did not permit local administrative offices to certify the employment status of workers.[9]

Bad debts created a potentially adversarial relationship between stores and their customers; shoplifting made it so in no uncertain terms. Shoplifting and employee theft were two activities which department stores had long sought to control. The economic hardship of the period, however, made it difficult to pay in any way and spurred more to break the law and risk prosecution. Christmas was peak season as shoplifters stole goods from department stores to provide holiday gifts for their loved ones. Department store managers stepped up their attention to the ever-present problem of shrinkage through employee and customer theft, spending large amounts of money hiring uniformed and plainclothes store detectives. Joining citywide organizations of department stores that kept track of shoplifters' identities, they attacked the problem, observing that the numbers had grown rapidly with the Depression.[10]

Simply put, store management had an increasingly difficult time controlling shoppers during the Depression. The copious advice provided by management and the retail industry on how to handle complaints and other problems suggested that customers were never passive. Women had long insisted on returning goods after they had been worn or used, for example. Customers at downscale department stores in the 1930s engaged in rowdy bargain-hunting behavior, a long-standing social practice among shoppers that physically disrupted operations. Opposition to store traditions and policies, however, became increasingly organized in the 1930s. In the late 1920s, protests by black consumers against discriminatory hiring practices in white-owned stores erupted in Chicago, spreading to other cities during the 1930s. "Don't Buy Where You Can't Work" campaigns targeted chain stores as well as independents like L. M. Blumstein's department store in Harlem. Some retailers in black neighborhoods, including Sears, responded to civil rights pressure and advertised changes in their racist hiring policies. In the Depression, it must have seemed even more imperative to satisfy those willing and able to spend money and maintain customer loyalty. This could mean taking a large step to overturn structural inequality through reform of hiring practices, or it could be as minor as changing personal behavior. During the 1930s, for example, the company newsletter of Gold's department store in Lincoln, Nebraska, advised employees on how to "keep valuable old customers." Salespeople were instructed on how to avoid arguing with difficult customers. "Gold Tips" suggested: "When you find yourself at odds with customers, agree with them by remaining silent or veering to other points."[11]

Not only did shoppers have less to spend, they were changing the context in which they spent, leaving town to do so. The decentralization of the retail environment that had begun in the 1920s continued in the Depression decade. Department stores in Boston's central business district, for example, including such well-known names as Jordan Marsh and Filene's, had dominated the city's retail trade prior to the Depression. During the 1930s, though, shoppers increasingly chose their individual automobiles over the city's public transportation system, spending their money across the broader metropolitan area of Boston. Elsewhere, firms like Saks Fifth Avenue and I. Magnin in California chose to locate outside their city's central business district when the economy began to recover in the late 1930s, an ominous stop that foreshadowed the massive decentralization of postwar suburbia.[12]

Low-price department stores in which expenses were cut to the bone would have been one possible model for the industry during this period of economic hardship. But during the 1930s, the self-service, low-price model of downtown department store selling was still on the fringes. The department store industry did not advocate that path in the Depression. While the grocery trade increasingly employed self-service in the 1930s, department store shopping for the most part still required the service of a skilled salesperson to bring out the desired goods, assist with fitting or selection, and advise on purchases. Shoppers could browse at will, but obtaining items to purchase involved extensive personal interaction with a salesclerk, as it had since the nineteenth century. Only a few downscale department stores experimented with lesser degrees of customer assistance by the 1930s. In New York City, discount department stores like Klein's and Ohrbach's introduced freely accessible racks and shelves to display garments and

FIGURE 14. Established in 1876 and remodeled in 1925, this family-run Beale Street institution in Memphis identified as both a department store and a general store. Shoppers like these photographed in 1939 would have found an array of low-priced goods at A. Schwab's. Author's collection.

provided a communal dressing room. Customers were not catered to with lavish store interiors or sales help. At these low-priced, high-volume stores, shoppers picked their own garments, tried them on unaided, and then proceeded to a cashier to pay and have the goods wrapped.[13] Discounters would cash in on this mode of selling two decades later, but most department stores hung on to older, tried and true methods.

In the face of the economic crisis and the changes that accompanied it, many department stores tried to hold fast to their traditional female, white, middle-class base by offering their customary level of service and amenity. Consumers—women shoppers, it was understood—would help determine which type of retail system prevailed. By the late 1930s, the department store trade press could say the "consumer [was] in the saddle and riding high." She (the feminine was always used) had the power to shape their industry, determining whether mass distribution based on low prices would predominate or the traditional retail mode would survive. If it were chains that could consistently give her the lowest price, one prescient editor of the *Department Store Economist* argued, then they would succeed and the anti-chain movement would fail. But the industry clung to the idea that this group had traditionally been style conscious rather than price conscious, a better fit for these institutions saddled with high operating costs and large gross margins.[14]

Market studies in the 1930s, however, revealed that low price, or good value as it was more commonly described, was important to women shoppers. One 1938 study of Buffalo, New York, housewives found that women stated their preference for their independent department stores over standardized chains like Sears, yet in practice they shopped at both, favoring chains for mundane goods and independents for prestige items.[15] Another market study, conducted in 1936 for B. Altman & Co. (Mrs. Al Smith's favorite store), documented the shopping habits of women in a fashionable retail district yet found good value to be important. The stores were all independents catering to different markets, from the luxury B. Altman & Co. to the price-cutter Macy's. Other competitors included were Bonwit Teller, Franklin Simon, Lord & Taylor, Saks, Stern Brothers, and Mc-Creary's. The study drew on households in Manhattan, Brooklyn, Queens, and the Bronx with a range of annual incomes from $1,800 to $9,000. The interviewees were certainly not representative of female shoppers nationally. In fact, most fell in the prosperous middle of this range, between $3,000 and $4,999 and between $4,500 and $5,999, with only eight interviews conducted in the lowest income range of $1,800–$2,900. Even middle-class and well-to-do shoppers in the B. Altman study showed indications of price consciousness in the Depression. At department stores, most shoppers in the study pursued lower prices and good value on regular priced and sales items. The women rated Macy's very highly for its low prices and good value. Macy's also ranked above other New York retailers for its advertising, selection, and quality. Most women in the B. Altman study preferred shopping in department stores (62 percent), with only 38 percent preferring smaller stores, a choice perhaps linked to their stated belief that prices were not necessarily higher and that service was better in larger emporia.[16]

Traditions of high levels of customer service continued throughout the 1930s, even though the growing demand for low prices and the competitive retail environment might have swayed department stores to shift to the chain store selling model. Department stores experienced higher labor costs than chains in part because they staffed their selling floors with skilled salespeople, available to help customers with information and advice. Not surprisingly, given the high expectations for personal interaction between salesclerks and customers, conflicts emerged. Customer service, one of the hallmarks of the full-service department store, had always been a social interchange, subject to power imbalances, prejudices, and personality. Paradoxically, the social and economic gap between salesclerks at upscale department stores and their customers was both necessary for the high-service model of selling and disruptive to it. In his work on retail unionization in the 1930s, for example, historian Daniel Opler demonstrated how the elite shopping experience was predicated upon the class and sometimes ethnic hierarchy between women shoppers and salesclerks. The in-house study at B. Altman's supports his observation. Although only a small percentage of the middle-class and upper-class women who frequented department stores in New York City's fashionable districts complained about the behavior of salesclerks, when they did take issue with department store service across New York City they chose words like "lazy," "rude," "impatient," "impersonal," "too busy or rushed," "too slow," or "not courteous," language that signaled their privilege and class expectations. According to one 1938 survey of customers in sixteen cities, over a third of shoppers' grievances were related to the conduct of clerks.[17]

Committed to the high-service, high-cost model of selling, the department store industry experienced increased pressure from its labor force in the context of the 1930s. Empowered by the New Deal's Wagner Act, salesclerks across the country were pushing back against low wages and the conditions of their work. Store clerks joined unions in greater numbers than ever before. In the late 1930s, strikes swept urban department stores from Tacoma, Washington, to Cleveland to New York City. Some progressive middle-and upper-class women offered their support to the labor movement, forming the League of Women Shoppers of New York during a strike at Ohrbach's. Through appeals like "Use Your Buying Power for Justice," they put their social status and purchasing power behind striking workers. For the most part, upscale store customers opposed the labor movement sweeping big-city retail workers during the decade. They often treated salesclerks with disdain and made unreasonable demands, not paying attention to closing times or exacting great services with little expenditure. Customers made "extreme demands," according to Irving Fajans, a

salesclerk who had worked at Macy's, the May department store, and Ohrbach's and was a member of the Department Store Workers Union, local
1250. Recounting his recent trying experiences in New York City to a WPA
interviewer, he noted that politeness "got to be natural" in his line of work,
though "when customers is out of earshot" he was able to say what he
really thought, classifying his customers into nine types, all of which wasted
the salesclerks' time or created unnecessary hassles and annoyances.[18] These
were age-old problems for department store salesclerks that federal policy,
for the moment, promised to alleviate. From the perspective of managers,
however, the pressure to solve their conflicts with both labor and customers
increased in the context of falling department store performance.

Surviving the Depression

Against a backdrop of falling prices, contractions in production, widespread
unemployment, and declining purchasing power, retailers suffered great
losses. Specialty retailers were hit the hardest, while retailers of lower-priced
lines fared better in general. Variety stores, for example, recovered by 1935
and then outpaced their pre-Depression figures. Department store sales
dropped 41 percent between 1929 and 1933. For the most part, department
stores faced abysmal net profits, though there were some variations across
the industry. Luxury stores did not necessarily fare worse than middle-
market or lower-end department stores during the Depression. Some big
independents with lavish facilities, like the Art Deco Bullock's in Los
Angeles, flourished. But many were forced to close their doors. Between
1935 and 1939, the number of department stores fell from 4,201 to 4,074
(a deceptively high number overall, however, since it incorporated retailers
that the census would later not count as department stores, when the way
merchandise line sales were reported changed). Department stores also
continued to lose market share to other types of retailers. As a group, their
share of total sales, which stood at 10 percent in 1933, continued to slip,
for the most part, until the United States entered World War II.[19]

Economic conditions in the 1930s favored firms that kept their costs
down or were able to cater to the market for low-priced goods. Downscale
department stores in New York City, for example, actually increased their
profits during the Depression, benefiting from a rise in bargain hunting. In
Boston, Filene's bargain basement allowed the firm to survive the Depression. In an era of diminishing purchasing power, some retailers lowered

prices to increase volume. Stern Brothers, then on 42nd Street, for example, tried to appeal to a wider range of customers. Department stores like Hengerer's in Buffalo, which had traditionally not carried bargain goods, introduced budget departments and thrift shops. In 1938, Macy's adopted the slogan "it's smart to be thrifty."[20]

Many took the opposite path, however, increasing their expenditure on store improvement and expansion plans in order to shore up their image as purveyors of luxury and service. Businesses did not envision relocating as a solution to their problems at this point. Reflecting a broader commitment to downtown, merchants and their associations reinvested in Main Street during the 1930s. Modernization came to be seen as central to economic recovery, receiving broad support from independent retailers and chains. Marking the National Retail Dry Goods Association's (NRDGA) anniversary in 1936, the organization published *Twenty-Five Years of Retailing*—over 250 pages of photos and essays written by prominent experts and professionals in the field that celebrated "progress" in merchandising, accounting, store operations and physical plant, and salesmanship. Written as the organization's official coming-of-age statement, it was an embodiment of the industry's modernization ideal in the 1930s. Amid declining profits, in fact, many chose to update fixtures and facades, adding escalators and elevators, expanding selling-floor space, and adding departments or special features like tearooms. Across the country, independents and units in department store groups modernized even as sales and profits fell. In Buffalo, for example, independents like J. N. Adam and Hengerer's embarked on expensive Depression-era remodeling plans costing $500,000 and $1 million respectively. Several chains stores opened new branches in downtown Buffalo, reflecting their belief in the centrality of Main Street. The federal government also demonstrated its support of modernization as a tool for economic recovery. Merchants across the country modernized their small store fronts with the support of federal loans issued under Title I of the Federal Housing Administration and its "Modernize Main Street" initiative.[21]

While big renovations and expansions received lavish attention in the trade press, providing inspirational stories for struggling merchants, countless modest or mundane modernizations were undertaken by smaller Main Street department stores across the country during the Depression. The trade press documented these efforts in a variety of ways. Advertisements for the Grand Rapids Store Equipment Company, for example, used before and after photographs that graphically demonstrated how display, lighting, and spatial arrangements had changed since the stores were first built. Before modernizing, many of the company's clients looked like general stores—dark, cluttered, and unattractively arranged. Ads argued a "drab, old-fashioned and uninteresting setting" would make shoppers go elsewhere. New Grand Rapids display equipment, ad copy suggested, would pay "dividends" and investment would quickly be repaid and doubled.[22] The trade press also sent editors out to "the field" to document the minor improvements made by local retailers in the provinces. Remodeled elevators at H. Leh & Co. in Allentown, Pennsylvania, they reported, connected four selling floors and could take visitors to the roof for a view of the city. An escalator from the first to second floor at Glosser Bros. in Johnstown, Pennsylvania, and the installation of indirect lighting at the People's Store in Charleston, a unit of the West Virginia department store chain, were just a few other updates reported by the field editor for the *Department Store Economist* in 1938. Some firms received extensive "face-lifting" the same Depression year. A typical case was Chase's in Pontiac, Michigan, first built in the teens. Advertised as "the largest store in Oakland County," it had a self-serve grocery department and offered to pay high prices for produce brought to the store. Such stores likely looked old-fashioned by the 1930s, leading to a $200,000 expansion program that added two new selling floors and modernized the building facade with glass brick between pilasters of black granite for a streamlined effect.[23]

Even for these smaller stores, modernization was a capital investment that had the potential to repay itself over time. But facing competition from other mass retailers and chains, merchants were desperate for short-term ways to bring in the crowds. To counter their declining share of the retail market, they increased expenditure on advertising and publicity campaigns. Traditional department stores made their first forays into national advertising in the 1930s, the first being the prominent independent retailer Neiman Marcus of Dallas, whose ads would appear in the national magazines *Vogue* and *Harper's Bazaar*. Individual merchants had long engaged in spectacle, from loudly advertised sales extravaganzas to rooftop weddings. Some crowd-drawing techniques in the 1930s sought to preserve a store's respectable image. Halle's in Cleveland invited authors to hold autograph parties, their book buyer consciously trying to elevate readers' tastes. In 1930, downtown merchants across the country sought to pull in potential customers with such middle-class entertainments as bridge clinics, piano

FIGURE 15. H. Leh & Co. of Allentown, Pennsylvania, called itself "the new daylight department store." Postcards were advertisements. This one featured a store directory on the back outlining each department and amenity, from the restaurant and soda fountain in the basement to the ladies' waiting room on the third floor. Storage work rooms and the men's room were relegated to the fourth and fifth floors. Author's collection.

recitals, and student debates. The South Center Department Store, which served black Chicago, exhibited paintings by African American artists during this period.[24] In the Depression, however, many stores were pushed to expand the boundaries of their middle-class identity, to seek new markets or capture the customers leaving them for chain stores.

Department stores went to extreme measures to draw in potential shoppers during this period, providing free performances and spectacles that undercut their conservative reputation and stately image. Entertainments that sought a broader appeal drew negative attention from industry experts. One 1930s academic analyst of the retail industry condemned the "ballyhoo" he saw: "poorly conceived and blatantly executed circuses and parades, 'movies,' and side shows, which represent the sound and the fury behind which they camouflage the excessive cost and loosely controlled activities of their business." In the Depression, however, "ballyhoo methods" were advocated in trade press articles and by merchandising managers. They included a range of highly publicized free events, such as Wild West shows, magicians, clowns, silhouette artists, minstrel entertainments, exhibits, festivals, and product displays. Ballyhoo followed in "Barnum's footsteps," according to the assistant merchandise manager of the Bon Ton Department Store in Hazleton, Pennsylvania. Bringing in the crowds was "practically the entire problem of the department store," she argued, not acknowledging that once there, most had little to spend.[25]

These promotions contributed to the rising cost of doing business during this period. Stores like Higbee Company, whose Santa and holiday parade would later be featured in the popular nostalgic film *A Christmas Story*, engaged in the common Depression-era practice of spending more on advertising than was financially justified. Efforts failed as rising advertising budgets did not translate into improved sales or profits. As retail scholars Peter M. Scott and James T. Walker have argued, advertising was no solution to the deep problems of interwar department stores. Focused on competition within their own sector and engaged in a competitive spiral of advertising expenditure with other stores, they "left themselves vulnerable to competition from the expanding chains stores and specialty retailers, who operated on a lower-cost model (which included much lower ratios of advertising to sales)." As a result, department stores became "locked into a high-cost regime," their rising ad budgets raising costs and eroding competitiveness.[26]

Hearn's of New York City was one such firm. In 1932, under the new ownership of Maurice Levin and Jacob Kaplan, New York City's Hearn's began an aggressive campaign to shore up its declining fortunes. Founded in 1827, it originally catered to the carriage trade, at some point allegedly selling such things as a camel's hair shawl for $10,000 or laces at $1,000. By the early twentieth century, it had become a department store and had a reputation for catering to bargain hunters. Its saleswomen, for example, earned lower salaries than those in more upscale New York stores like Lord & Taylor, reflecting the different status of the two establishments. With the hiring of Bernard Katz, who became the advertising and promotion director in 1932, the store upped its institutional advertising and turned to ballyhoo promotions to draw in crowds. The advertising department pushed "showmanship," and publicity campaigns became increasingly elaborate. For example, Hearn's offered free entertainments that tipped the scales in ballyhoo with such things as a circus with elephants and horses, a "Toy World," and both an Eskimo and a "Midget Village." An aggressive promotional campaign in 1934 began to advertise its goal of becoming the "Biggest Bargain Store in America." At the instigation of the store's president, Maurice Levin, the store itself became a spectacle. Levin widely publicized his decision to cut prices by taking in no profits during the economic crisis, as well as his decision to eliminate his salary and issue no dividends to manager-owners. This "Hearn Plan of 1934," under which the store would halt profits for a year in order to provide lower prices to customers, was not unprecedented but had never been publicized to such effect before. A *Time* magazine article on the announcement of the stunt noted dryly that "since Hearn's publishes no income statement, no man knew last week whether there were any profits to sacrifice."[27]

Hearn's publicity stunt reflects the store's recognition of consumers' increased price consciousness during the period. Management appealed to women, suggesting that it was women "who suffer the most" when there were no jobs or income. Newspaper ads, for example, featured a "motherly" woman shopper proclaiming "I'll Tell You What We Want—We want LOWER prices!" Others, directed at "Mrs. Housewife," informed consumers that Hearn's was "going to revolutionize" its department store business. The "Hearn Plan of 1934" was publicized in newspapers and magazines nationally. Endorsed by politicians like Al Smith and the National Recovery Administration (NRA) chief, Hugh S. Johnson, it represented a cooperative effort by business to help economic recovery.[28]

As the Depression wore on, Hearn's management decided to go further and transform their firm into a high-volume bargain store—their "New

Deal" for consumers. A confidential statement of Hearn's policy for 1938 noted that the store was "at the crossroads" and had to take action to survive. To achieve its ambitious goal of $30 million sales volume for the year, it planned to shift to popular-priced merchandise and employ aggressive selling techniques. This commitment to lowering prices was vigorously publicized in trade journals, newspapers, on billboards, radio flashes, and "five million circulars to blanket metropolitan New York and New Jersey in the most complete coverage that has ever been attempted." The appeal to women and the demand for lower prices culminated in the store's promotion of a consumer rally in Madison Square Garden on March 21, 1938, the "first in the history of New York," according to internal documents. Consumer groups attended, swelling the numbers to eighteen thousand. The actress Mary Pickford and politicians, such as the governor of Pennsylvania and a congressman from New York, lectured on the need for lower prices.[29]

Promotional schemes like this took place within a larger political and social context. Managerial decisions of particular firms could help a firm like Hearn's survive the Depression (a last, much diminished store in the Bronx closed in 1979).[30] But outside forces also played a role. During the 1930s, department stores had to contend with more than high operating costs and low or nonexistent profits. Over the decade, department stores struggled to define their relationship with an increasingly regulatory state and a growing anti-chain movement. How the industry responded during this period would affect the future contours of the commercial landscape.

Department Stores and Government during the Depression

One month after the stock market crash, the president of the venerable Arnold Constable & Company of New York City sent President Hoover a telegram urging him to convene a conference of department store and retail merchants as he had done with industrial and railroad leaders. The head of this luxury department store on Fifth Avenue, Meyer Liberman, wrote that retail business was the "crux of America's commercial life," something that affected more people and involved more money than any other industry. With the millions of dollars his industry spent on advertising, Liberman believed that department stores had the ability to "restimulate confidence" and help "dispel the pessimistic psychology" that threatened the country.[31]

A conference could do this by appealing to manufacturers and merchants to refrain from cancelling orders, cutting advertising expenditure, curtailing buying, or reducing staff. Of course, these rollbacks were exactly what happened in the months and years after the crash of 1929, but at this particular moment it seemed to progressive merchants and their trade organizations that state-supported business cooperation and voluntary efforts were all that was needed to recover from what seemed like a crisis of confidence.

While he did not organize a special retail conference in 1929, Hoover did send a personal message to be read at the 1930 annual meeting of the NRDGA. Hoover had already proven himself a friend of big retailers and their organizations as well as an advocate of chain organization, affinities demonstrated by the numerous pioneering federal studies of distribution initiated during his years in the Commerce Department. While Hoover often praised small businesses, he sought their modernization and favored big business. He preferred to work with business elites and collaborate with their trade associations. His pre-presidential businessman identity and his distance from the antitrust segment of the Republican Party made him at home with the leaders of large enterprises, such as J. C. Penney, with whom he was close. Perhaps in response to Liberman's urgent telegram, President Hoover praised the members of the NRDGA for their cooperation and their role in maintaining "economic stability." Likely intending to instill confidence and optimism that recovery was just around the corner, he pointed out that studies of retail stores revealed the "sustained buying power of the people."[32] Not surprisingly, Hoover's message to the NRDGA gave no indication of the harsh realities facing the retail sector in 1930, including deflation, declining consumer demand, and increasing hostility to big business. Instead, Hoover's brief words signaled his broader belief that voluntary solutions were all that were necessary.

Merchants largely concurred with Hoover's emphasis on volunteerist remedies. The NRDGA, marketing experts, and merchants across the country attempted to face this crisis on their own during Hoover's years, reflecting their deeply held suspicion of government intervention. Private consumption was upheld as a local solution to a national problem. Merchants encouraged local spending in newspaper ads and in organized events highlighting their community identity. Hosting events like Buffalo Day and Rochester's Pledge for Prosperity, merchants sought to make consumption a civic activity. They called consumers who waited for prices to fall "hoarders" and blamed them for the Depression. During the Hoover years,

National "Buy Now" campaigns urged these reluctant consumers—
especially housewives—to loosen their purses to alleviate stores overstocked
with inventory and factories desperate for new orders. (After the election
of Franklin Delano Roosevelt, the National Recovery Administration
launched a campaign as well. Edward Filene, a lifelong Democrat, led its
"Buy Now" campaign in Massachusetts.)[33]

The department store industry, however, largely opposed Hoover's protectionism. At issue was the Smoot-Hawley Tariff. The campaign to buy
American-made products and boycott imported goods, such as French
clothing and Irish linens, gathered strength through the efforts of William
Randolph Hearst and his newspaper empire, as well as through support
from upper-class women and consumers. But department store executives
and even some manufacturers feared that targeting imported goods could
have negative consequences as other countries retaliated by doing the same
to U.S. exports. Most retailers condemned the Smoot-Hawley bill for its
potential to instigate trade reprisals abroad and for isolating the American
economy. As the bill to raise tariffs substantially on imported goods worked
its way through the Senate, the NRDGA urged the president to veto the
measure. Its fears were published in the *New York Times,* making this
influential body's position well known among consumers, who were understood to bear the brunt of higher prices if the tariff passed. The "merchants'
point of view" expressed in the *New York Times* in 1932 was that "the
spread of nationalism and the tariff war" brought about by the bill was a
"major contributing factor" to retailers' woes.[34]

As many retailers realized, a solution to the Depression had to address
the problem of underconsumption, which was the result of a lack of purchasing power. Some turned their local efforts toward that end. Prominent
mass retailers embraced the scrip movement as a local solution to the con-
traction of currency in circulation following the crash and bank failures.
For example, in Atlanta, Walter Rich of Rich's department store offered
cash scrip to teachers in 1930, when the city council was unable to pay their
salaries. In Mason City, Iowa, local department stores and even the chain
J. C. Penney took part in an ambitious scrip scheme. Business leaders were
also called on to help stabilize purchasing power by maintaining wages.
Hoover pressed the business community to hold existing wage levels, but
in the department store industry, payroll was the first expense to be cut
back. Store employees, like those at Halle Brothers in Cleveland, received
salary cuts, were asked to work fewer hours, or were discharged. As the city

lost population and as residents' purchasing power declined, the store cut back its regular employees from 2,100 in 1929 to 1,500 in 1933. Even advocates of increased purchasing power like Filene's department store cut wages, just as the no-wage-reduction plans of major industrialists like Henry Ford and firms like U.S. Steel faltered. Policy makers needed to lift wages and prices at the same time, a dilemma that Hoover's volunteerist approach was unable to solve but that the New Deal would attempt.[35]

With the election of Franklin Delano Roosevelt (FDR) in 1932 and the potential for reform under the New Deal, the department store industry looked forward to the possibility of new solutions to old problems. Retailers at first hailed the 1933 National Industrial Recovery Act (NIRA) and its agency, the National Recovery Administration (NRA). The business press and national newspapers rallied behind the NRA and its promise of economic recovery, as did major business organizations like the U.S. Chamber of Commerce. Supporting it became a patriotic act in the 1930s as towns staged NRA parades and businesses across the country proudly displayed its emblem, the Blue Eagle, which signaled "We Do Our Part." Boston's Edward Filene, a strong supporter of FDR and the New Deal, praised the program. Other leading merchants who were more critical of the administration, like Lew Hahn, president of the NRDGA, also pledged support and offered their cooperation. The act seemed to offer something for everyone—labor, business, and consumers. Industries were to draft codes of fair competition that would rationalize a chaotic economic system through industry-wide agreements on working conditions and minimum wages, prices, and production standards. Purchasing power would return and the downward spiral of the economy would be halted. In fact, over the two years the codes were in operation, women, who were the main labor pool for department stores, benefited substantially. Margaret Allen in the lingerie department at Halle's in Cleveland, for example, remembered the NRA giving her a "tremendous raise." The Code of Fair Competition for the Retail Trade, or Retail Code, also addressed department store workers' historically long workday, limiting selling employees to a forty-four-hour week and nonselling workers to forty-eight hours, though regional and seasonal concessions blunted the impact on workers.[36]

For retailers in particular, the code promised to address price-cutting, long a contentious issue among department store merchants. By 1933, according to one study of large and small department stores across the United States, about 74 percent of stores used loss leaders occasionally or for special events, while only a little over 8 percent admitted to using them regularly. Analysts in the field hoped the NRA would clamp down on these "predatory activities."[37] In the hearings leading up to the Retail Code, representatives of the industry tried to level the playing field for smaller merchants in their competitive struggle with mass retailers. The retail trade took this opportunity provided by federal policy to try to eliminate wasteful price competition. The Retail Code's loss-limitation provision was understood as a way to do this. This portion of the code prohibited loss leaders, or the sale of merchandise at less than 10 percent above cost. In New York, where Macy's had long been engaged in price battles, competing department stores were especially active on behalf of the loss leader provision, with lobbyists on its behalf including the presidents of Namm's in Brooklyn and of Best's in Manhattan.[38]

For a very short period, retailers seemed to soften their stance on a regulatory state. Benjamin Namm, the chairman of the fair practice committee, which was composed of six national retail associations, turned his back on laissez faire. In a statement following the adoption of the code, he congratulated the NRA reforms: "It dawns a new era in the field of distribution. It means the end of that 'rugged individualism' which has all but destroyed the marts of trade and the beginning of that 'robust nationalism,' which is destined to bring us a new prosperity."[39] But this went only so far. For the most part department store executives were willing to turn to the government for legislation that would limit competition from chains or discounters, but they were never happy with the idea of a federally enforced minimum wage. In preliminary hearings for their code, retailers leveraged the labor prescriptions of the NRA to argue for regulations against loss leaders, saying one was necessary to uphold the other. Unless protections against "predatory price cutting" became effective immediately, the retailers argued, the burden of additional payroll would destroy tens of thousands of already "financially weakened concerns."[40]

Divisions that had emerged within the retail trade after the rise of chains in the previous decade emerged in the struggle over the industry's code. The decision to have each industry write its own code typically resulted in the largest companies or the most powerful national trade groups in each industry influencing their specifications and establishing provisions beneficial to them. Historian Ellis Hawley suggests that this was not exactly the case for the retail trade. There, he argued, code provisions favored small units, reflecting the fact that smaller retailers resented being forced to compete on price with mass retailers and sided with powerful manufacturers in favor of price maintenance.[41] This situation was fairly complex, in fact. Early versions of the code were drafted by committees made of representatives from all segments of the retail trade. Mass retailers—the ones accused of employing loss leaders and benefiting unfairly from economies of scale in other areas—were prominently represented. For example, the NRDGA, the Mail-Order Association of America, and a group for limited-price variety stores took part. Smaller retailers also held their ground for the moment, with numerous other national associations for single-line retailers and small business influencing the writing of the code, including leading representatives of retail furniture, hardware, clothiers and furnishers, shoes, and music merchants. Over the course of negotiations, however, the interests of mass retailers were preserved: when the final draft was submitted to the government it came out of a committee that lacked independent retailer representation as well as representation from the Consumers' Advisory Board.[42]

Divisions emerged over mass retailer's use of loss leaders, which the NRA now prohibited. The loss leader provision had emerged in the context of a broader-based opposition to costly competition and price-cutting. Hawley has argued that the NRA provision to eliminate loss leaders was intended to "maintain traditional methods of distribution and thus aid independent retailers and wholesalers in their struggle against the chain stores, mail-order houses, and vertically integrated manufacturers." Not all large-scale retailers used loss leaders, however. At the beginning of the Depression, many in the department store industry even condemned the practice, having come to believe that it was responsible for declining profit margins during the 1920s, as well as for costly interstore price wars and manufacturers' struggles to maintain retail prices.[43] Even though many engaged in it, department store merchants also understood that if all abstained from the practice, they would not be forced "against [their] will" into such aggressive and costly competition. The Depression made such aggressive competition seem "anti-social," as one trade writer put it. Those who sold loss leaders profited at the expense of others, rather than advancing the interests of the industry. According to one merchandise manager in 1932, loss leaders were "a definite out-and-out-evil" force. William T. Grant, who had engaged in the practice at his chain of variety stores, became a staunch opponent of loss leaders, calling it "one of the greatest curses that hangs over American business." A threat against profits was even a threat against "the security of the social structure," as one trade writer argued.[44]

Opponents of the NRA and its loss leader prohibitions, however, gained sway by early 1934. Before, opposition to the NRA provisions simply took the form of caution, as executives worried about the wording of the loss limitation section of the code, fearing that its characterization as an unfair trade practice was too confusing and vague. But retailers against the NRA soon grew increasingly organized. Between 1934 and early 1935, major retailers and their trade association, the NRDGA, the head of one of the largest department store chains, and prominent retail experts like Paul Nystrom all publically took a stand against the price-fixing agreements allowed by the NRA codes. Even Edward Filene, an early strong supporter, admonished those who maintained prices. The Retailers Protective Committee, led by Walter N. Rothschild of Abraham & Straus, a major Brooklyn department store, also lobbied against manufacturer control over prices, terms, and discounts. And Macy's challenged the Retail Code. A longtime opponent of price maintenance going back to its litigation with the book publishing industry at the turn of the century, Macy's led mass retailers in the fight. Big firms like Macy's with a reputation for low prices were loath to surrender the strategy of loss leaders. Others opposed the NRA for perhaps more ideological reasons. One future conservative presidential hopeful took down the Blue Eagle from Goldwater's, his family's department store in Phoenix, Arizona, protesting the "price dictates" of the retail codes. After the NRA was ruled unconstitutional in 1935, the industry continued to fear a New Deal resurrection of controls on prices, hours, wages, and output and lobbied against anything, according to the *Dry Goods Economist*, that would potentially allow "governmental invasion of all private business fields."[45]

Consumers who might support the higher wages promised by the Blue Eagle also turned their back on the NRA's toleration of price fixing and its prohibition of loss leaders. The Consumers' Advisory Board (CAB) voiced its opposition at a public forum called by the NRA administrator, General Hugh Johnson, arguing that "the consumer's interest requires that goods be turned out in large and increasing volume . . . [with] low prices." The CAB opposed the Retail Code's characterization of loss leaders as an unfair trade practice.[46] Though small retailers felt they fostered monopoly, from the point of view of shoppers, loss leaders were simply good buys or bar-gains, something that a rational consumer wanted, even though supporters of price maintenance did their best to convince them otherwise.

Even though popular opinion turned against the NRA, this short-lived experiment in government-industrial cooperation shaped the relationship between business, consumers, workers, and the state. For independent retailers in particular, according to political scientist Joseph Palamountain, the NRA gave merchants "a taste of a more protected life," although few received all that they wished in terms of code provisions. While the rela-tionship between business and the federal government was not permanently changed by the NRA, the experience did have an effect on the industry. As was the case with earlier debates and legislative pushes over resale price maintenance and minimum wage laws, department store managers, store founders, and the NRDGA gained experience lobbying the government to protect their interests. The experience of writing the Retail Code and arguing its merits or lack thereof in the trade press further solidified the identity of the department store industry, drawing more distinctly the lines between big and small retailer, independent and chain. And, overall, the issue of price became paramount. Who determined it? What was fair? And what role, if any, should legislators and policy makers have in answering these questions? Mass retailers' experience with the NRA convinced some that cooperation with government was necessary.[47]

After the Schechter decision ended the NRA in 1935, small retailers sought to salvage their former code provisions, especially those that would level the playing field between them and large-scale firms. The fiery anti-chain congressman from Texas, Wright Patman, gave them a way.[48] Depart-ment stores continued to engage the issues highlighted by the NRA but in a different way. Their efforts went to fighting the anti-chain store legislation and taxation advocated by Patman, and battling a proposed federal law on resale price maintenance.

As local institutions and sometimes small, family-run firms, department stores might have been eager members of the anti-chain movement. Pat-man and other supporters of a special chain store tax argued that redistri-bution was necessary because chains did not pay their fair share of taxes and drained money away from local economies. This was an argument that independent department stores used to spur support of their "buy local" campaigns in the period. And yet, even so, they did not join the efforts to level the playing field through taxation. In part this was because of the varied nature of their corporate structure. By definition, they were mass retailers, yet they varied widely in size. They could have hundreds of thousands of dollars in annual sales or many millions. Department stores could be independent businesses, quasi-independent members of department store groups, or part of national chains like J. C. Penney, Montgomery Ward, or Sears. As in the case of Sears and Montgomery Ward, department stores might even be members of a trade organization like the National Chain Store Association. Formed in 1928 in response to the wave of anti-chain store bills sweeping the country, it served as a lobby group for different types of multiunit retailers until the passage of NIRA led to code requirements that needed to be addressed by each industry or trade.[49]

In the context of the Depression, the NRDGA took a stand against chain store taxation. The national association, which historically represented independent department stores, argued that such legislation would hurt the larger independent department stores. In 1931, small merchants had won a victory over mass retailers with a Supreme Court decision legalizing chain store taxation. Over the next eight years, twenty-seven of the forty-eight states passed anti–chain store laws. As this anti-chain movement gained momentum over the 1930s, the NRDGA fought it.[50]

With the founding of a new trade association in 1935, the industry forged even closer ties with chains, pushing it further away from the anti-chain movement. Established by leading department store merchants Louis E. Kirstein of Filene's and Herbert J. Tilly, president of Strawbridge & Clothier, the new American Retail Federation (ARF) expected to pull in the combined power of one million merchants with an annual sales volume of $20 billion. Of unprecedented scale and scope, it proposed to act as a " 'unified voice' of the entire field of distribution on national and economic problems." Kirstein's recent experience on the NRA's advisory board had shown him the necessity for such an "authoritative group" that could speak for the industry as a whole and avoid divisions like those that had stymied the writing of the NRA's Retail Code. As ARF's executive committee shaped up, it drew from big urban independent department stores, department store chains, and national department store groups, as well as representatives of the retail drug, grocery, variety store, and shoe trade. Despite the major representation of chains in the group, ARF consciously tried to downplay the large corporate interests behind it, presenting itself in the press as "the voice of Main Street"—of the local merchant. Its founding gathered unfavorable attention in the press. The *New York Times* claimed that big retailers had formed a "superlobby" intent on destroying small business. The NRDGA, made up of independent merchants, also condemned it. Described as a "chain store lobby," ARF sparked tremendous opposition, and a congressional investigation was launched by Representative John J. Cochran, a Democrat from Missouri. As the investigation took shape, evidence emerged that department stores had been solicited as members as a way to claim representation from independents, but chains dominated the group. What was disclosed inflamed public opinion against the buying advantages of large-scale distributors. According to Godfrey Lebhar, editor of *Chain Store Age* and leading spokesman for the field, the scandal fueled Texas congressman Wright Patman's anti-chain crusade and helped secure the enactment of the Robinson-Patman Act, which was working its way through the House Committee on the Judiciary at the time.[51]

Described by one contemporary as the "Cracker-Barrel bill," the Robinson-Patman bill represented the efforts of traditional retailers and their political supporters to level the playing field between independents and large, vertically integrated, multiunit chains. Robinson-Patman proposed to modify the Clayton Act to limit the discounts available to chains. Since 1914, the Clayton Act had prohibited price concessions in interstate commerce, but it was written in a way that allowed large-scale purchasers to bypass it. In the 1920s and 1930s, for example, the chains Sears, Roebuck and Company and Montgomery Ward extracted significant discounts from tire manufacturers that allowed them to drive independent tire dealers out of business. Robinson-Patman sought to close that loophole. In particular, it called for the elimination of traditional large-quantity discounts or price concessions. It contained six provisions, the most important being Section 2(a), which prohibited sellers from discriminating in price between two or more competing buyers when selling commodities of like quality and grade where that discrimination substantially lessened competition, created a monopoly, or injured, destroyed, or prevented competition between those involved. Section 2(f) applied these principles to buyers. The other four sections of the act (b, c, and d) were designed to prevent sellers and buyers from circumventing the proscriptions of Section 2(a) and (f). They sought to prevent big firms from obtaining discriminatory discounts indirectly in the form of concessions or compensation for brokerage, advertising, and promotional allowances, or other services.[52]

The department store trade press excoriated the bill. Even though local department stores or independents were still dominant, the industry was largely hostile to anti-chain legislation. Mass distributors as a group saw it as a "drastic and dangerous interference with business." As Robinson-Patman moved toward passage, Edward Filene and Robert Wood, head of Sears, appealed to President Roosevelt himself, urging him to veto it. Filene told the president that the act was directly against what he was working for—"a better distribution of wealth for the masses." While FDR did not support the anti–chain store measures of the era, he did not veto them. Throughout the decade, moreover, many fair trade laws were passed at the state level "to help small retailers combat the increasingly vigorous competition of the chain stores."[53]

Soon after the enactment of Robinson-Patman, department store analysts predicted the end of the advantages they had previously enjoyed, but this was not to be the case. Department stores, one expert argued in 1937, relied on lower cost prices on most lines of merchandise to help offset their high costs of operation and would experience a particularly negative effect from the quantity discount prohibition. Robinson-Patman's effect on the department store industry, however, was not what was intended by the original framers. In several indirect ways, the anti-chain legislation in fact promoted bigness. Hawley argued that in practice it had a "boomerang effect" in that it "forced manufacturers and wholesalers to re-examine their discount structures, something that led many of them to realize that prices charged for small orders were insufficient to cover the costs of handling them." Its restrictions on advertising allowances and brokerage payments also hurt corporate chains less than others. In addition, the act never truly threatened the interests of big business as it was enforced by the Federal Trade Commission (FTC). In 1937, for example, a price-discrimination complaint brought against Montgomery Ward and a carpet manufacturer resulted in a decision that favored mass marketers. Throughout the late 1930s, the Robinson-Patman Act was only sporadically enforced, with the FTC prosecuting small firms that were easier to achieve victory against and acting cautiously against large corporations.[54]

In addition, retailers themselves found Robinson-Patman confusing and vague. It did not help that it was quickly followed by the passage of another, perhaps more important piece of federal legislation addressing their power, the Miller-Tydings Act of 1937. Long awaited by supporters of fair trade and finally passed in the context of 1930s deflation, Miller-Tydings exempted retail price maintenance agreements from federal antitrust laws. But department store managers struggled to follow the rulings of both

Robinson-Patman and Miller-Tydings. At Higbee Company in Cleveland, for example, executive-training courses included reports and lectures that addressed the effect of FTC rulings on both. Buyers were instructed that if a manufacturer registered his resale price with the commission, it became a federal offense to sell the article for less. Higbee's told its buyers about a state price commission that operated the same way. Rulings, the training course advised, were "varied and cover[ed] considerable ground" and were available "for your study" if required. Interestingly, the training report con-flated Robinson-Patman with Miller-Tydings, making it seem as if both addressed resale price maintenance. This was not really the case. The Robinson-Patman bill as it finally passed in June 1936 contained numerous qualifications to its prohibition of price discrimination that gutted the idea completely. The Miller-Tydings Act, on the other hand, addressed the issue of price explicitly, exempting resale price maintenance from antitrust pros-ecution under the Sherman Act and promising to eliminate loss leaders, those "weapons of monopoly" that purportedly destroyed the small, inde-pendent businessman.[55]

In the 1930s, the issue of prices divided the retail industry yet again, building on earlier battles. Not surprisingly, large department stores, chain stores, mail-order companies, and consumer advocates joined forces to fight against the Miller–Tydings Act, arguing it would limit price competi-tion and lead to an increase in the cost of living. Such coalitions against RPM had been successful against earlier fair trade bills, such as the Capper-Kelly bill of 1929. The story took shape differently at the state level during this period, however. After the passage of a fair trade law in California in 1931, such legislation swept the nation, brought about by the lobbying efforts of the National Association of Retail Druggists. By the end of 1936, fourteen states had fair trade laws. And, after the Supreme Court upheld these state laws at the end of that year, a new fair trade campaign led to twenty-eight more by the summer of 1937. Moving from the success of fair trade at the state level, the anti-chain movement sought to build on the dead Capper-Kelly bill and pushed for a federal law on RPM. Once achieved, the Miller-Tydings Act strengthened state laws. By 1941, RPM was on all statute books in the country except Missouri, Texas, Vermont, and the District of Columbia. By 1941, forty-five state fair trade laws had a nonsigner clause that bound all merchants (when notified of the agree-ment) to the terms of the resale price maintenance if only one merchant signed the contract.[56]

Mass retailers were unsuccessful in their campaign against RPM and restrictions on quantity discounts in the 1930s because the economic crisis had changed the context of the debate in several ways. Both Robinson-Patman and Miller-Tydings sought to limit the power of mass retailers to leverage their size to extract unfair advantages over small businesses and, in the case of the Miller-Tydings Act, manufacturers. During the Depression, big business had become increasingly suspect. Arguments for Miller-Tydings in particular reflected this, echoing, as they did, the decade's strong anti–chain store movement. Deflation in the early 1930s, moreover, provided "a macroeconomic climate favorable to RPM." As prices fell in the Depression, advocates of resale price maintenance won their battle. Forces in favor of RPM, led by druggists and other groups impacted by price-cutters or ideologically opposed to big business, were able to plug into the growing national concern for holding the line on prices.[57]

Some historians have argued that even though Congress passed the Miller-Tydings and Robinson-Patman Acts, their impact was largely symbolic. Meg Jacobs notes that Robinson-Patman "allowed ample room for retailers to justify their discounts and gave ultimate authority to the Federal Trade Commission." Largely supported by manufacturers of branded goods, especially book publishers, consumer electrical appliance manufacturers, cosmetics makers, and liquor dealers, it covered less than 15 percent of all goods, as both Jacobs and historian Jonathan Bean point out. Support could be spotty, moreover, undercutting the larger goal. While fair trade became near universal in the drug field, for example, it made few inroads in the grocery trade. Manufacturers were sometimes reluctant to put their products under price protection. Not surprisingly, consumers also opposed fair trade laws, siding with mass merchants and their low retail prices over protections for small business. Farmers objected to them too, fearing higher prices for manufactured goods. In addition, the legislation had unintended consequences. Not only did many find ways around Miller-Tydings, some, like Macy's, were able to turn it to their advantage. To the objection of manufacturers, Macy's issued advertisements that exposed the higher prices paid by consumers in fair trade states by running lists comparing price-protected goods with the ones they offered for sale. Department stores and large mail-order firms also issued their own private brands to compete with price-protected trademarked items.[58]

Consumer demand for low prices and department stores' need to cut costs might have launched a discount movement during the Depression, but they did not. The economic crisis of the 1930s did not change the department store industry's commitment to luxury and customer service. Even though modernization plans were put off and facilities declined, many individual firms went under, and retail market share declined overall, much about the department store as an institution stayed the same. Department stores continued to dominate downtown streets with their multifloored stone and brick buildings. In central locations accessible to pedestrians and public transportation, they still pulled in crowds off the city streets through spectacles and lavish displays, drawing in customers from surrounding areas through advertisements in local newspapers and radio. Their primary identity as local institutions that were central to the social and economic life of cities and towns remained unchanged.

The industry's efforts on behalf of progress and modernity, represented by its emulation of chain store efficiencies, also continued. Of course, the different context of depression rather than prosperity gave all this new meaning and weight. Challenges that had appeared in the 1920s had grown stronger. But even as competition with national chain stores intensified, the department store industry continued to work on behalf of bigness. Siding with chains, it fought the legislative reforms of the anti-chain movement in 1936 and 1937. The industry's main trade organization, the National Retail Dry Goods Association, also moved further away from its independent roots on Main Street during this period. And a new trade organization, the American Retail Federation, emerged to offer further support of mass retailers' increasingly powerful national agenda. The coming of World War II would only intensify these trends.

CHAPTER 5

An Essential Industry in Wartime

The retailer is quartermaster to the civilian population.
—David Craig, president, American Retail Federation, 1943

AFTER war broke out, President Roosevelt called on businesses and others to help turn the nation into a "great arsenal of democracy." American production revved up, bringing prosperity back and helping to win the war. Though largely overlooked, distribution was an important part of the war effort, and the success of this effort depended on the cooperation of business with the federal government. Department stores across the country assumed a new prominence in their communities in the weeks after the bombing of Pearl Harbor. They had made civic contributions for decades, but now their trade associations were able to argue that retailing was an "essential industry."[1] Individual merchants and their trade associations helped mobilize for war, following the directives of the Office of Price Administration (OPA), applying their considerable creative and economic resources to encourage popular support, and offering leadership both locally and on the national stage. In the process, the ties between the industry and federal powers grew stronger. Still, many resisted the needs of a command economy and instead pursued their self-interest, their dominant suspicion of any government oversight of their business affairs carrying over from previous decades into the debate over price ceilings and rationing in the war years.

During the war, the industry's pivot toward a large-scale retail identity continued. In fact, as happened in other industries, the war effort rewarded larger firms. The distance between department stores and chains also narrowed as department stores stripped away many free services and luxuries and began the shift toward self-service in the name of patriotism. But traditional merchants were only willing to go so far. They entered the postwar still burdened by a high cost of doing business and a commitment to downtown, two things that would not serve them well.

Department Stores as "Soldiers of Defense"

In December 1941, just days after the bombing of Pearl Harbor, the crowds of well-dressed people window-shopping, pushing through store aisles and onto elevators might have looked like those of any holiday season in a time of prosperity. But shopping had taken on a new urgency with the coming of war. Retail executives reported crowds at big downtown department stores like Macy's, Namm's, and Hearn's. Shoppers flocked downtown during the holiday rush to purchase their Christmas presents and the consumer goods they rightly feared might become scarce in the coming months. Americans began hoarding food, rubber goods, household supplies, clothing, and a range of miscellaneous items that could be subject to rationing. As the news of war sank in and as cities were shut down by air-raid drills, however, retail trade dipped below expectations.[2]

Nevertheless, in those first few weeks department stores played a special role in home-front preparation, setting the stage for later contributions to the war effort. San Francisco and New York stores met an urgent need for air-raid materials, such as flashlights, black fabric or crepe paper for windows, and other supplies, such as shovels and galvanized pails. Some even established blackout departments, selling materials and dispensing expert advice. As the need developed, local stores also sought to supply uniforms for a host of new war-related positions. Others, like the owners of Gimbels, a chain of eleven large department stores by this period, anticipated shortages and build up inventories of consumer goods like silk and nylon stockings.[3]

The war made itself evident at department stores in many different ways. Across the country, stores lost employees to the defense plants and the armed services. Store management did not fight this labor drain but in fact promoted volunteering and rewarded those who left. Employees who served were given much public recognition by local management. Small-town Bresee's department store demonstrated its wartime patriotism by granting former employees in the U.S. service a six-week bonus. The management of other upstate New York firms exchanged letters with personnel in the service and published honor rolls of those who had served or were serving in the armed forces, long lists of men and women that signaled the store's ongoing connection to the war effort and its deep community ties.[4]

Department store executives also volunteered their efforts and worked on behalf of the Allies in prominent ways. Some transformed their buildings into statements of support, draping fronts with patriotic buntings and enormous flags. And they raised money. Many department store owners like Meyer Poliakoff in Abbeville, South Carolina, were Jewish and took a special interest in fighting Hitler. Department stores supported federal efforts to raise funds, participating in the national War Savings Bonds and Stamps campaign, selling bonds and telling customers to "Take Part of Your Change in War Stamps." The Treasury gave retailers monthly war bond quotas; for the month of July 1942, Halle's alone was $50,000, which the well-known downtown Cleveland store outstripped five times. By Christmas of 1943, Halle's passed a one million milestone in war bond sales. Although in the business of selling, during the war stores pushed the anticonsumerist message, "Conserve for Victory." For example, J. L. Hudson Co. promoted women's role in conservation with ads such as "Needle and Thread Are Weapons on the Home Front," while Rike-Kumler Co. in Dayton advertised its "Commuter Committee," which organized employees to save gas and tires. Stores promoted salvage and engaged in it themselves, even going so far as scrapping their own electric signs.[5]

With the special needs of a command economy, retailers were compelled to go beyond the voluntary efforts and philanthropy they had traditionally favored. The pressure to take part must have been intense, and department store proprietors, like others, were pushed beyond volunteerism. At the beginning of the war, department stores served as a model of industry-government cooperation. As key local provisioners of necessary goods, but also as civic leaders, department store executives took their role in the war seriously. Many shouldered official patriotic duties on the home front. The Brooklyn department store magnate Benjamin Namm, who had headed a NRA code committee, became chairman of the retail advisory committee to the Treasury Department. In this new capacity, Namm ran the "Retailers for Victory" campaign for the sale of war bonds and stamps.[6]

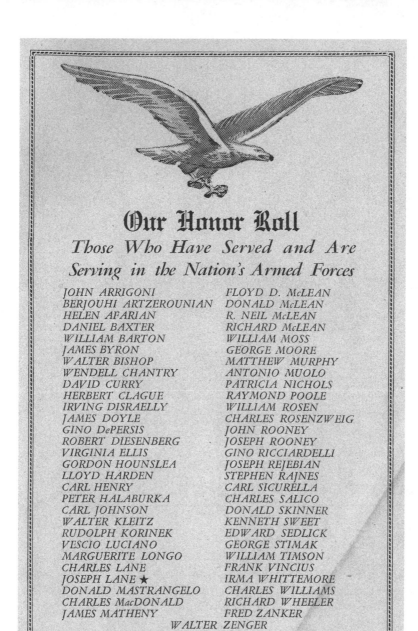

Our Honor Roll

Those Who Have Served and Are Serving in the Nation's Armed Forces

JOHN ARRIGONI
BERJOUHI ARTZEROUNIAN
HELEN AFARIAN
DANIEL BAXTER
WILLIAM BARTON
JAMES BYRON
WALTER BISHOP
WENDELL CHANTRY
DAVID CURRY
HERBERT CLAGUE
IRVING DISRAELLY
JAMES DOYLE
GINO DePERSIS
ROBERT DIESENBERG
VIRGINIA ELLIS
GORDON HOUNSLEA
LLOYD HARDEN
CARL HENRY
PETER HALABURKA
CARL JOHNSON
WALTER KLEITZ
RUDOLPH KORINEK
VESCIO LUCIANO
MARGUERITE LONGO
CHARLES LANE
JOSEPH LANE ★
DONALD MASTRANGELO
CHARLES MacDONALD
JAMES MATHENY

FLOYD D. McLEAN
DONALD McLEAN
R. NEIL McLEAN
RICHARD McLEAN
WILLIAM MOSS
GEORGE MOORE
MATTHEW MURPHY
ANTONIO MUOLO
PATRICIA NICHOLS
RAYMOND POOLE
WILLIAM ROSEN
CHARLES ROSENZWEIG
JOHN ROONEY
JOSEPH ROONEY
GINO RICCIARDELLI
JOSEPH REJEBIAN
STEPHEN RAJNES
CARL SICURELLA
CHARLES SALICO
DONALD SKINNER
KENNETH SWEET
EDWARD SEDLICK
GEORGE STIMAK
WILLIAM TIMSON
FRANK VINCIUS
IRMA WHITTEMORE
CHARLES WILLIAMS
RICHARD WHEELER
FRED ZANKER

WALTER ZENGER

FIGURE 16. During World War II, department stores like McLean's in Binghamton, N.Y., threw themselves into the war effort. Like many other stores, McLean's published a list of employees who served. One name was starred, denoting a casualty of war—Joseph Lane, a local seventeen-year-old submariner who received a Purple Heart. "We're in Our 64th year but We Don't Look It!" Box 1, McLean's Department Store Collection, Broome County Historical Society, Local History & Genealogy Center, Binghamton, New York.

FIGURE 17. Herbst department store in Fargo, North Dakota, participated in war bond campaigns as did many other department stores, big and small, across the nation during World War II. Institute for Regional Studies, North Dakota State University, Fargo (rs004917).

Experience in selling aided war bond campaigns; experience buying helped executives move into major wartime agencies. Donald Nelson, the editor of the Sears catalog and a vice president of the retail chain, held the most prominent position. A supporter of FDR and involved in defense planning since 1940, he was put in charge of the War Production Board (WPB) created in January 1942, where his experience in production and procurement was put to use. Nelson also pulled other chain retailers into leadership positions in his agency. Frank Folsom from Montgomery Ward became a liaison officer for the Navy's Procurement Division. Other prominent merchants also took on wartime roles, including Fred Lazarus Jr. of Federated fame, Irwin D. Wolf of Pittsburgh's Kaufmann stores, and David R. Craig, then president of the relatively new trade group the American Retail Federation (ARF). In Hartford, Connecticut, home of the Sage-Allen department store, Edward N. Allen also contributed to the war effort on the "Retailers for Victory" committee in 1942, likely drawing on his experience in the Great War as chairman of the merchants' division of the Liberty Loans campaigns (before he was commissioned as an officer in 1918). And Stanley Marcus of the prestigious Dallas store Neiman Marcus was responsible for the issuance of the War Production Board's order L-85, which rationed apparel and shaped fashion for the duration. Other major department stores, while not contributing executive leadership, signaled that they, too, were doing their part by advertising their adherence to limitation orders.[7]

In promoting an image of cooperation and patriotism, the department store industry helped shape the rhetoric on the role of business in wartime. More broadly, Depression-era criticism of business was replaced with greater sympathy as executives contributed their talents to wartime agencies. Right after the attack on Pearl Harbor, prominent retail executives spoke to the press on the role their industry would play. Experts like Paul Nystrom linked retailing with civilian morale, encouraging merchants to produce attractive window and store displays to hearten consumers and help maintain their optimism and patriotism. Similarly, the head of Hecht's, a Baltimore department store that also operated in Washington, D.C., and New York, cited retailers' role in keeping up "civilian morale at home" during past wars. With Pearl Harbor bringing it to "their own front yards," M. S. Hecht summarized how central the department store industry was to protecting the "bulwarks of the home": "Manufacturers who can provide a steady flow of these necessities . . . merchants who present them on display . . . and those behind the counter who sell them to the customer are all part of an almost endless chain of soldiers of defense." Hecht, who in earlier decades had lobbied against legislation, writing his congressman in 1921 to oppose a tariff bill, now advised merchants to "adhere strictly to all government regulations" and to "provide for the civilians' needs at the

FIGURE 18. The department store trade press highlighted industry-government cooperation during World War II. Patriotic images linking retailers to Allied success abounded in its pages. "Department Stores in the War," *Department Store Economist* (July 1942), 39. Rochester Public Library, Local History Division, New York.

lowest possible prices." His message also exhorted manufacturers to cooperate. Perhaps store magnates like Hecht saw the potential to tip the balance
of power in their favor in their relationship with suppliers. Breaks in the
supply chain plagued retailers even before Pearl Harbor, as shortages of
materials such as leather restricted production of shoes.[8] Self-serving or
not, merchants demonstrated their patriotism and willingness to cooperate
with the federal government after Pearl Harbor.

Department stores recognized that the war brought many opportunities
for new business. Furlough weddings became a specialty of some
department-store bridal salons. Davison-Paxon, a department store in
Atlanta, offered to do a "complete job on 6-hour notice." The store's bridal
service could plan for the "sudden" wedding in various price brackets, following a "prearranged routine" for dealing with florists, jewelry needs,
church arrangements, music, costumers, and ushers. Like others in the
wedding industry during the war, department stores promoted the traditional wedding, although stripped down due to wartime restrictions. Support for the long white gown and all it represented was evident in the
symbolic gesture made by Strawbridge & Clothier in 1943, in which forty
wedding gowns were sent to England via the American Friends Service
Committee so that British brides could "be traditionally gowned for their
'big day.'" The U.S. government even endorsed the ideal of the traditional
wedding after the bridal apparel industry fought for and received an exemp-
tion on restrictions from the War Production Board, arguing that bridal
gowns were vital for morale. Of course, such decisions were also good for
department store business.[9]

In addition to providing an opportunity to promote consumption in
new ways, the war created many obstacles to it. The local department store,
like other retailers, simply had to make do and cobble together acceptable
merchandise to sell an increasingly hungry public. Import and export firms
used by smaller department stores like Poliakoff's in Abbeville, South Carolina, offered substitutions when requested brand-name goods were unavail-
able. Manufacturers using scarce materials like rubber had to make stricter
demands on their customers, calling for shorter payment schedules that
small department stores must have found onerous. Many times, manufacturers simply had to write back "unable to enter your order" or "there will
be no more."[10] For the most part, department stores suffered a shortage of
brand-name goods created by rationing of materials and the conversion of
many industries to war production. Smaller or provincial stores had used

FIGURE 19. In promotional material for its sixty-fourth anniversary in 1945, McLean's department store in Binghamton listed five hundred brand-name products that it would carry when peacetime returned. Breaking with the tradition of large department stores, which relied on their own private brands, smaller stores or retail outlets in provincial markets sought the prestige of national brand-name goods and promoted the fact that they offered them. "We're in Our 64th year but We Don't Look It!" Box 1, McLean's Department Store Collection, Broome County Historical Society, Local History & Genealogy Center, Binghamton, New York.

brand-name goods to position themselves as fashion leaders. National brands in cosmetics, luggage, women's and men's apparel, stationery, gift wares, linens, rugs and carpets, and furniture elevated their image and had been a key part of their trade, while larger firms offered private-label goods. In this period of scarce resources, department stores that sold national brands continued to promote them, setting the stage for their postwar markets.[11]

Besides creating shortages of consumer goods, the war furnished an excuse for store management to strip away things that had contributed to rising operating costs. For example, delivery services, long abused and the bane of department stores, were severely cut back, permanently, retailers hoped. Many wanted to avoid returning to the "super-service era" of pre-war times, though they recognized that "department stores were built on service." Trade literature reported on their members' cutbacks almost with relief, with articles such as "Baby Shop Frills Are Out."[12]

World War II also changed the way department stores offered credit, with widespread implications for postwar consumption. Management cut back installment accounts as department stores complied with Regulation W, a federal policy intended to control consumer credit and curb inflation. But as the historian Louis Hyman has argued, retailers' attempts to both evade regulations and comply with them led to the emergence of new hybridized forms of charge accounts and new technologies. The Charga-Plate, for example, which actually expanded consumers' access to department store credit, acted as a stepping stone to the revolving credit system adopted widely by the early 1950s. Unintentionally, as was often the case, wartime regulations thus promoted a credit regime that later underwrote a huge postwar growth in sales and increased profits. More flexible credit options would allow postwar suburban consumers to borrow for prosperity. And again, it was the big department stores that benefited, as they were in the position to be most fully able to exploit the new charge systems and bring then to the suburbs.[13]

The many changes brought about by the war affected department store performance. Profits for stores with a volume over $500,000 rose from 0.7 percent in 1938 and 1.8 percent in 1939 to 7.6 percent of sales in 1942. Gross margins climbed to their highest ever—38.7 percent of net sales in 1942. The jump in gross margins as the nation approached the war reflected rising prices and stores stocking up and cutting back on markdowns. With the implementation of wartime price and inventory controls, gross margins subsided to a degree, though they remained high through the war. Stock turn, usually a key indicator of the health of a department store, soared over the period, from about 3.5 turns to 5.5 annually. Shortages in merchandise and the regulations applied to inventories in large retail stores, however, were behind this rise in stock turn, which returned to normal after the war. Major operating expenses like payroll dropped rapidly as a percentage of net sales. Department stores in the Harvard Bureau of Business Research study, for example, saw payroll go from a Depression high of between 15 and 19.5 percent of net sales to a low of between 13.5 and 16 percent of net sales around 1944. Advertising expenses as a percentage of net sales dropped from 3.5 percent before the war to 2.2 percent in 1944 and 1945, staying below 3 percent throughout the postwar period. The circumstances of the war, of course, limited advertising's potential. The advertising industry as a result focused on institutional ads that were designed to publicize the firm's name, promote the firm's patriotic efforts in the War Bond campaign, and dream about postwar consumer possibilities.[14]

Even in the face of rationing, labor shortages, and federal oversight of prices, department stores of all sizes fared well. Retailers of all stripes benefited from the fact that average family incomes soared above Depression levels. Dollar sales rose, with 1941 surpassing the department store industry's 1929 peak. Consumer spending as a whole rose by 22 percent in the United States, despite rationing and the diversion of resources for the war. Unable to spend their larger pay envelopes on many hard goods subject to wartime controls and scarcities, like automobiles, consumers spent money on entertainment and leisure and concentrated their buying in soft goods (nondurables like clothing or linens), a specialty of the department store. While competition from chain stores, specialty shops, and mail order remained a concern, department stores even met the chains on their own ground by developing their own basement stores during the war. Urged by the trade press not to return to the "service orgy" of the pre–World War II period, which had bloated their gross margins and made them less competitive with the leaner chains, retailers became more streamlined. They used wartime regulations to pare down permanently the costly free services they had traditionally offered, narrowing the gap between the traditional department store and the chain retailer.[15]

Department Stores Grapple with the OPA

Wartime price controls would do the same in a different way. A stronger wartime state renewed old fights and tensions within the department store field, favoring major firms. Industry-government cooperation would meet its strongest test with the introduction of widespread price controls under the Office of Price Administration. When first established in April 1941 to fight inflation, the OPA relied mostly on moral suasion and voluntarism, with mixed success. Big retailers had a long history of opposing price controls, but the war emergency changed that for the moment. Pearl Harbor

FIGURE 20. During World War II, the department store industry encouraged retailers to cooperate with the Office of Price Administration. The trade press commended retailers for their efforts in curbing credit and rising prices and dealing with shortages. *Department Store Economist* (July 1942), 8. Rochester Public Library, Local History Division, New York.

galvanized retailers' support for the Emergency Price Control Act of 1942, which empowered the OPA to enforce rationing, rent, and price controls. Executives from major firms even volunteered to head up local agencies of the OPA and then its retail distribution branch of the consumer goods price division, formed in 1943.[16]

Their efforts were encouraged and rewarded at all levels. The OPA heralded lowly salesclerks, depicting them as citizens fighting the war. OPA bulletins praised retail employees' efforts, stating: "The people at the fitting stool personally represent their government's shoe rationing for the consumers of this Nation. They are entrusted to handle ration currency and to sell only shoes that fit the customer's feet, his needs, and his pocketbook!" Department stores were seen as extensions of the agency. A July 1942 trade press article, "Department Stores in the War," argued that retailers helped sell the OPA to the public. Despite difficulties in complying and the sacrifices involved, they were seen as following "the spirit of regulation."[17]

Resistance among some executives, however, remained strong. Most famous in his opposition to government control was Sewell L. Avery, the head of Montgomery Ward. The elderly Avery resisted War Labor Board directives and was even photographed as soldiers bodily removed him from his office on order of President Roosevelt in 1944. Such a confrontational stance was not typical among retailers, but opposition was mounting as early as August 1942. Industry leaders like Fred Lazarus of Federated Department Stores feared inflation if the OPA was not able "to get better cooperation from retailers." Cooperation would not be left solely up to retailers, however. In April 1943, FDR bolstered the OPA's control over prices with his "Hold the Line" order, which rolled back prices, eliminated the agency's authority to allow price increases, subsidized agricultural producers, and standardized food ceiling prices. As the power of the OPA grew, so did opposition among a broad range of retailers. Prominent executives like B. Earl Puckett, the president of Allied Stores Corporation, a major department store chain, opposed "Hold the Line" as an unrealistic pricing policy and a bureaucratic control that hindered business. Similarly, small merchants resented the OPA as an intrusion. Even "corporate liberals" who might support government-business cooperation, such as Donald Nelson of Sears, wanted to preserve their autonomy.[18]

The OPA generated opposition among smaller retailers for many reasons. One was the advantages it seemed to give big business. As in the 1930s, mass retailers were better poised to pounce on new opportunities. Larger firms benefited from government contracts from the War and Navy Departments and from policies that they were better equipped to carry out. In response to this criticism, the Senate and the House formed Small Business Committees led by James Murray, a New Dealer from Montana, and the notoriously anti–chain store Texan Wright Patman. The trade press also expressed general concern for the plight of small retailers, publishing pleas on their behalf by Senator Murray, as well as numerous articles on the effect of the war on the "little store," broadly defined as a concern with sales between $100,000 and $1 million annually (a range that would have included many small-town department stores). The national department store trade association also addressed the popular issue. While the association had demonstrated its growing alliance with chain organizations during the Depression, a special-interest group within it still advocated for the smaller independent merchant. At the Smaller Stores Session of the NRDGA annual convention in 1943, the president of the group called for small stores to unite and to "recognize their importance and make use of it politically."[19]

Rather than focusing on chain activities and lobbying for legislation to protect their interests or level the playing field as they had done in the 1920s and 1930s, during the war smaller merchants now pointed to government regulation as the villain. State trade organizations egged them on. The Missouri Retailers Association, for example, pointedly told an audience of merchants and politicians: "We go beyond disgust to bitter resentment when our own government deliberately places us at a disadvantage with very rich and powerful competitors." The conflict also played out at the ground level. County price panels went to bat for their local retailers, writing to their district price officer when they were unfairly disadvantaged by particular OPA regulations. For example, arguing on behalf of a small local department store proprietor who lost money when a shirt wholesaler raised his prices, the county price panel chairman of Abbeville, South Carolina, wrote,

> Mr. Poliakoff is a merchant of long standing in this community. The community wishes to keep him in business. This cannot be done if Mr. Poliakoff is forced to operate at a loss. . . . Abbeville is located 15 miles from the nearest other shopping center. Any articles that the merchants in this town cannot handle would be almost prohibited from use by the people of Abbeville because under present gas and tire curtailments they would not be able to go this 15 miles to satisfy their needs.

OPA regulations raised concerns about cost at department stores of all sizes, however. Halle's, a major Cleveland institution, for example, had to hire five women to enforce OPA regulations, then add more to help them comply with rationing and wage stabilization measures. The family-run Hecht department store spent $110,000 yearly on a full-time staff of twenty-eight that was dedicated to compliance with the OPA. And Filene's, the famous Boston emporium, faced ceiling price lists for hundreds of items, just in one department.[20]

Trade writers, politicians, and merchants expressed growing concern over the unequal pressures the OPA put upon business. In particular, the OPA created varying burdens for merchants of different sizes. Big retailers were better able to afford OPA compliance, whereas the OPA was notoriously harder on the "little fellow," as one trade writer put it. On a day-to-day level, owners of small independent department stores faced many problems in fulfilling OPA regulations. In the fall of 1945, for example, the OPA brought suit against Derby's in Petersborough, New Hampshire, when the owner had a shortage of shoe ration coupons. Goodman's on the eastern shore of Maryland had a similar problem, resulting in the firm's suspension from dealing in rationed shoes for sixty days.[21]

Moreover, the bureaucracy created by the agency could be impenetrable to smaller department store managers, some of whom admitted to not knowing how many OPA regulations were in operation in their store or how they worked. Retailers had to contend with volumes of OPA directives, often written in language that they claimed required an attorney to decode. Price-control law required stores to post publicly the ceiling prices for all "cost-of-living" items sold by the store, to file this list with their nearest regional OPA office, and to label all goods with cards or pin tickets with the ceiling price noted alongside the store's price. The store's list of ceiling prices had to include a detailed description of each item, specifying material, size, finish, or other distinctive features to enable the OPA shopper to distinguish it from every other line in the department. Stores had to make copies available to customers upon demand. Business records reveal the day-to-day strain this put on small department stores. When South Carolina merchant Meyer Poliakoff received his OPA bulletin for "war models" of staple work clothing, for example, he first had to determine if he was a class 1 or 2 purchaser, then find the weight and finish of the material of the goods to be purchased, and then determine the retail price ceiling according to region—and do this for every staple item from bib overalls and overall jackets to waistband overalls and dungarees. Such complexity meant that larger firms, with their greater resources, were in a stronger position than the "country store-keeper who must wrestle with the identical regulations," according to the trade press.[22]

Some department stores, however, appear to have been little affected by OPA regulations and shortages and were even able to continue modest modernization programs, despite wartime restrictions. Such was the case at McLean's in Binghamton. As it and other independent department stores around the country competed for employees with other industries, some chose to share their profits with employees with onetime events like a Christmas bonus of a week's salary, or more permanent welfare schemes, such as a profit-sharing trust. Those independent department stores that had food departments or food service, however, were particularly hard-hit by OPA regulations. Most food items were regulated, and the cost of compliance cut drastically into net profits, even when sales increased, as they did at Leonard's in Fort Worth, Texas. Food department buyers had to get creative to procure supplies as well. One supplier, for example, offered Leonard's ten thousand pounds of bacon but required that it also buy five thousand pounds of spleens to finalize the deal. The store bought the lot, then sold the spleens to the Fort Worth Zoo with a price break. Wartime restrictions also left department stores with nonproductive floor space that dragged on their profits. Many firms found new ways to adapt to declining stocks of electrical appliances, toys, and other consumer goods by introducing departments featuring unrationed products. Department stores introduced fine food shops in this period, catering to expanding consumer tastes and affluence and introducing a market that would explode later in the century with the food revolution. The Florida department store Burdines, for example, introduced its Fine Foods Shop in 1944, finding its way around scarcities to sell such things as preserves, tea, coffee, meat sauces, relishes and pickles, anchovies, and a favorite at postwar weddings, chicken à la king.[23]

Independent department stores were also able to prosper during the war because they had help. Smaller family-run department stores that had adapted the methods of large-scale retailers or chains were not left alone by their industry to determine compliance. The NRDGA aided members by publishing bulletins to guide store heads through rationing, price freezes, and various WPB regulations. For smaller stores, organization could compensate. Buying groups, long a competitive tool for independents and smaller firms, helped member stores. Since 1930, McLean's department store in Binghamton had belonged to the large national buying office Arkwright, Inc., and during the war turned to it for assistance on WPB order

L219, an important regulation restricting inventories of consumer goods.[24] All of this meant that small retailers that were part of larger professional networks were in a better position to survive the strict regulatory environment necessary to protect against inflation and monitor scarce resources. The OPA was sensitive to the potential hardships created by its regulations. The pricing tables demonstrate that the agency used price to level the playing field between big and small retailers. For some lines, like hosiery, retailers were divided into classes based on their annual sales or the sales of their buying group. Maximum prices assigned to different product grades were set at different levels depending on the retailer's size class. Firms or groups with larger sales were assigned a lower maximum retail price, while those with smaller sales were allowed a higher maximum price for the same goods. As they were understood at the time, these price ceilings reflected that "operating methods and customary mark-ups vary as between different retail outlets."[25] Smaller firms sold lower volume of goods, sometimes carried higher operating costs as a percentage of sales, and engaged in higher markups, which the price tables for hosiery accommodated.

While smaller firms might have found the OPA more onerous and struggled to find ways to compete, all department stores, big and small, chafed under the power over prices it gave consumers. Aided by the required signage, consumers often blew the whistle on merchants who sold goods at prices above the government-sanctioned ceilings. New Deal political opponents called the price watching of consumers who volunteered to uphold OPA regulations "inexcusable, un-American, and absolutely unconscionable." But it was these shoppers, many of them women, who made the regulations work on the grassroots level. As a result of consumer actions, the OPA was able to file suit against numerous merchants. The well-known Washington, D.C., institutions Hecht's and Woodward & Lothrop, for example, were charged with violating price ceilings. Both countered that they had done everything they could to comply. While the OPA lost the case against Hecht's, it continued to prosecute big stores that were non-compliant, including Gimbels and Wanamaker's, as well as many others. Through their experience with the OPA, then, as the historian Meg Jacobs has argued, consumers came to expect cheap prices and more goods, an entitlement that would stretch into the postwar period. Massive chain department stores like Sears that were able to advertise prices below the OPA ceiling orders because of their lower distribution costs contributed to these expectations.[26]

As the June 1944 expiration date of the Emergency Price Control Act approached, the NRDGA supported further legislation to ensure the continuation of price controls. But by 1944, acceptance of wartime regulation had seriously declined, as expressed by a trade press article by mass retailer B. Earl Puckett, head of the nation's largest department store chain. In a list of liabilities for the industry going into the postwar period, Puckett included such things as a high tax burden on the wealthy and bureaucratic controls on reconversion, the switch from wartime to civilian production. Prominent in the laissez-faire American Retail Federation (ARF), which then represented half a million retailers, Puckett reflected its worldview in his assertion that "there must be unlimited faith in our proven, free enterprise system." Reflecting the agenda of the ARF for the coming decades, he told trade press readers that their job was to sell this free enterprise system. This was their own "product" that they were to sell, rather than their "competitor's product in this field—planned economy and government control."[27]

While we know now that the ARF's goals came to fruition later in the twentieth century and that Puckett's vision of retailing prevailed, the war provided a moment when the industry could have gone a different way— toward acceptance of greater government controls over price competition, wages, and the supply of goods. Patriotism and a desire to repair a reputation hurt by the Depression spurred early support of such things as the OPA. But quickly, older laissez-faire attitudes and hostility to the government emerged, even as business overall benefited from the tremendous revitalization of industry made possible by the federal agencies and efforts of workers to provide the arsenal of democracy. There were exceptions, like Edward Filene of Boston or Stanley Marcus of Dallas, who favored extending OPA controls into the postwar period, but most sought its demise.[28] Industry cooperation with federal regulators had reached its zenith. From 1945 on it would only decline.

CHAPTER 6

The Race for the Suburbs

The department stores did not create the downtown muddle
in America's large cities, and they cannot solve it singlehanded.
They can and should help; but in the meantime they had best roll
with the punch and head for the suburbs.
— *Fortune*, 1951

AT the first peacetime convention of the National Retail Dry Goods
Association (NRDGA), industry leaders praised their fellow merchants for keeping "the home fires burning and the ammunition flowing"
to help win the war. While concerns over shortages, continuing price controls, and labor troubles remained, it seemed to those speaking at New
York's Hotel Pennsylvania that the department store field was at an economic high point. An executive from Crews-Boggs Dry Goods Company
in Pueblo, Colorado, asserted proudly that "the modern department store
has become an institution throughout America," one that came into contact with so many people that it had an unprecedented "opportunity to set
an example for public spirited leadership and friendly relations."[1] Defined
in 1948 as retail establishments with twenty-five or more employees that
sold a broad line of merchandise, department stores numbered 2,590 in
November of that year and had 830,000 men and women on their payrolls.[2]

Small-town department store merchants, big urban independents, and
department store chain operators all entered the postwar period filled with
optimism, looking forward to a future in which they would profit from
consumers' "pent-up demand" and fulfill their long-delayed dreams of

expansion and modernization.[3] Most downtown department store executives had to shelve their plans to update or enlarge operations during the
war, but in the confident atmosphere of the postwar boom they were able
to move forward. Almost all department stores entered the period as corporations; older forms of organization like the proprietorship and partnership
had mostly died out.[4] These corporations aggressively pursued new avenues
of growth, urged on by their professional organizations and trade press.
Those that did not "chain up" or expand into the suburbs were seen as at
"risk of becoming an anachronism" due to the rise of discounters, suburban shopping centers, and the changing needs and desires of consumers.[5]

Modernization in the postwar era came to mean opening suburban
branches and developing shopping centers rather than updating or building
new downtown stores as in the 1920s. As has been well documented, this
corporate strategy changed the nation's retail environment. This strategy also
meant the ascendance of massive holding companies and department store
chains. Even stores located outside the metropolis changed, modernizing
their operations and joining larger department store groups, though in a
vastly different demographic context from the big-city or suburban stores.

These transitions began when the industry as a whole was in a strong
position, aligned with policy makers and with the dominant cultural, political, and economic values of the time. As the 1950s wore on, however, and
the civil rights movement gained support, downtown establishments
became highly visible symbols of both the promise and limits of the American dream. Resentment of the growing power of the federal government
during this period grew stronger over the early 1960s, even as industry
leaders supported policies that they hoped would strengthen the downtown
department store. Changes in federal tax policies, support for federally
funded highways and for urban renewal as a solution to downtown decline,
and an overarching commitment to an automobile-dependent suburban
landscape affected the fate of the downtown department store. Such policies, which received strong support across the spectrum of the department
store industry, helped retailers open suburban branches and develop the
massive new shopping centers and malls that would ultimately spell the
demise of Main Street.

The Shopping Center Revolution

It is an understatement to say that automobile-oriented suburbanization
transformed retailing in the postwar period. Between 1950 and 1955, the

suburban population grew seven times as fast as that of central cities. In the United States, decentralized residential patterns were tied to increased automobility as people relied on their personal vehicles to get to work or to travel downtown to shop or do business. American suburbs were low-density residential areas on the outskirts of larger cities where people of similar class and race lived amid trees and grass—with an automobile or two parked in the garage. Between 1946 and 1955, new car sales quadrupled in the United States.[6] By 1960, government reports described suburban shopping centers as "the inevitable byproduct of the automobile age." While not "inevitable"—central shopping districts continued to thrive in Europe, reflecting in part better support for public transit—in the United States the automobile contributed to the loss of downtown department stores.[7]

In the face of increased dependence on the automobile and this vast demographic shift, members of the department store industry became obsessed with parking. Not surprisingly, traffic congestion and scarce parking concerned both big-city and small-town retailers as more shoppers relied on their cars. Retailers' solutions to the problems created by decentralization focused on the automobile, doing little to improve public transit. The pedestrian mall was widely debated, but most major retailers viewed it with skepticism, reflecting the "innate conservatism" of department store executives in the early postwar period. The perceived need for enlarged parking capacity pushed many to open suburban branch stores with vast paved lots or hulking garages that could serve the massive new demand for goods and services outside of the central business district. As suburban shopping centers and branch department stores blossomed, they took more and more of their share of metropolitan retail trade—from 31 percent in 1948 to nearly 60 percent in 1961 in the country's ten biggest population centers.[8]

While it is a truism now that downtown local department stores were victims of suburbanization, the future was far from clear to contemporaries. The decade and a half after World War II was a tumultuous period for the industry. As things were shaking out, downtown retailers disagreed over the path they should take. The question of whether they should transport their "markets to the meadows" or recommit to their downtown parent stores filled the trade press and was the subject of numerous industry studies. Analyses of the situation were understandably mixed, even confused. A reorientation to the suburbs came hard for merchants and industry experts,

FIGURE 21. Florida's first branch of this New England department store opened in Miami in 1956. The store blended downtown and suburban elements. Multistoried and facing the street, it also catered to the automobile with a parking lot for three thousand cars, and had a swimming pool and a dock. Jordan Marsh was absorbed by Burdines in 1991. Author's collection. Photographer: Amadeus Rubel.

both intellectually and practically. One wartime trade article on department store planning noted that population loss in city centers would force the downtown retailers into a period of "major readjustment" but still maintained, "Central Store Very Necessary." Downtown shopping was a tradition that the industry, individual merchants, and even customers were unwilling to give up on entirely. One 1949 study of shopping habits in Philadelphia, for example, asserted that the vast majority of housewives favored downtown stores, though it suggested that these urban establishments were likely to decline in importance in future years.[9]

Indeed, in the late 1940s and early 1950s the industry revealed its devotion to the aging parent store. Big retailers across the country continued to expand their downtown operations. Brooklyn's Abraham & Straus, Newark's Bamberger's, Detroit's Hudson's, Richmond's Miller & Rhoads, and many others spent millions on expansion and renovation in the early postwar era. Major chains like Federated Department Stores also committed themselves to downtown by opening new outlets in medium and smaller cities that had seen significant population growth. Most remained loyal to their city's traditional central business district, even as they opened up their own suburban branches. Executives, like the publicity director at J. L. Hudson Co., an Associated Merchandising Corporation member, saw suburban branches and shopping centers not as competition for downtown but as a means of expanding into new, unserved markets. Few blamed their suburban children for the problems of downtown. Some, in fact, felt that the full-line branch store and the parent store reinforced each other. Downtown stores were the flagships that gave the firm its identity and appeal. Largely unable to see that what they had created was leading to their demise, downtown executives did not realize they were undercutting their central operations and sentencing themselves to suburbia.[10]

These negative implications were still unclear. As stores followed their markets to the suburbs in the 1950s, many merchants, academic observers, and consumers still saw downtown as the place to be. Decentralization did "not necessarily mean the extinction of downtown shopping areas," according to one contemporary expert. Another argued that branch stores resulted in no drop in downtown sales volume, even though they took away some of the business of regular downtown customers. Proponents of sprawl insisted that highways and suburbs did not endanger shopping in the central business district. A major marketing study in 1953, sponsored by the Highway Research Board of the National Research Council, reported on the continued strength of downtowns like that of Columbus, Ohio. Considering the highway board's pro-automobile perspective, it is not surprising that its report on suburban versus downtown shopping argued that it was too early to settle the question of "whether or not the central business district of American cities is a sinking ship, which business men should desert while something can still be saved." The Highway Research Board study did find that shoppers saw some disadvantage to shopping in downtown stores over suburban shopping centers, but that "whatever advantages there are downtown outweigh the disadvantages in their value scales." More forthrightly, a 1951 *Fortune* magazine article titled "Race for the Suburbs" asserted unequivocally that "the frontier of American retailing" was the suburban branch department store.[11]

Even in popular culture, the downtown department store ruled through the 1960s. In the popular imagination, these emporia were part of the downtown fabric. They made their appearance in a variety of genres. Their

invented traditions, such as the department store Santa, provided sentimen-
tal fodder for holiday movies that would become traditions in their own
right over the years. With their multiple floors and technological wonders,
such as pneumatic tubes, delivery chutes, elevators, and moving staircases,
they were the perfect backdrop for slapstick comedy. Filled with incongru-
ous items, they offered props for every situation. As places of luxury and
decorum that also permitted free entry, these downtown institutions had
the potential for hilarious comedic reversal and erasure of social divisions—
between people and animals, between children and adults, between the
native-born and immigrants. Bugs Bunny ran amok through department
store aisles on roller skates, bowling over headless mannequins. Comic
strip heroine Little Lulu drove a store floorwalker mad through her endless
testing of toys to exchange for a doll she no longer wanted. And groups of
immigrants and Native Americans, led by the Marx Brothers in an earlier,
though still popular movie, paraded through a luxurious furniture department to try out preposterously futuristic beds that moved up and down. As
a city within a city, the downtown department store provided an alternate
universe where a damaged stuffed bear like Corduroy came to life, got lost
at night alone in the store, and was saved by an African American girl. And
as long as the city retained the glamour and emotional pull expressed in
Petula Clark's 1964 hit song "Downtown," its department stores would as
well. The idea that "the lights were much brighter there" and that "everything's waiting for you" downtown was still strong, though the new glow
of low-slung shopping malls seen from the highway at night must have also
had its attractions.[12]

Despite its cultural pull, when the statistics came in it was clear that
downtown department stores simply could not compete. As suburban
branches first developed, industry concerns over downtown sales were
somewhat allayed by the belief that an expanding economy would "dull the
impact." In short order, however, central business districts across the country were hurt badly by the rise of the automobile as a form of mass transportation, the exodus to the suburbs, and the rapid growth of commercial
development outside the urban core. Well-planned shopping centers drew
consumers—especially women—away from downtown. By 1951, branch
store expenses were lower and their profits higher than those of downtown.
In the mid-1950s, anxiety about the declining fortunes of downtown retail
escalated with the publication of the 1954 business census. The census con-
firmed downtown's slipping sales. As an oft-cited 1954 history of the

department store commented, many felt that American retailers "cut their own throats" with suburban branches. Since 1948, total sales in forty-five metropolitan areas had increased 32.3 percent, whereas sales had only risen 1.6 percent in central districts. The market share of retail sales in the central business districts of seven middle-size cities fell from 34.3 percent in 1958 to 31.1 percent in 1963, while sales elsewhere rose during the same period.[13]

Beginning in the mid-1950s, department store firms began to close landmark downtown locations. Stores had always come and gone, victims of hard times, poor management, or superior competition. But, unlike earlier closures during the Depression and war years, the firms shutting down units in the postwar period were not inherently weak. The prestigious firm of John Wanamaker gave up on its big New York City complex in 1954. New York in fact saw the closure of eight major stores between 1952 and 1956. Throughout the rest of the decade, downtown Cincinnati, Washington, Baltimore, Boston, Brooklyn, Philadelphia, Pittsburgh, Buffalo, and Detroit all lost department stores. These closures were understood to be the result of many factors, both internal and external. Poor management and merchandising was blamed, as was competition from the suburbs. Many of the firms shutting down during the 1950s and early 1960s were lower-middle market and were thus more vulnerable to growing threats from discounters.[14]

To contemporary observers, postwar shopping center competition appeared to have sprung up by magic "from the meadows as though invoked by Aladdin's lamp." But this was not the case. Stores had begun establishing branches as early as the 1920s, beginning the movement out of traditional central business districts. Prestigious emporia like Saks Fifth Avenue and I. Magnin introduced resort shops in hotels in the 1920s. Marshall Field's established a presence in key locations outside downtown Chicago in 1929, and Philadelphia's Strawbridge & Clothier opened a branch in Germantown in 1931. On the West Coast, the famed Bullock's department store opened its landmark Art Deco branch in 1929. A few less prestigious department stores also began to open branches in this early period as the blue-collar population gained mobility through car ownership and began moving to suburbs. Contemporaries noted this early shift and its effect on retailing. In 1929, Christine Frederick observed that consumers seemed to be growing tired of shopping in "modern, crowded city conditions," a problem she believed the new "'mother store' system" of suburban branches would remedy. By the 1930s and 1940s, small department store outlets had appeared in a few shopping centers. Strawbridge & Clothier established a forty-thousand-square-foot branch in Suburban Square along Philadelphia's Main Line in 1930, while Frederick & Nelson built a sixteen-thousand-square-foot unit in Bellevue Square, east of Seattle, in 1946.[15]

Department store executives had been generally reluctant to set up branches in the undeveloped areas favored by shopping centers, choosing instead to build within established outlying business districts or in solo locations along highways. This changed slowly in the years following the end of World War II. Between 1946 and 1950, approximately sixteen made the move. Major department stores were in the position to act as developers for their own shopping centers, but still, some had to be convinced. As late as 1961, opening smaller branches known as "twigs," which carried specific merchandise classifications and could resemble bargain basements, was characterized by the business press as throwing "tradition and dignity to the winds."[16]

While the earliest shopping centers did not generally contain department store branches, by 1951, more than half of suburban branches were built within shopping centers. The number of shopping centers increased from a few hundred at the end of World War II to 7,100 by 1963.[17] Department stores as an industry benefited from this initial growth. Branch expansion into suburbia contributed to the higher percent change in department store sales volume between 1958 and 1963 than that experienced by other types of general merchandise retailers and even the retail trade as a whole. The department store industry grew from 2,761 establishments in 1954 to 3,157 in 1958, then to 4,251 in 1963. Sales more than doubled in the same period, rising 53.7 percent from 1958 to 1963 and outpacing total retail trade by 21.9 percent. By 1966, over half of department store sales were made in branch stores.[18]

This expansion into suburban shopping centers was aided by financial institutions, as developers found eager lenders in insurance companies and pension trusts. Developers and executives at first preferred that the majority of shopping center tenants be independents, but when investors began demanding the highest credit rating from the vast majority of a complex's occupants this changed. Finance needs gave national chains an advantage. Independents protested this tilted playing field to little effect, despite efforts of the Small Business Association on their behalf. By the late 1950s, massive chains like J. C. Penney were able to position themselves as major mall anchors.[19]

As their presence in suburban shopping centers expanded, the industry struggled to work out the proper relationship between parent and branch. Three standard types of branches with different relationships to the parent store emerged: full-line branches, basement-only branches, and the smaller branches called "twigs." Multiunit retailers grappled with the question of how much to centralize or decentralize management. The opening of suburban stores forced the downtown parent store to reconsider its management policy and organizational structure and the balance of power between the two locations. While some early branch stores in the 1930s operated with their own separate buying staffs, for example, they soon shifted to centralized purchasing for the majority of their branch merchandise in order to take advantage of potential efficiencies. Doing so not only cut operating costs, it gave individual branches access to a broader range of merchandise than would be available if they were autonomous units. The industry entered the postwar era in favor of centralized buying, with plans for "super" buying pools between stores like R. H. Macy and Company and the May Department Stores. Buying pools gave retailers more power over manufacturers and allowed them to clamp down on individual store's buyers as well. But some noted that centralization also created problems. Customers, for example, often perceived branch stores as having less stock than downtown stores, and they were right—branches were chronically out of items due to limited storage facilities, lax branch managers, and parent store buyers who sidelined their branch store duties and privileged their own downtown departmental needs.[20]

By the end of the decade, expert opinion shifted in favor of decentralized management, which granted more autonomy to branch store managers. Large department store ownership groups and holding companies during this period allowed each store to carry on most merchandising operations individually and independently. Even so, parent companies did not completely let go and still typically formulated policy and operating standards for their branches. Nonmerchandising functions also remained centralized in order to avoid duplication of facilities and personnel and to provide functional aid for each store and coordination of their various activities.[21]

Implicit in the debate over the centralization of management was the issue of standardization. While the American shopping mall would come to symbolize the homogeneity of suburban living, this was not clearly the case at first. Debates within the industry at the time show that there was

more than one potential path. Retail experts examining the particular problems of the suburban branch repeatedly brought up the issue of standardization, coming down on different sides in their analysis. In a series on the
topic written by a retail analyst for the *Department Store Economist* in 1951,
suburban branches were in fact presented as a potential counter to standardization. If outlets had their own independent management they were
believed to be more able to adapt to their community "with a distinctive
personality and a folksiness that is no longer possible downtown." A 1957
academic study out of Stanford's Graduate School of Business, however,
reached the opposite conclusion. The author recommended that branch
stores assert "some of the color and local prestige, as well as the reputation
for excellent service and value" enjoyed by the downtown parent store.
Advertising, public relations, sales promotions, and aggressive branch merchandising were needed, he argued, to prove "the suburban department
store branch is not of necessity a sterile operation."[22] Such disparate interpretations likely reflected their authors' aesthetic bias and occupational
position, but they also revealed that at stake was downtown's identity, as
well as its economic viability.

When they first appeared, shopping centers offered consumers a unique
experience distinct from that of the traditional downtown business district.
What distinguished this new way of distributing goods and services from
earlier forms was the fact that stores were "designed, built, and operated as
a single unit," populated by tenants who were selected for what they could
contribute to the whole. With grassy courtyards and parklike atmosphere,
shopping centers were expected to serve as both a commercial and a social
center. Shopping centers of the 1960s, like El Paso's Northgate, added community halls that hosted dances, meetings, and receptions. Some complexes
reflected the visionary, reform-minded perspective of their architects. The
most prominent of these, Austrian-born Victor Gruen, sought to provide
suburbanites with a new kind of urban experience. At Northland outside of
Detroit, Gruen introduced the department store J. L. Hudson to a suburban
market for the first time. Northland sought to have the appeal of a traditional downtown center but without its aggravations. Gruen designed it to
evoke a European city but with easy parking and less hustle and bustle. It
featured clusters of open spaces labeled courts, terraces, malls, and lanes,
decorated with colonnades, sculptures, and fountains.[23] Such ideas spread
across the country, framing the entry of downtown department stores into
suburban markets. Shopping centers like NorthPark, for example, which

FIGURE 22. When the Palm Beach Mall opened in 1967, it was the largest fully
enclosed, climate-controlled shopping center in the southeastern United States.
Anchored by department stores Jordan Marsh, Richard's, and J. C. Penney, the Florida
mall featured a lush, tropical landscaped interior concourse of one hundred thousand
square feet. After years of decline, it was torn down in 2013. © and ® John Hinde
Archive. Reproduced courtesy of Florida Photographic Collection, State Archives of
Florida. Photographer: E. Ludwig, John Hinde Studios.

opened outside Dallas in 1965, were advertised as "an attempt to counteract
the confusions of the city." By the mid-1960s, this view of the shopping
center as a solution to "the plight of cities" and "unplanned urban sprawl"
was widespread.[24]

Unlike downtown emporia, shopping centers and their branch department stores catered specifically to the needs and preferences of a more
homogenized group—middle-class, white suburban customers. Lower-end
urban department stores had long served working-class customers downtown. Luxurious "palaces of consumption" that furnished the carriage
trade and even small-town Main Street department stores had long had

bargain basements that served the needs of shoppers of lesser means. Unlike these downtown stores, however, suburban branches only occasionally featured a bargain basement; the first to be established was at the Hecht Company's Silver Spring branch in 1948. And shopping center developers single-mindedly sought a middle-class market. To pursue this market, department store branches in these shopping centers did things differently than their downtown parent store, cultivating a controlled, safe atmosphere that was believed to appeal specifically to white, suburban housewives. Suburban branches, as it was understood by the trade press, were "breaking away from downtown traditions," establishing evening hours, offering novel services, and even competing with the new mass merchandisers like the discount operation. The massive new complexes were also meant to appeal to families, not just women. Indeed, by the early 1960s they appeared to have had some success, as retail and marketing experts noted a change in family buying habits, with the husband becoming a "more active member of the family purchasing team."[25]

In spite of their early innovations and goals, shopping centers came to represent mass culture and the homogeneity of suburban living in American society. In part this was because of their appearance. Unlike the traditional downtown store, which was part of the heterogeneous city, shopping centers eventually became standardized in appearance. This was the result of a number of factors, both practical and strategic. Shopping center leases during the period sought to control the overall visual effect by requiring tenants to create unified color schemes and signage. Moreover, the centers as a whole had also been regularized into "a linear sequence of stores facing a front parking lot," laid out in a straight line or bent at one or two points to form a V or divided into two parts into an L shape. The overall effect was a low-slung shape built entirely around shoppers' love of their automobile. Increasingly they featured plain, windowless department stores—boxlike containers with low-key signs and entrances.[26]

These suburban configurations were increasingly ubiquitous, but they were not the only venue for department store retailing in postwar America. Department stores may have been racing for the suburbs by the 1950s, but they had another home, one that has been overlooked in the scholarly literature, for the most part. If the downtown and the suburban branch department store were children of the metropolis, the small-town Main Street merchant was a poor relation.

The Persistence of Localism in the Postwar Era

Suburbanization transformed the big-city department store during this period, but small-town establishments competed in a different demographic context. Regional variation, at least in store numbers, persisted relative to population density. Metropolitan areas supported relatively fewer but larger firms, while nonmetropolitan areas were served by larger numbers of small businesses.[27] Small-town retailers across the country faced similar problems. Urban yet nonmetropolitan, they had to contend with the fact that national demographic trends were leaving them behind. Metropolitan areas, as they were first defined in 1950, consisted of "a large population nucleus together with adjacent communities having a high degree of social and economic integrity." In 1950, the number of people living in such areas overtook those living beyond their limits, and by 1960, 63.3 percent of the population lived in relatively dense regions of the country. As suburban density increased, downtown populations declined. Nonmetropolitan density, however, remained relatively unchanged during this period. Facing a stagnant population and competition with larger trade centers and other forms of retailing, the nonmetropolitan small-town department store, some feared, was on its way to becoming a relic.[28]

Occupying a prominent place in the department store's origins narrative, the beleaguered small-town merchant received attention from the industry well into the postwar era. While the rise of the suburban branch store and shopping center dominated industry and academic discussions of postwar retailing, the problems of these nonmetropolitan merchants were still deemed significant in the trade press. In 1945, a trade article titled "Big Business Comes to Small Towns" sketched the turning of the familiar "wheel of retailing" from the peddler to the country store to the chain store. The author argued that small towns continued to provide significant markets. While the small town had once been "underestimated," big retail organizations were increasingly finding a place on Main Street.[29] Local and state trade organizations briefed smaller-store executives—many of whom would have been based in smaller communities—on topics of national interest that affected them as well, through industry clinics on changing employee-employer relations, fair employment practice legislation, credit problems, and buying habits. Such clinics attracted hundreds of participants.[30]

The number of small-town department stores surviving into the postwar period shows that industry attention was warranted. In 1963 it was not clear that the Main Street department store was on its way out. At that time, small-town department stores still commanded a significant proportion of establishments nationwide. Towns (or cities, as the census bureau labeled them) of fewer than 10,000 people were served by 218 department stores in 1963. Those cities with a population between 10,000 and 24,999 had many more department stores—764 to be exact.[31] Together, these smaller communities accounted for 23 percent of the nation's total number of department stores—certainly a less significant figure but one that did not yet turn the Main Street store into a museum piece. Adding in the stores serving cities with populations between 25,000 and 49,999, about 42 percent of all American department stores were located in relatively small markets. The census did not distinguish between independents and chain department stores like J. C. Penney, though. The number of independents had declined greatly over the decades, generating concern in the field. Between 1929 and 1954, almost 60 percent of independent department stores had either closed their doors or had been consolidated into other organizations, their numbers dropping from 2,166 to 905.[32]

Some of the problems experienced by postwar Main Street retailers were rooted in earlier decades, as we have seen. Like their big-city cousins, department stores in small communities struggled to adapt to the automobile. Parking and traffic congestion were of concern even in small towns. While decentralization was not a pressing issue for retailers serving these nonmetropolitan communities, since the 1920s the automobile affected small towns by easing travel to larger trade centers previously reliant on the railroads and their schedules. Inflationary trends after World War II made price an issue and played a role in motivating shoppers to drive in search of good value or bargains. The higher prices typically found in small communities certainly pushed some out to larger trading centers that were within casual driving distance.[33]

Within smaller communities themselves, the automobile encouraged decentralized commercial developments. As in bigger cities, the automobile allowed retailers to be drawn away from the central business districts, where department stores had traditionally made their home (and played a role in establishing in the first place). For example, automobile travel encouraged the growth of taxpayer strips consisting of rapidly built blocks of single-story commercial buildings radiating out from a town's center (road developments intended only to generate enough income to pay the taxes on the land until they became more lucrative investments). These now ubiquitous commercial strips made their appearance after World War I, when they emerged to serve the new residential neighborhoods that spread out from a town's Main Street or a city's downtown core. Taxpayer strips became "secondary Main Streets," but they housed retailers who were not direct competitors for Main Street's department stores. Increasingly, though, they took the shape of strip malls that would eventually pull significant trade away from the traditional central business district of towns and cities alike.[34]

A challenge specific to the small-town family-run firm came from chain department stores, which were rapidly growing in strength in the postwar era. Since their appearance in the 1920s, as we have seen, chain department stores were strong competition for family-run businesses. In particular, the threat of elimination was stronger for smaller independent department stores—those with annual sales in the range of $1 million to $10 million— that typically still lined Main Streets across the United States through the early 1960s. Over the years, chain department stores like Sears, J. C. Penney, and Montgomery Ward provided increasing competition for independents in provincial markets. By 1963, these three were the nation's largest and most well-established chain department stores, with combined annual sales of over $7 billion.[35] Still located downtown in smaller communities though also emerging in the outlying areas of metropolitan centers, they represented modern retailing in both appearance and in their methods of operation.

The small-town, independent establishment in some ways stood as the antithesis of these increasingly dominant department store chains. In an era where cost-cutting chain methods prevailed across much of the industry, the Main Street department store continued to engage in more individualized practices. For example, since the 1930s, big-city stores had cut delivery costs by coordinating their service with other area retailers and employing an outside contractor, such as the United Parcel Service, a move that resulted in the loss of their distinctive vans featuring store logos. But small-town independent stores depended on their own personalized delivery trucks into the postwar period. In addition, local stores emphasized their tradition of customer service. Indeed, personal connections between store owners and customers remained important to these firms. In small communities the two groups were more likely to include acquaintances, friends, or even relatives. When part of the same social networks as the store owners, customers sometimes exacted special favors, such as custom orders or rush delivery. Such personal attention certainly helped small-town independents distinguish themselves from Sears or J. C. Penney, which, despite their claims to localness, were standardized operations. Unlike chains, independent department stores typically reflected the personality and taste of their management, one generally built upon knowledge of local markets.[36]

Prescriptive sources also suggest that independents did not always want to or were not always able to follow the latest industry trends. Experts urged smaller stores to join buying organizations or mechanize their credit systems. In a similar vein, a management manual for independent department and specialty store owners criticized those who still used outdated accounting methods. As late as 1969, some independents were not in possession of up-to-date information about the retail value of their inventory provided by newer bookkeeping methods, following as they did the older system of accounting that relied on the physical counting of goods once or twice a year.[37]

Not surprisingly, the "electronic revolution" was slow to transform independent Main Street stores in the provinces. By the 1950s, some independents like Wellan's, the largest department store in central Louisiana, began to move in this direction. Change on Main Street, as was often the case, was not revolutionary. Founded in 1926, Wellan's modernized and mechanized its facility in downtown Alexandria in the 1950s, adding elevators, National Cash Register floor audit machines, and two-way radio systems in its trucks. It also mechanized its credit system. Firms like Wellan's that might have wanted electronic data processing (EDP), however, were simply too small or undercapitalized to afford an electronic computer or tabulating system. Instead, they turned to mechanical solutions. A Rol-Dex installation at Wellan's in 1962, for example, sought to rationalize its accounts receivable department. The system consisted of a mobile chair assembly in which the operator rolled back and forth between specially arranged files, a layout that allowed fewer clerks to access thousands of accounts.[38] Such arrangements were clearly inferior to the EDP available to large organizations.

The "electronic revolution" gave an edge to big players in the field. The great capital outlay required to set up electronic data-processing systems meant that the new technology was more accessible to large firms, giving them yet another advantage over the smaller Main Street operation. Department stores began to use punch-card equipment to handle payroll, sales audit, accounts payable, and accounts receivable. By the late 1950s, even some provincial "trail-blazer" department stores had installed their own IBM punch-card equipment. In El Paso, the White House installed its system in 1956 and benefited from a 50 percent reduction in credit department personnel. Others, like H. Leh & Company of Allentown, Pennsylvania, rented their equipment and boasted that a better responsiveness to customer preferences was the result. However, big chains like J. C. Penney would be the first to install computer systems that centralized more complex information about the cost of selling. With the exception of large department store chains like Penney's, retailers as a group in the early 1960s lagged behind other major users of EDP, such as banks and utilities. EDP systems began to run accounting and financial departments in the early 1960s and then slowly moved into the more complex task of monitoring inventories, sales, and profits at each outlet. By 1962, still only one out of eight respondents to a retail trade survey had installed EDP equipment.[39]

While independent department stores could not compete on their own with the EDP of massive chains like Penney's, experts at the time believed that their combined power would allow them to fight "the 'giants.'" In the early 1960s, independent department stores could turn to their buying offices for EDP services. Firms that could not afford the capital investment for equipment of their own participated "collectively" with other independent stores within their resident buying office network to control merchandise in the same efficient manner as much larger competitors. After 1965, computerization became more accessible to independent retailers with the introduction of group EDP programs by the smaller stores division of the national trade association. Using multistub punched tags that were processed at the buying office on IBM computer equipment, smaller stores monitored information about the items they sold. Punched tags became the receiving and sales reports and cumulatively provided the information for a summary inventory report. The success of EDP eliminated "guesswork," cutting costs and increasing productivity. While the EDP services of centralized buying offices allowed independents to achieve greater efficiencies, they could never do so on the scale of a true chain like Penney's, for example, which set up a computer system controlling inventory and merchandise decisions for thirty stores on the West Coast.[40]

At the time, however, EDP was received as a savior for the little guy. In the early postwar period, department store executives and the industry valued its potential for eliminating the competitive gap between small and big stores and between independents and chains. Some years later in 1973, the department store trade press heralded developments in computer hardware and software as a "new revolution" for retailing that made "changes of other years sound like the mouthings of midgets."[41] Widespread adoption of EDP meant more than an increase in operational efficiency and increased profits. It reflected the optimism of the postwar era. For the independents who invested in it, EDP represented an additional commitment to Main Street retailing.

During this period, many small-town department stores looked to the future in another way, committing capital resources to the modernization of their buildings and outdated facades. Small-town department stores like Bresee's in Oneonta, New York, modernized later than metropolitan retailers. So did southern department stores like Foley's in downtown Houston, which reportedly introduced the first store escalator in the South in its 1947 modern "store of tomorrow." By the early 1960s, over three-quarters of small stores—those doing $2 million to $5 million in sales—had undertaken some recent modernization. In small towns and provincial cities, renovations typically reflected a desire to rationalize stores' selling space—in effect to rid them of the older features that distinguished them from the modern suburban branch store. As big-city stores had done in the 1920s, the Main Street department store now eliminated such things as the Y-shaped staircase. Haak Brothers in Lebanon, Pennsylvania, replaced its staircase in 1950 with a single escalator that ran from the first to the second floor.[42] That same year, Buttrey's of Great Falls, Montana, modernized its exterior and also purchased three escalators, its president thinking "in terms of big city merchandising" for a population of thirty-nine thousand, according to the Otis advertisement. Everywhere, busy nineteenth-century Main Street facades were streamlined and windows covered up to create the flat, boxlike surface of new branch stores in suburban shopping centers.[43] These modernizations took place in the context of rising competition from chain department stores and larger trade centers but also reflected the era's optimism and belief in the continued viability of the Main Street enterprise.

Even firms that had little to fear from out-of-town or suburban competitors engaged in ambitious postwar modernization. Located on a railway line in upstate New York almost fifty miles from a larger market center, Bresee's department store celebrated its fiftieth anniversary in 1949 with parades, special window and interior displays, and much publicity in the

FIGURE 23. As did many older downtown department stores in the 1950s, Bresee's pursued an updated appearance, covering up its nineteenth-century storefront with a sleek, windowless facade in 1959. Attempts to redevelop the vacant building in 2009 resulted in the removal of the aluminum facade and dated signage, which many local residents perceived as inauthentic, if not ugly. Author's collection.

local newspaper. The Oneonta store had done very well during World War II and was poised to become a leading local retailer that could connect the town with the outside world, featuring the latest fashions in clothing, shoes, jewelry, housewares, appliances, and furniture. By the early postwar period, it had two hundred employees and forty-eight departments, including a lunch room, a bargain basement, and a credit department. The physical plant, however, was in dire need of modernization to bring it up to the standards set by urban retailers with larger markets. Under the leadership and boosterism of Fred Bresee, one of the store founder's three sons, the firm undertook a $100,000 store modernization project. Bresee's eventually

FIGURE 24. Bresee's advertised locally in Oneonta newspapers and on radio but featured national brands. In 1949, the store promoted Bendix automatic washers with a popular "Wash on the Air!" demonstration broadcast from the appliance department. Courtesy of Marc Bresee. Photo: Warnken Studio, Oneonta, New York.

gained new streamlined counters and cases, circular shadow box display windows, and the town's first and (still) only escalator. Fred Bresee also revamped the store's approach to advertising and merchandizing, reflecting his motto that "store business is show business." The store, for example, hosted appliance demonstrations and fashion shows. It invited the local Oneonta radio station WDOS to cover store events and sponsored a daily program titled "Brands That Please Are Found at Bresee's," which called attention to the store's many national brands, a selling feature for small-town stores that wanted to connect to big city trends.[44]

The modernization program and merchandizing methods developed by stores like Bresee's in the early postwar era were certainly not new within the industry as a whole. Major urban retailers had experimented with ways of bringing customers in the door as many as fifty years earlier.[45] Industry trends toward bigness came later to Main Street, a fact that is significant because it meant that the local and regional flavor of retailing associated with smaller, independent operations held on longer in nonmetropolitan areas than in suburbs or big-city downtowns, in spite of a rising national consumer culture. The different periodization for the Main Street merchant thus suggests that postwar American consumer culture was not monolithic but instead developed differently in all regions of the country and among various groups.[46]

As the gap between big city and small town, chain and local narrowed in significant ways in the early postwar era, many family firms continued to assert their own distinctive identity. In the face of postwar challenges, the industry increasingly deployed localism as a selling tool, a strategy for distinguishing the local brand from others. Privately held regional chains like the massive Belk department store organization, for example, promoted the individuality of its store partners until the late 1960s, even fostering a country store image to give it a local identity in the South.[47] Local department stores waxed nostalgic about their provincial roots in their advertisements and at their anniversary celebrations. Some romanticized their history, setting up generic "old-timey" promotional events like "Gaslight Gala" at M. Epstein, Inc., in Morristown, New Jersey.[48] In the 1950s, cooperative, citywide sales events, such as "Downtown Louisville Days" or a "Made in St. Paul Show," had met with great success. Perhaps in response to pressure from suburban shopping centers and branch department stores, celebrations of the local continued into the early 1960s. Localism was evident even in the face of consolidation. In 1962, for example, Saint Louis's Stix, Baer & Fuller launched a huge Mississippi riverboat promotion the same year it was bought by Associated Dry Goods. Over two weeks, the store served southern dishes and featured banjo players, soft-shoe dancers, and doormen dressed in rented southern colonial costumes. The main floor was transformed into a riverboat salon replete with Victorian arches, hanging baskets of moss and greenery, and potted palms; it featured a showboat stage for modeling fashions made out of new man-made fibers, ironically the purpose of the event.[49] Localism—in this case a celebration of "traditional" southern identity—became a way to market the firm's distinctiveness, setting it apart from national chains.

In smaller communities, however, it is clear that localism was more than just a promotional selling tool—that to some degree it reflected persistent regional tastes and consumer preferences within the national consumer culture. As late as the 1950s, small-town independent department stores still catered to local style preferences. Even though these firms relied on regional or national buying organizations by midcentury, they continued to instruct their buyers to find items that local customers wanted. Consumers themselves pushed retailers to stock items that fit needs and desires that might differ from national or big-city styles. The owner of Poliakoff's department store in Abbeville, South Carolina, for example, wrote to his buyer in Birmingham in 1956 that pleated "full skirts have been best with us," making reference to a fashion trend from earlier in the decade. The merchant's request likely reflected the conservative, or perhaps more practical taste of his shoppers, rather than the high fashion shift toward trimmer lines that would result in the tight pencil skirt by the end of the decade.[50]

The fact that Main Street stores continued to be "local" in the early postwar period, or that members of big holding companies continued to deploy localism as a selling tool, however, did not mean that department stores were isolated from national forces or trends. Department store management, workers, and shoppers interacted within a national framework created by government policies, a framework that they helped construct in significant ways.

Urban Renewal, Civil Rights, and the Postwar Department Store Industry

Since the Great Depression, the federal government had shaped the geography of retailing. By pumping money into the suburban housing market through programs that eased home financing, more Americans became homeowners. After World War II, federal policies continued to support the decentralization of cities. Federal and state financing to build highways facilitated the movement out of cities. By 1960, 62 percent of Americans owned their own homes.[51] Many of these homes were in new developments that needed the services a big shopping complex could provide. Aided by tax policy, such as the 1954 Internal Revenue Code that favored new construction, developers complied. The policy allowed investors to depreciate their commercial real-estate investments in a manner that encouraged new construction over maintenance or renovation of existing properties. Building a shopping center required a high level of initial investment with an extended payout time. By allowing accelerated depreciation, policy makers gave investors a tax break big enough to overcome these potential barriers. Moreover, the law encouraged turnover, as investors sought repeated deductions with new properties. According to historian Thomas Hanchett, this tax code underwrote shopping mall expansion in the postwar period and was a major contributor to decentralization, along with suburban home ownership, America's automobile culture, and rising racial tension in cities.[52]

Federally funded urban renewal programs demolished city neighborhoods, contributing to the demise of the downtown department store. The intention of these "redevelopment" projects was to strengthen traditional central business districts, but they ultimately destroyed homes and neighborhood businesses and turned Main Streets into vacant lots. While evicted homeowners and the small independent merchants that were negatively affected fought demolition plans, their voices were not as powerful as those of the industry leaders behind redevelopment. Actions taken in the name of commercial revitalization in fact had the opposite effect, increasing the challenges faced by downtown retailers and making suburban shopping centers even more attractive. In the end, urban renewal was a disaster for the downtown economy and the local department store.[53]

Ironically, department store executives themselves played a leading role in redevelopment plans. Top executives at Macy's supported it. The head of the major Atlanta store, Rich's, backed it. In Boston, the development chief Edward Logue recruited heads from Jordan Marsh, Filene's, and Gilchrist's to sit on the executive board of the Committee for the Central Business District, Inc., an organization in charge of planning downtown modernizations. From Sacramento to Chicago and from Rochester to Houston, department store management considered downtown redevelopment initiatives as a remedy for declining sales during this period.[54] Downtown retailers saw urban renewal as a means of "salvation"—specifically a strategy for fighting competition from the new discount stores that sprang up after World War II. Urban renewal was also a means of reclaiming their traditional role downtown. In the late 1950s, the president of Abraham & Straus described the "modernization of American cities, as a sequel to slum clearance projects" that assured the "continued dominance of the downtown department store over its suburban branches."[55]

This remedy required executives to turn once more to their government. For example, the Gimbels and Wanamaker's stores, which were deeply involved in efforts to promote Philadelphia, invested their own capital but also called for federal spending on urban renewal. In a 1953 advertising agency newsletter designed for the department store trade, downtown retailers were told they could not address "the troubles plaguing downtown" without federal help: "Retailers don't build arterial highways. Retailers don't clear downtown slum areas. Retailers can't underwrite lower transit fares by themselves—neither can they tear down slum areas to provide off-the-street parking."[56] As metropolitan areas became increasingly decentralized and downtown sales declined, normally government-averse downtown department store executives looked for state and federal funding. As early as 1944, speaking at the annual convention of the NRDGA, Albert M. Greenfield painted urban renewal as a means of "furthering the retailer's own interests." The head of City Stores Company and the chairman of the executive committee of the Urban Land Institute, Greenfield argued that the "business futures of retailers [was] vitally and inseparably tied up with the progress of their cities." Retailers, he told his audience, were to use their influence "in effecting eradication of the 'dirty collar strangling his city's center' and replacing it with a new forward looking and modern plan for reclaiming the land in the blighted area and putting it once more into productive use."[57]

Heads of major department stores supported urban renewal plans in their cities, and the industry as a whole supported redevelopment policy, but smaller department store merchants who faced losing their place downtown resisted. One such independent department store owner was at the center of a major judicial challenge to urban renewal. Max Morris's store on bustling Fourth Street, the commercial heart of Southwest Washington, was slated for the bulldozer as part of a revitalization plan instigated by the capital city's new Redevelopment Land Agency (RLA), established in 1945 by the federal District of Columbia Act of 1945. Invoking eminent domain, the District of Columbia's RLA planned to bulldoze Southwest Washington, a densely populated area just south of the National Mall that was home to immigrant Jews, African Americans, and the numerous mom-and-pop businesses that served them. Max Morris, who died during the ensuing litigation but whose family wanted to continue running the business, was replaced by Sam Berman, his executor, in the lawsuit. *Berman v. Parker* joined Max Morris's original legal challenge to the Redevelopment Land Agency with another case involving Goldie Schneider, the owner of a neighboring hardware store also slated for destruction. As decided by the Supreme Court in 1954, *Berman v. Parker* established the foundation for

eminent domain jurisprudence, one which broadened the definition of
"public use" to include commercial development for "public purpose."
The courts paved the way for the removal of Max Morris's department
store and other businesses and residences in the district in order to make
way for the privately developed, and ultimately unsuccessful, Waterside
Mall.[58]

While small, independent downtown businesses slated for the wrecking
ball opposed local urban renewal plans, by the mid-1950s, the department
store industry as a whole was placing its hopes for downtown revitalization
with the government. The NRDGA encouraged cooperation. It advised on
ways to take advantage of municipal, county, state, and federal support for
highway and traffic improvements—two issues that increasingly plagued
downtown retailers. Yet, retailers' attitude toward urban renewal was
shaped by their traditional support of state over federal action. The trade
organization endorsed President Eisenhower's recommendation in 1957
that financing fall largely to the states.[59] Few stepped forward to testify in
support of large-scale federal urban renewal grants after Eisenhower found
Section 57 of the housing and urban renewal bill excessive and vetoed it on
July 7, 1959. While leading retailers favored some federal financing for local
communities' urban renewal projects, they sympathized with the presidents' efforts to limit federal spending on such works. Instead, downtown
department store executives called for additional state and local aid to support their efforts to revitalize their business districts.[60]

As was often the case, they chose to ignore their reliance on government-
funded infrastructure and instead advocated "free enterprise" when it
suited their interests or improved their reputation. Department stores and
other downtown commercial interests benefited from eminent domain,
from downtown plans that drew on millions of dollars in federal loans and
grants, and from legislation like the 1954 National Housing Act and the
1956 Federal Highway Act, which made it possible to use those funds for
the rehabilitation of commercial areas. Yet business leaders and the press
celebrated some urban renewal projects as stellar examples of collabora-
tion between private capital and public interests, ignoring the state-
implemented legal and legislative infrastructure that made such massive
plans possible.[61]

One prominent project in Jacksonville reveals these underlying tensions. In 1963, the destruction of a section of this northern Florida port
city was undertaken to revitalize the downtown economy. Bulldozers made

way for the automobile there, as they had in countless communities across the country during this period of urban renewal. Docks and warehouses were torn down and replaced by a parking area for nearly two thousand automobiles that "signaled the rebirth of Jacksonville." The state of Florida was enlisted on behalf of the commercial interests involved, not the federal government, as the *New York Times* heralded in the title of its account of the project: "Renewal Pushed by Jacksonville: City Is Achieving Objectives without Federal Aid." The article made clear that the independent Jacksonville Expressway, which underpinned the entire redevelopment, was not funded federally but locally through county taxes and tolls. Big businesses were the beneficiaries. Chain department stores—both regional and national—were the anchors of Jacksonville's redevelopment initiative. The southern chain Ivey's department store was part of a rebuilt downtown center that included a stadium, theater, and revolving restaurant, as well as a new city hall and other public buildings. Sears also opened its largest outlet, while the May Company renovated the old Cohen Bros. department store.[62]

Although the Jacksonville project was praised at the time for being more than just "slum clearance," in fact the racial, gender, and class biases that emerged around it were typical of urban renewal. While accounts of department store involvement in urban renewal sometimes equated slum clearance with civic duty, building on a long tradition in which a city's merchants were also community leaders and philanthropists engaged in local charity, reports could also be explicitly racist. Racial attitudes of whites shaped the way in which urban renewal projects were presented to the public. A 1956 *New York Times* article argued that the redevelopment of aging downtown Baltimore was needed to counter "modern developments —the steady influx of new residents from the South, desegregation in housing, deterioration of the central city and a residential flight to the outlands," and the negative effect this had on city finances and taxes. A similar tone dominated the account of the Jacksonville project, in which shiny new chain department stores replaced what the press characterized as "small dingy shops huddled between bars frequented by carousing waterfront workers and sailors." Class and gender appeals were also part of the northern Florida project. As part of a larger redevelopment that included tourist attractions, public buildings, and parking, its new and refurbished downtown department stores were likely intended to draw middle-class suburban housewives back to Jacksonville.[63]

Urban renewal fit the department store industry's larger perspective on race relations, which in turn was closely tied to its "business conservative" economic and political worldview. To the business conservative, private investment led to increased productivity, creating desirable economic growth and prosperity. The department store trade press reflected this dominant perspective in its advocacy of "free enterprise."[64] The industry worked to overturn legislation it believed unfairly limited its freedom to make contracts with its labor force. When the government legislated higher costs or reduced retailers' flexibility to respond to changing market conditions, they pushed back, even if those higher costs and restrictions enabled justice and equality. Thus intervention on behalf of labor or consumer rights was opposed in the name of the free market. While not all department store executives went in this direction—in fact, one prominent merchant, Edward Filene, had advocated unionization as well as the consumer cooperative movement—most were highly committed to ideals of competitive individualism.[65] While other managers, executives, and business owners were beginning to be "at peace with the liberal order that had emerged," many in the industry held off on reform until legislation made change imperative.[66]

Anticommunism and Cold War fears shaped business conservatives' understanding of their relationship to state and federal government. Many department store leaders, like other business conservatives at the time, cooperated and even worked with their administration to uphold capitalism (by fighting communism). At the 1946 convention of the NRDGA, industry leaders expressed their belief in the superiority of "the competitive system" of distribution. Department stores were a key link in the chain of distribution that created what one Harvard professor assured the delegates at the opening meeting was the highest standard of living in history. Another prominent academic speaker exhorted department store management to use advertising media "to educate our people and tell them of the glorious achievements of American free enterprise."[67] Cold War values emerged in the postwar labor regime created by the Taft Hartley Act. With a few notable exceptions, department store executives were antiunion and supported the Taft-Hartley Act, which passed in 1947, over the veto of President Truman, to undercut the power given to unions during the New Deal.[68] Taft-Hartley damaged many unions, but the Congress of Industrial Organization's (CIO) Retail Wholesale and Department Store Union was hardest hit, losing its national leader and its largest locals in quick succession. The restrictions the act imposed were a huge setback for the CIO's retail union. Divisions over communism lead to a disastrous split and a lost opportunity for creating a powerful retail workers' union.[69]

In the early 1950s, several major department store promotions were even turned toward upholding capitalism and fighting communism. During this period, the NRDGA collaborated with the federal government to design import fairs meant to promote European economic recovery after the war. Fred Lazarus Jr. of Federated Department Stores, Ralph Straus of Macy's, and others contributed their expertise to the Economic Cooperation Administration, the agency that implemented the Marshall Plan. To promote American demand for European goods, they organized four major import fairs between 1950 and 1951 at Gimbels, Macy's, and Jordan Marsh. Cooperation with the government in this case served department stores well. "Buy European" succeeded as a marketing strategy.[70]

In spite of support for the Economic Cooperation Administration, some in the industry felt the administration was not going far enough. The shocks of 1949 were still fresh on the minds of business leaders. Republicans' rejection of President Truman's foreign policy was evident throughout the editorial voice of the department store trade press. Editorials in the leading trade press excoriated Truman for his indirect support of the Kremlin's alleged aim of "total domination, control of the world," and after North Korea crossed the thirty-eighth parallel, condemned him for his "softness" on communism.[71] In 1951, the industry went beyond attacking communism to take an active role in civil defense. The trade press proudly announced how suburban shopping centers were being considered bastions for civil defense—as evacuation points and shelters in the event of a nuclear attack.[72] The department store industry also looked within for threats. General Robert E. Wood, head of Sears, was one of the founders of the American Security Council in 1955, which sought to uncover communist activity in the business community and served members such as the well-known Chicago department store, Marshall Field's.[73]

Even though it advocated a powerful state for national defense and was even willing to turn to the government for urban renewal funding to help downtown compete with the suburbs, the industry continued to oppose other types of federal activism. True to its business conservative vision, the industry opposed the civil rights legislation on the horizon, which threatened to affect who could work and shop at its stores. Its history of race relations had always been extremely poor. With one notable exception—

Chicago's South Center Department Store—retailers maintained occupational segregation along racial lines. White-owned emporia had long barred blacks from management and sales, offering employment only in service positions. At Halle's department store in Cleveland, for example, the first African American to join the 25-Year Club was a footman in 1942. Hiring practices in the North began to change only under pressure during the 1940s. In Philadelphia, an interracial coalition began a persuasion campaign for job equality right after World War II. Facing resistance from management, the campaign to open job opportunities for blacks was forced to adopt a more public form of pressure. By 1948, Lit's, Strawbridge & Clothier, Wanamaker's, and Snellenburg's had hired some black saleswomen. In the South, however, department stores like Foley's in Houston continued to hire African Americans only for service positions. They, like other southern stores, also segregated black customers in fitting areas in the shoe department and in restrooms, and denied blacks service at their lunch counter.[74]

Alongside the civil rights movement came a growing recognition of black consumer power among the department store industry and the business community more generally. Although resistant to civil rights legislation, department store executives were willing to think about changing the way they served their African American market as it became clear it might be profitable. Self-interest pushed change forward by small degrees. By the early 1950s, for example, retail trade journals like *Women's Wear Daily* began to take a positive interest in the black consumer market. By the next decade, articles on general retail problems contained sections that addressed white migration to the suburbs and provided census figures on growing black populations in major cities across the country and comparative statistics on black and white family income.[75] Some simply asserted black consumers' preference for name brands that conveyed prestige or their major contribution to apparel industry sales. Such articles signaled a growing awareness and recognition but contained little valid analysis and buried it within larger discussions of merchandising or retail trends. A few experts asked whether department stores in large urban centers could "afford to neglect the Negro sales potential" and were told by one marketing research head that "the Negro could prove downtown's salvation."[76]

Industry leaders, however, continued to resist more substantial change in the name of free enterprise. They opposed federally mandated desegregation of public accommodations and asserted their preference for "voluntary programs" that were allegedly already under way in department stores across the South. The national trade press painted Kennedy's civil rights bill as a "disruptive threat to retail business," one that if passed would bring "the full might of the Federal Government into every corner variety store, every five-and-dime, every department store from 34th Street on."[77] Department store executives, for the most part, did not see integration as a way to fight the Cold War and spread democracy at home as did the black educator, Mary McLeod Bethune. At an after-dinner address in 1947 attended by Chicago's mayor and a gathering of the South Center department store's executives and employees, Bethune made reference to the "tense world situation," noting that the store's integration was a "brave step forward" that brought together "people of all races in a common battle for justice and equality among men."[78]

When department store executives and many of their white shoppers refused to take that step, black consumers pushed back. In addition to the well-known protests at dime store lunch counters, department stores with segregated lunch counters like Burdine's in Miami, Rich's in Atlanta, and Foley's in Houston were also subject to picket lines, sit-down protests, and outraged letters from professional groups and shoppers.

Shoppers who had been prevented from trying on clothes and hats at Thalhimer's and Miller & Rhoads in Richmond, Virginia, joined picket campaigns.[79] Reverend Martin Luther King Jr. himself was arrested at a protest at Rich's department store in Atlanta. At his hearing King noted that that he and his family had spent $4,500 there in 1959 and stated "we are welcome at all counters but the lunch counter." The retail trade press and others reported on the economic damage caused by the widespread boycotts, revealing how dependent many downtown merchants were on African American trade. One study of Atlanta showed African Americans taking their business elsewhere or cutting down their shopping overall after the boycotts of Rich's and Davison-Paxon. The Birmingham boycott, for example, revealed that Pizitz's department store pulled in half of its trade from black customers.[80] Along with other businessmen, department store executives and industry experts made the leap to desegregate in the early 1960s, but with their eyes on their bottom line rather than on the prize of equality and justice. And opposition from the white community continued. While desegregation happened uneventfully in some cases, in one instance it generated extreme violence from whites. Loveman's department store in Birmingham was bombed in August 1963 after it opened up its lunch counter to black customers. With the coming of the Civil Rights Act of

FIGURE 25. In addition to the well-known Woolworth lunch counter sit-ins, the Congress of Racial Equality (CORE) organized sit-ins at segregated department stores throughout the South. This particular protest, which was not associated with CORE, took place outside the lunchroom at Burdines department store in Miami. After the police blocked a group from entering the luncheonette, a leading minister, Rev. Carl E. Yaeger, produced his metal Burdines Charga-Plate and asked if he could use it to enter. After he was refused, Yaeger crumpled it in his fist, threw it to the ground, and stated: "Then I have no further use for this" ("Police Bar Burdine's Sitdown," *Miami News* [March 4, 1960], 3A). Florida Photographic Collection, State Archives of Florida.

1964, department store integration continued to garner both support and opposition from customers.[81]

Throughout the early 1960s, department store leaders hammered out their relationship with the liberal state. The summary of resolutions adopted at their annual convention in 1962 reveals an industry forging a combative relationship with federal policy makers. From their resolutions, it is clear that the "free enterprise" perspective could flex in a different direction when regulations gave the industry a competitive edge. Department store executives put their foot down on all federal policies or measures except for changes to parcel post regulation. They voiced opposition to the Credit Control Bill, the use of federal funds for health and unemployment benefits, and even the creation of a federal agency for consumer protection. States' legislation on Sunday closings, however, received strong support.[82]

Invited speakers also split on the issue of regulation. Senator Barry Goldwater, who was chairman of his family's Phoenix department store, spoke out against an activist state and advocated a market-driven economy. Specifically, Goldwater criticized the Kennedy administration's fiscal policy and pushed for a balanced budget. That year, the firm founded by his grandfather was acquired by the massive department store chain Associated Dry Goods, following an increasingly familiar trajectory in the industry.[83] In contrast, Senator Hubert Humphrey, who was also the president of a family-owned drug store and advocate of the small businessman, pushed for regulations or policies that fought bigness. Addressing a large audience at the convention, he advised independent retailers on ways to compete with discounters and also commented on the hearings being held with Senator John Sparkman on shopping centers. An advocate of protection for independent businesses, Humphrey stated that he wanted "to see that the old family enterprises get a chance to compete in the new central selling locations." Shopping center developers were notorious for favoring national chains and large department stores at the expense of smaller retailers who could not receive the highest AAA credit rating required by the lending institutions financing new developments. On a related issue, John E. Horne, head of the Small Business Administration (SBA), addressed the session of the smaller stores division and outlined the efforts of his agency on behalf of independent merchants.[84] Humphrey's and Horne's agenda failed. Big department stores and chain stores, with their AAA credit ratings required by lending institutions, dominated suburban shopping centers at the expense of downtown department stores and small-town Main Street firms.

In their fight for a place in the important new shopping centers, smaller independents could not compete with chain retailers or big independent department stores and turned to the government for help. Echoes of the old conflict between specialty merchants and department stores emerged, only this time a federal agency was in place to advocate for the weaker party. The SBA, which had been created by Congress in 1953, took up the cause and began to explore ways to improve conditions at shopping centers for independents. Humphrey, who chaired the Senate Small Business Committee's Subcommittee on Retailing, examined the problems faced by smaller stores in shopping centers and sought to remedy them. In the early postwar period, not all department stores were "big business," and some even benefited from the SBA.[85] Getting a toehold in shopping centers was crucial to expanding into important suburban markets. The SBA in this way fostered the development of shopping centers. As they had before, government actors underwrote the trajectory toward bigness and chain organization.

From the end of World War II to the early 1960s, the overarching conservative politics of the industry's leadership increasingly deflected attention away from other challenges facing members. Earlier industry leaders had offered at least initial, or qualified, support of such things as protective legislation for women, the NRA, and the OPA. But by the early 1960s, with the exception of its support for the government's position on anticommunism and the antiunion Taft-Hartley legislation, cooperation between business and the federal government dwindled to a (then) all-time low in the retail trade. The industry continued to favor voluntary over legislative solutions to social inequalities, opposing civil rights legislation for African Americans and women employees even in the face of powerful grassroots movements. Industry leaders protested all liberal reforms affecting workers, consumers, or the business environment, blaming the government for problems generated by the interplay between their own industry and other forces. Downplaying the effect of the new discounters and suburban shopping centers on their Main Street trade, the president of the National Retail Merchants Association and head of Zion's Cooperative Mercantile Institution (a Utah department store) admonished conventioneers in 1963 that "the most grave of all ills with which business must contend is the apparent move toward a form of controlled economy." Over time, it would become clear that such political posturing was a red herring. Only two years later, a very different message came out of the NMRA's annual meeting. The president of Allied Stores, Theodore Schlesinger, who had succeeded B. Earl Puckett's twenty-five-year tenure in 1959, described the great transformation he had recently observed in the industry. Schlesinger had been with Allied Stores for thirty years and was a seasoned merchant in 1965. Speaking to an audience of department store buyers, he heralded American shopping centers and discounters as the era's "dynamic forces."[86] Unknown to Schlesinger and his audience, this was only the beginning of the discount world.

CHAPTER 7

The Postwar Discount Revolution

The discount store will never fully replace the department store or specialty shop or supermarket; the U.S. consumer market is too huge and varied and complex for any form of retailing ever to predominate.
—*Fortune*, 1962

LOOKING back over his career at King's department store in a 1970 interview, Aaron Goldberg observed that "past experience was of very little value" in the early days of discount selling. This vice president in charge of sales promotion and merchandising and his colleagues at the Massachusetts discount chain felt they were "making their own rules" as they went along, since there were "no historical methods of operation . . . there were no books to read." Founded in 1949 in an abandoned Old Indian Motorcycle factory in Springfield, Massachusetts, King's broke with standard practice in several ways, as did the many other discount operations sprouting up after World War II. Stores like King's eschewed the services, amenities, and luxury typical of downtown department stores in favor of low overhead costs. Self-service general merchandisers that featured national brands, they operated with distinctively low margins, following a merchandising strategy to "pile it high, sell it cheap."[1] Convenience took precedence over the customs established by downtown merchants. Discounters taught consumers not only to expect cut prices but also to be able to shop whenever they wanted, successfully challenging blue laws and forcing department stores to open on Sundays.[2]

Discounters' merchandising model struck a chord with postwar shoppers, rapidly making them the era's dominant retail form. As discount stores mushroomed across suburbia in the postwar era, contemporary observers described them as "a retail revolution." While much about the discount phenomenon seemed radically new to contemporary observers, in fact they had a lot in common with mass retailers that came before them. Like the traditional department stores it challenged, King's was a multiple-line retailer, offering disparate lines of goods under one roof, such as toiletries, shoes, housewares, millinery, jewelry, sports and automotive equipment, and small appliances. More quickly than the department store industry, however, entrepreneurial discounters soon expanded into national chains. By 1966, for example, King's was operating forty-two stores across the country and grossing more than $100 million annually. Housed in sleek purpose-built single-story buildings—a far cry from the motorcycle factories and old armories of their earlier decades—King's and other discount chains even came to mimic suburban branch department stores in appearance. Along with the new suburban shopping centers, they established themselves in outlying business districts or on low-cost land. Advertising its abundant free parking, King's and other discounters would compete with suburban branches of traditional department stores, further linking automobility and retailing in American consumer society.[3]

If shoppers had not preferred the low-price, mass-consumption model supported by legislators and regulators, the postwar explosion of discount markets would not have been possible. The discount industry catered to the era's growing consumerism, enabling larger proportions of the population to partake of the "good life," even as the promise of low prices came at the expense of high wages and a producer ethic. Structures were in place to hold this explosion back, but a weak enforcement of regulations in the early postwar period allowed discount operators to flout fair trade legislation prohibiting loss leaders and price cuts on fair trade–protected brand-name merchandise. By the early 1970s, severe inflation changed the context for opponents of fair trade, making consumer interests paramount over those of small stores. After the 1975 passage of the Consumer Goods Pricing Act, all fetters were removed. The subsequent rapid expansion of general-merchandise discounters like Kmart, Target, and Wal-Mart drew shoppers further from Main Street. At the same time, increasing concentration of the discount industry—itself supported by policy makers' support of big business and free markets—contributed to the demise of the local department store.

The Rise of the Discounter

The first discount merchants experimented with a wide variety of retail formats. After World War II, membership clubs began hawking discounted hard lines (consumer durables, such as appliances) in the Northeast, and "soft-goods supermarkets" opened up in old textile mills and warehouses. On the West Coast, another early branch of discounting emerged with closed-door membership stores catering to government employees and other large organized groups. Over the next few years, the number of both large and small discounters exploded on the East and West Coasts, then spread south in the 1950s to cities as large as Dallas and as small as Morrilton, Arkansas, where one of the early Wal-Marts was housed in an abandoned Coca-Cola bottling plant. Setting up in relatively cheap buildings on low-rent sites, minimally furnished with basic fixtures and equipment, and operating largely on a cash-only basis at first, these enterprises were able to cut costs to the bone.[4] They competed with supermarkets and department stores selling many of the same goods, such as food, health and beauty aids, and women's apparel. Their cost-cutting strategies enabled them to undersell traditional retailers in a growing number of lines of goods. Discounters quickly became known for selling appliances, radios, televisions, records, cameras, gardening tools, and sporting goods at prices significantly below the manufacturers' suggested "list" price.

On the face of it, the stately downtown department store had little in common with the seemingly fly-by-night operations of entrepreneurs like the "unorthodox" Brooklyn-born Eugene Ferkauf, who founded Korvette's in 1948. Ferkauf boasted of keeping no files, having no office or secretary, and making decisions based on his own judgment rather than that of experts. As entrepreneurs like Ferkauf met success, however, they expanded into chains, centralized their operations, and in many cases, sold their businesses to larger concerns. Korvette's, for example, quickly grew out of its one-thousand-square-foot second-floor walk-up selling discounted luggage, appliances, and jewelry to become a "promotional department store chain." In 1955 it went public and two years later reported $71 million in

FIGURE 26. Discount chain department stores like J. M. Field's, which opened in Tallahassee, Florida, in 1964, cut costs in many different ways, stripping down interiors and reducing the need for skilled labor through greater reliance on self-service. Discounters introduced innovations in self-service drawn from the grocery trade, including centralized front checkout and shopping carts. Florida Photographic Collection, State Archives of Florida. Photographer: Richard Parks.

sales. Though many discount operations were originally family businesses that started on a shoestring like Korvette's, literally on the margins of the retail scene, they soon became big business. By 1958, industry sales were at approximately $800 million, a figure that was 6 percent of general merchandise sales, the census grouping that included general and variety stores and the increasingly beleaguered department store. Within five years, discount numbers had risen to $9.3 billion or nearly a third of general merchandise sales. Korvette's alone had more than $622 million in sales in 1964 and was considered "the fastest-growing retailer in the modern history of retailing." Industry growth continued at a tremendous rate. By 1967, discount sales reached $17 billion—39 percent of general merchandise trade.[5]

Although both department store and discount retailing was big business, there were important differences between the two modes of distribution. Just how different the two were generated debate among retail scholars. While most perceived the changes wrought by postwar discounters as revolutionary, other contemporaries perceived them as evolutionary, the product of a process begun decades before. Writing in the 1950s, influential marketing scholar Stanley C. Hollander made the argument that since discounters operated before the post–World War II era, "they cannot be considered manifestations of a retailing revolution." He pointed to "two-price retailers, 'curbstone brokers,' buying clubs, 'backdoor wholesalers,'" and others. In addition, grocery chains that pioneered the major principles behind discounting had appeared in the 1930s. Rather than breaking with the past, they developed their business on the principles proven successful by the grocery trade in the 1930s, including minimal service, low markup, rapid turnover, and high volume. The term "discount house" itself appeared as early as 1937, applying to sellers of cut-price radios.[6]

The long view supports these evolutionary interpretations, particularly if department stores are brought into consideration. The idea of discounting a fixed price to promote further sales was nothing new. In the late nineteenth century, department stores developed the concept of "marking down" previously fixed prices for publicity or as an advertised sales promotion. Some, like Macy's, used the idea of the cut price to distinguish itself from the competition. And, as we have seen, it was the ability of department stores to undersell specialty retailers that sparked the "store wars" of the 1890s and fanned the flames of the fair trade movement over the following decades. In many ways, discount stores simply took long-standing department and chain store practices to the next level. While it is true that the discount house pared things down to an unprecedented level, organizing its operation around the principle of cutting costs as no department store had done before, to obtain those savings the discounter drew on the lessons learned by the conventional retailer.

Discounters shared the same general trajectory toward bigness as department stores, only at a later date. As had the department store industry before it, the discount industry became increasingly concentrated. The discount field still included numerous small entrepreneurs, but by the mid-1960s the industry was consolidating. Approximately half of the firms that controlled the industry operated one store, but several very large chains dominated the rest of the market, in terms in their total number of stores. Well-established chains, such as F. W. Woolworth, Grand Union, and S. S. Kresge, had moved into discounting by the early 1960s. Kresge, the second leading discount firm in the nation by 1965, operated 233 Kmart and Jupiter stores, with sales of $490 million. Discount department stores Arlan's and S. Klein, while also in the top ten, operated only fifty-six and ten stores, respectively.[7]

In this context, executives at traditional department stores had reason to fear the new discount merchants. Studies from the postwar period clearly show the expansion of discount sales methods. In the mid-1950s they were still no threat to the full-service independent department store or department store chain, as their numbers were relatively few and they competed with only a narrow range of merchandise. Discounters, however, quickly moved beyond consumer durables and added merchandise lines that competed directly with department stores, not to mention supermarkets, liquor dealers, and various specialty shops. The early 1960s saw the first tipping point for department stores in some markets. In Dallas, for example, discount store sales grew as a percentage of total retail sales during this period. Dallas department stores reported being hurt by discount competition in many of their major merchandise classifications. And in 1965, three years after the founding of Target, Kmart, and Wal-Mart, discount department stores' sales volume overtook that of conventional department stores for the first time.[8]

In the battle over consumers' pocketbooks, discounters hurt some department stores more than others. Size and market focus played a role. Those department stores that handled higher quality merchandise in competing classifications were affected less, as were the large full-line retailers who were able to be more flexible in their response. For example, in the Dallas study, so-called junior department stores (offering fewer lines of goods) were found to be at a disadvantage in the competition with discounters. Less flexible because of their fixed small size, they were not able to add as many lines to compete and lost market share as a result.[9]

Discounters' ability to pare down gross margins also gave them a competitive edge. In contrast to traditional department stores, discount firms energetically minimized services and cut labor costs, relying on high volume instead of high gross margins to make their profits. By cutting costs, the early discounters were able to maintain earnings with gross margins as slim as 20 to 22 percent. Significantly, the gross margin among discounters in the mid-1960s was 10 percent less than that of traditional department stores.[10] Since the nineteenth century, department stores had based their reputation on high levels of service, amenity, and even luxury, things that raised the cost of distribution. Significantly, they did not initially attempt to lower their gross margins, which is not surprising given the conservative nature of their industry. Another explanation for a lack of any early concerted effort to lower them is found in their pricing practices. Department stores met discount prices on some merchandise lines and then recouped them on others. High gross margins, moreover, were generally considered a good thing from the perspective of an investor, signaling high profits. But when low-margin competition entered the scene, the picture began to change. The fact that both discounters' margins and expenses were significantly lower than those of conventional retailers boded ill for department store earnings. To compete, department stores could choose to distinguish themselves, as did high-end retailers like Nordstrom's and Saks. As this trend developed, middle-market department stores like Macy's would eventually find themselves squeezed between these luxury retailers and firms with lower gross margins like J. C. Penney.[11]

Stock turn, long a measurement of retail health, was another area where discounters distinguished themselves from traditional department stores. While both department stores and discounters depended on rapid turnover of inventory, the discount house did so to a greater degree. A study of the organization and operation of department stores in the 1920s recorded on average a stock turn of 2.3 to 3.7 times a year, with bigger stores turning stock at higher rates. Yet some traditional department stores still carried more inventory than was optimal.[12] Discount merchants, on the other hand, bought goods that would sell quickly, priced them to move, and cut prices if they didn't. As a result, they had much higher stock turn rates than traditional retailers. Wal-Mart turned over its inventory five times a year by the 1980s. Not all discounters moved goods that quickly, as demonstrated by studies of the self-service discount department store industry, which found more modest stock turns within the range of 3.14 to 3.49 in the late 1970s and early 1980s. The most successful firms of this period, however, excelled in this area. Stores like Kmart, the large, full-fledged discount department store introduced by the variety chain S. S. Kresge Company in 1962, reaped great profits with their ability to move goods. In the 1960s, for example, Kmart turned over its inventory eight times annually. This national chain, which influenced Sam Walton in its early years yet ultimately was much less successful than Wal-Mart, was able to rip through its market in the 1960s, opening one hundred stores in its first three and half years.[13]

Self-service was another important area that pushed discounters ahead of the Main Street department store. Discount stores did not invent self-service, nor were they the only general merchandiser to use it. Traditional department stores in postwar suburban shopping centers were introducing more self-service in order to reduce their labor costs. In principle, self-service allowed a store to operate with fewer clerks and eliminated the need for skilled salespeople. But department stores, even suburban branches, were not fully self-serve. Unlike many discounters, they still relied on salesclerks to take merchandise out of display counters, stationing them (theoretically) throughout different departments to assist customers with their selection. Postwar department stores used fixtures that allowed self-selection of goods, such as pipe racking for hangers and open shelves or tables, but salesclerks were still supposed to be on hand to wait on the customer, suggest items, and ultimately influence the sale. Cashiers, moreover, were also scattered through different departments. In contrast, discount stores relied entirely on customers' own efforts in a way pioneered by chain grocers. In these new venues, a row of centralized cashiers was positioned at the front near the exit, as in grocery chains like Piggly Wiggly. These new methods contributed to a decline in distributive costs in the retail trade between 1949 and 1965.[14]

Lower-end retailers cut labor costs further by relying on part-time workers. Retailers of all stripes were increasingly reliant on part-timers. In general, the new suburban shopping centers of the postwar period accelerated this trend. At the Paramus malls in New Jersey, for example, two-thirds of new hires in the 1960s were part-time. Discount chains employed more part-time workers than department stores, contributing to the further downgrading of retail work. While both independent and department store chains had a ratio of 70 part-time to 30 full-time employees, discount chains increased their ratio to 80/20. Discounters were able to exact a lower payroll/sales ratio of 11 to 13 percent. Compared to full-time workers, part-timers provided a cost advantage because they typically received lower wages, fewer benefits, and could be scheduled in a flexible way conducive to the store's, not the employee's, needs. The first Wal-Mart employees in 1962—a staff of twenty-five—were paid fifty to sixty cents an hour, which was well below the federal minimum wage. By the end of the twentieth century, Wal-Mart's unjust labor practices would be well known. It is important to note that the "high cost of low prices" began much earlier, however, in this formative period in the discount industry.[15]

The growing power of the discount industry in the postwar period meant less stable and lucrative employment for increasing numbers of workers, who were largely female. The department store industry's historical relationship to women's employment was not unblemished, but it was distinct from that emerging in the new discount industry after World War II. Sales-clerking had long been a path of advancement for white women. While top executives were largely male, with a few standouts like Dorothy Shaver and Beatrice Fox, women could work their way up the ranks to become buyers, middle managers or department heads, and fashion advisors.[16] By the early 1980s, while only a handful of women were presidents or board chairs of department store organizations, as many as a third or more vice president positions were held by women. The discount industry culture, on the other hand, was an entirely masculine one from its very beginning. When recounting how one made it in the discount world, executives frequently made masculine references, using such phrases as "a boy with education" to describe the kind of person needed in the field. With few exceptions, such as Eve Nelson, who in 1958 was the first female executive hired by Korvette's, discount store management was all male and self-consciously so. Promotion policies that required managers to regularly uproot and move to new store locations put women at a disadvantage, something even Sam Walton recognized though did not ameliorate. His firm, which became the largest private-sector employer in the United States, historically promoted from within, routinely overlooking female employees for management positions or paying them less than male managers. (Wal-Mart's notorious labor practices eventually resulted in the largest gender discrimination class action lawsuit in history, *Wal-Mart v. Dukes.* In 2011, the Supreme Court ruled in favor of the retailer.)[17]

Despite this history, shoppers have flocked to discount stores in search of bargains, supporting their growth. According to a 1954 Chamber of Commerce address on discounting that was reprinted for several different audiences in the retail industry, "the public's response to these offerings (was) nothing short of phenomenal."[18] As retail experts, discount merchants, and the department store industry sought to explain the new rage for discount shopping, they highlighted the role of consumer choice. Pared labor costs, high rates of stock turn, and low gross margins may have contributed to the competitiveness of discounters, but customers had to be amenable to the new way of selling. Many attributed discounters' success to consumer demand for low prices. Others suggested that discounters played a role in shaping this demand—that cut prices made consumers more price conscious overall.[19] Postwar marketing studies in fact documented that high prices, or even the perception of high prices, kept many consumers from shopping at certain department stores.

Department stores were associated with quality merchandise and selection, while discounters like Kmart were known for their low prices. Without exploring the link between quality and price, however, contemporary surveys revealed that "good quality" and "good value" ranked high in importance for consumers, while poor quality or bad bargains put shoppers off. One study of five Philadelphia-area department stores and three discount stores linked the perception of low quality to store closure. Interestingly, however, this same study found that half of its customer informants gave the successful discounter, Korvette's, a low rating, likely a reflection of the class bias of the survey and not of popular opinion, or the store would not have flourished as it did then.[20] Certainly discounters needed to find the right balance between quality and price to attract these shoppers.

Consumers' price consciousness played a key role in the spread of discounting, but demand for low prices emerged in a particular postwar context, which retailers needed to understand in order to succeed. Obviously, price had always been a salient factor in a consumer's decision whether to buy or not, with shoppers seeking value for their money. Most had to stretch limited budgets to cover basic needs. The context in which these economic decisions took place, though, was always historical, contingent upon the interplay of different factors. Discount stores in particular appealed to their market in specific ways connected to economic, demographic, and geographic changes in American society after World War II. Discount entrepreneurs like Eugene Ferkauf understood this changing postwar market. Rather than just appealing to those of limited means who needed to stretch their budget, his discount selling model had broad appeal among new suburbanites and the growing numbers of young families. One marketing professor writing in 1962 characterized the growth of discounters as an "institutional innovation" tied to recent changes in the consumer market. Educated in the ways of self-service, expecting a higher standard of living characterized by ownership of durable goods, and forming new households at unprecedented rates, the postwar consumer was "ready" for the discounter. Others have linked discounters' success to the growth of the middle classes with more discretionary buying power. The suburban migration of young families interested in the type of "do-it-yourself" equipment and materials typically offered by discount houses was also understood to play a role. And, of course, contemporary concern over rising prices spurred their popularity.[21]

Discounters responded to shifting markets, but they also succeeded in altering the broader framework within which people shopped, forcing other retailers to move closer to their model. They changed consumers' relationship with the traditional department store, reshaping both their expectations and behavior. Marketing studies on the industry in this early stage concluded that discount houses had taught consumers to eschew department stores' higher margins. In areas like appliances, traditional retailers would either have to meet discount store competition or discontinue their lines. Consumer motivation expert Ernest Dichter advised the department store industry that shoppers were subconsciously punishing them for years of poor service and lack of courtesy from their clerks. Another expert pointed to psychological motivations, suggesting that suburban branches lacked the thrill and excitement of the discount house. Surveys of shoppers found they appreciated the low prices but also were motivated by convenient location, self-service, and discounters' evening and Sunday hours. Perhaps the varied architecture and often unusual locale or pioneering atmosphere of discount stores was a novel alternative to the windowless, sanitized suburban department store.[22]

Opposition to Discounters

Shoppers may have loved the bargains and excitement of places like King's or Korvette's, but their appearance after World War II initially unsettled conventional retailers. Given discounters' growing market share and the pressure they put on prices by cutting operating costs, it is not surprising that they met strong opposition from traditional merchants, as had department and chain stores before them. Though single-line retailers and department stores had been on different sides in the late nineteenth-century store wars, they both felt threatened by the burgeoning discount field. Newspapers and the retail trade press dramatized competition between this new form of distribution and traditional merchants, revealing deep concerns about changes taking place in the commercial landscape. Painted as revolutionary rather than just taking another approach to a tried and true retail format, discounters came under fire. Department store managers in these early years described them as unprofessional or even "illegitimate."[23] In fact, many undercapitalized and inexperienced operators went into this intensely competitive business and, not surprisingly, their failure rates were high.[24]

The language adopted to describe their practices, however, suggests that more was at stake and that this was not simply fly-by-night competition from the margins of the retail field. Discount houses were described as "an increasing annoying threat" to "'regular' retailers" and as the "pariah of American retailing."Price-cutters appeared as bootleggers, shady agents for shoddy merchandise, or otherwise engaged in dishonest sales practices. Competition between traditional retailers and discounters was imagined in terms of physical combat, with the two having "their sleeves rolled up" and "getting ready to slug it out." In language that evoked the antimonopolist imagery of the late nineteenth century, the *New York Times* asserted that "the discount ogre in the old-line retailers' nightmare [was] a multiheaded monster," attacking with club plans, industrial outlets, supermarket gimmicks, government buying clubs, and military store sales.[25] Retail tradition itself seemed under siege.

Merchants' opposition to discounters grew more intense and increasingly organized from the late 1940s to the early 1950s. While Senate testimony in 1958 on the effect of discounters on small business suggested that the industry's success was in part due to the lack of early response from traditional retailers, other evidence suggests this was not the case. One marketing expert who contributed to the government report criticized the "ostrich-like behavior of the department stores and many specialty chains" in the face of cut-price distributors. But across the board, retailers had taken note of this new form of distribution. Alarmed, department store managers held meetings to exchange information on discount competition and sent employees out to shop the competition. Specialized retailing publications, like the trade press for the house furnishing field, published article after article on the topic, beginning in the late 1940s with "Don't Discount the Discount House."[26] In *Retailing Daily*, advertisements sought to persuade other merchants and wholesalers of the perils of discounting and urged trade associations and manufacturers to help curb the practice. Campaigns directed at consumers warned of the dangers of discount sources of goods. Anti–discount store advertisements urged shoppers to patronize a familiar local dealer, to request warranty cards for goods, and to check for unaltered serial numbers on appliances before purchasing. By 1954 a national campaign against discounters was under way. Department stores played a major role in the fight against these "illegitimate" businesses. That same year the National Retail Dry Goods convention pledged to expose the discount industry.[27]

Opponents took aim at shopping centers, where most retail growth was to be found. Suburban branch stores lacked basement departments, and one 1960s marketing researcher contended that this missed opportunity helped open the door to discounters. Perhaps most potentially damaging to discount merchants was the effort of traditional retailers and chains to exclude them from the new shopping centers springing up across the suburban landscape.[28] The owners of new developments like El Paso's Northgate in the 1960s were selective and publicized the fact they only allowed "reputable firms" as tenants. In regional shopping centers, department stores and national chain stores typically received favorable leases and veto power over prospective tenants. Not surprisingly, they often barred stores that were perceived as "too aggressive or unorthodox in their merchandising practices," a description that more than likely included the low-margin mass retailers they most feared. Similarly, manufacturers sought to shut out discounters by barring sales to those firms that discounted their wares. In a way reminiscent of the opposition to department stores in the late nineteenth century, these manufacturers refused to sell in part out of respect for their long-standing traditional clients. As jewelry manufacturers had refused to sell their goods to department stores in the late 1890s, apparel manufacturers in the 1950s refused to sell to discount houses.[29]

Anti–discount store sentiment in this early era peaked with the publication in 1965 of Walter H. Nelson's *Great Discount Delusion*, a popular exposé of corrupt or shady practices in the industry. Presented as a sort of self-help manual with appended Federal Trade Commission guides, the book tapped into the growing consumer rights movement of the era, represented by figures like Ralph Nader, author of the influential *Unsafe at Any Speed* (1965). Nelson's book captured the rough-and-tumble entrepreneurial world of early discounting through its glossary of alleged insider terms used by discount merchants to describe their sales practices. As revealed in its glossary, advertisements lured customers in with loss leaders—"kickers" or "nail-downs." Management offered salesmen a bonus for making a "switch" to higher-priced goods, paying them a "spiff" for "putting them on the elevator."[30] As noted in a *New York Times* book review by a prominent business writer, discounters who read these accusations were "indignant, frustrated, and disgusted," denying that they ruined competition, exploited customers, and destroyed national brands. The chairman of Korvette's publically challenged the criticism, stating that "if the discounter lives and flourishes, it is only because he has won the vote of confidence from that highest tribunal—the American shopper."[31]

Even as this book gathered publicity, opposition to discount stores had already lifted in other quarters. Frank Kiefer, the editor of *Department Store Economist*, titled his January 1962 editorial "Are We Against Discounting?" and answered definitively no. Apparel manufacturers would lift their restrictions against discount sellers in 1962, the year of Wal-Mart, Kmart, and Target's founding, marking the field's growing legitimacy. By the time that the founder of Korvette's appeared on the cover of *Time* magazine in 1962, discounting had clearly advanced from the margins. Korvette's luxurious new location on Fifth Avenue and Thirty-Fourth Street signaled this shift as the company laid claim to tradition. In 1967, it moved into a nine-story glass and marble building on this historic retail site—right between Macy's and Gimbels at the site of the former Saks. In addition to entering into long-standing department store territory, discounters quickly colonized their more recent habitat. By 1970, after overcoming opposition from department store suburban branches, discounters made their way into shopping centers.[32]

The newly formed discount industry's trade association also played a role in bringing about acceptance. In response to opposition, discounters formed the National Association of Discount Merchants in 1954 "to tell their side of the story" and "combat unfavorable publicity." The industry's first trade journal, *Discount Merchandiser*, was established in 1961. Professionalization and the legitimacy it granted were also furthered by the scholarly attention discounting began to receive. By the early 1960s the academic community saw discounters as a topic for serious study, as reflected by numerous conferences, industry reports, and marketing dissertations. Demand for industry classifications reflected discounters' newfound legitimacy. The U.S. Census Bureau considered reporting discount store statistics separately from "orthodox" or "traditional" department stores in 1963 at the behest of the Retail Trade Committee, an advisory group composed of executives from the National Retail Merchants Association, among others. Difficulties of definition created by this still-fluid retailing format, however, hindered the bureau, and discounters remained buried within the General Merchandise Group through the end of the decade. The retail industry itself, however, conveyed the seriousness of the new form of distribution by publishing a special Discount Store Directory in 1962.[33]

As discounters traded up, moved next door, and captured increasing shares of department stores' merchandise lines, department stores in the early 1960s continued to look for ways to "strike back," as *Barron's* put it. Outright opposition became a less viable strategy. According to Theodore Schlesinger, president of Allied Stores, the department store industry had "passed the point of closing our eyes and wishing the discounters would go away. They are here, and the question is, what to do about them." Department stores instead began, in a limited fashion, to join their ranks. The stately downtown J. L. Hudson Co. fought discount chains moving into Detroit by opening "twigs," the smaller, limited-line suburban branches characterized by self-service and a "bargain basement atmosphere."[34] During the period, holding companies like Federated Department Stores, Allied Stores Corporation, Interstate Department Stores, and Dayton-Hudson, and the department store chain J. C. Penney established their own discount outlets. These operations ran under different names—for example, Allied operated Almart Stores, and Interstate Department Stores acquired White Front Stores, Topps Stores, and opened a new chain titled Family Fair.[35] To contemporary observers, it seemed as if the difference between the two retail forms had diminished within a couple of decades. In 1970, the president of Zayre Corporation, a discount department store chain, observed that "the department store today is so much more self-service and self-selection than it was twenty years ago" and asserted there was "really no difference between regular retailing and the so-called discount retailing."[36]

Department stores also responded to competition from the discount trade by cutting prices, thus fueling the low-price expectations that would eventually contribute to their own demise. In testimony against the discount industry relayed to a Senate small business committee in 1958, the American Fair Trade Council pointed out that department stores cut prices in the manner of discount houses while at the same time crying foul play when discounters did the same to them. In the early 1950s, so-called price wars broke out between major department stores and discounters in cities across the country.[37] The rise of the discount retailer after World War II changed the context within which department stores and manufacturers interacted. Accounts of price wars at the time noted that the growing sentiment of traditional merchants was "If you can't lick 'em, join 'em." If discounters were going to compete unfairly by selling goods below the manufacturer's suggested price, ran the thinking, then department stores would be forced to follow. Formidable retailers like Macy's in New York and J. L. Hudson in Detroit published price lists featuring manufacturer set prices alongside their own prices. Other local department stores followed suit. Department stores across the country made changes in their pricing policies, either generally lowering their prices to compete, offering to meet competition, or making public statements about not being undersold. Discount stores thus had the effect of making low prices a more prominent part of marketing strategies across the board. Such pricing policies accustomed shoppers to the idea of the bargain or cut price itself, making such a state seem normal rather than seasonal or periodic as before.[38]

By the mid-1970s, observers began to note the disruptive effect discounters had on central business districts. Though widespread opposition from consumers and nostalgia for the local department store would not emerge fully until later, by the mid-1970s hints of that loss began to emerge. In a 1975 interview, one Main Street restaurant owner recounted that before discounters had arrived, his small town of Alliance, Ohio, had two department stores: King's replaced the Boston Store and the Spring-Holtzworth Company. Moreover, in the early 1970s, shoppers still perceived traditional department stores as more civic-minded and progressive than chains or discounters.[39] At this point, it was clear that things were changing. Why and what it meant, however, was another matter.

While the energy and new ideas supplied by entrepreneurs like Eugene Ferkauf and Sam Walton changed the postwar retail landscape, the discount "revolution," as many called it, would not have been possible without the methods and principles of mass retailing forged by department stores. This discount model would have failed, moreover, if it were not for a larger cultural embrace of mass consumption and widespread demand for low-priced consumer goods. Both would contribute to the decline of Main Street and the local department store. Yet consumer demand and innovations in business were not the only factors in the evolution of retailing that gave birth to colossi like Wal-Mart.[40]

Department Stores, Discount Houses, and Regulation

As it had with the department store industry, local, state and federal policy played a role in the rise of discount selling, though not in a straightforward way. Through specific policies and the laws it engendered, through its idiosyncratic enforcement, and even through a lack of regulation itself, the state

interacted with the market and shaped distribution. As the discount industry expanded, traditional department stores looked to government for assistance in their battle with these "bootleg" operators. One approach was to
lobby for blue laws to prohibit late-night discount store hours and seven-
day openings. Discount department stores like King's, for example, typically
offered daily opening hours from 10 A.M. to 10 P.M.[41] Smaller family-run
stores found it difficult to man their businesses seven days a week. Even big
department stores were closed on Sundays, taking part as they did in a
traditional understanding of appropriate work times. As discounters gained
market share and continued to flout convention, the National Retail Merchants Association conveniently bypassed its typical antigovernment stance
to advocate for blue laws prohibiting Sunday selling of nonessentials. The
courts sided with traditional retailers over this issue. In a court case involving Two Guys, a New Jersey discount chain, and two traditional department
stores, Macy's and Bamberger's, a 1959 New Jersey law restricting Sunday
selling was upheld.[42] In May 1961, the U.S. Supreme Court upheld the right
of states to enact blue laws, but challenges from discounters continued. In
the months following the department store industry's victory, the Supreme
Court turned away five appeals against Sunday blue laws.[43]

Legislation addressing openings and hours had the potential to support
the traditions of large, full-price retailers and the smaller independents over
discounters. However, weak penalties and idiosyncratic enforcement of existing blue laws meant discounters could essentially keep any hours they desired.
Indeed, an earlier New Jersey blue law, which the 1959 legislation replaced,
had no penalty at all. Discounters continued to sell on Sundays. While
around-the-clock hours and Thanksgiving and Christmas openings were still
in the future, the shift toward shopping all day, every day had begun. In 1969,
Sears began opening on Sundays, leading prominent industry observers to
conclude that "the 'Never on Sunday' trend may be on the way out among
the nation's big stores." With blue laws still on the books, however, courts
across the country continued to deal with challenges by discounters.[44]

Legislation governing pricing was also on the books, which discounters
likewise ignored to their advantage. Many department stores had done the
same—since the Miller-Tydings Act of 1937, mass retailers' resistance to
fair trade laws had continued even as media interest in the subject diminished as the Depression lifted and war broke out in Europe. A variety of
retailers had continued to discount goods through strategies that skirted
the law, such as trade-ins, rebates, and bonuses. Macy's, a prominent

price-cutter in the department store industry, evaded book publishers' prices through book clubs that provided customers with discounts. More generally, department stores continued to use their own private labels to compete directly with fair trade brand-name products. Contention over the issue lessened on the home front during the war, when a changed economic climate helped manufacturers maintain minimum prices. The seller's market department stores enjoyed during the war, however, was quickly replaced by price competition in the late 1940s, and the issue of fair trade emerged again. Although department stores continued engaging in the practice, in the postwar period the issue refocused on the newcomers.[45]

Resale price maintenance legislation had the potential to prevent, or at least delay, the ascendance of discounting and industry concentration—as it did in Britain and France, for example—but not as it played out in the United States.[46] The Miller-Tydings Act of 1937 failed to contain the price wars of department stores and discounters for many reasons. First, it failed to give fair trade advocates a strong tool for maintaining minimum prices. It was not a federal resale price maintenance law, a goal that the National Association of Retail Druggists had abandoned in favor of a law more amenable to states' rights. Thus the Act did not directly authorize or require resale price maintenance. What it did was strengthen existing state fair trade laws by permitting interstate commerce for goods under state price maintenance contracts. Fair trade was limited to products with trademarks or brand names that were "in 'free and open competition' with similar goods on the market," restrictions that limited its application to between 4 and 20 percent of total retail sales. Second, Miller-Tydings contained a defect that would allow later critics to challenge it successfully in the courts. It lacked the nonsigner clause already present in many state fair trade laws, a clause that strengthened resale price maintenance agreements by requiring only one merchant to sign the contract to bind other merchants to its terms. Moreover, Miller-Tydings did not grant the federal government the power to enforce fair trade contracts, but left that to the manufacturer itself. Self-policing was a logistical impossibility for small firms and a costly nuisance for big manufacturers. And significantly, since it was not a federal mandate for fair trade, states were free to reject resale price maintenance. The side-by-side existence of fair trade and non–fair trade states opened the door for comparisons that hurt the case of price protectionism. Macy's department store, for example, publicized price comparisons of brand-name goods in fair trade and non–fair trade states to show how fair trade laws forced consumers to pay more. More generally, critics were able to use statistics about the higher cost of living in fair trade states to argue that the policy hurt consumers.[47]

From the beginning, discounters were strategically negligent of fair trade legislation. The New England discounter King's department store, for example, adopted a typical middle-of-the-road strategy against resale price maintenance. As recalled by executive Aaron Goldberg in an interview for a major study of the discount industry in 1970, King's used loss leaders "if necessary" but added, "We don't do it intentionally—only to meet competition." His firm also equivocated with its fair-traded products. As Goldberg told an interviewer, "No, we never paid any fine. Once we agree to stop, we stop. We prefer to stop before we get a court injunction because then, if we do it again through error, we aren't subject to contempt of court. If we think the manufacturer is serious we stop." While less flagrantly illegal than some discounters' strategy, King's still skirted the law in a way likely intended to force it to change. Others, however, "fought it to the hilt and settled it on the courthouse steps," as a founder of a Pennsylvania discount chain remembered. Perhaps with the benefit of hindsight and knowledge that resale price maintenance legislation would become largely inconsequential for their industry, discount store executives' memories downplayed the law's effect. One remembered fair trade as "somewhat of a headache," describing the cases against their lawbreaking as "harassment lawsuits."[48]

Traditional department stores did not help. Rather than uniting with manufacturers against price-cutters like King's, they ceded to the competition and joined its ranks, thereby further undermining any legislative effort at containment. At the time when discounters began to appear, only about 5 to 10 percent of the goods department stores sold were subject to fair trade agreements. Even though department stores were less affected by fair trade legislation than discounters, who built their business around selling below manufacturer's suggested prices, they were pulled into price wars. Initially, the powerful Macy's complied with pricing lists, but changed its strategy when faced with competition from discounters that were ignoring the suggested manufacturer prices. In May 1947, for example, Macy's went to General Electric (GE) with complaints that others were breaking rank and pressured the manufacturer to bring suit. GE secured injunctions instructing the price-cutters to stop but to no avail. Macy's caved to the competition, cutting prices on GE goods. After Macy's openly dared the manufacturer with a 20 percent reduction on two of its appliances, GE brought suit and won. As historian Thomas McCraw has argued, this established a "precarious modus vivendi" under which manufacturers would expend "substantial but still insufficient resources on policing RPM, while Macy's and hundreds of thousands of other distributors nationwide either followed or flouted the rules according to their business strategies."[49]

The 1951 Supreme Court decision *Schwegmann Brothers v. Calvert Distillers Corp.* fanned the flames of discount competition. The case was the product of a shift in thinking on fair trade. Opposition had been stirring in the federal government as concerns over monopoly and unfair price competition spurred new investigations into Miller-Tydings. Judicial thinking also shifted from upholding the constitutionality of fair trade to questioning it, first reflected in the 1949 Florida Supreme court case that nullified the nonsigner clause of its state fair trade law, and then two years later with the *Schwegmann Brothers* case, which freed nonsigning retailers from certain pricing restrictions. In this case, the U.S. Supreme Court took on the nonsigner clause of RPM agreements, arguing that because the Miller-Tydings Act did not include such a clause, it did not legalize their use in interstate commerce. The Court here construed the 1937 act as narrowly as possible, ignoring the fact that at the time of its passage, dozens of state laws contained a nonsigner clause and the act was assumed implicitly to recognize them.[50] The effect of the 1951 decision was immediate. In New York, one week after the announcement, Macy's publicized sweeping price cuts, followed quickly by its competitor Gimbels, then Bloomingdales, and in Brooklyn, Abraham & Straus and Namm's department store. A bargain mania swept customers into these stores, with the number of sales of cut-price goods soaring above normal. Over five thousand Palm Beach brand suits flew off the racks at Gimbels within three days, when the typical daily sales figure for that item was 150. As many Toastmasters were sold, when the standard was forty. Moreover, the effect of the *Schwegmann Brothers* decision was not limited to New York City. Stores in cities across the country followed suit in a price war that lasted over two months. National coverage in newspapers and on the radio spread the news of these price battles, likely encouraging greater expectations for cut prices and sales among consumers as a whole.[51]

The hiatus of federal control, however, was soon over. Up in arms over the price wars spurred by the *Schwegmann* decision, manufacturers and retail associations quickly lobbied for a stronger fair trade law and received one in 1952 with the McGuire Act. Support came from the National Association of Retail Druggists, the American Fair Trade Council, the Department of Commerce, and the Small Business Administration and focused on the rights of producers rather than of consumers. The bill's author argued in Congress that fair trade legislation was a means of fighting price-cutting, "the favorite device of the mass distributor to force the independent out of business and to obtain a monopolistic position."[52] Similarly, Senator Hubert Humphrey of Minnesota argued on its behalf, suggesting again that small retailers needed protection from monopolistic powers. As he countered criticism of the McGuire bill, however, Humphrey defined consumers as laborers, noting presciently that "the man who gets a cheap price and buys cheap goods will wind up getting cheap wages." But, at this point in time, the antilabor outcomes of mass retailing were not fully evident and arguments against discounters focused on their negative effects on independent retailers.[53]

Fair trade advocates might have won their battle with the McGuire Act, but discounting won the war in the 1950s. Just two years after the McGuire Act had reinstated fair trade, the number of participating manufacturers actually declined from sixteen hundred to nine hundred.[54] Within a few years of its passage, many manufacturers had abandoned the issue. In the lower courts, moreover, state fair trade laws began to collapse, followed by a series of U.S. Supreme Court decisions that weakened fair traders. As these court decisions in the late 1950s and early 1960s made it increasingly difficult for manufacturers to enforce fair trade agreements, more abandoned the practice. GE estimated that it spent from $300,000 to $500,000 annually in the early 1950s to enforce fair trade, while Sunbeam Corporation spent as much as $900,000 in one year. Price-cutting spread to so many retailers that it was impossible to litigate all into compliance. GE ended resale price maintenance in 1958, citing the impossibility of monitoring thirty thousand fair trade contracts and three thousand lawsuits against those who violated them. The volume of contracts inhibited enforcement, but in the end the sheer volume of sales by discounters like Korvette's and department stores like Gimbels and Macy's pushed manufacturers to abandon their commitment to fair trade. By the late 1950s, for the most part, only glassware, liquor, cosmetics, high-fidelity equipment, and drugstore goods were still fair-traded. Advocates for fair trade, however, continued to try to push through bills in the early 1960s, something the department store trade press observed from the fence, perhaps reflecting tension between its roots as the voice of the independent merchant and the increasing dominance of large-scale firms and chain department stores.[55]

At the time, there was some recognition that fair trade regulations as they stood were having unintended consequences. The McGuire Act protected price maintenance, and yet price-cutters had flourished. The Antitrust Division of the Department of Justice alleged in a 1958 Senate report on discounting that in fact fair trade laws "brought about the rise of the discount houses," providing "an umbrella" under which they could reside. The success of discounters depended on fair-traded national brands, they argued before the Senate in a somewhat tautological fashion, because these goods were susceptible to price-cutting.[56]

In this struggle over control of the postwar retail market, discounters and opponents of fair trade from within the department store industry succeeded in part because they had shoppers on their side. The discount industry turned to consumers for support in its offensive strategy, drawing attention to the price differentials between fair trade and non–fair trade states. If fair trade agreements remained behind the scenes, customers might have been unaware of which products they affected and to what degree they led to higher prices. But this was never the case. Court cases in which manufacturers sought injunctions against price-cutters were highly publicized and generated sympathy for the discounter. Consumers were also made aware of the high cost of fair trade. As we have seen, department stores advertised their cheaper private brands through price list comparisons with fair-traded brands. And even when discounters chose to comply with fair trade laws, they publicized the fact in a way that promoted their commitment to low prices. Prominent discounters like Korvette's, which had thirty-five fair trade lawsuits against it active in 1956, in fact embraced the fame their lawbreaking brought them. Korvette's executives boasted that the court cases were free advertising. And the massive chain Zayres displayed signs in the store saying it could not discount particular items because they were fair-traded.[57] In these ways, discounters tried to pull shoppers into their camp.

Discounters had inflation on their side. Rising inflation during this period galvanized opponents of fair trade. Inflation had risen 2 percent yearly during the postwar period, but it jumped to 6.7 percent a year after 1967. Spiraling inflation, set off by military spending in Vietnam and a massive increase in the money supply, brought prices to the fore. Businessmen interpreted it as the result of labor and union demands as well. In

August 1971, President Richard Nixon put in place a ninety-day price and wage freeze to try to "zap labor," in the words of his policy makers. Elimination of fair trade emerged as an additional way to counter inflation, one that spoke directly to consumers. Opponents of fair trade claimed the practice had pushed prices on protected goods up 18 and 27 percent and raised the consumer price index up by almost 20 percent. In the context of double-digit inflation, this was presented as an unacceptable burden.[58]

In 1974, as part of President Gerald Ford's "Whip Inflation Now" (WIN) program, Massachusetts Republican Edward W. Brooke introduced a bill that called for the repeal of fair trade legislation enacted between 1937 and 1952. Fair trade, according to President Ford, was "costly, inefficient, and obsolete"; repealing it was for the "benefit of the American consumer." The bill gained bipartisan support in Congress as market-oriented conservatives joined consumer-minded liberals to unite behind Brooke's argument that inflation was the "No. 1 enemy." Gone for the moment were concerns about the rights of small businesses or independents versus chains. Low consumer prices had won out over the older ideas of producer rights behind the fair trade movement.[59]

The Consumer Goods Pricing Act of 1975 signaled a reorientation of the American economy that undercut Main Street and contributed to the rise of discounting. The act squarely made it "illegal for manufacturers to fix the prices of consumer products sold by retailers." With this repeal of fair trade laws, discounters had carte blanche to expand legally into the territory of the traditional department store, an area they had entered illegally or on the fringes just years before. More broadly speaking, it was the neoliberal perspective behind the 1975 Consumer Goods Pricing Act that supported the creation of monoliths like the Macy's department store chain, Wal-Mart, Kmart, Target, OfficeMax, and Toys-R-Us. The Consumer Goods Pricing Act itself arguably played some role in the massive retail concentration that followed the legislation as stores merged or joined conglomerates in an attempt to counter unfettered low-price competition. But while the act certainly cleared the way for discounters and fostered the creation of large-scale retail chains to counter them, as we have seen, this transformation began much earlier. Opposition to fair trade at the state judicial and legislative level and ongoing resistance from mass retailers themselves had succeeded in seriously diminishing the power of fair trade long before. On the eve of the Consumer Goods Pricing Act, only eleven states still had such laws in effect.[60] Rather than a

turning point in a retail revolution, the 1975 act instead marked the cul-
mination of a process under way for several decades, in which independent department stores chained up or merged, department stores and
discount stores became more alike, and low prices and mass consumption
became a way of life.

CHAPTER 8

The Death of the Department Store

I . . . miss the old department stores Like May Company, Higbee,
O'Neills and Polskys by closing them down they hurt Cleveland and
Akron. All the Malls have died out and we are stuck shopping at
Walmart. It doesn't compare to shopping at these classic
department stores.
     —Boxer301977, YouTube.com post, 2008

AT the 1966 annual convention of the National Retail Merchants
Association in New York City, Malcolm McNair gave his predictions
for "retailing in the 1970s," a decade the department store industry was
looking forward to with some trepidation. Arguably the most prominent
figure in his field, this Lincoln Filene Professor Emeritus of Retailing at
Harvard had been analyzing department stores since the 1920s, when he
began collecting data on margins, expenses, and profits that contributed
to the industry's professionalization and modernization over the years. As
director of Allied Stores Corporation and a trustee of Wanamaker in Philadelphia, he was deeply vested in the continued success of his industry and
in promoting its legitimacy. And yet, McNair's vision of the coming decade
was a dark one for Main Street retailers. "The day of the single large store
is past," he warned. Department stores in the 1970s would be "multi-unit."
They would cease to be local institutions and would instead become
regional in identity. Jordan Marsh of Boston would become Jordan Marsh
of New England. Downtown locations would decline as markets became

"predominantly suburban," even more than before. Consumers would also be younger and more hedonistic as society grew increasingly affluent, meaning that department stores would have to change their traditional merchandising tactics. Reflecting his industry's antigovernment stance, McNair also cautioned against increased regulation. Department store executives were to watch out for more rules affecting hours, wages, pricing, advertising, credit, and mergers and acquisitions. Departing from the perspective of earlier decades, his speech showed none of the cooperative spirit that sputtered throughout the Depression and World War II in the department store industry. Instead, he advocated "questioning, resisting and heel-dragging" as a strategy to fight government control. In the face of all these changes, McNair was confident the "historical department store" would survive, but only, he told his trade association members in 1966, if the industry did not "stay pat."[1]

As the department store industry entered the 1970s, many of McNair's predictions came true. Like other industries, the department store field experienced a period of economic transformation. American manufacturing began moving operations outside the United States and the country began importing more goods than it exported. After the oil embargo of 1973, gasoline shortages and higher prices for petroleum products put new limits on American consumers who were used to driving big Chevys and Fords. For department stores in particular, the development of a rival discount industry and the expansion of suburban shopping centers cut into the traditional downtown retailer's profits. Younger, suburban families were more time-constrained and preferred the convenience of the new centers. Facing rising prices and stagnating wages, many chose convenience over service, low prices and mass consumption over luxury and amenity.[2]

Revisiting the condition of his field about ten years after his 1966 predictions, McNair and his longtime professional associate Eleanor May wrote that the department store remained "an urban institution." But they observed deep changes. By 1977, the "conventional department store" had become "the regional department store chain, an organization typically consisting of one store in the downtown section of a city and a number of outlying stores, all being managed and operated by one group of executives." Looking ahead to the 1980s, McNair and May predicted that this mode of distribution faced a "stiff challenge" from new competitors and different consumer demands, but also from increased governmental pressures.[3]

In fact, over the course of the 1980s and 1990s, weak regulatory oversight enabled the largest reorganization in the industry's history. The conventional department store entered the 1980s with only 40 percent of department store sales overall, a category which now included huge discount chains like Kmart and Wal-Mart. Traditional department stores that had once commanded between 8 and 10 percent of total retail sales before World War II had lost their hold on consumers by the early 1980s, pulling in only 3 percent of the country's total retail sales, a number that continued to fall into the next century.[4] Consolidation returned as a popular strategy for eliminating competition and achieving even greater economies of scale. In the pro-business climate of President Ronald Reagan's administration, the biggest deals in the industry's history up to that point were cut in the 1980s. The mergers and the drastic closures that followed, coupled with the rising market share of the discount general merchandiser and the new big-box store phenomenon, finally pushed the Main Street department store over the cliff it had been slowly approaching for decades. With the mega-merger of Federated and May in 2005, many more historic nameplates were lost, all reorganized as Macy's in a move that seems to have put an end to the local in the department store industry. Mirroring these transformations, the industry's trade associations also realigned and merged, reflecting the growing dominance of the mass retailers like Wal-Mart, which by the early twenty-first century was the biggest corporation in the world and one of the most controversial.[5]

Wall Street Comes to Main Street

For much of the twentieth century, mass retailers expanded either by opening new units or by consolidating with many large individual stores or with smaller chains to become massive multiunit firms. Internal expansion was the chosen method of growth for the major twentieth-century general-merchandise chains. Wal-Mart, Kmart, and, in its heyday, Sears, all expanded by building new units that replicated their success in a formulaic way. Kmart typically occupied a freestanding building that had a single large entrance/exit, centralized checkout, shopping cart self-service, and merchandise from Asian sources. Sears was still the nation's largest retailer in the late 1980s, though Wal-Mart was beginning to challenge that claim. Sam Walton's empire, which he took public in 1970, ballooned to 1,300 stores with nearly $20 billion in sales by 1989. Mergers and acquisitions, however, were a more typical method of growth for the conventional or traditional department store. After a period of consolidation activity in the 1920s, which diminished in the 1930s and 1940s, mergers picked up again in the 1950s with the expansion efforts of May, Federated, and Allied Department Stores. Postwar mergers significantly restructured the general merchandise field as the nation's twenty largest department store companies acquired seventy-three companies operating 168 establishments between 1951 and 1965. According to a 1956 *New York Times* article titled "Chains Absorbing the Big Store Too," the department store field, which had once been "a stronghold of independent operation" was now in "the thick of the march toward centralized ownership." Family-run institutions like Hecht's, which became a member of the May Department Store holding company in 1959, lost their independent status though they continued to operate under their own nameplate.[6]

Increasingly, what loyal customers would later lament as lost were in fact department store chains or members of massive holding companies. Since the first business census began keeping track in 1929, multiunit or chain department stores grew from around 17 percent of their market to just over half by 1948. By midcentury, chain organization was the dominant department store form, even though this period was looked on in recent years as a golden age for the industry, when local institutions still lined Main Street and kept downtown humming. In 1963, a year after the birth of Target, Kmart, and Wal-Mart, around 85 percent of department stores were in fact part of multiunit operations. Four years later that share had grown to just over 90 percent. By 1975, Sears, Montgomery Ward, and J. C. Penney together captured 43 percent of all department store sales—a whopping $22.6 billion of sales in this era of inflation. Almost all department stores were thus outlets of multiunit firms by 1982, when the percentage of chains in the industry reached 97.95 percent.[7]

Of course, not all multiunits operated on such a massive scale as Wal-Mart, Target, or Kmart, nor were they all cookie-cutter operations, indistinguishable from one another. Until 1982, four stores technically constituted a chain; after that time the number dropped to three establishments. Thus chains could be quite small and their numbers might include family-run businesses or firms with the strong local identity their customers valued. To some degree it was their mode of operation, rather than their size, that distinguished chains from traditional department stores. The census bureau, for example, defined a chain as any group of stores in the same field

FIGURE 27. In the early 1970s, the family-run Herbst department store expanded beyond Fargo, North Dakota, where it had operated since the late nineteenth century. It began opening branch stores in neighboring towns and cities and moved into a Fargo shopping center before it went out of business in 1982. Institute for Regional Studies, North Dakota State University, Fargo (rs001410).

of business or of the same general kind, operating under one ownership and management with largely centralized merchandising, purchasing, and warehousing. Defined in this way, multiunits were standardized in that the decisions of a central management determined the operation of all units. This was the case with true department store chains like Sears or, after it ended its decentralized operations in 1950, J. C. Penney.[8] Traditional department stores, however, which were owned by holding companies or affiliated with large department store groups were run in a very different way, as we have seen.

Before the mid-1980s, merger and acquisition did not mean the loss of individual identity for the bought-up store. Acquiring chains initially allowed stores to keep their nameplate and with it the loyalty of their customers. The earliest large department store groups like Hahn Stores, or even Federated, consisted of many different local stores running under their own management and nameplate. These chains, according to the retailing visionary Edward Filene in 1927, had "the fault of dissimilarity," not something they would be accused of at the end of the century. Some of this local flavor persisted into the 1980s in spite of the fact that the industry was highly concentrated. Consumers shopped in their favorite community department store without knowing their institution was no longer truly "local." As late as the mid-1980s, for example, Federated operated 238 department stores (units) with over $6 billion in sales, spread across many nameplates. Ten holding companies dominated the traditional department store market, each containing many local names that had long retail histories behind them. Of the top one hundred firms, ranked by annual sales, seventy were affiliated with these ten holding companies. Thirty other stores—fully one-third—were still independent.[9]

In the late 1980s, however, this changed as rising concentration in the department store industry meant less local flavor—a loss of retail diversity and a blander consumer experience as shoppers had fewer choices. Bigger chains came to mean fewer store nameplates. Their dominance also caused the loss of distinctive brands, holiday traditions or other public spectacles that had been brought back year after year, and of course the end of the institution's distinctive presence downtown. The ascendancy of national chains like Macy's, for example, meant that nationally televised traditions, such as the Thanksgiving Day parade and Fourth of July fireworks, replaced the numerous local customs of newly defunct department stores. Gone were the enchanted village at Jordan Marsh in Boston, the pink pig train at Rich's in Atlanta, and the Circus in the Sky at Burdines in Miami, to name just a few. Even suburban shopping centers, which housed the branches where three-quarters of all department store sales took place by the mid-1970s, became more standardized as a result of increased concentration in the industry. Widely seen as "bland" in recent years, shopping malls grew even more interchangeable as historic department store names were lost over the 1980s or were turned into Macy's in the early twenty-first century.[10]

The surviving independent department stores, once the backbone of the industry, had also changed. Historically, these were single-unit, downtown operations with the founding family owning the majority of the store's assets. By the mid-1980s, "independent" largely meant a department store chain run under a single nameplate with strong family ownership. The family-run, single-outlet Main Street department store was still in existence, but most independents had become multiunit, with all that came to imply. According to a 1985 directory of 1,327 department store companies operating 9,036 stores, 660 were one-store companies—about half of the total number of firms, but only 5 percent of all outlets. Two- and three-store companies were responsible for 573 stores. The largest proportion of department stores was operated by only five companies each consisting of at least 201 units. "Independent" had never necessarily meant small, but especially in this later period when department store companies typically had to be very big to survive, independents too were large entities. One independent department store—the Dillard's chain of Little Rock, Arkansas —made it into the top five with $847,485,000 in sales.[11]

As these figures demonstrate, smaller independent stores were still hanging on in the mid-1980s, serving their local economies, but they were greatly challenged on all fronts. Dependent on advertising and location for survival and limited by higher fixed costs per sales dollar, these often family-run independents followed a "break-even" plan rather than the "grow-or-die" philosophy of their big corporate competitors. Growth, in any event, was difficult as independents retained insufficient earnings and had fewer finance options for expansion compared to holding companies and retail chains, both of which enjoyed a favored status in capital markets.[12] Most independent firms in the mid-1980s were in the bottom half of one set of sales rankings for the industry, with only ten making it to the top fifty stores. Some relatively small firms still identified themselves as department stores as well. The ninety-ninth and one-hundredth ranking spots, for example, went to the Dry Goods in Aston, Pennsylvania, and to Stone & Thomas in Wheeling, West Virginia, each with $1 million in annual sales. Some of these firms prospered in the early 1980s, like the one-hundred-year old family-owned and operated Bresee's department store on Main Street in Oneonta, New York, operating in a building the family owned rather than leased, and with strong multigenerational commitment.[13]

While statistics show independents vastly outranked by stores affiliated with the likes of the massive Carter Hawley Hale, Mercantile Stores, and Batus, the range of surviving nameplates reveal a persistent local flavor in the mid-1980s. Historic stores like Donaldson's in Minneapolis and Carson

FIGURE 28. Independent small-town department stores like Bresee's were typically family businesses. Intergenerational commitment allowed this firm to prosper on Main Street in Oneonta, New York, between 1899 and 1994. "We're Telling You Macy's!" *Collier's* (November 12, 1949), 26. Photographer: Hans Knopf. Courtesy of Marc Bresee.

Pirie Scott in Chicago still served their communities. In Texas alone, shoppers in the mid-1980s were familiar with local stores like Joske's and the independent Frost Bros. in San Antonio; Foley's in Houston; the Dunlap Company, an independent department store, in Fort Worth; and Sanger-Harris in Dallas, all of which made it into the top one hundred sales ranking for the industry overall. And finally, even the ten giant holding companies that controlled the stores that were among the top one hundred in the nation also included smaller firms with historic nameplates—Strouss of Youngstown, Ohio, with just over $1 million annual sales, for example, was owned and operated by the giant May.[14] Such local flavor, however super-ficial, would be conspicuously absent only fifteen years later. At the beginning of the second decade of the twenty-first century, only a handful of single-unit Main Street emporia remained—local institutions like the 130-year-old Wilson's department store in Greenfield, Massachusetts, and Weaver's department store, a longtime downtown anchor for Lawrence, Kansas.[15]

The decline of local department stores during this period was in part the product of federal policies that fostered business concentration. The connection between policy and the survival of traditional department stores, however, was never straightforward. Limitations on postwar consolidation, for example, inadvertently had the opposite effect as corporations pushed for ways around regulations and found them. This was the case with the Celler-Kefauver Act in 1950, antitrust legislation that eliminated opportunities for merger and helped give birth to the conglomerate movement of the 1960s. Also called the Anti-Merger Act, its intention had been to close a legal loophole in the 1914 Clayton Antitrust Act "by forbidding those mergers in which one company purchased the assets, rather than the stocks, of another." Celler-Kefauver's clear and strong prohibitions on horizontal and vertical mergers were coupled with less clear directives on the anticompetitiveness of conglomerates. The FTC, for example, moved to limit the number of merger opportunities for retailers with sales of $500 million or more but left the door open for mergers with unlike firms. With vertical and horizontal mergers limited, diversification became a popular alternate avenue for rapid growth.[16]

Department stores joined the conglomerate movement in droves. Some independents, like the southern Miller & Rhoads, merged with specialty retail apparel firms. Others diversified into totally unrelated areas or product fields. For example, in 1964, when Federated Department Stores acquired Bullock's, then the seventeenth largest chain of department stores, the FTC tried to clamp down on its growth. Federated had to agree to refrain from further acquisitions of any department store or apparel or furniture store for five years, unless gaining prior FTC approval. Following this ruling, Federated adopted a conglomerate strategy and in 1968 acquired its own supermarket chain. Discount department store chain Korvette's did the same, expanding yet staying in compliance with federal regulations. Conglomeration also brought non–department store retailers into the industry. Gamble-Skogmo of Minnesota, for example, grew from a little-known automobile accessory franchise operation into a retail giant by 1969. After a few mergers before the postwar period, Gamble-Skogmo began to acquire a wide variety of firms, from Grigg's Department Store in Lima, Ohio, in 1965 to variety stores, a women's apparel chain, a supermarket chain, and a bank in the late 1960s. Gamble-Skogmo capped off the decade by acquiring the J. M. McDonald Company chain of eighty-five to ninety department stores.[17]

Massive merger attempts in the 1960s garnered attention from the FTC, but ultimately they were allowed, and in spite of stricter antitrust regulations the industry became increasingly concentrated by the 1970s. Again, federal regulation did not work to contain this type of growth. The Hart-Scott-Rodino Antitrust Improvements Act of 1976 had signaled Congress's intent to block anticompetitive mergers more aggressively. The act required "parties to large mergers to notify the FTC and Department of Justice (and supply substantial amounts of information) prior to consummating the transaction." Following Hart-Scott-Rodino, local department stores continued to be swallowed up. Just in the South, for example, two prominent local institutions were taken over by massive national holding companies: Federated Department Stores acquired Rich's in 1976, and Allied Stores took over Miller & Rhoads in 1981.[18]

In the 1980s, loose federal oversight of the financial sector and the explosion of leveraged buyouts allowed a wave of "retail-merger mania" that took consolidation in the department store industry to new heights and left far fewer firms standing. Just as Wal-Mart's incredible growth was fostered by the conservative era's economic environment, which, as historian Nelson Lichtenstein has argued, "relieved employers, especially the retailers and fast-food restaurants, of hundreds of billions of dollars in annual labor costs," big players in the department store industry were able to grow even bigger because of the same pro-business climate.[19]

One particularly disastrous merger sequel in the mid to late 1980s stands out. Robert Campeau's acquisitions of Allied and Federated created the largest department store holding company in the country, with $15 billion in sales (Sears was still larger, with $23 billion in annual sales that year). This relatively miniscule French-Canadian investor and his real estate firm first acquired Allied Stores Corporation in 1986 (which then included the Bon Marche, Jordan Marsh, and Stern's) for the inflated price of $3.6 billion. Two years later, he acquired Federated Department Stores (consisting of Abraham & Straus, Bloomingdale's, Burdines, Lazarus, and Rich's) for the even more inflated price of $6.6 billion. Campeau's reckless invest-ment decisions—and the man himself—have been blamed for destroying the American department store industry. However, it was the era's embrace of freewheeling investment practices that enabled Campeau.[20]

Campeau's deal was the product of financing and stock market transac-tions that challenged long-standing practice. To acquire Allied in the first place, for example, Campeau made use of the street sweep, a stock market tactic popular in the mid-1980s made possible by the Second Circuit's loos-ening of Securities and Exchange Commission (SEC) restrictions. Street sweeps were part of the mechanics for a leveraged buyout. They were blitz-kriegs that combined aggressive open-market purchasing with privately negotiated transactions "to gain control of enough stock to end contested takeover contests." The SEC found that tender offer rules had been broken when Campeau's company had withdrawn its tender offer and then imme-diately gone to the open market and purchased 48 percent of Allied stocks. Yet the courts allowed it to stand.[21] Then, having borrowed far beyond what the company's earnings would support, as was common in the Reagan-era junk bond boom, Campeau sold off portions of Allied to pay for his initial acquisition. Just the Allied deal alone required a return of 12 percent, an unrealistic amount for any retail industry investment at that time. The com-pany's average return was between 6 and 7 percent. As a result, immediately after purchasing Allied, Campeau had to sell sixteen of its twenty-four divi-sions, including Donaldson's, Block's, Joske's, and Bonwit Teller. Stores like Richmond's one-hundred-year-old Miller & Rhoads, which was part of the Allied chain, were sold off to nonretail companies like real estate developers. These firms then closed outlets and mismanaged others (Miller & Rhoads, for example, went into bankruptcy in 1989 and closed in January 1990).[22]

The acquisition of Federated in 1988 simply threw good money after bad, with Campeau borrowing over $6.5 billion after having already borrowed $4 billion to purchase Allied. While the acquired department stores and their customers suffered, advisors and bankers in the deal earned hundreds of mil-lions of dollars in fees, more than Federated earned in a year. And Campeau immediately sold off two Federated stores, Houston's Foley's and the historic Boston firm Filene's. As the dust cleared and it became evident there was no way out of the firm's massive debt, the Campeau Corporation's board of director removed Campeau and put Allied, Federated, and sixty-five subsidi-aries into Chapter 11 bankruptcy. Federated, moreover, had to liquidate its discount stores, which put it at a long-term disadvantage.[23]

By allowing such takeover strategies to stand, federal regulators helped open the door for further consolidation, contributing to the closure of many historic local or regional names in retailing. Earlier consolidations preserved the nameplates of local department stores, but after the mergers and bankruptcies of the 1980s and the subsequent reorganization of the industry this was no longer the case. By the 1990s, merger clearly came to mean a loss of local identity and the removal of a traditional retailing name from the commercial scene. Over and over again in this period, department stores with a local history and regional presence were bought up by national chains and renamed, sometimes repeatedly as firms were resold. A Texas institution, Sanger-Harris—itself a product of a 1961 merger when Federated purchased the two competing one-hundred-year-old Dallas firms—became Foley's in 1988. Family-owned firms like Strawbridge & Clothier became Hecht's and Lord & Taylor and finally Macy's. Likewise, Dayton-Hudson stores were all converted to Marshall Field's.[24] And in the early 1990s, when the huge May chain expanded, consolidating a number of old department stores into one of its own companies, the southern Thalhimer's became Hecht's; Rochester's Sibley's was combined with Famous-Barr; and the Los Angeles May Company and Robinson's were merged to form Robinson-May.[25]

Wanamaker's story illustrates the industry's increasing consolidation over the last few decades. In 1979, descendants of John Wanamaker, the "merchant prince," sold their one-hundred-year-old firm to the department store chain Carter Hawley Hale. The chain had just tried and failed to buy Marshall Field's, blocked by the FTC, and had also unsuccessfully tried to do the same to Wanamaker's. After fighting two hostile takeover attempts and incurring much debt, Carter Hawley Hale sold the historic Philadelphia store to a real estate developer in 1986. In such inexperienced hands, Wanamaker's was stripped down and divided up. A shadow of its former self, it operated as a department store until 1994, when it was put into bankruptcy by its real estate developer–owner. The May chain acquired thirteen Wanamaker outlets in 1995 and renamed them Hecht's, itself a well-known traditional department store chain from the Baltimore/Washington region. All were renamed Macy's. Wanamaker's eagle and famous pipe organ, both from the St. Louis World's Fair, now belonged to the national chain Macy's. Still centered in the Market Street building's graceful atrium in 2012, where Macy's had attempted to enliven an otherwise slightly depressed scene with a lavish flower show throughout the shoe department on the atrium floor, the eagle was a busy spot, with tourists taking photographs of themselves with the historic icon. The organ rising up along one wall was also a point of interest for tourists, giving the atrium a museum-like feel rather than helping to make it the vibrant commercial space it once was. Retail activity took place only on the lower levels; the upper floors opening onto the atrium were darkened and unused, giving the rest of the store a sad look.[26]

In many ways, merger mania in the 1980s and beyond augmented the department store field's late twentieth-century woes, as evinced by the journey from Wanamaker's to Macy's. Family-run firms, which had survived for over a century, could no longer compete in a market that had been changing for decades. In the 1990s, Main Street department stores across the country closed their doors.[27] Those that survived changed. Regionally identified retailers focused on specific markets became identical national chains intent only on pleasing shareholders. Industry consolidation pushed department stores to shed lines, turning them into glorified apparel stores with only a few nonapparel lines, such as fragrances and cosmetics.[28] Department stores became more standardized in the 1990s, losing the last vestiges of local or regional identity they had forged as downtown institutions a hundred years before. Due in large part to the disastrous business moves of the 1980s, the last decade of the twentieth century was characterized by store closures and name consolidation.

Federated's history in particular exemplified how the traditional department store industry increasingly turned its back on the local in the 1990s. After a 1994 merger with Macy's, many of Federated's affiliates ceased to operate under their own nameplates. Macy's had sought to acquire Federated in 1988, but in 1994 it was in the weaker position, a direct result of its bidding war with Robert Campeau. Both Macy's and Federated had been bankrupted by their dealings with the Canadian investor. Federated had emerged from bankruptcy in 1992, the year Macy's was forced to file Chapter 11. Macy's was saddled with debt from its purchase of the Federated divisions of Bullock's and I. Magnin, all it could get out of its bidding war. Debt coupled with leadership turnover and disastrous sales meant it could no longer remain independent so it agreed to be acquired by Federated.[29]

The 1994 Federated-Macy's merger created the biggest department store company at the time, with 460 stores and $13 billion in annual sales. Such size brought efficiencies; it was estimated the merger would save the firm $50 million a year. While Federated had not decided whether nameplates would change after the consolidation, from the beginning, closures were part of the merger agreement. In spite of the size of the new company formed by the merger, the FTC had approved it with no strings attached, but New York's state attorney general, G. Oliver Koppell, feared the merger would lead to monopoly and price effects. Koppell pressured the new company to close stores, claiming it would "open competition and bring new department stores into the area." The divesture was necessary, he argued, to avoid "a virtual lock on the department store business." In this particular case, however, his efforts on behalf of competition in fact removed several local stores from the market mix in New York's metropolitan area. Two Abraham & Straus locations, two Stern's, a Bloomingdale's, and a Macy's were closed in response to the merger. In 1995, the Abraham & Straus name was no more, its stores becoming first Stern's then Macy's.[30]

By destroying so many historic nameplates, the 1994 merger between Federated and Macy's led to widespread industry standardization. The enlarged Federated consolidated many of its regional chains into geographically organized Macy's divisions. Some acquired chains like I. Magnin's were dissolved. Others, like the Broadway Stores in 1995, and Jordan Marsh in 1996, were converted en masse to the Macy's nameplate. To capture a higher-end market, the Bloomingdale's nameplate was expanded.[31] Department store names thus became less distinct as a direct result of this huge merger. Standardization of merchandising was another result. After the Federated–Macy's merger in 1994, analysts predicted the company would increase its selection of private-label merchandise across all stores, drawing on Macy's large product-development unit.[32] Such efficiencies lay behind growing criticism that department store merchandise was all the same. The historic battle between manufacturers and department stores over national brand-name goods was finished as well.

In 2005, the industry was again transformed when Federated Department Stores, Inc., acquired May Department Stores for $17 billion. When the two prepared to merge, the FTC conducted a six-month investigation of the planned merger but ultimately permitted the Macy's deal to go ahead without modification. This massive merger fit into a larger context, one that included Wal-Mart, the dominant retailer of the time. Retail experts drew parallels between Wal-Mart and the 2005 merger of Federated and May. According to Wharton marketing professor Z. John Zhang, "People have learned from Wal-Mart that size does matter." The merged department store company's greater size allowed it to cut costs and achieve greater power over suppliers. As Nelson Lichtenstein has ably demonstrated, Wal-Mart had famously been able to squeeze "billions of dollars out of a once-bloated system of manufacture, transport, distribution, and sales" and thus lower prices, but at a high cost for American society. The loss of American jobs as production shifted overseas and the appalling global exploitation of factory workers were just two consequences of the rise of a Wal-Mart world. Adding to this the environmental impact of Wal-Mart and the political and corporate corruption associated with the firm's expansion in markets like Mexico, this "retail revolution" was clearly a negative one. From the management perspective, though, Wal-Mart's model was one to emulate.[33]

For the department store industry too, bigness brought cost benefits. The 2005 merger meant national mass media was possible, which was a more efficient way of communicating to consumers. National ad campaigns for Macy's on television, like Wal-Mart ads, would become ubiquitous, a change from department stores' historic dependence on advertising media like local newspapers and radio, or local television. The merger also created a truly national network of stores that could compete with national discount chains like Target and Wal-Mart, as well as the powerful specialty apparel chains and home furnishing stores.[34]

The highly publicized merger of Federated and May marked the end of an almost century-long process of consolidation, which according to the FTC's investigation created "by far the largest chain of 'traditional' or 'conventional' department stores in the country." May Department Stores had become the first department store holding company in 1910, when it acquired the Schoenberg Mercantile Company of St. Louis, the May Company of Cleveland, and a Denver shoe and clothing company.[35] Federated had been formed in 1929, the biggest merger of its decade. This merger of the two largest department store chains in the United States put it in fifth place behind Wal-Mart, the newly merged Sears and Kmart, Target, and Costco, with almost one thousand stores and $30 billion in annual sales. The traditional department store industry now had a national department store brand of unprecedented size—Macy's. Adding to the list of regional department stores Federated had already converted to Macy's, including Burdines, Goldsmith's, Lazarus, and the Bon Marche, the merger addressed overlap between its department store companies and those owned by May. Still more local nameplates fell before the Macy's brand, while overlapping Federated and May outlets were closed. With almost a quarter of a million employees between the two prior to the merger, many were affected negatively by the deal. In 2007, Federated's corporate name changed to Macy's Inc., reflecting the fact it was no longer a federation of individual department stores as it had once been. While many saw the merger of Federated and May as the death of the department store, the chairman and CEO of Federated (Macy's), Terry Lundgren, framed it as a commitment to the future of his field. Lundgren had worked his way up at Federated in Bullock's Los Angeles division between the mid-1970s and 1987, a time when members still operated under their own nameplates. The 2005 merger changed all that. In a press release announcing the acquisition, however, Lundgren asserted the continued importance of the downtown flagship store in Herald Square and boasted they were "proving that department stores can be a vibrant, very much alive form of retail."[36]

The Rise of Big Boxes

Changes in the associational organization of the retail industry mirrored the rising power of Wal-Mart and its ilk. The National Retail Merchants Association (NRMA) had been the main trade group for independents since its inception in 1911 as the National Retail Dry Goods Association. In its typically conservative fashion, the organization changed its name only in 1958, long after the era of the dry goods merchant. As discount competition exploded, the new field also got its own trade group. Not surprisingly, Sam Walton was behind the first discount trade association, the Mass Retailing Institute (MRI). The MRI was formed in direct opposition to the national department store group in 1969 after Walton had tried to join the NRMA but had been rebuffed, allegedly because "department store owners didn't want to mix with a discounter." Walton and twenty other firms cofounded their own organization to provide workshops and executive seminars for member companies. Without a presence in Washington, the influence of the MRI was limited at first. Eventually, after a few name changes it became in 2004 the Retail Industry Leaders Association (RILA), a trade association representing some of the largest chain retailers, big-box stores, and category killers in the United States, among them Wal-Mart, Target, Safeway, Staples, Whole Foods, and Lowe's.[37]

Similarly, the department store trade press reorganized in ways that mirrored larger shifts in the retail field. Beginning in the early 1960s, retail experts described a narrowing of the gap between the conventional department and discount store, a change that was soon reflected in the names of the main trade journal. The longtime *Department Store Economist* had simply updated itself to become *Department Store Management* in 1968. But, in 1973, without explanation, *Department Store Management* changed its name to *Retail Directions*, a title that effectively erased the Main Street department store. Perhaps reflecting opposition to this erasure, in 1975 the old title returned and it again became *Department Store Economist*, now published by *Retail Directions*. In any event, the reinsertion of "department store" shows that in the 1970s the industry still held on to its traditional roots, a small point, but one that helps periodize the decline of the much-beloved local institution. Some in the field still resisted closer ties with mass retailing. One reader of *Retail Directions* wrote to the editors in 1973 that they were "making a big mistake in aiming (their) magazine to the mass retailing industry . . . the department store market is desperately in need of good publications." The editors responded defensively, revealing that they too still identified with the department store field. They noted their publication went back 127 years and stated they would not neglect "the Federated's, the Macy's, the Magnin's, the Halle's," but added that big chains like Sears, Korvette's, and Ohrbach's were also "important factors in retailing," signaling the growing influence of the discount industry in the postwar period.[38]

The journal's response revealed the distance the industry had come. In fact, in 1973 there was little difference, in terms of corporate structure and size, between traditional department stores and the mass retailers listed by the editors. A closer look at the stores listed by *Retail Directions* in its defense shows just how things had changed—and become more the same. Sears was one of the original department store chains and well known for its moderate pricing and staple, rather than fashion, goods, while Korvette's represented the relatively recent shift toward discount department store chain retailing. Ohrbach's was a more established bargain department store. Opened on Union Square in New York in 1923, it expanded after World War II and was eventually bought up in 1962 by a Netherlands-based chain. None of these three chains, however, offered a full line of services as did conventional department stores, nor did they sell high-fashion items in a luxurious setting. Of the other traditional department stores mentioned, while all had origins as single unit, family-run independents, by the 1970s they too had become multiunit enterprises that had either been purchased by or merged with a larger firm.

As defined by *Retail Directions*' choice of firms to represent "the department store field," "traditional" meant big holding company or ownership group, not the single-unit downtown palace of consumption or Main Street merchant of yore. What was deemed a true department store in 1973 had actually grown much closer to its chain competitors. For example, one of the traditional firms held up by *Retail Directions*—Halle's of Cleveland— had been purchased in 1970 by Marshall Field. By the end of the decade, it still operated under its original name but had grown to ten units with about $75 million in annual sales. Thus, by 1973, the single-unit independent was no longer considered a meaningful constituency by the department store trade press. Only one article in *Retail Directions* in 1973 addressed the topic, one which interestingly was deemed "inspirational" by another reader who was motivated enough to write to the editors.[39] The traditional independent department store may have held a special place in such readers' memories, but the trade press clearly now had a broader scope and audience, signaled by its name changes over the years and its choice of news coverage.

The growth of mass retailing—with Wal-Mart leading—was evident in further changes in retail trade organization in the 1970s and 1980s. The lobby group for the discount industry began to broaden its reach during this period. In 1976, the Mass Retailing Institute founded by Sam Walton and other discounters changed its name to reflect better its widening scope, becoming the National Mass Retailing Institute (NMRI). This organization served the burgeoning self-service discount department store industry, sponsoring the publication of a long series of operating results and analysis by Cornell University until 1986, when the trade association again shifted. Historically, trade associations for the discount or low-price retail industry broke down along size, reflecting the different interests of large mass retailers and smaller store formats like variety stores. But beginning in the 1980s, the push toward bigness changed even this.[40]

As discounters consolidated in the 1980s, so did their professional organizations. In 1986, the NMRI merged with an older organization, the Association of General Merchandise Chains (AGMC). With this merger, the new organization pulled in the lobbying power and economic might of all segments of the retail trade, except food chains and the traditional department store. The trade group for general merchandise chains (AGMC) that merged with the national discount group (NMRI) had consisted of smaller-format retailers like variety stores. The new organization threatened to swallow smaller stores. During the merger, the head of the NMRI advised new members that the organization would continue to cater to small stores through separate divisions. It would also provide information on how the issues facing mass retailers applied specifically to them. The association, which encompassed specialty discount merchandisers and general merchandise discount chains, needed a new name. NMRI members in 1987, considering a name change for the enlarged organization, bandied around the idea of calling themselves the "non-department store association," an unfortunate title which perhaps would have unnecessarily rubbed the competition the wrong way.[41] Instead, in 1988 the NMRI became the International Mass Retail Association, then after years of expansion it became the Retail Industry Leaders Association (RILA). Although the awkward "non-department store" nomenclature did not stick, the suggestion itself signaled the association's oppositional identity, as well as the cultural and economic decline of the traditional department store by the late 1980s.

At a time when mergers were transforming the department store field, professional organizations for this industry were also consolidating. Traditional department stores followed a different timeline than discounters' associations, but the trajectory was the same. By the mid-1980s, the old NRMA saw itself working "in behalf of large chains, department stores, and specialty stores involved in general merchandise retailing in the United States." The association also provided "governmental representation." Still based in New York City like its predecessor the National Retail Dry Goods Association, the NRMA had grown. Members operated over forty-five thousand stores with annual sales volume greater than $150 billion. Continuing to grow, in 1990 it merged with the American Retail Federation (ARF), forming the National Retail Federation (NRF). Historically, the NRMA had represented the independent department store and was a foe of the ARF, an organization formed in 1935 in spite of much opposition and cries of monopoly. The 1990 merger created an organizational umbrella headed up by the CEO of J. C. Penney. The new NRF claimed to be the world's largest retail trade association. It covered much of the retail industry in the United States, including independent and major chain retailers, fifty state retail associations, and twenty-seven national retail associations. Discount general merchandisers and the rapidly growing big-box retail industry were not part of this group but instead were represented by the powerful RILA (the former NMRI). In 2013, however, the NRF achieved a major "coup" when Wal-Mart finally joined its ranks.[42]

RILA and the NRF presided over the shifting retail landscape at the close of the last century and the beginning of the new. Each came out of different traditions yet joined forces to lobby on behalf of the interests of big business. Both trade organizations were agents of neoliberalism, advocating free-market principles and fighting to destroy all remaining vestiges of the New Deal. As Nelson Lichtenstein has shown in his study of Wal-Mart, RILA paired with the retailing giant—its most powerful member—to minimize the influence of the federal government over its industry. RILA lobbied for Wal-Mart against minimum wage increases under President George W. Bush, failing only after Democrats took control of Congress and made a deal with the president. In these years, RILA also worked on behalf of Wal-Mart and big-box discounters to fight health insurance mandates, living wage pay standards, port security regulations, and clean air standards that might have increased retail shipping costs. RILA also vigorously opposed the Democratic Party's efforts to facilitate union organizing. During this period, the NRF joined RILA, uniting against external forces affecting the industry, such as labor laws and unionization efforts, credit card regulations, and tax policies. The two trade associations also worked together on internal problems, such as organized retail crime.[43]

In 2009, NRF and RILA, two historic foes, considered merging, a move that would have created a retail lobby group of unprecedented size and influence. Both organizations worked on behalf of the interests of giant retailers, with Wal-Mart extending its reach over the NRF, even before it added its membership to the group. Wal-Mart's CEO, Lee Scott, addressed the NRF convention before he retired in 2009 and top Wal-Mart executives moved into leadership roles in the trade organization. More important, the two collaborated on issues affecting retail, maneuvering together against both labor and consumers. Yet, some differences remained. While the NRF's membership had grown more diversified over the decades, consisting of fewer department stores, it still maintained an identity distinct from RILA, which may have played a role in keeping the two associations apart in this merger attempt. In 2009, the NRF was composed of 2,500 national chains, independents retailers, restaurants, and online retailers. RILA's two hundred members included retail suppliers, service providers, and sixty mass chains. Of the two, RILA was understood to represent more the interests of big-box retailers. When talks on the merger of these two former competitors broke down, it was to the satisfaction of many smaller retailers still in the NRF. Differences on some key early twenty-first-century issues, such as the Affordable Care Act, also divided the two.[44]

Although the proposed 2009 merger between the NRF and RILA broke down, the effort to consolidate the two professional organizations in the industry signaled the growing influence of the big-box retailers, chains, and discounters that dominated both trade groups. Wal-Mart's eventual joint membership in the NRF and RILA only underlines this point. Traditional department stores no longer had a powerful trade voice as they had earlier in the twentieth century, when presidents sent messages to their annual conventions or appointed merchants to head important wartime agencies or consult on national policy. Beginning in the 1980s, professional organizations themselves no longer upheld distinctions between the department store industry and these newer modes of distribution. Under their watch, the Main Street institution had disappeared.

Remembering Downtown Department Stores

A S the local department store—the Main Street retailer—seemingly met its demise at the turn of the twenty-first century, widespread nostalgia and regret for a lost commercial culture emerged. There were more than nine thousand department store outlets in the United States in 2002,[1] but customers felt the loss of distinctiveness connected to historic nameplates. In the era of Wal-Mart, which many had come to see as a monopoly that destroyed local markets, department stores had joined ranks to create their own oligopoly. Even region seemed to matter no longer. As shoppers lamented the death of their department stores, traditional Main Street retailers became nostalgic artifacts consumed in opposition to global-ization and a perceived loss of unique community identity.

Traditional trade practices have generated nostalgia in the past. The economist Barry Bluestone observed in his 1981 study of the department store that "the folksy, unsophisticated management style of the old-time general store" continued to live on in the imaginations of consumers in spite of vast transformations in distribution. Department stores had long emphasized their putative old country store roots. Celebrating its fortieth anniversary in 1921, the Binghamton firm Hills, McLean & Williams looked back with nostalgia on its "horse and buggy days." The independent retailer celebrated its recently achieved modernity and looked forward to future expansion, but it also played up "the store's traditions." After the rise of chains in the 1920s, department store advertising, anniversary window displays, and promotional materials show individual family firms inventing themselves as small-town community traditions, wrapping themselves in a cloak of nostalgia. Independent retailers infused nostalgia into their "brand" or store identity even as they emphasized their progressiveness. Merchants published romanticized origin narratives about the founding of their business that demonstrated how far they had come over the years. Store displays and promotional literature featured images of a horse and buggy or nineteenth-century fashions to celebrate their roots. By World War II, sentiment for lost modes of distribution, such as peddlers and country stores, had a sort of evolutionary place in the profession's public image, helping to define it as modern and progressive.[2] As the industry consolidated in the postwar period, and as urban renewal and newer forms of retailing destroyed central business districts of cities across the country, control over the nostalgic image of the Main Street department store shifted from the businesses themselves to the public.

Since Bluestone's writing in 1981, the traditional department store came into its own as a nostalgic cultural symbol, taking the place of the general store. Beginning in the 1980s, nostalgia for lost downtown retailers emerged in popular culture, part of a broader feeling about America's industrial past.[3] Shopping malls emerged as a countersymbol for everything that was wrong with American culture. In the 1980s and 1990s, the postindustrial shopping mall became a common setting for a wide range of anti-nostalgic films, providing the backdrop for everything from marital breakups, romance, and teenage angst to crime, time travel, and zombie marauding.[4] In contrast, downtown department stores provided nostalgic settings for movies representing an idealized past of urban community and social space.

The 1983 film that became a holiday tradition for many, *A Christmas Story*, reflected this shift in meaning. The movie featured Higbee's, a well-known Cleveland department store that became part of the Dillard's chain in 1992 before closing ten years later.[5] Structured around the 1940s childhood memories of the narrator, Ralphie, now grown, the movie depicts the downtown department store as part of the vibrant urban setting of his youth. Scenes included elaborate window displays of toys for Christmas, a nighttime parade with the department store Santa, bustling Christmas shopping scenes, and children lining up in the store to tell Santa what they wanted for Christmas. In the film, the department store fit into the nostalgic, though wryly and even bitingly humorous, memories of the narrator's childhood dreams and learning experiences. Tempting window displays

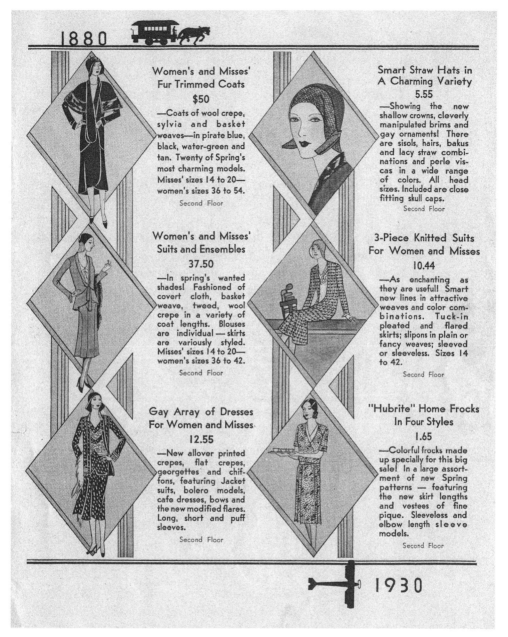

1880

Women's and Misses' Fur Trimmed Coats

$50

—Coats of wool crepe, sylvia and basket weaves—in pirate blue, black, water-green and tan. Twenty of Spring's most charming models. Misses' sizes 14 to 20— women's sizes 36 to 54.

Second Floor

Smart Straw Hats in A Charming Variety

5.55

—Showing the new shallow crowns, cleverly manipulated brims and gay ornaments! There are sisols, hairs, bakus and lacy straw combinations and perle viscas in a wide range of colors. All head sizes. Included are close fitting skull caps.

Second Floor

Women's and Misses' Suits and Ensembles

37.50

—In spring's wanted shades! Fashioned of covert cloth, basket weave, tweed, wool crepe in a variety of coat lengths. Blouses are individual — skirts are variously styled. Misses' sizes 14 to 20— women's sizes 36 to 42.

Second Floor

3-Piece Knitted Suits For Women and Misses

10.44

—As enchanting as they are useful! Smart new lines in attractive weaves and color combinations. Tuck-in pleated and flared skirts; slipons in plain or fancy weaves; sleeved or sleeveless. Sizes 14 to 42.

Second Floor

Gay Array of Dresses For Women and Misses

12.55

—New allover printed crepes, flat crepes, georgettes and chiffons, featuring Jacket suits, bolero models, cafe dresses, bows and the new modified flares. Long, short and puff sleeves.

Second Floor

"Hubrite" Home Frocks In Four Styles

1.65

—Colorful frocks made up specially for this big sale! In a large assortment of new Spring patterns — featuring the new skirt lengths and vestees of fine pique. Sleeveless and elbow length sleeve models.

Second Floor

1930

FIGURE 29. Before their decline, department stores used nostalgic images of the past to signal progress and demonstrate their modernity. Typical anniversary promotions, like this one at the Rhode Island department store Shepard's, paired horse-drawn streetcars with airplanes to signal the store's longevity and place in history. "50th Anniversary Sale." Shepard Stores–Providence, R.I., Box 1, McLean's Department Store Collection, Broome County Historical Society, Local History & Genealogy Center, Binghamton, New York.

encouraged Ralphie's passion for a Red Ryder BB gun, despite his mother's admonitions that he would shoot his eye out. Based on Jean Shepherd's far less nostalgic 1966 book about his mill town childhood, *In God We Trust: All Others Pay Cash*, the 1983 film version of *A Christmas Story* had a different message, coming out as it did in a very different historical context. Shepherd's book featured the department store Goldblatt's, but the child-like amazement of the toy wonders in the window displays and Ralphie and his brother's fear of the large department store Santa Claus were the same. Unlike the book, the later film version worked through the viewers' juxta-position of their own very different lives with the simpler, more innocent period fondly portrayed by the narrator—one reason the film became such a popular Christmas ritual in the United States. Though Higbee's was still in operation in downtown Cleveland at the time of the novel's filming, store closures across the country must have made the Higbee's parade, lavish downtown Christmas window displays, and even the department store Santa seem already more a part of the idealized past, as in the story, than the present. And as the movie passed into classic status over the years since 1983, this was even more the case.[6]

At the same time as idealized representations of downtown department stores became popular in film, store closures were hurting shoppers and affecting communities across the country. Nostalgic newspaper articles doc-umented the personal effect store closures had on ordinary people. King's in Johnson City, Tennessee, was remembered fondly by former employees, who sadly recounted lifelong careers that came to an end when the store was shuttered in 1984.[7] In some cases it meant that old habits of downtown shopping were disrupted. Upon the closure of the Jerry Cox department store in Aiken, South Carolina, in 1992, Covel C. Moore, who had been shopping there for over twenty-five years, stated, "I just don't see why they're going out of business. What am I going to do? Where will I go now?"[8]

As the nameplates of local institutions disappeared from downtown streets and from shopping malls across the country, they emerged more prominently in the memories of older generations and in the dreams of new devotees on the Internet. Store closures coincided with this new medium for capturing or remembering this past. The expansion of the Web in the late 1990s allowed the public a broader voice in constructing the past. Along with many other types of nostalgia sites, department store memory Web sites abounded by the early twenty-first century where fans of department store architecture and historic brands, as well as loyal former customers, shared their memories or appreciation. Former employees of local department stores who lamented their passing used these Web sites to connect with one another. Countless personal pages and fan sites emerged, where people posted photos of lost local institutions, including photographs and postcard images of store buildings, window displays, and promotional events. Nostalgic accounts of former department stores appeared on Web sites devoted to particular locales or heritage. All of these generated numerous comments—posts on childhood memories of Christmas shopping trips and visits to the soda fountain and shopping with mothers or grandmothers. With the rise of YouTube, fans of these old stores uploaded clips of lost department store TV ads, even elevator and escalator rides, generating thousands of hits and many nostalgic comments and references to "oldtimers" remembering.[9] In these posts, the traditional department store represented the vibrant industrial city, perceived to be lost. A YouTube film of Petula Clark singing "Downtown" in 1964 generated posts that waxed nostalgic about urban commercial culture. One included the local department store, L. S. Good & Co., which went bankrupt in 1980:

> Christmas 1964–65. I was ten yrs old and in 5th grade . . . this was a huge hit and it reminded me of the love for SHOPPING we had in WHEELING, WV. . . . a real Mecca for shopping in those days . . . nothing there today . . . the smells of the city . . . Black diesel smoke from the big old busses. Stone & Thomas alley Tea Room Vent, Mr. Peanut and L. S. Good's Air door and the cosmetic counter as you entered. . . . She was such a hit and we all went shopping to this song!!!!![10]

Online expressions of nostalgia for local department stores were often intertwined with social and economic critiques of suburbanization, deindustrialization, or globalization. Sometimes these online sites or individual posts explicitly espoused oppositional politics and local activism. Celebration of the independent retailer and laments over the loss of local department stores fit into a larger activist agenda dedicated to rebuilding urban spaces.[11] The Macy's (Federated) acquisition of Marshall Field's was a focal point for much of this kind of feeling. The subsequent name change of the nineteenth-century firm in fact brought protesters into the city streets. Angry Chicagoans cut up their store credit cards and gathered outside the store chanting the slogan on their placards, "Boycott Macy's/Field's is Chicago!" YouTube clips of Marshall Field's television commercials posted at the time generated many online protests of the merger, including calls to "Boycott Macy's," "Macy's Sucks," and "Death to Macy's."[12]

More typically, nostalgia for the local department store was and is a way for consumers to express cultural dissatisfaction with globalization and the world of Wal-Mart. In many cases, it originated as a middle-class, aesthetic response to changes in the urban landscape—as opposition, for example, to the "malling" of America. It reflects a growing sense that globalization has destroyed the city-specific or regional identities that evolved around these older commercial forms.[13] Some, for example, condemned the rise of "corporate blandness" as their favorite stores were "taken over by Federated." Articles on the closing of local stores invariably contained quotes from former customers comparing the distinctiveness of their favorite stores to the standardized nature of chain store shopping.[14] People lamented the loss of private department store brands, like Marshall Field's Frango Mints, which had become closely connected to the local identity of the Chicago store since they were first introduced in 1929. Local department stores like the Crescent in Spokane in the 1960s were remembered as having a "unique atmosphere" that contemporary retailers lacked. One fan of the Crescent posted in 2010, "Holiday shopping does not have the magic it used to have for me." People also valued the personal services they received at these independent stores, something they believed they would not find anywhere else. Such views, retail experts believed, were behind the decline in department store performance across the 1980s and early 1990s.[15]

These virtual communities and other popular accounts reiterated the seeming inevitability and finality of downtown's decline in the metaphors of death that pervaded their accounts of store closures. Descriptions of store closures typically envisioned the event as the passing of a loved one or likened the last day of the store to a funeral. For example, before the closing of Newman's in Emporia, Kansas, according to the store president, former customers and employees stopped by to "express their sorrow" and "to see it one last time," while others stayed away because they "want[ed] to remember it the way they knew it." Local newspaper accounts of the closure described customers as mourning, with some red-eyed or even crying. The demolition of historic shopping centers like the 1967 Palm Beach Mall elicited similar emotions.[16]

FIGURE 30. The downtown Chicago institution Marshall Field's became "Macy's on State Street" in 2005 after the biggest merger in department store history. Author's collection.

Even the Federal Trade Commission framed the massive merger of Federated and May in terms of inevitable loss or death. The commission defended its decision not to take action against the unpopular transaction, stating that it recognized "that many individual consumers mourn the gradual disappearance of individual department stores in their hometowns. . . . These changes, however, have been ongoing for many years." This seemingly innocuous metaphor of death allowed retailers, consumers, and government regulators to extract this economic process from its particular history. In effect, it popularized a critique of "bigness" that actually naturalized consolidation and justified its negative outcomes. In the case of the Federal Trade Commission, the metaphor of death papered over a highly politicized antitrust decision that ruled in favor of monopoly. We can be sad about the changes to our hometowns, the commission tells us, but that is just the way things are; we don't like death, but there is nothing we can or should do about it, except mourn. As one fan of the defunct Cleveland department store memorialized in *A Christmas Story* posted on an Internet venue, "I know we have to move into the future, but sometimes the past is just a bit more comforting. How can shopping at Walmart ever compare to the magnificence of stepping into Higbee's and its sea of red carpet and crystal chandelier grandeur."[17]

While such nostalgia is understandable and even moving, it fails to note that while death is inevitable and natural, store closures are not. Concentration in the industry and the subsequent loss of local nameplates were enabled by particular political, social, and economic contexts that changed over time. These were historical events and were influenced by historical actors, including consumers, department store executives and their trade associations, and federal, state and local policies. The industry's pursuit of bigness, consumers' preference for low prices and mass consumption in the suburbs, and government policies that favored chains, automobility, shopping centers, and mass discounters, all led to the diminishment of both local institutions and the local identity of their communities. All of these factors were necessary, though not sufficient, conditions on their own. Together, they contributed to the rise of a Wal-Mart world.

While some Internet commentators see the underlying economic and political forces at work behind the demise of local retailing, for the most part their nostalgia for the lost department store has a conservative edge, evident in its tendency to uphold the status quo rather than offer solutions. Predominantly a cultural critique rejecting the aesthetics of the new commercial environment, nostalgia is not an avenue of transformation. It offers no way out of the challenges facing central business districts today.

In recent years, solutions to the widespread decline of the local have emerged out of grassroots organizations and their practical efforts. Main Street and community groups across the country have taken some responsibility, running "buy local" campaigns and promoting local sourcing of food and other products. Cooperatives have sprung up—one small town in the Adirondacks even created its own community department store in an attempt to fend off a proposed Wal-Mart. Dead shopping malls have been repurposed, turned into medical centers, gyms, or even schools. Many, however, see no solution to our discount world and simply accept it. In their view, the death of the downtown department store was inevitable, rather than the product of a complex interaction between business, the state, and consumers in a neoliberal context. As one city official in upstate New York put it, "I think most people are nostalgic about what Bresee's [department store] was. But I think most people are realistic and know that it's an era that has passed." On the occasion of a new county museum exhibit in Lehigh, Pennsylvania, "local nostalgia fans" are told humorously to "unite! Hess's makes return." As the newspaper article on the exhibit noted, the area's favorite landmark department store was "back, if only in pictures, memorabilia."

Today, the nostalgic image of the local department store remains locked in a vague critique of the changes brought about by globalization and corporate culture, rather than as a part of direct action. Such accounts see the decline of the department store as a natural process, part of progress, rather than as deeply connected to historical developments such as federal policies that promoted suburbanization and dependence on the automobile, rules and regulations that governed corporate practice, and consumers' own demand for low prices—at any cost.[18]

NOTES

The following abbreviations of frequently used material appear in the notes.

MANUSCRIPT COLLECTIONS

BAC   B. Altman Collection, New-York Historical Society, New York, NY

BC   Bresee's Department Store, Oneonta, New York, Private Collection of Marc Bresee, Oneonta, NY

BKP   Bernard Katz Papers, Manuscripts and Archives Division, New York Public Library, New York, NY

FBMC   Falk-Bloch Mercantile Co., Idaho State History Society Library and Archives, Boise, ID

FC   Foley's Department Store Records, 1845–2006, University of Houston Libraries, Houston, TX

HC   Higbee Collection, Baker Library, Harvard Business School, Boston, MA

MDSC   McLean's Department Store Collection, Broome County Library, Binghamton, NY

OC   Outlet Company Records, Rhode Island Historical Society, Manuscripts Division, Providence, RI

PC   Poliakoff Collection, South Caroliniana Library, Columbia, SC

RC   Resseguie Collection, Baker Library, Harvard Business School, Boston, MA

RGC   Rudge & Guenzel Collection, Nebraska State Historical Society, Lincoln, NE

RRC   Richard H. Rich Collection, Manuscript, Archives, and Rare Book Library, Emory University, Atlanta, GA

SCC   Strawbridge & Clothier Collection, Hagley Museum & Library, Wilmington, DE

ZDSC   Zahn Department Store Collection, Archives and Area Research Center, Library/Learning Center, University of Wisconsin–Parkside, Kenosha, WI

JOURNALS AND NEWSPAPERS

ASF   *Advertising & Selling Fortnightly*

DGE   *Dry Goods Economist*

DSE   *Department Store Economist*

JOM   *Journal of Marketing*

JOR   *Journal of Retailing*
NYT   *New York Times*

INTRODUCTION

1. "Foley's Due to Open New Houston Store," *NYT* (September 11, 1947); photo of 1947 crowd in "Macy's Will Soon Make Final Sale in Downtown Building," *Houston Chronicle* (January 3, 2013), http://www.chron.com/business/real-estate/article/Macy-s-to-make -final-sale-in-downtown-building-4166141.php; "Macy's Building Comes Down with a Bang," *Houston Chronicle* (September 22, 2013), http://www.chron.com/default/article/ Macy-s-building-comes-down-with-a-bang-4834076.php ; "Shoppers Who Lunched," *NYT* (February 7, 2013).

2. Susan Porter Benson may have been the first historian to talk about departments stores as palaces of consumption, meaning "the world of bourgeois gentility and lavish service." Benson, *Counter Cultures: Saleswomen, Managers and Customers in American Department Stores, 1890–1940* (Urbana: University of Illinois Press, 1988), 81. See also William Leach, *Land of Desire: Merchants, Power, and the Rise of a New American Culture* (New York: Pantheon Books, 1993); Robert Hendrickson, *The Grand Emporiums: The Illustrated History of America's Great Department Stores* (New York: Stein and Day, 1979), 428; "Shoppers Who Lunched," "all-day affair" quote; "Foley's and Macy's: A Downtown Houston Timeline," *Houston Chronicle* (January 3, 2013), 1, http://www.chron.com/busi ness/article/Foley-s-and-Macy-s-A-downtown-Houston-timeline-4166213.php; "Deep in the Heart of Houston," *NYT* (February 27, 2000); Finding Aid, FC, University of Houston Libraries, Houston, TX; The terms *shopping center* and *mall* are used interchangeably now, but Richard Longstreth provides a useful clarification: "Strictly speaking a shopping mall is a shopping center whose stores are primarily oriented to one or more pedestrian walkways instead of the parking lot or street; that is, a complex with an internalized more than an externalized configuration." Longstreth, *City Center to Regional Mall: Architecture, the Automobile, and Retailing in Los Angeles, 1920–1950* (Cambridge, Mass.: MIT Press, 1997), 170.

3. Richard Longstreth, *The American Department Store Transformed, 1920–1960* (New Haven: Yale University Press, 2010), 51.

4. Alison Isenberg, *Downtown America: A History of the Place and the People Who Made It* (Chicago: University of Chicago Press, 2004), 8–9. Isenberg argues that Main Street was a cultural as well as an economic artifact, one that has continually been remade through the contests of different historical actors. She also asserts that "decline itself has multiple meanings, depending on one's perspective" and that the vacant stores of recent decades "symbolized not death and decline but another stage in the ongoing struggle to define urban commercial values amid proclamations of decline."

5. "What's Next for Downtown?" *CultureMap Houston* (January 4, 2013) http://hous ton.culturemap.com/newsdetail/01-03-13-23-44-whats-next-for-downtown-houston-offi cials-hope-for-a-smaller-macys-after-iconic-building-is-torn-down/; Longstreth, *The American Department Store Transformed*, 51–53; Benson, *Counter Cultures*, 8.

6. On Lazarus's commitment to cities, see Dero A. Saunders, "Department Stores: Race for the Suburbs," *Fortune* (December 1951), 173; "Federated Department Stores, Inc. History," *Funding Universe*, http://www.fundinguniverse.com/company-histories/fede

rated-department-stores-inc-history/ (accessed February 8, 2013); Longstreth, *The American Department Store Transformed*, 51; "Let's Talk About Foley's," *Houston Architecture Info* (April 30, 2009), http://www.houstonarchitecture.com/haif/topic/20187-lets-talk-about-foleys/page-5; "RIP Foley's Department Store," *Off the Kuff* (July 29, 2005), http://www.offthekuff.com/mt/archives/005887.html; *Department Store Museum* (blog), http://departmentstoremuseum.blogspot.com/2010/05/foley-brothers-dry-goods-co-houston.html (accessed February 9, 2013); Heritage Society at Sam Houston Park, http://www.heritagesociety.org/calendar.html (accessed February 8, 2013), "more than a department store" quote.

7. Isenberg, *Downtown America*, 271–72, 283; "Gallery at Market East: Philadelphia, PA," Deadmalls.com (January 9, 2011), http://deadmalls.com/malls/gallery_at_market_east.html.

8. U.S. Census Bureau, *2011 E-Stats* (May 23, 2013) http://www.census.gov//econ/estats/2011/2011reportfinal.pdf; *U.S. Census Bureau News* (May 15, 2014), Table 1: Estimated Quarterly U.S. Retail Sales Total and E-Commerce, http://www.census.gov/retail/mrts/www/data/pdf/ec_current.pdf; "Loss of Shoppers Drives Federated/May Merger," *Forbes* (January 20, 2005) http://www.forbes.com/2005/01/20/cx_mt_0120federatedmay.html; Robert Spector, *Category Killers: The Retail Revolution and Its Impact on Consumer Culture* (Boston: Harvard Business School Press, 2005), 110–11.

9. "Loss of Shoppers Drives Federated/May Merger."

10. Earle Dunford and George Bryson, *Under the Clock: The Story of Miller & Rhoads* (Charleston, S.C.: History Press, 2008), 97, 100; Robert M. Grippo, *Macy's: The Store, the Star, the Story* (Garden City Park, NY: Square One, 2009). On the wheel of retailing, see Stanley C. Hollander and Glen S. Omura, "Chain Store Developments and Their Political, Strategic, and Social Interdependencies," *JOR* 65 (Fall 1989), 316; Stanley C. Hollander, "The Wheel of Retailing," *JOM* 25 (July 1960), 37–42; Homer H. Johnson and Sung Min Kim, "When Strategy Pales: Lessons from the Department Store Industry," *Business Horizons* 52, no. 6 (2009), 587.

11. A good summary of various approaches is Gareth Shaw, "The Study of Retail Development," in *The Evolution of Retail Systems, c. 1800–1914*, ed. John Benson and Gareth Shaw (Leicester: Leicester University Press, 1992). On the role of Wanamaker's and Marshall Field's department stores in the larger transformation of America into a consumer society, see Leach, *Land of Desire*. On Marshall Field's, see Nancy F. Koehn, *Brand New: How Entrepreneurs Earned Consumers' Trust from Wedgwood to Dell* (Boston: Harvard Business School Press, 2001). On department stores as sites of consumption and women's labor, see the seminal work of Susan Porter Benson, *Counter Cultures*. On New York City luxury and down-market department stores and the labor movement, see Daniel J. Opler, *For All White-Collar Workers: The Possibilities of Radicalism in New York City's Department Store Unions, 1934–1953* (Columbus: Ohio State University Press, 2007).

12. Alan Trachtenberg, *The Incorporation of America: Culture and Society in the Gilded Age* (New York: Hill and Wang, 1982), 131; Leach, *Land of Desire*; Michael B. Miller, *The Bon Marché: Bourgeois Culture and the Department Store, 1869–1920* (Princeton: Princeton University Press, 1981); David Monod, *Store Wars: Shopkeepers and the Culture of Mass Marketing, 1890–1939* (Toronto: University of Toronto Press, 1996); Geoffrey Crossick and Serge Jaumain, eds., *Cathedrals of Consumption: The European Department Store, 1850–1939* (Aldershot, UK: Ashgate, 1999); Longstreth, *City Center to Regional Mall*; Ted Ownby,

American Dreams in Mississippi: Consumers, Poverty, and Culture, 1830–1998 (Chapel Hill: University of North Carolina Press, 1999), chapter 4; Victoria Buenger and Walter L. Buenger, *Texas Merchant: Marvin Leonard and Fort Worth* (College Station: Texas A&M University Press, 1998); Mark L. Gardner, "Rich's of Atlanta: Does a Change of Ownership Affect Corporate Culture?" *Essays in Economic and Business History* 11 (1993), 272–82. Western and southwestern studies are also rare: see Henry C. Klassen, "T. C. Power & Bro.: The Rise of a Small Western Department Store, 1870–1902," *Business History Review* 66, no. 4 (1992), 671–722. Similarly, see June Webb-Vignery, *Jacome's Department Store: Business and Culture in Tucson, Arizona, 1896–1980* (New York: Garland, 1989); Stephanie Dyer, "Markets in the Meadows: Department Stores and Shopping Centers in the Decentralization of Philadelphia, 1920–1980," Ph.D. diss., University of Pennsylvania, 2000; M. Jeffrey Hardwick, *Mall Maker: Victor Gruen, Architect of an American Dream* (Philadelphia: University of Pennsylvania Press, 2004); Lizabeth Cohen, "From Town Center to Shopping Center: The Reconfiguration of Community Marketplaces in Postwar America," *American Historical Review* 101 (October 1996), 1050–81.

13. Important recent historical work by Sarah Elvins on regionalism and retailing in western New York and by Richard Longstreth on architectural change in major department stores in the nation's sixty largest cities has broadened the scope of department store scholarship to a considerable degree. See Sarah Elvins, *Sales and Celebrations: Retailing and Regional Identity in Western New York State, 1920–1940* (Athens: Ohio University Press, 2004); Longstreth, *The American Department Store Transformed.*

14. On small-town department stores, see Vicki Howard, "'The Biggest Small-Town Store in America': Independent Retailers and the Rise of Consumer Culture," *Enterprise & Society* 9, no. 3 (2008), 457–86. On retail revolutions, see Nelson Lichtenstein, *The Retail Revolution: How Wal-Mart Created a Brave New World of Business* (New York: Metropolitan Books, 2009); Barry Bluestone, Patricia Hanna, Sarah Kuhn, and Laura Moore, *The Retail Revolution: Market Transformation, Investment, and Labor in the Modern Department Store* (Boston: Auburn House, 1981); Sandra Stringer Vance and Roy Vernon Scott, *Wal-Mart: A History of Sam Walton's Retail Phenomenon* (New York: Twayne Publishers, 1994), 18; Meg Jacobs, *Pocketbook Politics: Economic Citizenship in Twentieth-Century America* (Princeton: Princeton University Press, 2005), 18; Leonard Nakamura, "The Measurement of Retail Output and the Retail Revolution," *Canadian Journal of Economics / Revue Canadienne d'Economique* 32 (April 1999), 408.

15. Joyce Appleby, *The Relentless Revolution: A History of Capitalism* (New York: W. W. Norton, 2010), 222, 306. Numerous economic studies document the negative impact of Wal-Mart on local businesses. For example, see Carlena Cochi Ficano, "Business Churn and the Retail Giant: Establishment Birth and Death from Wal-Mart Entry," *Social Science Quarterly* 94 (March 2013), 263–91. Also see several studies by economist Kenneth E. Stone; for example, "Competing with the Discount Mass Merchandisers" (Iowa State University, 1995); Stone, Georgeanne Artz, and Albert Myles, "The Economic Impact of Wal-Mart Supercenters on Existing Businesses in Mississippi" (Iowa State University, 2002). For the counterargument that there exists a mutually beneficial relationship between different types or sizes of stores, see Chip E. Miller, James Reardon, and Denny E. McCorkle, "The Effects of Competition on Retail Structure: An Examination of Intratype, Intertype, and Intercategory Competition," *Journal of Marketing* 63 (August 1999), 107–20.

16. Sam Walton with John Huey, *Sam Walton, Made in America: My Story* (New York: Doubleday, 1992), 228. Interestingly, Walton's words echo those of merchants protesting an anti–department store law in Missouri in 1899, quoted in chapter 2. See "The Department Store: A Protest against the Hostile Law Enacted in Missouri," *DGE* (September 2, 1899), 5; news clipping, Anti–Department Store Legislation, Case 1, RC.

17. See David Harvey, *A Brief History of Neoliberalism* (New York: Oxford University Press, 2005), quotes 2, 3, 16–17, 34–35; "Family Fortune: The Twentieth Richest Families in America" (November 26, 2013), http://www.therichest.com/rich-list/nation/the-20-richest -families-in-america/ 20. On the vast increase in wealth inequality during this period, see Thomas Piketty, *Capital in the Twenty-First Century* (Cambridge, Mass.: Belknap Press of Harvard University Press, 2014).

CHAPTER 1. THE PALACE OF CONSUMPTION

1. Merchandising was undergoing expansion, concentration, and incorporation as were other areas of the late nineteenth-century economy. Mass retailers like department stores challenged single-line merchants who specialized in one type of good, like jewelry. Leach, *Land of Desire*, 19. Alfred D. Chandler, Jr., *The Visible Hand: The Managerial Revolution in American Business* (Cambridge, Mass.: Harvard University Press, 1977), 237–38.

2. Raymond A. Mohl, *The New City: Urban American in the Industrial Age, 1860–1920* (Arlington Heights, Ill.: Harlan Davidson, 1985), 40–44. Department store founders were prominent philanthropists. For example, see the Lincoln and Therese Filene Foundation, http://www.filenefoundation.org/lincoln-therese/, or the Altman Foundation, http://www .altmanfoundation.org/about/history/index.

3. "Thinks Letters Beat Newspaper Advertisements," *Printers' Ink* 64 (September 9, 1908), 29.

4. Chandler, *The Visible Hand*, 224–29; Susan Strasser, *Satisfaction Guaranteed: The Making of the American Mass Market* (Washington, D.C.: Smithsonian Institution Press, 1989), 65.

5. Chandler, *The Visible Hand*, 215–16; Harry E. Resseguie, "Alexander Turney Stewart and the Development of the Department Store, 1823–1876," *Business History Review* 39 (Autumn 1965), 318; Strasser, *Satisfaction Guaranteed*, 58–59, 80–82, 204. The grocery trade was a different story. See Susan V. Spellman, "Trust Brokers: Traveling Grocery Salesmen and Confidence in Nineteenth-Century Trade," *Enterprise & Society* 13 (June 2012): 277–78.

6. On A. T. Stewart, see Strasser, *Satisfaction Guaranteed*, 206–7; John Ferry, *A History of the Department Store* (New York: Macmillan, 1960), 41–45; Chandler, *The Visible Hand*, 215; Christopher Gray, "The A. T. Stewart Department Store: A City Plan to Revitalize the 1846 'Marble Palace,'" *NYT* (March 20, 1994).

7. Resseguie, "Alexander Turney Stewart," 303–4, 312, 317; Strasser, *Satisfaction Guaranteed*, 204–6.

8. Strasser, *Satisfaction Guaranteed*, 204–6; Porter Benson, *Counter Cultures*, 15–16; Wayland A. Tonning, "Department Stores in Down State Illinois, 1889–1943," *Business History Review* 29 (December 1955): 343.

9. Resseguie, "Alexander Turney Stewart," 303, 317, 322; Gray, "The A. T. Stewart Department Store"; Jan Whitaker, *Service and Style: How the American Department Store Fashioned the Middle Class* (New York: St. Martin's Press, 2006), 55.

10. Regina Blaszczyk, *American Consumer Society, 1865–2005: From Hearth to HDTV* (Wheeling, Ill.: Harlan Davidson, 2009), 75–76; Porter Benson, *Counter Cultures*, 17–18; Katherine C. Grier, *Culture and Comfort: Parlor-Making and Middle-Class Identity, 1850–1930* (Washington, D.C.: Smithsonian Institution Press, 1988), 161; Sarah A. Gordon, *Make It Yourself: Home Sewing, Gender, and Culture, 1890–1930* (New York: Columbia University Press, 2006, Gutenberg-e), 7; Wendy Gamber, *The Female Economy: The Millinery and Dressmaking Trades,1860–1930* (Urbana: University of Illinois Press, 1997), 194.

11. "Christmas Crazy Town," *NYT* (December 23, 1894), "bread-winning" quote, 2; Porter Benson, *Counter Cultures*, "Adamless Eden" quote, 76, 79, and chapter 3; "A Great Firm Fails," *NYT* (August 27, 1896), "women's club" quote, 1, 6.

12. During the Civil War, Stewart's sales were $36 million. Resseguie, "Alexander Turney Stewart," 314, 306; "Some Hit and Miss Chat: Stray Bits of Gossip from an Observer's Note Book. Stories of A. T. Stewart and the Oldtime Dry Goods Business Recalled by the Death of H. B. Claflin," *NYT* (November 29, 1885); Harry A. Resseguie, "The Decline and Fall of the Commercial Empire of A. T. Stewart," *Business History Review* 36, no. 3 (1962): 255; Jonathan J. Bean, *Beyond the Broker State: Federal Policies toward Small Business, 1936–1961* (Chapel Hill: University of North Carolina Press, 1996), "merchant" quote, 22; Ferry, *History of the Department Store*, 44; Chandler, *The Visible Hand*, 218.

13. "Some Hit and Miss Chat," "free from all airs" quote; "Associated Merchants' Company Organized," *NYT* (April 10, 1901), 2; Hollander and Omura, "Chain Store Developments," 304; "Kings County Supervisors—Meeting of the Law Committee—Investigation of the Jail Swindle," *NYT* (December 13, 1870); "Law Reports: The Case of H. B. Claflin & Co. Motion to Quash the Indictments against Them," *NYT* (October 21, 1875).

14. Leach, *Land of Desire*, 24–26; Hollander and Omura, "Chain Store Developments," 304; Longstreth, *The American Department Store Transformed*, 11; "Inhaled Too Much Chloroform," *NYT* (May 1, 1889), 10.

15. Resseguie, "Decline and Fall of the Commercial Empire," 256–61, 267, 272–74, 277, 283; "Hilton, Hughes & Co.," *NYT* (December 2, 1894), 1; Stewart's remains were stolen in 1878 and held for $200,000 ransom. His widow, Cornelia Stewart, did not comply with the ransom demands on advice of Hilton. In 1881, she was able to obtain bones that were allegedly her husband's, but their identity remains controversial. The grave robbers were never caught. See J. North Conway, *Bag of Bones: The Sensational Grave Robbery of the Merchant Prince of Manhattan* (Guilford, Conn.: Glove Pequot Press, 2012), xiii–xiv.

16. Resseguie, "Alexander Turney Stewart," 303, 310, 322. Resseguie makes a convincing case for Stewart's importance as a transitional firm. Popularly, though, Stewart's has been called the first department store. See Gray, "The A. T. Stewart Department Store."

17. Resseguie, "Decline and Fall of the Commercial Empire," 284.

18. *A Visit to Hilton, Hughes & Co., Broadway, New York: Leaves from an Artist's Sketch Book* (New York: Giles Company, lith., ca. 1895), Baker Library, Harvard Business School; Resseguie, "Alexander Turney Stewart," 311; "Bids Shoppers Welcome," *NYT* (November 17, 1896), 9; "Wanamaker Buys a Store," *NYT* (September 29, 1896), 9; "An Opening of Much Interest," *NYT* (October 7, 1894), "inconveniently crowded" quote, 16.

19. *A Visit to Hilton, Hughes & Co.*; "An Opening of Much Interest," "commodious" quote, 16; Resseguie, "Alexander Turney Stewart," 321.

20. Resseguie, "Decline and Fall of the Commercial Empire," 284; "Of Value to Advertisers," *NYT* (October 2, 1895), "expert" quote, 5; "Manly M. Gillam Dies at 79 Years," *NYT* (March 24, 1925), 23; J. Russell Doubman and John R. Whitaker, *The Organization and Operation of Department Stores* (New York: John Wiley & Sons, 1927),43; Leach cites Manly Gillam as a nationally known copywriter who worked for Wanamaker's at the turn of the century, though Gillam's obituary puts his work there earlier and names his title as advertising manager, *Land of Desire*, 43–45, 51; "Working on Pay Rolls," *NYT* (August 28, 1896), 16; Gillam went on to become general manager at Hilton, Hughes & Co. in March 1896 and in that capacity gave the press announcement of the firm's failure, which he attributed to the stringency of the money market and to the recent depression; "Big New York Failure," *NYT* (August 27, 1896), 5; "The Financial Markets," *NYT* (August 27, 1896), 12.

21. On the Wanamaker style, see Doubman and Whitaker, *The Organization and Operation of Department Stores*, 43–44; "Where Shoppers May Be Happy," *NYT* (October 8, 1893), "best stores," "American kings," and "suitable for the women" quotes, 12; "An Opening of Much Interest," *NYT* (October 7, 1894), 16.

22. "Hilton, Hughes & Co." ads, *NYT* (December 12, 1892), 8; (May 18, 1893), 8; (February 5, 1893), 9. "Almost Like Monday," 6; "The Great Attractions of Our Magnificent Store," *NYT* (December 2, 1894), 17. For additional examples of this new advertising style, see *NYT* (November 11, 1894), 28; (March 25, 1895), 4.

23. "An Opening of Much Interest," "sidewalk" quote, 16; "Big New York Failure," 5; Resseguie, "The Decline and Fall of the Commercial Empire," 286. In spite of such appeals and all efforts by Manly Gillam, Hilton, Hughes & Co. went under and its building and inventory were bought up by John Wanamaker, who reopened the store in November 1896, advertising it as "John Wanamaker. Formerly A. T. Stewart & Co." See Leach, *Land of Desire*, for more in-depth discussion of the consumerist aspects of late nineteenth-century department store innovation.

24. On the path from hardware to department store, see Vicki Howard, "The Rise and Fall of Rudge & Guenzel: From Independent Retailer to Department Store Chain," *Nebraska History* 89 (Fall 2008): 102–19; Leach, *Land of Desire*, 126; Some of these future department store merchants gained experience as traveling salesmen, like Louis Kirstein, who worked for Filene's. Kirstein sold men's shirts and optical supplies. Benjamin M. Selekman, "Louis Edward Kirstein," *American Jewish Yearbook* (1943–44): 37–38, http://www.ajcarchives.org/AJC_DATA/Files/1943_1944_3_SpecialArticles.pdf; Ferry, *History of the Department Store*, 111; "Risen from the Ranks: Pen Portraits of Successful Merchants," *DGE* (June 5, 1926), 11; "Honoring Louis Pizitz," *DSE* (September 1943), 58.

25. Howard, "The Biggest Small-Town Store in America," 457–86; "From Clothing Shop to Department Store," *DGE* (April 3, 1915), 293. Most department stores got their start as dry goods emporia. For examples of this path, see Tonning, "Department Stores in Down State Illinois," 335, 339; Chandler, *The Visible Hand*, 225–26; Lloyd Wendt and Herman Kogan, *Give the Lady What She Wants! The Story of Marshall Field and Company* (Chicago: Rand McNally, 1952), 312, 322–24. Field's maintained its wholesale operations long after other department stores had got out of the business, eliminating its historic sector in 1935. Koehn, *Brand New*, 129.

26. This popular account labels Field's achievement a "revolution," however. Wendt and Kogan, *Give the Lady What She Wants!* 203; Koehn, *Brand New*, 107, 110, 117, 119–21. When Marshall Field died in 1906, he left a fortune of $100 million, the equivalent of about $1.9 billion in 2001 (Koehn, *Brand New*, 129); Porter Benson, *Counter Cultures*, 16, chapter 3.

27. Porter Benson, *Counter Cultures*, 13, 16; Koehn, *Brand New*, 116, 123–24, 129; Wendt and Kogan, *Give the Lady What She Wants!* "ad" quote, 204, "specially attractive" quote, 204.

28. Porter Benson, *Counter Cultures*, 18–19, "iron" quote, 39; John Henry Hepp IV, *The Middle-Class City: Transforming Space and Time in Philadelphia, 1876–1926* (Philadelphia: University of Pennsylvania Press, 2003), chapter 6; Koehn, *Brand New*, 18–19, 127, 203, 218–19; Hrant Pasdermadjian, *The Department Store: Its Origin, Evolution and Economics* (London: Newman Books, 1954), 25; Wendt and Kogan, *Give the Lady What She Wants!* 203, "exposition" quote, 218, 219.

29. "A Story of Forty Years," n.p., pamphlet, Hills McLean & Williams, Inc., MDSC; Doubman and Whitaker, *The Organization and Operation of Department Stores*, ad, 158, 211; "Electric Delivery Is the Coming Vogue," *DGE* (January 23, 1915), 6; "Be Posted on What Your Competitors Are Doing," *DGE* (January 23, 1915), 5; "This May Happen Any Day to Your Horses," *DGE* (August 24, 1912), "horse-flesh" quote, 10; Elvins, *Sales and Celebrations*, 19, 25; Leach, *Land of Desire*, 123, 281; Edward F. Gerish, *The Retailer and the Consumer in New England* (Washington, D.C.: Domestic Commerce Division, United States Department of Commerce, Bureau of Foreign and Domestic Commerce, 1928), 10–11, 20, in *Prosperity and Thrift: The Coolidge Era and the Consumer Economy, 1921–1929*, Library of Congress http://memory.loc.gov/ammem/coolhtml/coolhome.html.

30. Koehn, *Brand New*, 123; "Bernheimer's Striking Advertising Methods," *Printers' Ink* 65 (December 2, 1908), 22, "undignified" quote, 22–24; Rachel Bowlby, *Carried Away: The Invention of Modern Shopping* (New York: Columbia University Press, 2000), 7–8; Benson, *Counter Cultures*, 76–77.

31. Ownby, *American Dreams in Mississippi*, 94; Doubman and Whitaker, *The Organization and Operation of Department Stores*, 19; Tonning, "Department Stores in Down State Illinois," 336; "Improving the Service," *DGE* (August 24, 1912), 19; On the Lincoln, Nebraska, stores, see Howard, "Rise and Fall of Rudge & Guenzel," 106; *The 1985 Directory of Department Stores* (n.p.: Business Guides, Inc., 1984), 336; Interview, Walter Dannenberg, March 9, 2004, transcript, William Breman Jewish Heritage Museum, Jewish Oral History Project of Atlanta; "A Story of Forty Years," "McLean's" quote, MDSC.

32. "Negro Actors Are Shut Out," *Columbia (SC) State* (December 24, 1903), 9; John M. Matthews, "Black Newspapermen and the Black Community in Georgia, 1890–1930," *Georgia Historical Quarterly* 68 (Fall 1984): 375.

33. The ad for Samuel W. Trice Department Store appears in D. A. Bethea, *Colored People's Blue Book and Business Directory of Chicago, Ill.* (Chicago: Celerity Printing Co., 1905), 95, https://archive.org/details/coloredpeoplesbl1905beth; "Negro Department Stores-Colored Residents of Newark, N.J. Subscribe to the Scheme," *NYT* (August 12, 1903), 2. "Negro Department Store in Gotham," *Pawtucket Times* (November 28, 1906), 1. One was proposed in Chicago by the black leader Rev. J. M. Townsend. See "A Negro Department Store," *Boston Daily Advertiser* (August 17, 1900), 4; "Negro Department

Store: Remarkable Scheme Suggested by a Chicago Man," *Columbus (GA) Ledger* (April 30, 1903), 7. For a discussion of race businesses as they had developed by the 1920s in Chicago, see Lizabeth Cohen, *Making a New Deal: Industrial Workers in Chicago, 1919–1939* (New York: Cambridge University Press, 2008), 149–52.

34. Elsa Barkley Brown, "Womanist Consciousness: Maggie Lena Walker and the Independent Order of Saint Luke," *Signs* 14 (Spring 1989): 624–26.

35. Lewis Atherton, *Main Street on the Middle Border* (Bloomington: Indiana University Press, 1954), 44–47; see also Thomas D. Clark, *Pills, Petticoats and Plows: The Southern Country Store* (Norman: University of Oklahoma Press, 1964).

36. Under $100,000 qualified in 1929 but not by 1933. U.S. Department of Commerce, *Census of American Business: 1933, Retail Distribution*, vol. 1, *United States Summary: 1933 and Comparisons with 1929* (Washington, D.C.: U.S. Government Printing Office, May 1935), 15, 35, 62.

37. This was the case for Monnig's Dry Goods Company (1890) in Fort Worth, Texas, which did not change its name until the 1940s. Victoria Buenger and Walter L. Buenger, *Texas Merchant: Marvin Leonard and Fort Worth* (College Station: Texas A&M Press, 1998), 54; "Stewart's Department Store Celebrates 125 Years," *Oneonta Daily Star* (August 22, 2008); "George Stewart," obituary, *Oneonta Daily Star* (October 21, 2011).

38. "4 Boast 20 Years Service at Bresee's," *Oneonta Star* (January 9, 1919), 6. Run by one man, general stores typically had little capital for growth. But when proprietors like Frank Bresee incorporated their business, they gained the resources for expansion, becoming more like their big-city cousins. The Oneonta department store incorporated in 1908 with authorized stock set at $35,000 and by 1919 had 178 people on its regular payroll. Howard, "Biggest Small-Town Store in America," 457–86; U.S. Department of Commerce, *Census of American Business: 1933, Retail Distribution*, vol. 1, *United States Summary: 1933 and Comparisons with 1929*, 1, 40; "Washington Alert," *DSE* (June 1950), 64. The tradition of the general store hung on in rural areas as late as the postwar era, though some felt it lingered for "mostly for sentimental reasons." "Big Business Comes to Small Towns," clipping, circa 1945, Small City Trends folder, case 13, RC.

39. Ed. D. Hirshey entry, circa 1899, Black ledger, pp. 107, 112–13, Roy Adams entry, 1904–5, Black ledger, p. 151, BC; Strasser, *Satisfaction Guaranteed*, 253–54; "Sensational Sacrifice of the Fair Store Stock," November, 6, 1913, handbill in the possession of the author; Webb-Vignery, *Jacome's Department Store*, 41. T. C. Power & Brothers in Montana provides another example of a department store engaging in barter exchanges. Klassen, "T. C. Power & Bro.," 680.

40. Klassen, "T. C. Power & Bro.," 675; "The Power Behind the Throne CASH," *The Star* (June 17, 1905), 2; "The Power of Cash," *The Star* (June 20, 1905), 2; "Cash and Independence," *The Star* (June 22, 1905), 2; "Think It Over," *The Star* (December 2, 1905), 2; "Forward," *The Star* (December 5, 1905), 2.

CHAPTER 2. CREATING AN INDUSTRY

1. Bean, *Beyond the Broker State*, 18–19; Lendol Calder, *Financing the American Dream: A Cultural History of Consumer Credit* (Princeton: Princeton University Press, 1999), 170; Juliet E. K. Walker, *The History of Black Business in America: Capitalism, Race, and Entrepreneurship*, 2nd ed. (Chapel Hill: University of North Carolina Press, 2009), 271; Blaszczyk, *American Consumer Society*, 61; Gamber, *The Female Economy*, 37.

2. Leach, *Land of Desire*, 19, 26–32. Chandler, *The Visible Hand*, 209–33, 237–38; Jacobs, *Pocketbook Politics*, 15–16.

3. On retail wars, see Leach, *Land of Desire*, 27; Monod, *Store Wars*; Jacobs, *Pocketbook Politics*, 29; Trachtenberg, *The Incorporation of America*, 39.

4. Chandler, *The Visible Hand*, 229.

5. Leach, *Land of Desire*, 27–29; Wendt and Kogan, *Give the Lady What She Wants!* 217, 245–46; Monod, *Store Wars*, 27; Nancy F. Koehn, *Brand New: How Entrepreneurs Earned Consumers' Trust from Wedgwood to Dell* (Boston: Harvard Business School Press, 2001), 129.

6. Leach, *Land of Desire*, grocers' quotes, 27; Jerome Gilbert Meyers, "Reactions of the Independent Retailer to the Evolution and Development of the Department Store, the Mail Order House, and the Discount Operations" (MBA thesis, Ohio State University, 1962), 14; Bean, *Beyond the Broker State*, 22.

7. George Sweet, *The Whitesmiths of Taunton: A History of Reed & Barton, 1824–1943* (Cambridge, Mass.: Harvard University Press, 1943), 210–12.

8. "Chase of the Octopus," *DGE*, circa 1900, p. 14. "The Big Store War," *DGE* (April 3, 1897), "country stores" quote, 7, news clippings, Anti–Department Store Legislation, Case 1, RC; "Occupation Tax Bill," *Saint Paul Globe* (March 17, 1897), 5.

9. "The Department Store: A Protest against the Hostile Law Enacted in Missouri," *DGE* (September 2, 1899), 5, news clipping, Anti–Department Store Legislation, Case 1, RC.

10. "Review Retail Methods," *DGE* (January 25, 1913), "crusade" and "cross roads" quote, 39.

11. "A Changed Order in Merchandising," *NYT* (October 22, 1916), "crossroads" quotes, E8.

12. Strasser, *Satisfaction Guaranteed*, 204; Boris Emmet and John E. Jeuck, *Catalogues and Counters: A History of Sears, Roebuck and Company* (Chicago: University of Chicago Press, 1950), 204, 187; Minute Book, Rudge & Guenzel Co., Board of Directors, January 22, 1915, p. 96, RGC; Bean, *Beyond the Broker State*, "colossus" quote, 22, 23; "Books & Stationery," *DGE* (June 8, 1901), 41.

13. Citing Hower (1943), Thomas K. McCraw, "Competition and 'Fair Trade,'" *Research in Economic History* 16 (1996), 230 n. 13.

14. "Books & Stationery," 41.

15. *Bobbs-Merrill Company v. Straus et al. Doing Business Under the Firm Name and Style of R. H. Macy & Company*, 210 U.S. 339 (1908); McCraw, "Competition and 'Fair Trade,'" 188–90.

16. *Federal Anti-Trust Decisions: Cases Decided in the United States*, Index-Digest, vols. 1–6, (Washington, D.C.: U.S. Government Printing Office, 1918), 62; *Straus v. American Publishers Association*, 231 U.S. 222 (1913); "Right to Restrict Re-Sale Price," *DGE* (July 13, 1912), 25.

17. Leach, *Land of Desire*, Federal Industrial Commission quote, 30; Bean, *Beyond the Broker State*, 22–23.

18. Here I am equating professionalization, formal organization, and political identity with "industry" creation. The earliest example I've found of trade writers consciously talking about the existence of a politicized department store industry was in a 1927 editorial

by the market editor. See W. D. Darby, "As It Looks to Me," *DGE* (January 8, 1927), 25; Porter Benson, *Counter Cultures*, 31.

19. W. B. Phillips, *How Department Stores Are Carried On* (New York: Dodd, Mead, 1901).

20. The *Retail Ledger* was another trade paper. Porter Benson, *Counter Cultures*, 49; Fred Andersen, *The Miracle Merchant: How I Built My Department Store in a Town of 1300 to an Annual Volume of Over $300,000* (Cozad, Neb.: n.p., 1925), 92.

21. Images of this department store can be found in the Jones Store Company photographs, circa 1900, Missouri Valley Special Collections, Kansas City Public Library.

22. "The Department Store: A Protest Against the Hostile Law Enacted in Missouri," *DGE* (September 2, 1899), "political quack" quote, 5; "The Department Store: A Protest Against the Hostile Law Enacted in Missouri," *DGE* (September 2, 1899), "cheap paper" quote, 5, news clippings, Anti–Department Store Legislation, Case 1, RC.

23. "The Department Store: A Protest against the Hostile Law Enacted in Missouri," 5.

24. *Twenty-Five Years of Retailing* (National Retail Dry Goods Association, 1936), 48–49; Porter Benson, *Counter Cultures*, 48–49; "Want Minimum Wage," *DGE* (March 29, 1913), 35.

25. *Twenty-Five Years of Retailing*, 52, 48; Godfrey M. Lebhar, *Chain Stores in America, 1859–1962* (New York: Chain Store Publishing Corporation, 1952), 184–85.

26. Minute Book, Rudge & Guenzel Co., February 23, 1912, p. 25, box 3, RGC; Howard, "The Rise and Fall of Rudge & Guenzel, 56; "What Was Said and Who Said It at the N.R.D.G.A. Convention," *DGE* (February 19, 1927), 13; *Twenty-Five Years of Retailing*, 56.

27. M. Browning Carrott, "The Supreme Court and American Trade Associations, 1920–1925," *Business History Review* 64 (Autumn 1970), 320–21; Porter Benson, *Counter Cultures*, 54; "How Retailer Keeps Trade at Home," *DGE* (March 1, 1913), "efficiency" quote, 45. Among smaller Canadian shopkeepers during this period, as historian David Monod has argued, trade organization was "less about survival than about controlling competition and increasing profits." In the Canadian context, the activism of Main Street retailers challenged mass merchandisers, such as department and chain stores, and fought encroaching immigrants' and women's backstreet shops by promoting modernization—by accommodating the mass market rather than trying to go back in time. Monod, *Store Wars*, 231–32.

28. The War Industries Board worked through the trade association to allocate materials and fixed prices and production. Carrott, "The Supreme Court and American Trade Associations," 321; *Twenty-Five Years of Retailing*, "governmental interference" quote, 63.

29. Melvin T. Copeland, *And Mark an Era: The Story of the Harvard Business School* (Boston: Little, Brown, 1958), 221, 222; Leach, *Land of Desire*, 288; Longstreth, *The American Department Store Transformed*, 7. In the economy overall, the excess profits tax instituted in 1917 to help cover war expenses encouraged advertising expenditure (as a tax deduction). See Martha L. Olney, *Buy Now, Pay Later: Advertising, Credit, and Consumer Durables in the 1920s* (Chapel Hill: University of North Carolina Press, 1991), 4. On Lew Hahn and Thanksgiving, see Robert F. Blake, "Talk of the Town," *New Yorker* (September 2, 1939). The Thanksgiving date change has also been attributed to Fred Lazarus Jr. of

Federated; "Federated Department Stores International Company," Lehman Brothers Collection, Contemporary Business Archive, Baker Library, Harvard Business School, http://www.library.hbs.edu/hc/lehman/company.html?company=federated_department_stores_international_company (accessed June 23, 2004).

30. As late as 1926, a convention of 3,500 Dayton, Ohio, merchants and salespeople held at the National Cash Register Co. plant was admonished, "All obsolete methods must go." "Thoughts on Merchandising Problems," *DGE* (June 5, 1926), 87; Gerish, *The Retailer and the Consumer in New England*, 19–21.

31. Porter Benson, *Counter Cultures*, 64. One scientific retailing method devised in response to the war experience was Edward Filene's model stock plan, designed to streamline stocks and increase turnover. See Porter Benson, *Counter Cultures*, 65. See also Christopher T. Martin, "Edward A. Filene and the Promise of Industrial Democracy" (Ph.D. diss., University of Rochester, 2002), 80–82; Doubman and Whitaker, *The Organization and Operation of Department Stores*, 214; Pasdermadjian, *The Department Store*, 42.

32. *Twenty-Five Years of Retailing*, "local or state responsibility" quote, 64, 72–73; Jacobs, *Pocketbook Politics*, 54–57, "forbade hoarding" quote, 60, 61–62.

33. *Twenty-Five Years of Retailing*, 72–73; Lew Hahn, "Retailers Must Organize for Their Protection," *Dry Goods Guide* (August 1920), quote, 9.

34. *Twenty-Five Years of Retailing*, 64, 66–67, 72–73; Porter Benson, *Counter Cultures*, 64–65, 97; Doubman and Whitaker, *The Organization and Operation of Department Stores*, 213.

35. For example, on taxes, freight rates, and tariff rates, see "The National Retail Dry Goods Association," *DGE* (February 8, 1913), 27; on the minimum wage, see "Retail Merchants Discuss Trade Problems," *DGE* (February 13, 1915), 35, 38.

36. As business historian Thomas K. McCraw put it, "Brandeis exemplified the antibigness ethic without which there would have been no Sherman Act, no antitrust movement, and no Federal Trade Commission." McCraw, *Prophets of Regulation: Charles Francis Adams, Louis D. Brandeis, James M. Landis, Alfred E. Kahn* (Cambridge, Mass.: Harvard University Press, 1984), 81, quote 82, 122–24; Bean, *Beyond the Broker State*, 20.

37. McCraw, "Competition and 'Fair Trade,'" 102, 195, 104.

38. Strasser, *Satisfaction Guaranteed*, 278. From Miles's perspective, a higher maintained price acted as an incentive for small shopkeepers, in an era without self-service, to promote his elixirs. Lower prices did not mean higher volume from his point of view. Instead, "cut-rate" or "cut-price" department stores hurt his business and pulled down the reputation of his product. McCraw, "Competition and 'Fair Trade,'" 192; Leach, *Land of Desire*, 179–80.

39. Jacobs, *Pocketbook Politics*, 33–34; Fisher, "Ohio Fair Trade: Fair or Foul?" *Ohio State Law Journal* 28 (Fall 1967), 565.

40. "Resale Price Bill," *DGE* (January 16, 1915), 163; "Retailer and Manufacturer Discuss Stevens Bill," *DGE* (November 13, 1915), "cash discount" quote, 39; McCraw, "Competition and 'Fair Trade,'" 196–97; William Hard, "Better Business," *Overland Monthly* 66 (August 1914), 200–201.

41. "The Case For and Against Coupons Laid Before Advertising Men," *Printers' Ink* 91 (May 20, 1915), 108.

42. "Retailers' Views on Resale Price Control Bill," *DGE* (December 11, 1915), 38; "Retailer and Manufacturer Discuss Stevens Bill," *DGE* (November 13, 1915), Straus quote, 38, 40; "How Dry Goods Retailers View Stevens Bill," 26; "Retailers' Views on Resale Price Control Bill," 38.

43. *Printers' Ink* 91 (April 1, 1915), 108; "How Dry Goods Retailers View Stevens Bill," *DGE* (December 4, 1915), 26; "Stevens Bill and Manufacturing Monopolies," *DGE* (November 27, 1915), 34; "Answer to Arguments against Price Maintenance," *DGE* (November 20, 1915), 30; "Retailer and Manufacturer Discuss Stevens Bill," 38.

44. "How Dry Goods Retailers View Stevens Bill," 26; "Stevens Bill and Manufacturing Monopolies," 34;"Answer to Arguments against Price Maintenance," 30; "Retailer and Manufacturer Discuss Stevens Bill," 38; "distribution trust" quote in Jacobs, *Pocketbook Politics*, 34–35; "Resale Price Bill," 163; "Stevens Bill and Manufacturing Monopolies34–35; "Answer to Arguments against Price Maintenance," "limited means" quote 30. For a discussion of brands, marketing, and resale price maintenance, see Strasser, *Satisfaction Guaranteed*, 269–84.

45. "Answer to Arguments Against Price Maintenance," "business efficiency" quote, 30; "Price Fixing, Not Price Maintenance Bill," *DGE* (November 6, 1915), "line of goods" quote, 34.

46. "California Merchants against Stevens Bill," *DGE* (November 6, 1915), 35; "Price Fixing, Not Price Maintenance Bill," "Cheney's" quotes, 34; "Stevens Bill and Manufacturing Monopolies," 34; "Retailers' Views on Resale Price Control Bill," "American progress" quote, 38; "Retailers' Views on Resale Price Control Bill 39. The Stevens bill failed to pass in 1915 but national bills would be introduced in each Congress until 1933, when resale price maintenance came in with the National Recovery Act, and following 1935, the Miller-Tydings Act of 1937. Fisher, "Ohio Fair Trade: Fair or Foul?" *Ohio State Law Journal* 28 (Fall 1967), 565.

47. McCraw, "Competition and 'Fair Trade,'" 193, 194, 201–2.

48. Landon R. Y. Storrs, *Civilizing Capitalism: The National Consumers' League, Women's Activism, and Labor Standards in the New Deal Era* (Chapel Hill: University of North Carolina Press, 2000), 46.

49. *Twenty-Five Years of Retailing*, 55; "The Minimum Wage," *DGE* (March 15, 1913), 51; Porter Benson, *Counter Cultures*, 136.

50. Storrs, *Civilizing Capitalism*, 73; "Retail Merchants Discuss Trade Problems," 39; Kim McQuaid, "An American Owenite: Edward A. Filene and the Parameters of Industrial Reform, 1890–1937," *American Journal of Economics and Sociology* 35 (January 1976), 77–94. On Filene more broadly, see Martin, "Edward A. Filene and the Promise of Industrial Democracy."

51. "The Minimum Wage," "intense interest" quote, 51; Porter Benson, *Counter Cultures*, 23, 25, 136; collection description, R. H. Macy & Company Collection, Women, Enterprise & Society, Baker Library, Harvard Business School, http://www.library.hbs.edu/hc/wes/indexes/alpha/content/1001954460.html (accessed June 23, 2014); Sarah L. Malino, "Behind the Scenes in the Big Store: Reassessing Women's Employment in American Department Stores, 1870–1920," in *Work, Recreation & Culture: Essays in American Labor History*, ed. Martin Henry Blatt and Martha K. Norkunas (New York: Garland, 1996), 26; "The Minimum Wage," "consumers" quote (emphasis in original), 51.

52. Porter Benson, *Counter Cultures*, 125, 136; Storrs, *Civilizing Capitalism*, 14, "recruiting" quote, 20.

53. Storrs, *Civilizing Capitalism*, 2, 20; Porter Benson, *Counter Cultures*, 134–35, 193–94; Val Marie Johnson, "'Look for the Moral and Sex Sides of the Problem': Investigating Jewishness, Desire, and Discipline at Macy's Department Store, New York City, 1913," *Journal of the History of Sexuality* 18 (September 2009), 457–85; Christopher J. Cyphers, *The National Civic Federation and the Making of a New Liberalism, 1900–1915* (Westport, Conn.: Praeger, 2002), "whitewash" quote, 88; Malino, "Behind the Scenes in the Big Store," 17–37; Leach, *Land of Desire*, 117–18. For a detailed account of the poor conditions of store work, see Louise de Koven Bowen, *The Department Store Girl: Based upon Interviews with 200 Girls* (Chicago: Juvenile Protection Association, 1911).

54. *Twenty-Five Years of Retailing*, quotes, 54; "The Minimum Wage," 51, 58–59; Porter Benson, *Counter Cultures*, 136, 151–53; Leach, *Land of Desire*, 158–59.

55. *Twenty-Five Years of Retailing*, quote, 57; Elaine S. Abelson, *When Ladies Go A-Thieving: Middle-Class Shoplifters in the Victorian Department Store* (New York: Oxford University Press, 1989), 98–102; Beth Kreydatus, "'You Are a Part of All of Us': Black Department Store Employees in Jim Crow Richmond," *Journal of Historical Research in Marketing* 2 (2010), 110, 119; Porter Benson, *Counter Cultures*, 194–95; Howard, "The Rise and Fall of Rudge & Guenzel," quote 112–13. On Mandel Bros. see "Happenings Among Retail Stores," *DGE* (February 1, 1913), 37; on turnover rates see Opler, *For All White-Collar Workers*, 27.

56. *Twenty-Five Years of Retailing*, 74; "Dry Goods Men See Great Prosperity," *NYT* (February 9, 1926), 5.

57. Leach, *Land of Desire*, 364–65; Paul H. Nystrom, "An Estimate of the Volume of Retail Business in the United States," *Harvard Business Review* (January 1, 1925), 150–51; Gerish, *The Retailer and the Consumer in New England*, 4–5.

58. "Dry Goods Men See Great Prosperity," *NYT* (February 9, 1926), 5.

CHAPTER 3. MODERNIZING MAIN STREET

1. Trachtenberg, *The Incorporation of America*, 133; *A Friendly Guide to Philadelphia and the Wanamaker Store* (Philadelphia: n.p., 1926). Library of Congress, *Prosperity and Thrift: The Coolidge Era and the Consumer Economy*, http://memory.loc.gov/ammem/cool html/coolhome.html (accessed March 22, 2011); "Vote for Frank H. Bresee," *The Star–Oneonta* (November 13, 1919), 3; Howard E. Covington, Jr., *Belk: A Century of Retail Leadership* (Chapel Hill: University of North Carolina Press, 1988), 52.

2. Doubman and Whitaker, *The Organization and Operation of Department Stores*, 19; Gerish, *The Retailer and the Consumer in New England*, 9; Hollander and Omura, "Chain Store Developments," 299 n. 2, 302.

3. Chicago, Ill., South Central Dept. Store A118873-A119976 (production file), Illinois Digital Archives, http://www.idaillinois.org/cdm/ref/collection/lakecou02z/id/3525; "Two Ambassadors Named," *NYT* (May 21, 1955), 8; Interview with Dick Jones, Illinois Writers Project, "Negro in Illinois" Papers, 5–6, box 35, folder 5, Chicago Public Library; "The Defender Winning Its Fight," *Chicago Defender* (March 31, 1928), A2. South Central is the only large-scale black-owned department store my research could bring to light. The store became black owned in 1963, when the prominent manufacturer/entrepreneur Samuel B.

Fuller bought the deteriorating building complex with intentions to rehabilitate the storefront as well as the Regal Theatre. According to this account, Fuller declared bankruptcy in 1969. At the time of Fuller's acquisition, the store had 110 employees across seventy-six departments. Rachel Kranz, *African-American Business Leaders and Entrepreneurs* (New York: Facts-On-File, 2004), 98. Clovis E. Semmes, *The Regal Theatre and Black Culture* (New York: Palgrave Macmillan, 2006), 193–97; according to Semmes, when the store opened, fourteen African Americans were hired in nonmanual positions out of 220 employees. According to this account the store had fifty-four departments and ninety thousand square feet of floor space; Fuller went bankrupt in 1968 (and not 1969) (ibid., 18). According to another source, when the store opened, a third of its 114 employees were black, a percentage that soon rose to half. See Arvarh E. Strickland, *History of the Chicago Urban League* (1966; Columbia: University of Missouri Press, 2001), 94–95. On African Americans and department stores, see Traci Lynnea Parker, "The Work of Consumption, the Consumption of Work: Integrating American Department Stores and Shaping a Modern Black Middle Class, 1890–1991" (Ph.D. diss., University of Chicago, 2013).

   4. Jacobs, *Pocketbook Politics*, 28–29; Theodore Dreiser, *Sister Carrie* (1900; reprint, New York: New American Library, 1961), 26–27; Bowlby, *Carried Away*, 24–25; Abelson, *When Ladies Go A-Thieving*, 148.

   5. Porter Benson, *Counter Cultures*, 215; "American standard" quote in "Business: Dry-Goods Men," *Time* (February 22, 1926), http://www.time.com/time/magazine/article/0,9171,721672,00.html.

   6. Leach, *Land of Desire*, "consumptionism" quote, 265, 266–69, 272; Christine Frederick, *Selling Mrs. Consumer* (New York: Business Bourse, 1929), "machine-like" quote, 291, 296.

   7. Sinclair Lewis, *Babbitt* (New York: Harcourt Brace Jovanovich, 1922), 59; "Books: Again, Tarkington," *Time* (June 10, 1929), http://www.time.com/time/magazine/article/0,9171,751958,00.html.

   8. Longstreth, *The American Department Store Transformed*, 13; Pasdermadjian, *The Department Store*, 16–17; Dyer, "Markets in the Meadows" 30–34; Malcolm P. McNair, "Trends in Large-Scale Retailing," *Harvard Business Review* (1931–1932), 32; Richard S. Tedlow, *New and Improved: The Story of Mass Marketing in America* (New York: Basic Books, 1990), 288.

   9. Meredith Clausen, "Department Stores," *Encyclopedia of Architecture, Design, Engineering, and Construction*, vol. 2 (New York: Wiley, 1988), 215–16; Malcolm McNair and Eleanor May, *The American Department Store, 1920–1960*, Bureau of Business Research Bulletin No. 166 (Boston: Harvard University Graduate School of Business Research, 1963), 62; Longstreth, *The American Department Store Transformed*, 13, 15–31, 202–3; Dyer, "Markets in the Meadows," 30; "Gimbel Bros. Open $8,000,000, Twelve Story Addition to Philadelphia Store," *DGE* (January 22, 1927), 58. On Gimbel Brothers, see Hepp IV, *The Middle-Class City*, chapter 6.

   10. "Last Step Made in Hahne Improvement," *Westfield Leader* (August 24, 1927), 3; *The 1985 Directory of Department Stores*, 352; "All Over the World," *DGE* (January 29, 1927), 184–85; Porter Benson, *Counter Cultures*, 39; Longstreth, *The American Department Store Transformed*, 26, 28, 47; Leach, *Land of Desire*, 73–74; Hepp, *The Middle-Class City*, chapter 6; "Otis Escalators in Scranton," *DGE* (January 22, 1927), equipment section,

cover; "Escalators Relieve Rush at Maison Blanche Store," *DGE* (January 22, 1927), equipment section, 64; "Gimbel Bros. Open $8,000,000, Twelve Story Addition to Philadelphia Store," 58.

11. Pasdermadjian, *The Department Store*, 25; Covington, *Belk*, 24, 82, 84; "N. C. R. Clerk-Wrap Plan Speeds Up Service, Cuts Expense, and Protects Cash and Merchandise," *DGE* (February 27, 1915), 99; "Store Transactions Speeded by Modern Communications Systems," *DSE* (April 1948), 14–15; Elvins, *Sales and Celebrations*, 13, 23–25; National Cash Register ad, *DGE* (February 22, 1913), 76; Lamson Carrier Service Systems ad, *DGE* (January 25, 1913), 74–75.

12. *Public Documents*, West Virginia, vol. 3 (Charleston, W.V.: Tribune Printing Company, 1915), 303; "This Flooring Appeals to Stores," *DGE*, equipment section, (January 22, 1927), 51; "Last Step Made in Hahne Improvement," 3.

13. Lewis, *Babbitt*, 21; Leach, *Land of Desire*, 42; Geoffrey Jones and Jonathan Zeitlin, eds., *The Oxford Handbook of Business History* (Oxford: Oxford University Press, 2008), 409.

14. Vicki Howard, "Department Store Advertising in Newspapers, Radio, and Television, 1920–1960," *Journal of Historical Research in Marketing* 2 (2010), 61–85.

15. Noah Arceneaux, "A Sales Floor in the Sky: Philadelphia Department Stores and the Radio Boom of the 1920s," *Journal of Broadcasting and Electronic Media* 53 (2009), 76–89; Susan Smulyan, *Selling Radio: The Commercialization of American Broadcasting, 1920–1934* (Washington, D.C.: Smithsonian Institution Press, 1994), 100, 103; Whitaker, *Service and Style*, 136. For more on the Wanamaker organ, see Linda L. Tyler, " 'Commerce and Poetry Hand in Hand': Music in American Department Stores, 1880–1930," *Journal of the American Musicological Society* 45 (Spring 1992), 75–120.

16. Elvins, *Sales and Celebrations*, 23; Buenger and Buenger, *Texas Merchant*, 59; Porter Benson, *Counter Cultures*, 53, 85. On department store bridal consultants, see Vicki Howard, *Brides, Inc.: American Weddings and the Business of Tradition* (Philadelphia: University of Pennsylvania Press, 2006), 116, 121, 105; *The 1985 Directory of Department Stores*, 2.

17. Elvins, *Sales and Celebrations*, xiv-xv.

18. "Float of the J. B. Wahl's Department Store in Tulip Festival Parade—May 2, 1921," photography, 1921, Wilbur J. Sandison, 1997.0017.00033, Whatcom Museum, Bellingham, Washington; Howard, "The Rise and Fall of Rudge & Guenzel," 110; Buenger and Buenger, *Texas Merchant*, 53, 109; "Jewish Institutions Get Share in Bequests Left by Colonel Friedsam," *Jewish Telegraphic Agency (JTA)* Archive, the Global Jewish News Source (April 21, 1933), http://www.jta.org/1933/04/21/archive/jewish-institutions-get-share-in-bequests-left-by-colonel-friedsam. Michael Friedsam, the heir to Benjamin Altman, and head of the store, supported a wide range of groups and charities.

19. "A Real Minstrel," *DGE* (June 5, 1926), "mob" quote, 53; For other similar examples, see Elvins, *Sales and Celebrations*, 152.

20. Robert S. Lynd and Helen Merrell Lynd, *Middletown: A Study in Modern American Culture* (New York: Harcourt Brace Jovanovich, Publishers, 1929), 45; McNair, "Trends in Large-Scale Retailing," quotes, 30, 31; Edward Filene periodized the transformation in distribution the same way as McNair, evident in the chapter title, "From Shopkeeping to Mass Distribution," in his 1937 book on retailing; Manufacturers had many complaints

against department stores in the 1920s, all of which arose out of the size and power of these distributors. Manufacturers resented department stores seeking bargain lots or closeouts only, forcing discounts and special accommodations, not placing orders early enough, and not treating manufacturer representatives respectfully. See "The Charge Against the Department Store," *ASF* (July 29, 1925), 18, 58, 60.

21. Strasser, *Satisfaction Guaranteed*, 230; See Gerish, *The Retailer and the Consumer in New England*, 3. Figures are from the Census of Business: Retail Trade, taken from Louis P. Bucklin, *Competition and Evolution in the Distributive Trades* (Englewood Cliffs, NJ: Prentice-Hall, 1972), 105; Nystrom, "An Estimate of the Volume of Retail Business in the United States," 158. For the 1923 statistic, see Nystrom, p. 151.

22. David J. Hess, *Localist Movements in a Global Economy: Sustainability, Justice, and Urban Development in the United States* (Cambridge, Mass.: MIT Press, 2009), 114. The Hudson's Bay Company predated this in North America. Chartered in 1670, it established trading posts throughout the eighteen and nineteenth centuries in Canada, where it had ten modern department stores by the late 1930s. Theodore Beckman and Herman Nolen, *The Chain Store Problem* (New York: McGraw Hill, 1938), 14–15; Marc Levinson, *The Great A&P and the Struggle for Small Business in America* (New York: Hill and Wang, 2012); Cohen, *Making a New Deal*, 119; Lewis Eldon Atherton, *Main Street on the Middle Border* (Chicago: Quadrangle Books, 1966), 240; Hollander and Omura, "Chain Store Developments," 307; Cohen, *Making a New Deal*, 152–54. Leach, *Land of Desire*, 273, 274. Kresge Department Stores, Inc. only had two stores in the mid-1920s. Doubman and Whitaker, *The Organization and Operation of Department Stores*, 20; Emmet and Jeuck, *Catalogues and Counters*, 321.

23. "About Us," *Chain Store Age* (CSA), http://www.chainstoreage.com/about-us (accessed August 13, 2012).

24. By 1980, a department store chain was a corporation with eleven or more units. Bluestone et al., *The Retail Revolution*, 15; Elvins, *Sales and Celebrations*, 92. On the South, see chapter 4 in Ownby, *American Dreams in Mississippi*, and Covington, *Belk*, chapter 2. On credit offered by country stores in rural areas in New England, see Gerish, *The Retailer and the Consumer in New England*, 3; United States Federal Trade Commission, *Chain Stores: The Chain Store in the Small Town*, 73rd Congress, Second Session, Senate, Document No. 93 (Washington, D.C.: U.S. Government Printing Office, 1934), 1, 17–18. A 1934 federal study of the effect of chains on independent businesses in 30 small towns with a population of two to five thousand showed the power of large-scale, corporate retailing. In 1926, these small communities had an average of 8 chain department stores and 23 independent department stores—roughly a quarter were chains at this early stage. Only five years later, independents had shrunk to 19, while the number of chain department stores grew to 15, or 44.1 percent of the total. *Chain Stores: The Chain Store in the Small Town*, 1, 17–18.

25. J. C. Penney instituted a centralized purchasing office, personnel department and sales, advertising, real estate and research, and testing departments. Montgomery Ward, too, was highly centralized. Sears, however, experimented with decentralization under General Wood and later. For more on the complicated chronology of Sears's movement from centralization to decentralization, see Alfred D. Chandler, "Management Decentralization: An Historical Analysis," in *Alfred P. Sloan: Critical Evaluations in Business and Management*, ed. John Cunningham Wood and Michael C. Wood (New York: Routledge, 2003), 365–67;

Emmet and Jeuck, *Catalogues and Counters*, 195, 321; Buenger and Buenger, *Texas Merchant*, 54–55; Bluestone et al., *The Retail Revolution*,15–16: "After World War II Sears followed the population shift to the suburbs, but continued to maintain many of its downtown stores." Ownby, *American Dreams in Mississippi*, 87; Doubman and Whitaker, *The Organization and Operation of Department Stores*, 20, 292.

26. Elvins, *Sales and Celebrations*, 79–80, 102–3.

27. Bucklin, *Competition and Evolution*, 98; Hollander and Omura, "Chain Store Developments," 315; Bluestone et al., *The Retail Revolution*, 64–66; Leach, *Land of Desire*, 272.

28. *The 1985 Directory of Department Stores*, 167; Cohen, *Making a New Deal*, 115, 117–19; Elvins, *Sales and Celebrations*, chapter 4.

29. Cohen, *Making a New Deal*, 118; Elvins, *Sales and Celebrations*, 84–85; "local store" quote in "Were You Ever Told," J. C. Penney ad, *Oneonta Daily Star* (July 6, 1926); Bluestone et al., *The Retail Revolution*, 23–24.

30. "Our Objectives," *Lincoln State Journal* (January 25, 1929), quote 3; *The Cornhusker*, 1938, Nebraska State Historical Society; Covington, *Belk*, 80–81; "Birthday Candle Lighted," *Lincoln Evening Journal* (May 1, 1929), 5.

31. As defined in 1929, they consisted of "a number of unit retail stores operating under a common ownership and management and following common policies and utilizing common methods of operation which are determined by the central management." "Chain Stores," *Encyclopaedia Britannica*, 14th edition, volume 5 (New York: Encyclopaedia Britannica Company, 1929), 190. Chains are defined by the Federal Trade Commission during this period as "an organization owning a controlling interest in two or more establishments which sell substantially similar merchandise at retail." The Bureau of the Census defined chains in the mid-1930s as "groups of 4 or more stores in the same general kind of business, owned and operated jointly, with central buying, usually supplied from one or more central warehouses." Beckman and Nolen, *The Chain Store Problem*, 2–3; U.S. Department of Commerce, *Census of American Business: 1933, Retail Distribution*, vol. 1, *United States Summary: 1933 and Comparisons with 1929*, May 1935, 15, 35, 62.

32. Koehn, *Brand New*, 118, 129; Doubman and Whitaker, *The Organization and Operation of Department Stores*, 19, 20. Harvard's Bureau of Business Research reports on operating results divided stores according to volume of sales, not type of organization. It can be assumed that the reporting stores were independents at this early date.

33. "They Protected Stock Values: Merchants in Three Cities Find Ways to Salvage Surplus Merchandise," *DGE* (July 1932), 67; Monod, *Store Wars*, 184; Ownby, *American Dreams in Mississippi*, 86–90.

34. Elvins, *Sales and Celebrations*, 79–80, 102–3; "Is the Independent Merchant Doomed?" *DGE* (February 26, 1927), "doomed" quote, 11; "Another Consolidation," *DGE* (January 8, 1927), 12.

35. McNair, "Trends in Large-Scale Retailing," 31; McNair and May, *American Department Stores*, 22–23, 51.

36. Bluestone et al., *The Retail Revolution*, 13. Gross margins were the "aggregate price markups over net purchase costs." Peter M. Scott and James Walker, "Sales and Advertising Expenditure for Interwar American Department Stores," *Journal of Economic History* 71

(March 2011), 54; Pasdermadjian, *The Department Store*, 36, 39. Pasdermadjian provides the following average operating figures for the period 1860 to 1880: gross margin 20 percent, expenses 15 percent, and net profit 5 percent (ibid., 18–19).

37. Scott and Walker, "Sales and Advertising Expenditure," 41, 48, 51; Pasdermadjian, *The Department Store*, 90; McNair, "Trends in Large-Scale Retailing," 32. For a table on annual operating results of department stores, 1920–1960, see McNair and May, *American Department Stores*, 22. For a discussion of fluctuating total expenses over the period, see ibid., 52.

38. Edward A. Filene with Werner K. Gabler and Percy S. Brown, *Next Steps Forward in Retailing* (New York: Harper & Brothers, 1937), 19; Porter Benson, *Counter Cultures*, 66. "Business Volume Still Large, but Distinct Recession is Under Way," *DGE* (June 5, 1926), 18; Frank Thomson Hypps, "The Department Store—A Problem of Elephantiasis," *Annals of the American Academy of Political and Social Science* 193 (1937), 84, 86, 87.

39. When the Nebraska firm of Rudge & Guenzel merged with Hahn Department Stores in December 1928, it had experienced a profitable decade after very poor sales in the depression of 1920–21. But when compared to the store's earlier performance during the World War I era, profits seemed flat and even slipping in 1927. Owner Carl Guenzel and the board may have seen the opportunity to merge with Hahn as a remedy, while from the chain's perspective, the Nebraska store was a good prairie city property, making solid, if not spectacular profits. Howard, "The Rise and Fall of Rudge & Guenzel," 111, 112; "Hahn Department Stores, Inc.," Lehman Brothers Collection, Contemporary Business Archives, Baker Library, Harvard Business School, http://www.library.hbs.edu/hc/lehman/company .html?company = hahn…department…stores_inc (accessed June 23, 2014); Longstreth, *The American Department Store Transformed*, 12.

40. See Bluestone et al., *The Retail Revolution*, for a useful taxonomy of the department store industry, 15–29; Leon Harris, *Merchant Princes* (New York: Harper and Row, 1979), 20–21; "Associated Merchandising Corporation," entry in "Target Through the Years," https://corporate.target.com/about/history/Target-through-the-years (accessed January 10, 2013); "Founder's Biographies," Lincoln and Therese Filene Foundation, http://www .filenefoundation.org/lincoln-therese/ (accessed January 10, 2013).

41. For more on these individuals and the merger, see Martin, "Edward A. Filene and the Promise of Industrial Democracy," 309–13; McQuaid, "American Owenite," 78–79; see also Leach, *Land of Desire*, 266, 291–58, 283. Lincoln Filene's experience with the AMC, economist Barry Bluestone has argued, led to the adoption of this corporate form as the merchant "recognized the need to stabilize earnings through a geographical dispersion of risk," something achieved by the formation of a national retail holding company. Bluestone et al., *The Retail Revolution*, 11, 23; *The 1985 Directory of Department Stores*, 472–73, 258, 365; Ferry, *A History of the Department Store*, 120.

42. Leach, *Land of Desire*, 292; Leach incorrectly calls the AMC the American Merchandising Corporation. McNair and May, *The American Department Store*, 37.

43. Richard Longstreth has argued that it was not clear that consolidation was the best path for department store merchants. Consolidation remained in "a nascent state and was yielding mixed results," with "no clear model [emerging] to demonstrate that consolidation could substantially reduce operating costs and generate an effective system of large-scale

buying." Longstreth, *The American Department Store Transformed*, 12–13; "Is the Independent Merchant Doomed?" *DGE* (February 26, 1927), 11–12. As the Depression decade began, retailers began blaming the problems facing the industry on a too strict adherence to centralized buying, as in the case of Hahn department stores. Its movement toward decentralization in 1932 was heralded as the beginning of a "new era." See "Initiative for Buyers Hailed as Significant," *NYT* (August 14, 1932), F9; Filene, *Next Step Forward in Retailing* (New York: Harper and Brothers, 1937), 57; Daniel M. G. Raff, "Robert Campeau and Innovation in the Internal and Industrial Organization of Department Store Retailing," *Business and Economic History*, 2nd series, 20 (1991), 54–55.

44. See Letters, 1939–1941, folder: "Various loose materials," box 7, RGC.

45. Raff, "Robert Campeau and Innovation," 55–56; "Initiative for Buyers Hailed as Significant," F9.

46. "A Changed Order in Merchandising," *NYT* (October 22, 1916), E8; Harris, *Merchant Princes*, 20–21; Bluestone et al., *The Retail Revolution*, 11.

47. "Live Merchants Are Not Overlooking This Proposition," *DGE* (July 20, 1912), 88; Doubman and Whitaker, *The Organization and Operation of Department Stores*, "financed and controlled" quote, 120, 121–22.

48. Gerish, *The Retailer and the Consumer in New England*, 2; "Frederick Atkins, Inc.," in *International Directory of Company Histories*, vol. 16 (Chicago: St. James Press, 1997); "Frederick Atkins Honored by Stores," *NYT* (December 8, 1938), 42; "Frederick Atkins," obituary, *NYT* (November 18, 1946), 21; James M. Wood, *Halle's: Memoirs of a Family Department Store, 1891–1982* (Cleveland, OH: Geranium Press, 1987), 175; *The 1985 Directory of Department Stores*, 110.

49. Bluestone et al., *The Retail Revolution*, 11; Harris, *Merchant Princes*, 21; "Can You Manage a $40,000,000 Business?" *DGE* (January 29, 1927), 183. On foreign buying offices, see Doubman and Whitaker, *The Organization and Operation of Department Stores*, 123–24. The AMC grew to be the largest buying office and merchandising research center in the United States by the post–World War II period, including big independents like Rich's in Atlanta, a member from 1943 through the mid-1970s; "Frederick Atkins, Inc." On Rich's membership, see finding aid, "Scope and Content Note," Richard H. Rich Papers, Emory University, http://findingaids.library.emory.edu/documents/rich575/series3/. (Accessed October 5, 2014)

50. Loren Miller to Mr. E. J. Zahn Sr., November 27, 1928; Central States Department Stores Association: Agreement of Members to Continue Membership, March 11, 1930, box 12, folder 9, ZDSC; Doubman and Whitaker, *The Organization and Operation of Department Stores*, ad, 45, 120.

51. Andersen, *The Miracle Merchant*, 90; "Oneonta Dept. Store Affiliates with New York Buyer," *The Daily Star* (January 13, 1926), 6; Doubman and Whitaker, *The Organization and Operation of Department Stores*, 119–20, 122.

52. Alfred Fantl, "What Retailers Are Buying," *DGE* (June 5, 1926), 26. This was a regular feature. For example, see "What Retailers Are Buying," *DGE* (April 18, 1925), 87.

53. While the United States technically became an urban nation in 1920, a quarter still farmed, only a third of homes had electricity, and one in five had indoor flush toilets. Family expenditures also shifted slightly, as the percentage of income spent on food declined and the percentage spent on housing increased. Thomas K. McCraw, *American*

Business Since 1920: How It Worked, 2nd ed. (Wheeling, Ill.: Harlan Davidson, 2009), 4–5; Nystrom, "An Estimate of the Volume of Retail Business in the United States," 154–55; *The Buying Habits of Small-Town Women* (Kansas City: Ferry-Hanly Advertising Company, 1926), 68–73. Major durable goods purchases rose in the 1920s, while minor durable goods were purchased in lower proportions than before. See Olney, *Buy Now, Pay Later*, 1; Hypps stated that department stores were not serving "the wants of the buying public" satisfactorily. Hypps, "The Department Store—A Problem of Elephantiasis," quote, 74, 409; Gerish, *The Retailer and the Consumer in New England*, 7–8; "Ford Owners!" Macy's ad, *New York Sun* (August 24, 1915), 16; Frederick, *Selling Mrs. Consumer*, "deserted" quote, 290. On Grayson-Robinson, see Hardwick, *Mall Maker*, 49.

54. Calder, *Financing the American Dream*, 71; Joseph G. Knapp, "Credit Costs in Nebraska Retail Stores," *University Journal of Business* 2 (March 1924), 170–71; De Leslie Jones, "What Price Installment Selling?" *ASF* (September 9, 1925), 19–20, 54.

55. W. T. Grant, "The Price Problems of the Chain Store Industry," in *Addresses before the Second Annual Convention of the National Chain Store Association, September 23–24, 1929* (Printed and Bound for Association of Teachers of Marketing and Advertising), 3; Frederick W. Walter, *The Retail Charge Account* (New York: Ronald Press Company, 1922), 245–46; Gerish, *The Retailer and the Consumer in New England*, 2; Calder, *Financing the American Dream*, 200–201, 276–77; Knapp, "Credit Costs in Nebraska Retail Stores," 169; Lizabeth Cohen, *A Consumers' Republic: The Politics of Mass Consumption in Postwar America* (New York: Knopf, 2003), 282.

56. "This Playroom Is Paying Its Way," *DGE* (June 5, 1926), 12; "Service is By-Word in Joslin's Baby Shop," *DGE* (June 5, 1926), 14; Porter Benson, *Counter Culture*, 66, 100–101; "Club Women Attest Appreciation of Pfeifer's Service at Unusual Sale," *DGE* (June 5, 1926), 20; Leach, *Land of Desire*, 112–14, 133–38.

57. James M. Campbell, "How One Small City Department Store Buys and Sells," *ASF* (May 6, 1925), 26, 28; Gamber, *The Female Economy*, 195; Porter Benson, *Counter Cultures*, 106–9; "Relating Stock to Sales," *DGE* (December 1932), 20; Covington, *Belk*, 74, 84; "Building Corset Business in Small Stores," *DSE* For Buyers and Their Assistants (March 20, 1915), 35; "Building Ribbon Business in Small Town," *DSE* For Buyers and Their Assistants (February 20, 1915), 105–7; Koehn, *Brand New*, 122. Introduced in the 1920s, a new unit system of stock control was a "record system for arriving at customer demand through an analysis of customers' purchases." Gerish, *The Retailer and the Consumer in New England*, 20; "Merchandise Type Promotion to Gain," *NYT* (October 6, 1929), 21; Roland Marchand, *Advertising the American Dream: Making Way for Modernity, 1920–1940* (Berkeley: University of California Press, 1986), 120.

58. Gamber, *The Female Economy*, 200; Frances Donovan, *The Saleslady* (Chicago: University of Chicago Press, 1929), chapter 5, "improve their taste" quote, 46; *Prosperity and Thrift: The Coolidge Era and the Consumer Economy*, http://memory.loc.gov/ammem/coolhtml/coolhome.html (accessed March 28, 2011). On Donovan, see Porter Benson, *Counter Cultures*, 50; John J. Kelley, "Ready-to-Wear," *DGE* (April 18, 1925), "old-fashioned" quotes, 27.

59. Claudia Kidwell, *Cutting a Fashionable Fit* (Washington, D.C.: Smithsonian Institution Press, 1979), 98–99; Gamber, *The Female Economy*, 10, 194, 197, 227; "Effective Costumes and Hats for the Trousseau of the January Bride," January 7, 1911, scrapbook of

news clippings, series 8, box 76, SCC; Margaret Oliver Holmes to Sarah Hawley, box 2, folder 12, news clipping, *New York Herald* (March 11, 1914), and box 2, folder 13, news clipping (March 22, 1914), Sarah Davis Hawley Papers, Rosenberg Library, Galveston, Texas; Ferry, *A History of the Department Store*, 86.

60. Porter Benson, *Counter Cultures*, 110–11.

61. Beckman and Nolen, *The Chain Store Problem*, 156–57; *The Buying Habits of Small-Town Women*, 25–27; Gerish, *The Retailer and the Consumer in New England*, 3–4; Frederick, *Selling Mrs. Consumer*, quote, 209; "Not Chaos, but Transition," *DGE* (April 1933), 16. Filene observed that retailers in the early 1920s often said that customers were not interested in prices but wanted quality and fair treatment. Experts like Filene or Christine Frederick were interested parties, vested in promoting services and quality, which they believed distinguished department stores from "cut-rate" stores, or chains.

62. "How Retailer Keeps Trade at Home," *DGE* (March 1, 1913), 45; "Keeping Trade at Home," *DGE* (December 4, 1915), 23; "Another Message to the Merchant Who Wants to Hold the Business He Is Now Losing to the Mail Order Houses," *DGE* (November 6, 1915), 85; "We Don't Have to Go Out of Town," *DGE* (March 29, 1913), 7; Mamie Louise McFaddin, diary, April 28–30, 1919, Family Papers, McFaddin-Ward House, Beaumont, Texas; Gerish, *The Retailer and the Consumer in New England*, 2, "trend" quote, 8.

63. The study found that of the 394 families from Kansas and Missouri, 249 travelled to larger trade centers nearby to spend their money. A closer look at the statistics of this shopping study, however, shows that even though most did travel to larger trade centers, they did so rarely. In some towns, many shopped out of town only once or twice a year or not at all. The tiny number of child-related out-of-town purchases, moreover, was likely a factor of shoppers not wanting to travel with children. It also was a reflection of the study's sample composition, which was biased toward small families (a class and cultural indicator), including couples without any children at all. *The Buying Habits of Small-Town Women*, foreword, n.p.; "Purpose and Scope of the Survey," 4–52, 59.

64. Gerish, *The Retailer and the Consumer in New England*, quote, 11–12, 19; Longstreth, *City Center to Regional Mall*, 111, 251; Matthias Judt, "Reshaping Shopping Environments: The Competition Between the City of Boston and Its Suburbs," in *Getting and Spending: European and American Consumer Societies in the Twentieth Century*, ed. Susan Strasser, Charles McGovern, and Matthias Judt (Cambridge: Cambridge University Press, 1998), 329.

65. *The Buying Habits of Small-Town Women*, 55, 57–58. By the mid-1980s, only the Jones Store Co. survived, having grown into a regional chain of seven units in Kansas City, Missouri. Owned by Mercantile Stores Co., its annual sales then reached $170 million. *The 1985 Directory of Department Stores*, 314–15. On Emery, Bird, Thayer, see *Kansas City Star*, April 7, 1973.

66. Paul T. Cherington, "What Is Happening to the Rural and Small Town Market," *ASF* (May 20, 1925), 15–16; *The Buying Habits of Small-Town Women*, 11–14; Gerish, *The Retailer and the Consumer in New England*, 18.

67. *The Buying Habits of Small-Town Women*, "I should say" quote, 19–20, "price is the important thing," "expressed the conviction" quotes, 21.

68. Cherington, "What Is Happening to the Rural and Small Town Market," 16; Porter Benson, *Counter Cultures*, 103; Frederick, *Selling Mrs. Consumer*, quote 286, 287–89; "Chicago Christmas: Marshall Field's Original Frango Mints: A Holiday Tradition Missed by

Many," *Huffington Post* (December 23, 2012) http://www.huffingtonpost.com ; "Kenmore: America's Favorite Household Appliance Brand," Sears Archives website, http://www.sears archives.com (accessed June 23, 2014).

69. Dyer, "Markets in the Meadows," 29–32.

70. Scott and Walker, "Sales and Advertising Expenditure," 48; Elvins, *Sales and Celebrations*, 79.

71. James H. Madison, "Changing Patterns of Urban Retailing: The 1920s," *Business and Economic History* 5 (1976), 102–11; Leach saw the end of the 1920s as a turning point, when department stores "long resistant to the need to centralize resources, began to move toward merger and national store organization." Leach, *Land of Desire*, 265.

CHAPTER 4. A NEW DEAL FOR DEPARTMENT STORES

1. Robert S. McElvaine, *The Great Depression* (New York: Random House, 1993), 74; Jacobs, *Pocketbook Politics*, 135; For discussion of different stores' responses to the Depression, see the study of Wanamaker's, Strawbridge & Clothier, Shipley's, City Stores, and Lit Brothers in Philadelphia in Dyer, "Markets in the Meadows," chapter 2; Scott and Walker, "Sales and Advertising Expenditure," 40–69.

2. Porter Benson, *Counter Cultures*, 97; Wood, *Halle's*, 146; By the mid-1980s, only B. Altman and Lord & Taylor remained. *The 1985 Directory of Department Stores* (n.p.: Business Guides, Inc., 1984), 380, 395–96.

3. B. Altman & Co. charge account records, Mrs. Alfred Smith, Biltmore Hotel, December 1928–June 1930, BAC; Robert A. Slayton, *The Empire Statesman: The Rise and Redemption of Al Smith* (New York: Free Press, 2007), 339, 393.

4. Mandel's in Chicago and Wanamaker's in Philadelphia also had this service. Whitaker, *Service and Style*, 254–59; Leach, *Land of Desire*, 134.

5. Susan Ware, *Holding Their Own: American Women in the 1930s* (Boston: Twayne, 1982), 3.

6. David M. Kennedy, *Freedom from Fear: The American People in Depression and War, 1929–1945* (New York: Oxford University Press, 1999), 58–59, 65; Ware, *Holding Their Own*, xii–xiii.

7. Calder, *Financing the American Dream*, 276–77; *The 1985 Directory of Department Stores*, 466; E. H. Stewart to C. L. Bradley, February 21, 1934, p. 6. box 3, HC; handwritten and typed collections lists for Falk's Department Store, box 1, folder 27, FBMC.

8. Fifteenth Census of the United States, *Census of Distribution, Small City and Rural Trade Series: Analyzing the Small City and Rural Market Area* (Washington, D.C.: U.S. Government Printing Office, 1933), 1; "Report of Twin Falls, Collections," January 12, 1934, box 1, folder 27, FBMC. For an account of a customer's objection to his collection techniques see [illegible] Darling to Jennie M. Nicholson, December 18, 1933, box 1, folder 27, FBMC.

9. *Falk's Forum* (November 1945), 13, box 1; J. E. Warner to Mr. Darling, December 30, 1933; J. E. Warner to Mr. Darling, December 18, 1933, box 1, folder 27, FBMC.

10. Opler, *For All White-Collar Workers*, 23; "Shoplifters of Every Type Mingle with the Shoppers," *NYT* (December 13, 1933).

11. Porter Benson, *Counter Cultures*, 96–98; Opler, *For All White-Collar Workers*, 23; Cohen, *A Consumers' Republic*, 44–53; "Gold Tips" Newsletter, folder 1, 1937, RG2018: AM Gold & Co., Series 1, Nebraska State Historical Society.

12. Longstreth, *City Center to Regional Mall*, 204; Matthias Judt, "Reshaping Shopping Environments," 328–31; "Modern Trends in Department Store Planning," *DSE* (November 1944), 16.

13. *The 1985 Directory of Department Stores*, 408; Opler, *For All White-Collar Workers*, 22.

14. "Patman's Allies May Backslide," *DSE* (February 10, 1938), 45.

15. A 1938 study of Buffalo, New York, shoppers, for example, showed that women preferred independent department stores over chain department stores like Sears. Elvins, *Sales and Celebrations*, 166.

16. *A Study of Shopping Habits and Attitudes toward Department Stores*, 1936 report made for B. Altman & Co., 1–9, 18, 21–26, BAC.

17. *A Study of Shopping Habits and Attitudes toward Department Stores*, 12–17; Opler argues that salesclerks' grievances with these types of customers in upscale emporia were central to white-collar unionization in the 1930s. Opler, *For All White-Collar Workers*, 82–83.

18. Opler focuses on New York City, but in the summer of 1937, strikes hit the West Coast retail sector as well. See "Merchants, Clerks Sign Agreement," *Bellingham Herald* (November 13, 1937), 1; "Business Resumed," *Bellingham Herald* (September 1, 1937), 1. The strike involved Sears, Roebuck, Montgomery Ward, two Woolworths, and a number of independent department stores, for a total of ten firms. An International Ladies' Garment Workers' Union strike also hit Halle Bros. Co. in 1934. Wood, *Halle's*, 142–43; Cohen, *Consumers' Republic*, 35; Irving Fajans interview, February 1, 1939, Living Folklore, Library of Congress, Manuscript Division, WPA Federal Writers' Project Collection; Opler, *For All White-Collar Workers*, 82–83.

19. Ferry, *A History of the Department Store*, 173; *Operating Results of Department and Specialty Stores in the Pacific Coast States: 1935*, vol. 33, no. 5, Bulletin Number 102 (Harvard University Graduate School of Business Administration, July 1936), 10–12; McNair and May, *The American Department Store*, 12, 14–15, 41–43. McNair and May defined gross margin as "net sales in owned departments less the applicable net delivered cost of goods sold, after crediting cash discounts taken on purchases, after charging net alteration and workroom costs, and after allowing for stock shortages and merchandise depreciation" (ibid., 20); U.S. Department of Commerce, *Fifteenth Census of the United States: 1930 Distribution*, vol. 1, *Retail Distribution*, Part 1 (Washington, D.C.: U.S. Government Printing Office, 1933), 47, 49; U.S. Department of Commerce, *Census of American Business: 1933, Retail Distribution*, vol. 1, *United States Summary: 1933 and Comparisons with 1929*, May 1935, A-1, A-12, A-13, 15; Scott and Walker, "Sales and Advertising Expenditure," 40–41, 50, 54; *Historical Statistics of the United States*, vol. 4, table De73–109, Retail establishments, by type of business: 1929–1982, 4–720; *U.S. Census of Business—1948, Trade Series, Department Stores*, 5; For a discussion of Bullock's, see William Ramsey Scott, "Dressing Down: Modernism, Masculinity, and the Men's Leisurewear Industry, 1930–1960" (Ph.D. diss., University of California, Berkeley, 2007), chapter 2.

20. Opler, *For All White-Collar Workers*, 18; Harris, *Merchant Princes*, 15; Ferry, *A History of Department Stores*, 76–77; Elvins, *Sales and Celebrations*, 146; Hendrickson, *The Grand Emporiums*, 290; Scott and Walker, "Sales and Advertising Expenditure," "thrifty" quote, 44.

21. Ferry, *A History of the Department Store*, 169, 155; Elvins, *Sales and Celebrations*, 144–48; Gabrielle Esperdy, *Modernizing Main Street: Architecture and Consumer Culture in the New Deal* (Chicago: University of Chicago Press, 2008), chapter 2.

22. "A Sure Thing," *DGE* (November 23, 1937), "dividends" quote, 5; "Ring Out the Old!" *DSE* (January 25, 1938), 67; "Store Should Have Sales Appeal," *DSE* (April 10, 1941), back cover.

23. "Improvements Going Ahead," *DSE* (February, 10, 1938), 43; *The 1985 Directory of Department Stores*, 506; Digitized pamphlet, *Premium List of the Thirty-Ninth Annual Exhibition of the Oakland County Milford Fair* (Milford, Michigan, September 16–19, 1919), "largest store" quote, Google Books online; "Chase's Plan &200,000 Expansion Program," *DSE* (February 10, 1938), 42; "Why People Buy at Neighborhood Stores," *DSE* (January 25, 1939); "San Francisco Stores Solve Parking Problem," *DSE* (May 25, 1941), 20; Richard P. Doherty, *Trends in Retail Trade and Consumer Buying Habits in the Metropolitan Boston Retail Area* (Boston, Mass.: Bureau of Business Research, Boston University College of Business Administration, 1941), 14.

24. Porter Benson, *Counter Cultures*, 51, 104; Ferry, *A History of the Department Store*, 49–50; Wood, *Halle's*, 129–33, 147; Whitaker, *Service and Style*, 140, 149–50; *The Buying Habits of Small-Town Women*, 19–21; the black Texan painter Cornelius W. Johnson had an exhibit there in 1932. See "Johnson, Cornelius W.," entry, *The Handbook of Texas*, http://www.tshaonline.org/handbook/online/articles/fjoht (accessed November 3, 2013).

25. Hypps, "The Department Store—A Problem of Elephantiasis," 84; "Following in Barnum's Footsteps," *DGE* (June 1933), 20–21, 74; for examples in Buffalo and Rochester department stores, see Elvins, *Sales and Celebrations*, 151–53.

26. Porter Benson, *Counter Cultures*, 104; E. H. Stewart to C. L. Bradley, February 21, 1934, p. 6. box 3, HC; Scott and Walker, "Sales and Advertising Expenditure," 49, 65, quote, 66.

27. "Business & Finance: Profitless Hearn," *Time* (September 3, 1934); Porter Benson, *Counter Cultures*, "showmanship" quote, 104, 190; untitled talk, circa 1938, p. 5, Personal: Miscellaneous, Hearn Department Store, BKP; "I'll Tell You What We Want—We want LOWER prices!" Display Ad, *NYT* (August 28, 1934), "biggest bargain store" quote, 9; "Hearn plan" quote in Memo, February 17, 1938, Hearn's Policy for 1938, BKP; Untitled talk, circa 1938, Personal: Miscellaneous, Hearn Department Store, BKP; "Hearns to Give Up Profits for Year," *NYT* (August 24, 1934), "income statement" quote, 17.

28. Untitled talk, circa 1938, "suffer most" quote, 7–8, Personal: Miscellaneous, Hearn Department Store, BKP; "I'll Tell You What We Want—We want LOWER prices!" Display Ad, *NYT* (August 28, 1934), "motherly" quote, 9; "Mrs. Housewife!" Display Ad, *NYT* (September 3, 1934), "revolutionize" quote, O8; "Says Al Smith: I'm Proud of Hearns!" *NYT* (August 31, 1934), 7; "Hearns Opened By Smith," *NYT* (September 7, 1934), 41.

29. "Tomorrow–Thursday at 9:30 a.m. The Hearn Plan Swings into Action," *NYT* (September 5, 1934), "crossroads" quote, 11; Memo, February 17, 1938, Hearn's Policy for 1938, "five million circulars" quote, 2, BKP; Untitled talk, circa 1938, "first in the history of New York" quote, 8, Personal: Miscellaneous, Hearn's Department Store, BKP.

30. Hearn's in New York City closed down in the 1950s. See Whitaker, *Service and Style*, 28. However, the Bronx unit survived until 1979. See "42 Franklin Stores and Hearn's Are Closed," *NYT* (August 17, 1979), D3.

31. "Urges Retail Conference," *NYT* (November 22, 1929), 2; Hoover responded with a pro forma letter that he would consider Liberman's suggestion. Letter, November 22, 1929, Herbert Hoover to Meyer Liberman, John T. Wooley and Gerhard Peters, *The American Presidency Project* [online], http://www.presidency.ucsb.edu/ws/?pid + 2214.

32. Corey Lewis Sparks, "Locally Owned and Operated: Opposition to Chain Stores, 1925–1940" (Ph.D. diss., Louisiana State University, 2000), 105–6, 127; Leach, *Land of Desire*, 357; Letter, November 22, 1929, Herbert Hoover to Meyer Liberman.

33. Elvins, *Sales and Celebrations*, chapter 5; "Mount Vernon Had Lost Sales to New York," *DGE* (March 1933), 28; "What Policy Can We Best Follow during the Next Few Months?" *DGE* (October 1932), "hoarders" quote, 21; Jacobs, *Pocketbook Politics*, 96, 112; On Edward Filene's politics, see McQuaid, "American Owenite," 85.

34. Elvins, *Sales and Celebrations*, 133–34; "What Think Business Men About 'Buy American'?" *DGE* (January 1933), 34; "'Buy American' in Retail Disfavor," *DGE* (February 1933), 30–31; "Tariff Foes Open Final Senate Fire," *NYT* (June 10, 1930), 2; C. F. Hughes, "The Merchant's Point of View," *NYT* (May 1, 1932), quote, N6.

35. Ferry, *A History of the Department Store*, 160; Sarah Elvins, "Scrip, Stores, and Cash-Strapped Cities: American Retailers and Alternative Currency during the Great Depression," *Journal of Historical Research in Marketing* 2 (2010), 86–107; Sarah Elvins, "Scrip Money and Slump Cures: Iowa's Experiments with Alternative Currency during the Great Depression," *Annals of Iowa* 64 (Summer 2005), 236, 241; "Economies Are Not 'Temporary,'" *DGE* (November 1932), 28; Wood, *Halle's*, 140, 144; Jacobs, *Pocketbook Politics*, 96, 98; McElvaine, *The Great Depression*, 74.

36. Ferry, *A History of the Department Store*, 121; On Chamber of Commerce, see Kim Phillips-Fein, *Invisible Hands: The Making of the Conservative Movement from the New Deal to Reagan* (New York: W. W. Norton, 2009), 8–9, 16–17; "Retailers' Views Mingled on Code," *NYT* (October 24, 1933), 17; Opler, *For All White-Collar Workers*, 29; Roger W. Babson, "Recovery Act Hailed as Boon to Retail Trade," *Washington Post* (August 20, 1933), R6; Jacobs, *Pocketbook Politics*, 109, 130; Wood, *Halle's*, quote, 142; Kenneth Dameron, "Retailing under the NRA," *Journal of Business of the University of Chicago* 8 (January 1935), 4, 9–10; Ware, *Holding Their Own*, 38.

37. R. C. Hollander, "The 'Economic Criminal'" *DGE* (January 1933), 20–21; Hypps, "The Department Store—A Problem of Elephantiasis," "predatory" quote, 74.

38. Ruth Prince Mack, *Controlling Retailers: A Study of Cooperation and Control in the Retail Trade with Special Reference to the NRA* (New York: Columbia University Press, 1936), 188–90; Ellis W. Hawley, *The New Deal and the Problem of Monopoly: A Study in Economic Ambivalence* (Princeton: Princeton University Press, 1966), 58–59; Dameron, "Retailing under the NRA," 18–19. The NRA codes prohibited "sales below invoice cost plus a percentage mark-up," something also known as "stop loss" or "selling below cost."

39. "Namm Lauds Retail Code as Dawn of a New Era," *Brooklyn Daily Eagle* (October 23, 1933), 11.

40. Letter to the President, October 20, 1933, from Hugh S. Johnson, front matter to National Recovery Administration, *Codes of Fair Competition for the Retail Trade*, no. 60, in *Codes of Fair Competition*, nos. 58–110, vol. 2 (Washington, D.C.: U.S. Government Printing Office, 1934), 29.

41. Hawley, *The New Deal and the Problem of Monopoly*, 83.

42. Letter to the President, October 20, 1933, 28; Dameron, "Retailing under the NRA," 8; Jacobs, *Pocketbook Politics*, 113.

43. Hawley, *The New Deal and the Problem of Monopoly*, quote 59; Hendrickson, *The Grand Emporiums*, 191; R. C. Hollander, "Merchandise Murder," *DGE* (February 1933), 23.

44. Murray C. French, "Am I My Brother's Keeper," *DGE* (September 1932), 21.

45. Jacobs, *Pocketbook Politics*, 109, 113, 127; "Retailers' Views Mingled on Code," *NYT* (October 24, 1933), 17; On NRA parades, see Robert S. Lynd and Helen M. Lynd, *Middletown in Transition: A Study in Cultural Conflicts* (New York: Harcourt, Brace, 1937), 23; "NRF Turns 100," *Stores* (February 2011); Mack, *Controlling Retailers*, chapter 3; Rick Perlstein, *Before the Store: Barry Goldwater and the Unmaking of the American Consensus* (New York: Hill and Wang, 2001), "price dictates" quote, 20; "Flash a Red Light in the Path of the Court Plan Steam Roller," *DGE* (July 20, 1937), "invasion" quote, 13.

46. Jacobs, *Pocketbook Politics*, quote, 127; On the CAB, see also Cohen, *Consumers' Republic*, 28–29; Dameron, "Retailing under the NRA," 9.

47. Joseph C. Palamountain, *The Politics of Distribution* (Cambridge, Mass.: Harvard University Press, 1955), quote,192; Sparks, "Locally Owned and Operated," 207.

48. The *A.L.A. Schechter Poultry Corporation vs. United States* (1935) rendered NIRA unconstitutional. Hawley, *The New Deal and the Problem of Monopoly*, 249–51.

49. Lebhar, *Chain Stores in America*, 175–90.

50. Sparks, "Locally Owned and Operated," 267; Lebhar, *Chain Stores in America*, chapters 8–12, 175–90; Beckman and Nolan, *The Chain Store Problem*, chapter 14; Paul Ingram and Hayagreeva Rao, "Store Wars: The Enactment and Repeal of Anti-Chain Store Legislation in America" *American Journal of Sociology* 110 (September 2004), 448.

51. Lebhar, *Chain Stores in America*, "*New York Times*" quote, 192, 193–94, 197, 201, 215–16, 234–35; "Retailer's Voice," *Time Magazine* (April 29, 1935), 72; Sparks, "Locally Owned and Operated," 201, 211, "voice of Main Street" quote, 208; Charles G. Daughters, *Wells of Discontent: A Study of the Economic, Social, and Political Aspects of the Chain Store* (1937; reprint, New York: Arno Press, 1979), 78.

52. Sparks, "Locally Owned and Operated," quote, 244, chapter 6; Bean, *Beyond the Broker State*, 17–18, 31–33; Lebhar, *Chain Stores in America*, 233, 277; Donald S. Clark, "The Robinson-Patman Act: General Principles, Commission Proceedings, and Selected Issues," Federal Trade Commission, June 7, 1995, http://www.ftc.gov/public-statements/1995/06/robinson-patman-act-general-principles-commission-proceedings-and-selected.

53. Sparks, "Locally Owned and Operated," chapter 6, 241, 258–59, 293, 304–8; Elvins, *Sales and Celebrations*, 104; *Twenty-Five Years of Retailing*, 37; Roosevelt signed the bill, arguing that it clarified antitrust legislation and was an important protection for small business. Hawley, *The New Deal and the Problem of Monopoly*, "drastic" quote, 251, 258; David A. Horowitz, *Beyond Left and Right: Insurgency and the Establishment* (Urbana: University of Illinois Press, 1997), "better distribution" quote, 121; Bean, *Beyond the Broker State*, 33, 42; Vance and Scott, *Wal-Mart*, 26.

54. Hypps, "The Department Store—A Problem of Elephantiasis," 81; Hawley, *The New Deal and the Problem of Monopoly*, 267; Bean, *Beyond the Broker State*, 40–42.

55. McCraw, "Competition and 'Fair Trade,'" 207–8; "Pricing Purchase," Mr. C. P. Walker, May 13, 1938, Higbee Company Records, 1932–44, box 1, quote, 17, Baker Library,

Harvard Business School; Hawley, *The New Deal and the Problem of Monopoly*, 253; Bean, *Beyond the Broker State*, "weapons" quote, 73; Stanley M. Fisher, "Ohio Fair Trade: Fair or Foul," *Ohio State Law Journal* 28 (Fall 1967), 568.

56. Benjamin C. Butcher, *Fundamentals of Retailing* (New York: Macmillan, 1973), 36–37; Bean, *Beyond the Broker State*, 73; Hawley, *The New Deal and the Problem of Monopoly*, 254–55;"The Present Status of Fair Trade Laws," *Survey of Current Business* (May 1933), 11–12; Sparks, "Locally Owned and Operated," 293–94; Vance and Scott, *Wal-Mart*, 26. In spite of opposition from the NRDGA and mass retailers who opposed it, Miller-Tydings stood unchanged until 1951.

57. McCraw, "Competition and 'Fair Trade,'" quote, 207–8.

58. Jacobs, *Pocketbook Politics*, 162; Lebhar, *Chain Stores in America*, 115; "Use of Fair Trade Urged," *NYT* (September 1, 1939), 37; Sparks, "Locally Owned and Operated," 302–3; "Investigation of Concentration of Economic Power," *Price Behavior and Business Policy*, Monographs No. 1–3, Temporary National Economic Committee (Washington, D.C.: U.S. Government Printing Office, 1941), 380; Bean, *Beyond the Broker State*, 75.

CHAPTER 5. AN ESSENTIAL INDUSTRY IN WARTIME

1. For a discussion of government-business cooperation under FDR, including relevant figures such as Donald Nelson of Sears, Roebuck and Company, see Richard E. Holl, *From the Boardroom to the War Room: America's Corporate Liberals and FDR's Preparedness Program* (Rochester, NY: University of Rochester Press, 2005), 6–7, 49–53, 134–35; John Morton Blum, *V Was for Victory: Politics and American Culture during World War II* (New York: Harcourt Brace Jovanovich, 1977), 105, 16; David R. Craig, "Retailing—An Essential Industry," *Vital Speeches of the Day* 9, no. 15 (1943), 477.

2. "War Fails to Cut Holiday Trading," *NYT* (December 9, 1941), 53; "Tighter Control on Goods Is Seen," *NYT* (December 8, 1941), 39; "Holiday Trade Still Off but Better Than Tuesday," *NYT* (December 11, 1941), 44; Blum, *V Was for Victory*, 94.

3. "Department Stores Check Stock for Blackout Line Demands," *Christian Science Monitor* (December 13, 1941), 26; "Stores Prepare Blackout Plans," *NYT* (December 14, 1941), F6; "Newark Store Prepares a Blackout Shop," *NYT* (December 13, 1941), 18; "Women Get Ready to Aid Blackouts," *NYT* (December 11, 1941), 36; Blum, *V Was for Victory*, 105.

4. Buenger and Buenger, *Texas Merchant*, 107; light brown ledger, record of annual stockholder meetings and corporation business, 1908–51, 119 BC; "We're in Our 64th Year but We Don't Look It!," MDSC. For letters from servicemen to their former department store employer, see box 3, four folders of World War II letters, MDSC. For another example of an honor roll, see the sixty-five men and women listed in a Falk's department store company newsletter and also honored in a store plaque. *Falk's Forum* (November 1945), 19; See also Wood, *Halle's*, 162, an honor roll that provided the addresses of those in the service so employees could write to them; "Joseph Melvin Lane," *On Eternal Patrol-Lost Submariners of World War II*, http://www.oneternalpatrol.com/lane-j-m.htm (accessed June 8, 2011); Those remaining to work at the stores experienced a "guilt complex," according to one industry member, though they had "a fine, patriotic job to do." "Smaller Stores Full of Fight!" *DSE* (February 1943), 14.

5. Joseph Goldhaber to Poliakoff Bros., January 27, 1942, PC; Wood, *Halle's*, 156, 158; Lew Hahn, "Backing Our Faith!" *DSE* (May 25, 1942), 31; "Take Part of Your Change in War Stamps," *DSE* (May 25, 1942), 30; "Conserve for Victory," *DSE* (July 1942), 44–45; Mary Firestone, *Images of America: Dayton's Department Store* (Charleston, SC: Arcadia Publishing, 2007), 71.

6. Whitaker, *Service and Style*, 154; Meyer Poliakoff, an Abbeville, South Carolina, department store proprietor, was for all intents and purposes impressed into service as an auxiliary fireman, receiving a letter from his local County Council for National Defense explaining his "duty and obligation." F. D. West to Meyer Poliakoff, January 7, 1942, PC; Longstreth, *City Center to Regional Mall*, 294–98; Hardwick, *Mall Maker*, 86–88; "War Bond Day Set By Nation's Stores," *NYT* (May 26, 1942), 19; "War Bond Sales in Stores $699,185," *NYT* (July 3, 1942), 19.

7. Noel F. Busch, "Donald Nelson," *Life* (July 6, 1942), 81–82; "Among Retailing's Contributions," *DSE* (July 1942), 41; Wood, *Halle's*, 156, 158; Blum, *V Was for Victory*, 121; Donald Nelson first headed the Supply Priorities and Allocation Board, which merged into the War Production Board. Kennedy, *Freedom from Fear*, 478, 618; "Among Retailing's Contributions," *DSE* (July 1942), 41. On Edward N. Allen, see *Jewelers' Circular Weekly* (September 11, 1918), 75d, and *Biloxi Daily Herald* (March 12, 1942), 7; Many clothing stores flaunted Order L-224. See Kathy Peiss, *Zoot Suit: The Enigmatic Career of an Extreme Style* (Philadelphia: University of Pennsylvania Press, 2011), 38–39.

8. Phillips-Fein, *Invisible Hands*, 32; Hardwick, *Mall Maker*, 60; "Bulwark to Civilian Morale Seen as Retailers' War Role," *Washington Post* (January 2, 1942), Hecht quote, F11; "Smaller Stores Full of Fight!"; "American Valuation Plan Best under Present Conditions, Officials Say," *Boot and Shoe Recorder* 80 (December 3, 1921), 69; Roberts, Johnson & Rand to D. Poliakoff, January 15, 1941, PC.

9. "War Brides Find Davison-Paxon Ready," *DSE* (January 1942), 17; Leader's department store bridal room photo, 1949, Lima, Ohio, Gottscho-Schleisner Collection, Library of Congress Prints and Photographs Division, Washington, D.C. For background on the role of department stores in the formation of the wedding industry, see Howard, *Brides, Inc.*, chapters 4 and 5, 168; "One Thousand Brides," *DSE* (July 1944), 36; "Our Wedding Gowns Go to 40 Christmas Brides," *Store Chat* (December 1943), 5, SCC.

10. Manufacturer quotes on supply problems in the following letters: Leonard Krower & Son, Inc. to D. Poliakoff, January 19, 1942; Bata Shoe Company, Inc. to D. Poliakoff, January 29, 1942; Archer Hosiery Mills to D. Poliakoff, January 21, 1942; Richmond Dry Goods Co., Inc. to D. Poliakoff, February 4, 1942, PC. Also, see Wear Well Co., to D. Poliakoff, January 19, 1942; Daniel Miller Company to D. Poliakoff, January 24, 1942, PC.

11. "We're in Our 64th Year but We Don't Look It!" MDSC. See also Howard, "'The Biggest Small-Town Store in America,'" 477.

12. "Stiff Post-war Competition Facing Department Stores," *DSE* (November 1943), "super-service" quote, 11; "Baby Shop Frills Are Out," *DSE* (June 1944), 27; "More Stores Join Baby Development Clinic," *DSE* (Marsh 1944), 91; "Department Doubles As Birth-Rate Soars," *DSE* (August 1943), 34; "Charm and Convenience Ideal Baby Shop Theme," *DSE* (August 1943), 35; C. F. Hughes, "The Merchant's Point of View," *NYT* (October 4, 1942), F6.

13. Federated Department Stores became the first to offer unlimited credit payable over time, and others quickly followed. Louis Hyman, *Debtor Nation: The History of America in Red Ink* (Princeton: Princeton University Press, 2011), 109–10, 118–20, 122–27, 129–33, 155. Before the Korean War, large department stores in major eastern cities had revolving credit. After the war, the practice spread and by 1955 some department stores were doing away with installment plans entirely, consolidating sales into revolving credit plans or charge accounts (ibid., 129–30).

14. As Malcolm McNair and Eleanor May point out in their Harvard study of department store performance, gross margins followed a mostly level trend from 1933 to 1960, countering contemporary impressions among store managers that retail distribution costs rose steadily over a long period. For the Harvard study, gross margin was defined as net sales less the net delivered cost of goods sold, after cash discounts taken on purchases were credited and after net alteration and workroom costs were accounted for, and after allowing for merchandise depreciation and stock shortages. Gross margin was expressed as a percentage of net sales in owned, as opposed to leased, departments. McNair and May, *The American Department Store*, 20, 22–25, 32, 40, 44, 47, 61; Hardwick, *Mall Maker*, 50; Blum, *V Was for Victory*, 100; Emmet and Jeuck, *Catalogues and Counters*, 472–73.

15. Blum, *V Was for Victory*, 92, 95, 98; McNair and May, *The American Department Store*, 32; McCraw, *American Business since 1920*, 77; Sears catalogue omitted many hard line goods during the war, things such as aluminum cookware, copper boilers, electrical appliances, stainless-steel cookware and tableware. Toys were scarce and children's books seemed to replace them, with sales doubling. Emmet and Jeuck, *Catalogues and Counters*, 430, 434; "The Evolution of the Basement!" *DSE* (July 1944), 15; "Stiff Post-war Competition Facing Department Stores," *DSE* (November 1943), "service orgy" quote, 10–11.

16. Jacobs, *Pocketbook Politics*, 183–90; "Gitchell to Head OPA Retail Branch," *NYT* (October 3, 1943), S12.

17. Jacobs, *Pocketbook Politics*, 183–90; "Gitchell to Head OPA Retail Branch," S12; Retailer's OPA Bulletin, no. 48 (Washington, D.C.: Department of Information, Office of Price Administration, December 1943), PC, "fitting stool" quote, 1; John Guernsey, "Department Stores in the War," *DSE* (July 1942), 9.

18. Richard S. Tedlow, *New and Improved: The Story of Mass Marketing in America* (New York: Basic Books, 1990), 337; "Urges Policy Changes in OPA Management," *NYT* (August 6, 1942), "cooperation" quote, 28; Jacobs, *Pocketbook Politics*, 194; Blum, *V Was for Victory*, 122; B. Earl Puckett, "Post-war Assets and Liabilities," *DSE* (October 1944), 96; Holl, *From the Boardroom to the War Room*, 53.

19. Bean, *Beyond the Broker State*, 43–44; Senator James E. Murray, "What about Small Business?" *DSE* (July 1944), 48; W. H. Wright, "Little Store—What Now?" *DSE* (March 10, 1942), 2; W. H. Wright, "An Inventory in Chaos," *DSE* (April 10, 1942), 8; "Smaller Stores Full of Fight!" *DSE* (February 1943), "recognize their importance" quote, 14.

20. Price panel letter quote: Ralph C. Segee to George W. Tomlin, June 25, 1943, PC; "Urges Policy Changes in OPA Management," *NYT* (August 6, 1942), 28; Wood, *Halle's*, 157; "OPA-Hecht Price Ceiling Hearing Begin," *NYT* (January 15, 1943), B14; Jacobs, *Pocketbook Politics*, 194.

21. Derby's Department Store World War II Ration Records Scrapbooks, box 1, Milne Special Collections, University of New Hampshire; "OPA Suspends Three Maryland Shoe Dealers," *NYT* (April 13, 1945), 3.

22. Smaller Stores Full of Fight!" *DSE* (February 1943), 54; "OPA Decrees Hit by Small Stores," *DSE* (June 1943), 24; "Says OPA Orders Hard on the Little Fellow," *DSE* (October 1943), 58, quote 62; "Post Your Ceiling Prices," *DSE* (May 25, 1942), 30; "Digest of Amendment No. 3 to Maximum Price Regulation No. 208, Staple Work Clothing," May 4, 1943 (Office of Price Administration Regional Office, Fourth Region, Atlanta, Ga.), PC.

23. "We're in Our 64th Year but We Don't Look It!"; McLean's *Storoscope* (May 8, 1942), MDSC; Howard, "'The Biggest Small-Town Store in America,'" 477; *Falk's Forum* (November 1945), 8, box 1, FBMC; Buenger and Buenger, *Texas Merchant*, 107–8; "A Fine Food Shop in a Department Store," *DSE* (March 1944), 89.

24. Report, Arkwright Inc., New York, January 14, 1943, folder 2: WWII National Bulletins, 1942–44, box 3, MDSC; "We're in Our 64th Year but We Don't Look It!" MDSC; NRDGA April 4, 1942, April 13, 1942, May 29, 1942, folder 2: WWII National Bulletins, 1942–44, box 3, MDSC.

25. "Retailers' Digest on How to Set Ceiling Prices as Governed by Maximum Price Regulation 339—Women's Rayon Hosiery," Prepared by the South Carolina State Office, Columbia, SC. May 15, 1943, PC. "Customary" quote in "Price Ceilings in Rayon Hosiery Effective April 15th," *Underwear & Hosiery Review* (March 1943), PC.

26. Jacobs, *Pocketbook Politics*, 194, quote 196–97, 203–4, 220; "Special Bulletin: Price Posting Procedure for Shoe Retailers," June 7, 1943 (Office of Price Administration, Liberty Life Building, Columbia, South Carolina), PC; Cohen, *Consumers' Republic*, 75–83, 361; "Loss of Hecht Case Not to Deter OPA," *NYT* (February 21, 1943), R3; "Five Big Philadelphia Stores Accused by OPA of Price Violations," *NYT* (July 12, 1945), 3; Emmet and Jeuck, *Catalogues and Counters*, 473.

27. "Thirty-Third Annual NRDGA Convention," *DSE* (February 1944), 85; B. Earl Puckett, "Post-war Assets and Liabilities," *DSE* (October 1944), 37, 96, "free enterprise" quote, 121. For information on the ARF, see "Fear of the Future," *Time* 43, no. 11 (March 13, 1944), 92.

28. Harris, *Merchant Princes*, 194; "Retailer Wins Merchants' Award," *DSE* (February 1946), 122, 124.

CHAPTER 6. THE RACE FOR THE SUBURBS

1. Ira K. Young, "The Challenge to the Small Store," *DSE* (February 1946), 17.

2. United States Department of Labor, Bureau of Labor Statistics, *Employment Outlook in Department Stores*, Bulletin No. 1020 (Washington, D.C.: U.S. Government Printing Office, 1951), 1–4; See *Historical Statistics of the United States*, vol. 4, Table De73–109, Retail establishments, by type of business: 1929–1982, 4–720; Determining the number of department stores across time is difficult, given the changing criteria. According to the 1910 United States census, there were 8,970 department store merchants in the country and 88,059 general stores. Dun & Bradstreet, however, in the teens listed a much smaller number, approximately 1,800 department stores. Dun statistic and 1910 statistics from Paul Nystrom, *Economics of Retailing* (New York: Ronald Press Company, 1919), 248–49.

3. "Highlights of the 35th NRDGA Convention!" *DSE* (February 1946), 33; "The Challenge to the Small Store," *DSE* (February 1946), 17.

4. In 1948, of the total 2,580 department stores, only 99 were partnerships, 26 were individual proprietorships, and one was another "legal form" (perhaps the cooperative department store started by Edward Filene). Table 9.–Department Stores–Legal Form of Organization–United States: 1948, *U.S. Census of Business—1948: Trade Series: Department Stores*, vol. 3, part 44, (Washington, D.C.: U.S. Department of Commerce, Bureau of the Census), 16.

5. "Anatomy of a Modernization," *DSE* (June 1963), 22.

6. James D. Tarver, "Suburbanization of Retail Trade in the Standard Metropolitan Areas of the United States, 1948–54," *American Sociological Review* 22 (August 1957), 427; definition of suburbia drawn from Becky M. Nicolaides and Andrew Wiese, eds., *The Suburb Reader* (New York: Routledge, 2006), 7; Cohen, *A Consumers' Republic*, 123.

7. *Impact of Suburban Shopping Centers on Independent Retailers*, Report of the Select Committee on Small Business United States Senate, 86th Congress, 1st Session, Report No. 1016 (Washington, D.C.: U.S. Government Printing Office, January 5, 1960); Pasdermadjian, *The Department Store*, 149.

8. J. Edward Johnston, "The Economic Value of Parking," Conference on Downtown Parking, Purdue University, September 3, 1958, Series V, Conferences, Acc. 1960 U.S. Chamber of Commerce, Hagley Museum and Library, Wilmington, Delaware; "Kenneth C. Welch, "Modern Trends in Department Store Planning!" *DSE* (November 1944), 16–17; "Getting to the Downtown Store," *DSE* (November 1950), 58, 68; Longstreth, *The Department Store Transformed*, 226–30, "innate conservatism" quote, 231; "Cohen, *A Consumers' Republic*, 257.

9. Editorial Comments, *DSE* (November 1951), 136; Frank Kiefer, "Branch Store: Their Future Looks Bright If You Look before You Leap," *DSE* (April 1963), 15; Welch, "Modern Trends in Department Store Planning!," "major readjustment" quote, 16; Longstreth, *The American Department Store Transformed*, 128; Myron S. Heidingsfield, "Why Do People Shop in Downtown Department Stores?" *JOM* 13 (April 1949), 510–12.

10. "Fedway Stores Planned for Smaller Cities," *DSE* (December 1951), 50; Isenberg, *Downtown America*, 163; Tarver, "Suburbanization of Retail Trade," 433; "'Selling the Advantages of Downtown Shopping,' a Talk by Mr. Chess Lagomarsino, Jr., Presented at the A.M.C. Publicity Directors' Group Meeting," Report #6925, June 19, 1953, 2, FC; Longstreth, *The American Department Store Transformed*, 221, 219; Whitaker, *Service and Style*, 105–6.

11. Tarver, "Suburbanization of Retail Trade," "extinction" quote, 433; John Guernsey, "Suburban Branches: Their Merchandising, Management and Control," *DSE* (August 1951), 52; According to the highway research board study, consumers chose downtown Columbus over the suburbs because they appreciated its greater selection of goods, its convenience for conducting several errands at once, and its cheaper prices. C. T. Jonassen, *Downtown Versus Suburban Shopping*, Special Bulletin No. X-58 (Columbus: Ohio State University Bureau of Business Research, 1953), *Fortune* quote, 1, 58–59.

12. *Miracle on 34th Street*, 1947; *The Big Store*, 1941; *Corduroy*, 1968; Little Lulu in "Bargain Counter Attack," 1946; Bugs Bunny "Hare Conditioned," 1945; Isenberg, *Downtown America*, cites Petula Clark's song, 182–83, 312.

13. Dero A. Saunders, "Race for the Suburbs," 168, "dull the impact" quote, 170; Bart J. Epstein, "Evaluation of an Established Planned Shopping Center," *Economic Geography* 37, no. 1 (January 1961), 20; John Guernsey, "Suburban Branches: Sites, Parking, Financing, Construction, Equipment," *DSE* (September 1951), 102; Pasdermadjian, *The Department Store*, 148; Isenberg, *Downtown America*, 174; Bucklin, *Competition and Evolution*, 106.

14. Longstreth, *The American Department Store Transformed*, 220; Bucklin, *Competition and Evolution*, 107.

15. Frank Kiefer, "Branch Store: Their Future Looks Bright If You Look Before You Leap," *DSE* (April 1963), "Aladdin" quote, 15; The pastoral image "markets in the meadows" was used during this period to describe the appearance of shopping centers in outlying areas. For a 1949 example, see Longstreth, *City Center to Regional Mall*, 222; see also the title of Stephanie Dyer's 2001 dissertation, "Markets in the Meadows"; Longstreth, *The American Department Store Transformed*, 110–11, 113–17, 119, 121–24, 126–27, 172; Frederick, *Selling Mrs. Consumer*, 312.

16. Guernsey, "Suburban Branches: Sites, Parking, Financing, Construction, Equipment," 43; "Is 12% Enough?" *DSE* (June 1962), 130; Hardwick, *Mall Maker*, 105–6; Longstreth, *The American Department Store Transformed*, 173.

17. Guernsey, "Suburban Branches: Sites, Parking, Financing, Construction, Equipment," 41; Blaszczyk, *American Consumer Society, 1865–2005*, 210; Shopping centers founded their own professional association in 1957. The International Council of Shopping Centers was an association of owners, developers, investors, brokers, and retailers in this new industry. See "Historical Timeline," ICSC website, http://www.icsc.org/about/historical-timeline (accessed October 6, 2014).

18. *1963 Census of Business*, vol. 1, part 1, Retail Trade-Area Statistics, 1–6 U.S., Retail Trade-Area Statistics, Table 1: United States: 1963 and 1958; Daniel M. G. Raff, Table De73–109: Retail establishments, by type of business: 1929–1982, 4–720, *Historical Statistics of the United States*, vol. 4, part D: Economic Sectors, ed. Susan B. Carter, Scott Sigmond Garner, Michael R. Haines, Alan L. Olmstead, Richard Sutch, Gavin Wright (Cambridge: Cambridge University Press, 2006); Table De268–290 Retail store sales, by type of business: 1929–1998, 4–733, *Historical Statistics of the United States*, vol. 4, part D: Economic Sectors (Cambridge: Cambridge University Press, 2006); Cohen, *A Consumers' Republic*, 273.

19. Guernsey, "Suburban Branches: Sites, Parking, Financing, Construction, Equipment," 100; Longstreth, *The American Department Store Transformed*, 195; Mary Elizabeth Curry, *Creating an American Institution: The Merchandising Genius of J. C. Penney* (New York: Garland, 1993), 312.

20. "How About Future Planning For Branches," *DSE* (April 1963), 16; "Department Stores Strike Back: Bargain Basements and 'Twigs' Help Old-Line Merchants Recapture Markets," *Barron's National Business and Financial Weekly* (September 4, 1961), 3; Clinton L. Oaks, *Managing Suburban Branches of Department Stores* (Stanford: Graduate School of Business, Stanford University, 1957), 30, 40–42, chapter 2; Store buyers had long resisted group buying organizations, which took away much of their purchasing discretion. Under these new "super buying pools" they were given power over high-style merchandise, but the pools focused on staple goods in durable and soft goods categories. About 15 percent of department store stocks came from the joint buying scheme. Resident buyers working

for outside firms that served independent stores urged their clients to adopt similar buying pools, and expected the type to spread in the postwar, which it did. "Super Buying Pools Broaden Program," *NYT* (December 17, 1944), S8. See also "How About Future Planning for Branches," *DSE* (April 1963), 18.

21. Saunders, "Race for the Suburbs," 168; "How About Future Planning for Branches," 16; Oaks, *Managing Suburban Branches*, 1, 30–32, 37–38, 40–42, 86, chapter 2.

22. Guernsey, "Suburban Branches: Their Merchandising, Management and Control," "personality" quote, 33; Oaks, *Managing Suburban Branches*, "sterile" quote, 88.

23. Longstreth, *The American Department Store Transformed*, "single unit" quote, 170; Hardwick, *Mall Maker*, 85, 128–30. See also Cohen, *A Consumers' Republic*, 262–63; Bucklin, *Competition and Evolution*, 109; "Northgate Sets Pace in Area," *El Paso Herald Post* (August 1, 1966), 3; *Retailing in the 1970s: A Collection of Papers Presented at the National Retail Merchants Association* (New York: National Research Institute, 1966), n.p.

24. "Nasher Concept for Northpark," News Release, box 28, folder 27, FC.

25. Saunders, "Race for the Suburbs," 101; Cohen, *A Consumers' Republic*, 265, 267; Low-income families in 1948 spent 60 percent of their income for housing, food, and other necessities, with only approximately $690 left annually for other purchases. E. R. Richer, "Who Buys in Department Stores?" *DSE* (November 1950), 54; Jonassen, *Downtown Versus Suburban Shopping*, 59; Isenberg, *Downtown America*, 176; Patricia Cooper, "The Limits of Persuasion: Race Reformers and the Department Store Campaign in Philadelphia, 1945–1948," *Pennsylvania Magazine of History and Biography* 126 (January 2002), 124; "Is 12% Enough?" *DSE* (June 1962), "breaking away" quote, 130; "Administration by Crisis," *DSE* (January 1962), "family purchasing team" quote, 20.

26. Isenberg, *Downtown America*, 198; Longstreth, *The American Department Store Transformed*, 155, quote 178.

27. In 1963, for example, the South had more department store establishments than the Northeast and not many fewer than the north central states. Large relative numbers of department stores in the South certainly reflected the census counting small, family-run department stores that would have been more like departmentalized general stores than the massive emporia in cities like New York, Boston, or Chicago. See *1963 Census of Business*, vol. 1, part 1, United States Retail Trade-1963, Table 9: Regions, Division, and States, page 1.44. The northeastern states had 892 establishments; the north central states had 1, 462; the South had 1,193; the West had 704. Annual sales of department stores also varied regionally, with north central states ranking highest, followed by the northeastern states, the South, and the West.

28. Frank Hobbs and Nicole Stoops, *Demographic Trends in the Twentieth Century*, U.S. Census Bureau, Census 2000 Special Reports, Series CENSR-4 (Washington, D.C.: U.S. Government Printing Office, 2002), "population nucleus" quote, B-4, 32, 37–39. By 1950, 56.1 percent lived in metropolitan areas and their cities. In 1960, the proportion of the total U.S. population living in the suburbs (30.9 percent) was almost equal to the proportion of the population living in the central cities (32.3 percent). By 2000, the metropolitan population (226 million) was four times the size of the nonmetropolitan population (55 million) (ibid., 32–33).

29. "Big Business Comes to Small Towns," clipping, circa 1945, Small City Trends folder, Case 13, RC.

30. "Illinois Clinic for Small Stores," *DSE* (November 1946), 85.

31. *1963 Census of Business*, vol. 1, part 1, Retail Trade-Area Statistics, 1–135, Table 16: City Size—United States by Kind of Business: 1963.

32. Ernest A. Miller, "Can Independent Stores Survive in Tomorrow's Mass Merchandising?" *JOR* 39 (Winter 1963–64), 27.

33. John Claire Smith, "Advertising for a Small Town Department Store" (thesis, June 5, 1953, University of Cincinnati, Ohio), 3–4; Bucklin, *Competition and Evolution*, 126. Bucklin suggests that "some of this may be due to the absence of sufficient competitive pressures to drive out less efficient firms."

34. Esperdy, *Modernizing Main Street*, 20, 27, 28. Chain stores and the new combination supermarkets were often housed there.

35. Miller, "Can Independent Stores Survive in Tomorrow's Mass Merchandising?" 27, 30–32. The SBA considered a department store a small business if its annual sales did not exceed $2 million in 1964, up from an earlier $1 million limit (ibid., 28).

36. Photo, Bresee's department store delivery truck on Main Street, Oneonta, N.Y., 1949, BC; Ferry, *A History of the Department Store*, 39–40; Nathan Vigodsky to Meyer Poliakoff, October 9, 1956, PC.

37. "The New Approach to Old Problems," *DSE* (June 1962), 54–56; "Big Business Comes to Small Towns," circa 1945, news clipping, Case 13, RC; Miller, "Can Independent Stores Survive in Tomorrow's Mass Merchandising?" 34; "The New Approach to Old Problems," *DSE* (June 1963), 54; Seymour Helfant and Beatrice Judelle, *Management Manual for Independent Stores: A Handbook for the Head of the Owner-Operated Department or Specialty Store* (New York: National Retail Merchant Association, 1969), 11–13.

38. "The New Approach to Old Problems," 54–56.

39. *1985 Directory of Department Stores* (New York: Business Guides, Inc., 1984), 231, 506; McNair and May, *The American Department Store*, 10. McNair and May note in 1963 that EDP will begin to handle these departments in the not very distant future, though by the time their book came out there were already such accounts in the trade press; "Electronic Data Processing and the Smaller Store," *DSE* (September 1963), 26, 28–29; Bluestone et al., *The Retail Revolution*, 18; Harvey M. Sapolsky, "Organizational Structure and Innovation," *Journal of Business* 40 (October 1967), 502; "Economist Outlook," *DSE* (May 1962), 7; Helfant and Judelle, *Management Manual for Independent Stores*, 251–52.

40. Helfant and Judelle, *Management Manual for Independent Stores*, 251–52; "Automatic Control Systems Can Benefit Smaller Stores, Too," *DSE* (January 1963), 32–33. See also "Electronic Data Processing and the Smaller Store," 29. This account describes the use of an outside service bureau by Craig's in Houston; McNair and May, *The American Department Store*, 10; "Economist Outlook," *DSE* (May 1962), 7.

41. Editorial viewpoint, "Retailing's New Revolution," *Retail Directions* (October, 1973), 8.

42. "Biographical Note," Finding Aid, Foley's Department Store Records, 1845–2006, University of Houston Libraries; "Among Smaller-Size Stores, a Large-Size Trend," *DSE* (July 1962), 32; Otis Escalators advertisement, *DSE* (June 1950), 99.

43. Otis Escalators advertisement, *DSE* (September 1950), 125. See also the Smith Bridgman Company modernization pictured in "A New World of Shopping Satisfaction," *DSE* (November 1963), 20.

44. Howard, "'The Biggest Small-Town Store in America,'" 475–77.

45. See Elvins, *Sales and Celebrations*, for discussion of 1930s modernizations in Buffalo and Rochester stores. For turn-of-the-century innovations, see Leach, *Land of Desire*.

46. For a discussion of rural consumerism, see Ronald R. Kline, *Consumers in the Country: Technology and Social Change in Rural America* (Baltimore: Johns Hopkins University Press, 2000); Ownby, *American Dreams in Mississippi.*

47. Covington, *Belk*, 405; As of 2009, Belk was the largest privately held department store company in the United States. Jay Diamond and Sherri Litt, *Retailing in the Twenty-First Century*, 2nd edition (New York: Fairchild Publishers, 2009), 7.

48. "50 Years in the Morristown Area," *DSE* (January 1963), 87. See also "1862–1962: A Century of Business Growth," *DSE* (March 1963), 46.

49. Downtown Louisville merchants coordinated their event with bus and taxicab companies, parking lot operators, and the police department. See "Louisville Event Boosts Volume 34%," *Women's Wear Daily* (August 16, 1955), Case 13, RC; Made in St. Paul was a joint promotion of different firms, industries, and colleges, sponsored by The Emporium and the St. Paul Junior Chamber of Commerce. "Briefing . . . The Retail News," *DSE* (January 1963), 53; "Big Store System to Buy Stix, Baer: Associated Dry Goods Corp. Seeks St. Louis Concern Associated Dry Goods to Buy Stix, Baer Stores of St. Louis," *NYT* (August 4, 1962), 23; "Aboard the Fashion Showboat," *DSE* (July 1962), 82–83.

50. Myer Poliakoff to Bob Lapidus, July 11, 1956, "full skirts" quote, PC; Kay Inglis-Jones, "Fashion Trends Abroad," *NYT* (February 4, 1956), 22; "California's Stripes Star in New Casual Clothes," *NYT* (February 18, 1956), 22. For a northern example, see Howard, "'The Biggest Small-Town Store in America.'"

51. Nicolaides and Wiese, *The Suburb Reader*, 4; The federal government, however, also supported the modernization of smaller, Main Street stores through the Federal Housing Administration's Modernization Credit Plan. Esperdy, *Modernizing Main Street*, chapter 2; Cohen, *A Consumers' Republic*, 122–23; In addition, during World War II, the federal government promoted the new commercial format, engaging directly in shopping center development. Even though federal plans failed, historian M. Jeffrey Hardwick has suggested that these wartime shopping centers, which were publicized and analyzed in architectural magazines, "paved the way for more ambitious postwar retail facilities." Hardwick, *Mall Maker*, 86–87.

52. Kenneth T. Jackson, "All the World's a Mall: Reflections on the Social and Economic Consequences of the American Shopping Center," *American Historical Review* 101 (October 1996), 1115; Thomas W. Hanchett, "U.S. Tax Policy and the Shopping-Center Boom of the 1950s and 1960s," *American Historical Review* 101 (October 1996), 1082–110.

53. "Rochester Renewal Uprooting Stirs Loud Merchants Hooting," *Women's Wear Daily* (March 4, 1965), Urban Renewal folder, Case 15, RC. Also see Isenberg, *Downtown America.*

54. On David L. Yunich's support at Macy's, New York, see *Women's Wear Daily* (May 27, 1964), clipping, Urban Renewal folder, Case 15, RC. On Rich's, see "R. H. Rich Backs Ike's Urban Policy," *Women's Wear Daily* (June 26, 1957), clipping, Urban Renewal folder, Case 15, RC; Lizabeth Cohen, "Buying into Downtown Revival: The Centrality of Retail to Postwar Urban Renewal in American Cities," *Annals of the American Academy of Political and Social Science* 611 (May 2007), 82–85, 89; And in Chicago as early as 1947, Marshall

Field's contributed to downtown urban renewal plans that affected Loop merchants. Arnold R. Hirsch, "Urban Renewal," *Encyclopedia of Chicago*, http://encyclopedia.chicagohistory .org/pages/1295.htmlaccessed August 24, 2011); "Selling the Advantages of Downtown Shopping," A Talk By Mr. Chess Lagomarsino, Jr., Presented at the AMC Publicity Directors' Group Meeting," Report #6925, June 19, 1953, 2, 5, FC.

55. David A. Loehwing, "Department Stores Strike Back," *Barron's National Business and Financial Weekly* (September 4, 1961), "salvation" quote, 15–16; "Rebuilt Cities Held Retailers' Downtown Key: Called Way to Keep Lead Over Suburbs," *Women's Wear Daily* (March 22, 1959), Abraham & Straus president's quotes clipping, Urban Renewal folder, Case 15, RC.

56. Cohen, "Buying into Downtown Revival, 82–85; Grey Matter department store edition, February 1954, quotes n.p., box 10, folder 20, FC.

57. "33rd Annual NRDGA Convention," *DSE* (February 1944), 91.

58. Charlotte Allen, "A Wreck of a Plan," *Washington Post* (July 17, 2005), http://www .washingtonpost.com/wp-dyn/content/article/2005/07/15/AR2005071502199.html; Amy Lavine, "Urban Renewal and the Story of *Berman v. Parker*," *Urban Lawyer* 42 (2010), 423, 425–26, 444, 451, 465; Spector, *Category Killers*, 146.

59. 54th Annual Convention Report," *DSE* (February 1965), 63. The NRMA urged members to support the government in its urban renewal efforts; "Downtown Areas Not Without Hope," *NYT* (June 21, 1955), 43; "R. H. Rich Backs Ike's Urban Policy," *Women's Wear Daily* (June 26, 1957), clipping, Urban Renewal folder, Case 15, RC; "NRF Turns 100," *Stores* (February 2011), 25–26.

60. "Reluctance to Testify on Bill Seen Limiting Urban Renewal," *Women's Wear Daily* (August 17, 1959), clipping, Urban Renewal folder, Case 15, RC; "Government Aid Stressed to Redevelop Downtown," *Women's Wear Daily* (May 27, 1964), Urban Renewal folder, Case 15, RC; on Section 57 see Dwight D. Eisenhower, "208—Veto of the Second Housing and Urban Renewal Bill," September 4, 1959, *The American Presidency Project*, http://www .presidency.ucsb.edu/ws/?pid = 11499.

61. The New Haven downtown renewal plan in 1957 called for nearly $40 million in federal loans and grants, while private investment came in at $34 million. Longstreth, *The American Department Store Transformed*, 231; Cohen, *A Consumers' Republic*, 272; R. Hart Phillips, "Renewal Pushed by Jacksonville: City is Achieving Objectives without Federal Aid," *NYT* (April 14, 1963), 6.

62. "Ivey's Seventh Store: Downtown Center, Jacksonville, Florida," *DSE* (February 1963), 62; Phillips, "Renewal Pushed by Jacksonville," 1, 6; William F. Freeman, "Retailing Gains Noted for South," *NYT* (October 1, 1961), F12.

63. Phillips, "Renewal Pushed by Jacksonville," "slum clearance" and "dingy" quotes, 1; Isenberg, *Downtown America*, 175–87; Laurence Stern, "Renewal Stirs Hagerstown," *Washington Post and Times Herald* (May 19, 1957), A20; James Connolly, "Baltimore Tries to Renew Itself," *NYT* (January 12, 1959), "modern developments" quote, 136.

64. Cohen, *A Consumers' Republic*, 114; For a discussion of conservatism and businessmen, see Phillips-Fein, *Invisible Hands*.

65. Edward Filene proposed the plan in 1936. "Cooperatives See Their Plans Gain," *NYT* (November 13, 1936), 44; After founding the Consumer Distribution Corporation, he opened the first cooperative unit in 1947, making plans (which failed ultimately) to open

one hundred. "The First Customer-Owned Department Store in the U.S. Is Now Under Way," *Washington Daily News* (September 25, 1947), 34, news clipping, Case 3, RC.

66. Phillips-Fein, *Invisible Hands*, 33. Phillips-Fein does not document these political divisions within the industry under study here, but her broader observations apply.

67. "Highlights of the 35th NRDGA Convention!" *DSE* (February 1946), 14.

68. Nevertheless, union leaders and store employees pushed to organize retail workers. Between 1954 and 1958, District 65 of the Retail Wholesale and Department Store Union reached beyond the downtown New York stores in which they had been active. Gimbels, Sterns's, Saks Thirty-Fourth Street, Hearn's, Bloomingdale's, Namm's, and Loeser's all held contracts with District 65. Building on this success with downtown stores, organizers sought to incorporate the suburbs. They focused their efforts on branches of Bloomingdale's, Abraham & Straus, and Stern's. The union began informational picketing and leafleting and engaged in home visits, and in some cases when organizers were fired, in strikes. Such drives were largely unsuccessful, reflecting the difficulty of organizing a part-time female labor force and the broader political and economic context of the postwar, which increasingly favored big business over labor interests. Minna P. Ziskind, "Labor Conflicts in the Suburbs: Organizing Retail in Metropolitan New York, 1954–1958," *International Labor and Working-Class History* (Fall 2003), 56, 60–63.

69. It set up rules about which unions could participate in National Labor Relations Board (NLRB) elections, forcing union official to abandon militant tactics, sympathy strikes, and secondary boycotts, and requiring all officials who wished to use the NLRB to sign affidavits stating that they were not Communists. Opler, *For All White-Collar Workers*, 3–4, 159, 173, 208–9; See also Cohen, *A Consumers' Republic*, 153.

70. Stephanie M. Amerian, "'Buying European': The Marshall Plan and American Department Stores," *Diplomatic History* (2014): 1–26.

71. James West Davidson et al., eds., *Nation of Nations: A Narrative History of the American Republic* 4th edition (New York: McGraw-Hill, 2001), 922; Domination Quote in "No War! That's Almost a Certainty Now," *DSE* (February 1951), 29. Similarly, as Tracy Deutsch argues, supermarkets "as positioned by policymakers and trade associations," were "vehicles for establishing the superiority of America, and more broadly, of capitalism itself." *Building a Housewife's Paradise: Gender, Politics, and American Grocery Stores in the Twentieth Century* (Chapel Hill: University of North Carolina Press, 2010), 192. "High Time We Cracked Down!" *DSE* (August 1950), "softness" quote, 3.

72. "Quit Fiddling: Rome Is Burning!" *DSE* (September 1950), 3; "Wouldn't Seem Normal without a Crisis," *DSE* (December 1950), 5; "Washington News," *DSE* (June 1951), 5; "Free Enterprise: The Continuing Force for Shaping America's Greatness," *DSE* (January 1963), 48–49.

73. Phillips-Fein, *Invisible Hands*, 58; Sara Diamond, *Roads to Dominion: Right-Wing Movements and Political Power in the United States* (New York: Guilford Press, 1995), 24, 47.

74. Beth Kephart, "South Side Portraits," *Chicago Tribune* (March 23, 2003); Wood, *Halle's*, 157; Cooper, "The Limits of Persuasion," 97–99, 124. For discussion of black service workers in southern department stores from 1890–1965, see Beth Kreydatus, "'You Are a Part of All of Us,'" 108–29.

75. Isenberg, *Downtown America*, 207; "A Gold Mine for Retail Research," *DSE* (October 1962), 39. For a broader discussion of business, the black consumer market, and market-driven civil rights reform, see Robert E. Weems, *Desegregating the Dollar: African*

American Consumerism in the Twentieth Century (New York: New York University Press, 1998).

76. "Administration by Crisis," *DSE* (January 1962), 21; "Sales potential" quote in "A Gold Mine for Retail Research," *DSE* (October 1962), 39; Isenberg, *Downtown America*, 206, 227; "The Negro Consumer Dynamic Force in Urban Marketing," *DSE* (August 1965), 25.

77. David R. Heinly, "Washington Alert," *DSE* (September 1963), 5.

78. "An after-dinner address delivered to a gathering of executives and employees of the outstanding South Center Department Store, Chicago, Ill., September 22, 1947," 00217–18, Reel 2, Speeches and Writings, 1946–47, Mary McLeod Bethune Papers (microform): The Bethune Foundation Archive, Bethune-Cookman College Campus, Daytona Beach, FL.

79. Memo from Mr. Stephenson to Mr. Shiffick, "Restrooms," September 10, 1958, box 11, folder 11, FC. For a letter of protest against the lack of lunch counter service for blacks, see Letter from Retired Teachers Association of Houston to the Management, November 26, 1955, box 11, folder 12, FC. On segregated shoe department service, see Letter from Mrs. Jacob T. Stewart to Sales Manager, February 11, 1957, box 13, folder 15, FC. On sit-down protests at the soda fountain, see Memo to Mr. Dundas, September 10, 1958, box 14, folder 16, FC. On pickets at Rich's, see Whitaker, *Service and Style*, 47. On trying on clothes and hats, see "Oral History Interview with Cecelia T. Tucker," (March 6, 2009), interview by Karen Vaughan, Perry Library, Digital Collections, Old Dominion University, Norfolk, VA, http://www.lib.odu.edu/specialcollections/oralhistory/oduhistory.

80. Beth Kreydatus, " 'You Are a Part of All of Us,' "110; "Demonstrators Jailed Awaiting Trial in Georgia," *Anderson Daily Bulletin* (Indiana) (October 20, 1960), "welcome" quote, 34; John V. Petrof, "The Effect of Student Boycotts upon the Purchasing Habits of Negro Families in Atlanta, Georgia," *Phylon* 24 (1960): 266–70; Isenberg, *Downtown America*, 206, 215, 218. For a broader discussion of commercial investment in downtown and the civil rights movement of the early 1960s, see Isenberg, chapter 6.

81. Letter from Dr. & Mrs. Charles Weinaug to Personnel Manager, January 9, 1964; Memo from Mrs. Cayler to Mrs. Cipriani, November 14, 1964, Re: Colored Model in Terrace, box 21, folder 18, FC. Isenberg, *Downtown America*, 225, 215–16.

82. "The Challenge of Change," *DSE* (February 1962), 40, 43; Department stores continued to oppose the creation of a Consumer Protection Agency in the 1970s, lobbying as did Sears through the Business Roundtable, an organization of CEOs from the Fortune 500. Phillips-Fein, *Invisible Hands*, 190, 195.

83. "The Challenge of Change," *DSE* (February 1962), 40, 43; "Big Store System To Buy Stix, Baer," *NYT* (August 4, 1962), 23.

84. *Impact of Suburban Shopping Centers on Independent Retailers*, 4; "The Challenge of Change," *DSE* (February 1962), Humphrey quote, 43, 48.

85. Bean, *Beyond the Broker State*, 83; "A Report on Lease Guarantees in Shopping Centers for Smaller Stores," *DSE* (July 1962), 19; Miller, "Can Independent Stores Survive in Tomorrow's Mass Merchandising?" 28; Robert W. Bell and John M. Peterson, *Business Budgeting for Small Department Stores* (Washington, D.C.: Small Business Administration, 1963). While large independent department stores and department store chains could have

the high credit ratings that allowed them exact preferences in shopping center development, they could also be small enough to merit studies funded by the SBA and publications addressed to their specific needs.

86. *DSE* (February 1963), "controlled economy" quote, 24–26; "54th Annual Convention Report," *DSE* (February 1965), "dynamic" quote 61; On the history of Allied Stores, see "Campeau Corporation," in *International Directory of Company Histories*, ed. Paula Kepos and Paul Derdak (Chicago: St. James Press, 1992), 25–28.

CHAPTER 7. THE POSTWAR DISCOUNT REVOLUTION

1. Robert Drew-Bear, *Mass Merchandising: Revolution and Evolution* (New York: Fairchild Publications, 1970), 17, vice president's quote, 52; Bluestone et al., *The Retail Revolution*, 13. The founding date was 1948 in "King's Opens New Store in Manchester Tuesday," *Hartford Courant* (March 21, 1966), 9C; Myron Kandel, "The Discount House," *NYT* (November 9, 1961), 47. Whereas department stores had their own Standard Industrial Classification definitions, discount stores did not in the early 1960s. For a detailed definition of a discount store, see Russell Alan Porter, "An Investigation of the Effects of Discount Department Store Competition on Selected Retail Establishments" (Ph.D. diss., University of Arkansas, 1966), 2–3; David Usborne, "Pile It High, Sell It Cheap, Make the Parking Lot Big Profits Grow," *Independent* (June 15, 1999), http://www.independent.co.uk/news/pile-it-high-sell-it-cheap-and-make-the-parking-lot
-big-the-profits-grow-1100209.html; Hannah Liptrot, "Tesco: Supermarket Superpower," *BBC News* (June 3, 2005), http://news.bbc.co.uk/2/hi/business/4605115.stm.

2. Alan Raucher, "Sunday Business and the Decline of Sunday Closing Laws," *Journal of Church and State* (Winter 1994), 46–51; "Hartford's Newest Discount Store," *Hartford Courant* (November 14, 1957), 9.

3. "King's Opens New Store in Manchester Tuesday," *Hartford Courant* (March 21, 1966), 9C; Reference to suburban locations on low-cost land in Bluestone et al., *The Retail Revolution*, 20.

4. Some were membership stores requiring membership cards, though such cards were given freely at businesses and at the store itself. By the mid-1960s, a few discount firms still used membership cards. Isadore Barmash, *More Than They Bargained For: The Rise and Fall of Korvette's* (New York: Chain Store Publishing Corporation, 1981), 7; Bucklin, *Competition and Evolution*, 88–89; Porter, "An Investigation of the Effects of Discount Department Store Competition," 9, 14; Vance and Scott, *Wal-Mart*, 30, 48; Kandel, "The Discount House," 47; Cohen, *The Consumers' Republic*, 381.

5. "Retailing: Everybody Loves a Bargain" *Time* (July 6, 1962), http://www.time.com/time/magazine/article/0,9171,940052,00.html; Hendrickson, *The Grand Emporiums*, 199–200, quote, 201, 202; "Discount Houses Add to Stature," *NYT* (January 6, 1958), 64.; Barmash, *More Than They Bargained For*, 29, 35–36; Bucklin, *Competition and Evolution*, 88–89. In 1950, Korvette's had a volume of $2 million.

6. Isadore Barmash, "The Discount Triumph," *NYT* (June 26, 1967), 47; Leonard Stone, "Discount Stores Broaden Inroads," *NYT* (July 19, 1964), *F1*; On this "retail revolution," see Bluestone et al., *The Retail Revolution*, 18; "Discount Houses: Big, National and Maybe a Retail Revolution," *Tide* (May 8, 1954), 21, clipping, box 10, folder 20, FC; Kandel, "The Discount House," 47; Vance and Scott, *Wal-Mart*, 23; On earlier precedents, see

Lebhar, *Chain Stores in America*, 357; "The Revolutionists of Retailing," *Fortune* (April 1962), 265; Discounters in the 1950s saw parallels at the time between the discount store and the transformation of the food business in the 1930s. Drew-Bear, *Mass Merchandising*, 182; Stanley C. Hollander, "The Discount House," *JOM* 18 (July 1953), 1937 "discount house" quote, 58, "manifestations" and "two-price" quotes, 59.

7. Vance and Scott, *Wal-Mart*, 30, 35–36; Porter, "An Investigation of the Effects of Discount Department Store Competition," 13.

8. Porter, "An Investigation of the Effects of Discount Department Store Competition, 12, 13, 16, 43–51; Bluestone et al., *The Retail Revolution*, 18.

9. Porter, "An Investigation of the Effects of Discount Department Store Competition," 43, 54.

10. Isadore Barmash, "Discount Stores Cite Price Study," *NYT* (April 28, 1965), 69; Bluestone et al., *The Retail Revolution*, 13.

11. McNair and May, *The American Department Store*, 42, 73–74; Sacha Joseph, "Ethnicity, Personality, and Values: Exploring the Consumer Exodus from Department to Discount Department Stores" (Ph.D. diss., Florida State University, 2006), 3–4. See also Robert Berner, "This Rising Tide Won't Lift All Boats," *Businessweek* (January 12, 2004), 114–16.

12. Doubman and Whitaker, *The Organization and Operation of Department Stores*, 273; Harris, *Merchant Princes*, 109.

13. Scott and Vance, *Wal-Mart*, 49, 61, 116, 119; Gene German and Gerard Hawkes, *Operating Results of Self-Service Discount Department Stores, 1983–84* (Cornell University, 1984), 25; Lebhar, *Chain Stores in America*, 361; "Kresge's Detroit Discount House," *Wall Street Journal* (February 19, 1962), 6; "K-Mart Corporation History," Company Profiles_Fundinguniverse http://www.fundinguniverse.com/company-histories/kmart-corp oration-history/ (accessed June 14, 2012); "Kresge to Open 23 K Mart Stores in Next Two Months," *Wall Street Journal* (September 1, 1965), 3.

14. Tracey Deutsch, "Untangling Alliances: Social Tensions Surrounding Independent Grocery Stores and the Rise of Mass Retailing," in *Food Nations: Selling Taste in Consumer Societies*, ed. Warren Belasco and Philip Scranton (New York: Routledge, 2001), 156–74; Bucklin, *Competition and Evolution*, 300.

15. Cohen, "From Town Center to Shopping Center," 1075–76; Bluestone et al., *The Retail Revolution*, 20, 23, table 2.3, p. 30; Scott and Vance, *Wal-Mart*, 44; *Wal-Mart: The High Cost of Low Prices* (2005; director, Robert Greenwald) popularized the phrase associated with Wal-Mart.

16. Bluestone et al., *The Retail Revolution*, table 2.3, p. 30; For example, see the case of the fashion advisor, Tobe. "The Lady Boss Who Bosses the Bosses," *DSE* (February 1962), 46; See also Kay Brownlee, who was style expert for the B. F. Dewees Department Store in Philadelphia in 1939 and then its personnel director from 1940 until the store's closing in the late 1960s. Kay Brownlee/ Dewees Department Store Papers, Hagley Museum and Library, Wilmington, Delaware. For an example of an influential middle manager, see the case of B. Eugenia Lies, director of planning at Macy's in New York City in the early twentieth century. Laurel Graham, "Lillian Gilbreth and the Mental Revolution at Macy's, 1925–1928," *Journal of Management History* 6 (2000): 285–305. In the early 1950s, Clara E. Clark became perhaps the first African American woman to become a personnel director. She was hired by the South Center Department Store in Chicago, which would later be a

black-owned firm. "Clara E. Clark," Obituary, *Chicago Tribune* (April 24, 1998), http://art
icles.chicagotribune.com/1998-04-24/news/9804240153_1_mrs-clark-chicago-home-sales
-clerk. For a broader discussion of female department store employees to 1940, see Benson,
Counter Cultures.

17. Myron Gable, Karen R. Gillespie, and Martin Topol, "The Current Status of
Women in Department Store Retailing: An Update," *JOR* 60, no. 2 (Summer 1984), 90–91.
For a discussion of the conservative Christian ethos behind Wal-Mart's expansion, see Beth-
any Moreton, *To Serve God and Wal-Mart: The Making of Christian Free Enterprise* (Cambridge, Mass.: Harvard University Press, 2009); Drew-Bear, *Mass Merchandising,*
"education" quote, 81; Barmash, *More Than They Bargained For,* 59–61; Sam Walton, *Made
in America,* 218; "Female Wal-Mart Employees File New Bias Claim," *NYT* (October 27,
2011).

18. John W. Wingate and Arnold Corbin, *Changing Patterns in Retailing* (Homewood,
Ill.: Richard D. Irwind, 1956), "public's response" quote, 11.

19. For more on consumer acceptance, see Drew-Bear, *Mass Merchandising,* 60, 85;
Vance and Scott, *Wal-Mart,* 34, 37; Porter, "An Investigation of the Effects of Discount
Department Store Competition," 81.

20. D. A. Doyle, et al., *A Report on the Cornell Co-eds Image of Rothschild's Sportswear
Department,* report prepared for Jim Rothschild, Cornell University, 1964, 7–8; Charles B.
McCann, *Women and Department Store Newspaper Advertising: A Motivational Study of the
Attitudes of Women toward Department Store Newspaper Advertising* (Social Research, Inc.
Report, 1957), 107–25; F. E. Brown and George Fisk, "Department Stores and Discount
Houses: Who Dies Next?" *JOR* (Fall 1965), 17–19. A consumer study performed for Rich's
department store outlined perceived differences between department stores and discounters
(Kmart) and chains. Part V—Image Characteristics, Graph 1–8, circa 1970, series 3, box
29, folder 15, RRC.

21. M. S. Moyer, "The Roots of Large-Scale Retailing," *JOM* 26 (October 1962), "insti-
tutional" and "ready" quotes, 55–56; Porter, "An Investigation of the Effects of Discount
Department Store Competition," "do-it-yourself" quote, 11; "Eugene Ferkauf, 91, Dies;
Restyled Retail," *NYT* (June 6, 2012); Vance and Scott, *Wal-Mart,* 24.

22. F. W. Gilchrist, "The Discount House," *JOM* 17 (January 1953), 267–72; David A.
Loehwing, "Department Stores Strike Back," *Barron's National Business and Financial
Weekly* (September 4, 1961), 15; Kandel, "The Discount House," 47; Drew-Bear, *Mass
Merchandising,* 130.

23. Such descriptions were reported by a Los Angeles department store appliance manager in 1949, cited in Gilchrist, "The Discount House," 267. See also accounts included in
Wingate and Corbin, *Changing Patterns in Retailing,* 12.

24. Many discount operators expanded rapidly with little cash reserves or assets, borrowed at high interest rates, and bought on extended credit terms. Vance and Scott, *Wal-
Mart,* 35.

25. Hollander, "The Discount House," 59; Gene Boyo, "Discount Houses Face Retail
Fight," *NYT* (February 14, 1954), "annoying" and "sleeves" quotes, F1; Discounters were
remembered as "the postwar bogy of conventional retailers." See "Discount Houses Add
to Stature," *NYT* (January 6, 1958), 64; Kandel, "The Discount House," "pariah" quote,
47; Ben Gordon, executive Vice President of Rich's department store in Atlanta and an

active member of the NRDGA was attributed with the much repeated epithet "bootlegger." See Boyo, "Fair Trade Legal but Will It Last?" *NYT* (November 14, 1954), F1; Boyo, "Cut-Rate Menace Takes Many Forms," *NYT* (September 5, 1954), "monster" quote, F1.

26. *Discount-House Operations: Report of the Select Committee on Small Business, United States Senate*, 85th Congress, Second Session, Report Number 2504 (Washington, D.C.: U.S. Government Printing Office, 1958), "ostrich" quote, 4; memo from C. F. Luft to Misters Dundas, Kaim, Friedman, Brawn, and Cuevas, May 14, 1954, "Discount Houses in Houston on Jewelry," May 26, 1954, L. C. McCulley, Report, box 10, folder 20, FC; "Globe Discount Store #2," Comparison Office report, July 29, 1961, box 17, folder 21, FC; summary of *Retailing Daily* titles in Hollander, "The Discount House," 57.

27. Hollander, "Discount Retailing: An Examination of Some Divergences," 251–52, 257; Boyo, "Discount Houses Face Retail Fight." F1.

28. Porter, "An Investigation of the Effects of Discount Department Store Competition," 13; Drew-Bear, *Mass Merchandising*, 57.

29. "Northgate Sets Pace in Area," *El Paso Herald Post* (August 1, 1966), "reputable firms" quote, 3; Morris L. Sweet, "Tenant-Selection Policies of Regional Shopping Centers," *JOM* 23 (April 1, 1959), "aggressive" quote, 399; Drew-Bear, *Mass Merchandising*, 100.

30. Walter Henry Nelson, *The Great Discount Delusion* (New York: David McKay Company, 1965), 205–8. For a broader discussion of consumer activism during this period, see Daniel Horowitz, *The Anxieties of Affluence: Critiques of American Consumer Culture, 1939–1979* (Amherst: University of Massachusetts Press, 2004), chapter 6.

31. Isadore Barmash, "New Book Opposes Methods by Cut-Rate Stores," *NYT* (July 12, 1965), 39–40.

32. "Are We Against Discounting?" *DSE* (January 1962), 17; Myron Kandel, "The Discount House," 47; Myron Kandel, "Apparel Men Ease Stand on Discounts," *NYT* (July 20, 1962), 29; Hendrickson, *The Grand Emporiums*, 200–201; "Retailing: Discounter on 34th Street," *Time* (November 10, 1967) http://www.time.com/time/magazine/article/0,9171,837555,00.html; Barmash, *More Than They Bargained For*, 75–77, 137, 150–151, 161; Vance and Scott, *Wal-Mart*, 27; Drew-Bear, *Mass Merchandising*, 73, 57, 128.

33. Retail scholars first began writing about this new institution during World War II, but in the early 1950s marketing expert Stanley Hollander still lamented the lack of scholarly attention to the topic. Several years after discounters had first appeared on the scene, the retail industry was still figuring out whether the phenomenon was something peculiar to the special context of the World War II era or whether it represented a new direction in the field. Most soon agreed, however, that discount selling had become "a serious challenge to conventional retailers." Boyo, "Discount Houses Face Retail Fight," "side of the story" quote, F1; Hollander, "The Discount House," 57–58. The first article in the *JOR* on the topic was in 1943 (ibid., 58); Drew-Bear, *Mass Merchandising*, 16; Lebhar, *Chain Stores in America*, 358.

34. Loehwing, "Department Stores Strike Back," "strike back" quote, 3, "twigs" quote, 15.

35. Bluestone et al., *The Retail Revolution*, 32; Lebhar, *Chain Stores in America*, 361–62; by 1962, in a list of 109 companies obtaining sales of at least $10 ten million in their discount stores, four department store chains made it into the top ten. The editors of *The*

Discount Merchandiser, Discount Retailing in the U.S.: A Detailed Marketing Study of a Dynamic New Force-the Discount Store (New York: Super Market Publishing Co., 1963), 216–17.

36. Drew-Bear, *Mass Merchandising*, 181.

37. *Discount-House Operations: Report of the Select Committee on Small Business, United States Senate*, 85th Congress, Second Session, Report Number 2504 (Washington, D.C.: U.S. Government Printing Office, 1958), 16; Macy's had long been a major player in these contests over pricing power. In the mid-1930s, Macy's tried to sell General Electric–brand refrigerators without being a franchised dealer. Stanley C. Hollander, "Discount Retailing: An Examination of Some Divergences from the One-Price System in American Retailing" (Ph.D. diss., University of Pennsylvania, 1954), 249–50.

38. Boyo, "Fair Trade Legal but Will It Last?" *NYT* (November 14, 1954), "lick 'em" quote, F1; Bluestone et al., *The Retail Revolution*, 32; Porter, "An Investigation of the Effects of Discount Department Store Competition," 54–55. In Dallas, for example, nine out of city's twelve department stores changed their pricing policies because of discounters.

39. "Reminiscences of Frank Peters," p. 26, interview by Harriet F. Miller, prepared for Rodman Public Library for the Oral History Project, Alliance, Ohio, August 6, 1975,Alliance Memory, http://www.alliancememory.org/cdm/ref/collection/voices/id/135; Rich's department store in Atlanta outranked Sears and Kmart in these areas (progressivism and civic-mindedness), though perhaps the study did not include those affected by its long history of segregation. Part V—Image Characteristics, Graph 1–8, circa 1970, Series 3, box 29, folder 15, RRC.

40. The implications are that a different result might have been possible with different policies or enforcement regimes. In other words, the discount "revolution" or its "evolution" in the mid-twentieth century was not inevitable. In no way should this be interpreted as an argument against government regulation.

41. "Hartford's Newest Discount Store," 9.

42. "54th Annual Convention Report," *DSE* (February 1965), 63; "1959 Sunday Law Upheld in New Jersey," *NYT* (April 5, 1960), 39, 41.

43. For more on this decision, see "Similarly Situated under the Sunday Closing Law," *University of Pennsylvania Law Review* 119 (November 1970): 190–99; "5 Blue Law Pleas Blocked by Court," *NYT* (Jun 20, 1961), 18.

44. "1959 Sunday Law Upheld in New Jersey," 39, 41; "54th Annual Convention Report," 63; "5 Blue Law Pleas Blocked by Court," 18; "Reform of State Sunday-Selling Curbs is Sought," *NYT* (March 19, 1973), 39. See also "Judge Bars Harassment of Texas Discount Store That Stays Open Sunday," *Wall Street Journal* (January 11, 1963), 10; Isa-dore Barmash, "A Shift in Policy by Retailers Widens as J. C. Penney Acts," *NYT* (October 8, 1969), "never on Sunday" quote, 61.

45. Bean, *Beyond the Broker State*, 75–77. Bean argues that competition from the private brands of department stores and chain stores and from discounters' low prices under-cut fair traders and led to the policy's demise, 81. For a discussion of Macy's and book publishers in the postwar period, see Laura J. Miller, "Saving Books from the Market: Price Maintenance Policies in the United States and Europe," in *Citizenship and Participation in*

the Information Age, ed. Manjunath Pendakur and Roma Harris (Aurora, Ontario: Garamond Press, 2002), 222.

46. Britain maintained fair trade much longer than the United States. According to Helen Mercer, the 1964 Resale Prices Act, which made resale price maintenance illegal, led to dominance by large retailers. See "Retailer-Supplier Relationships before and after Resale Prices Act, 1964: A Turning Point in British Economic History?" *Enterprise & Society* 15 (March 2014): 123–65; "French Lawmakers on Both Sides Unite to Spear Amazon" (October 3, 2013), *France 24,* http://www.france24.com/en/20131003-national-assembly -amazon-book-law-free-shipping-competition-ump-socialist-lang/.

47. Palamountain, *The Politics of Distribution*, 248; Vance and Scott, *Wal-Mart*, 26; McCraw, "Competition and 'Fair Trade,'" 209–11; FDR opposed the legislation, but signed it after its managers out-maneuvered a veto by attaching it as a rider to an important D.C. revenue bill; Bean, *Beyond the Broker State*, 75–76, 205 n. 28.

48. Drew-Bear, *Mass Merchandising*, 51, 56, 58, 60, 79–80, 83, 93, 126.

49. The independent department store, Jacome's in Tucson, used their state fair trade laws to attack new discounters in their market. Webb-Vignery, *Jacome's Department Store*, 146–148; "Competition and 'Fair Trade,'" quote, 211; Hollander, "Discount Retailing: An Examination of Some Divergences," 235, 290.

50. Bean, *Beyond the Broker State*, 77–78. As Bean has demonstrated, the period 1945–51 saw challenges to fair trade from the Federal Trade Commission, a newly formed Antitrust Subcommittee charged with investigating monopoly, and the courts; McCraw, "Competition and 'Fair Trade,'" 211.

51. Ralph Cassady Jr., "The New York Department Store Price War of 1951," *JOM* 22 (July 1957), 4, 6–7, 9; McCraw, "Competition and 'Fair Trade,'" 212.

52. "Remarks of Rep. John A. McGuire Introducing H.R. 5767," in *The Legislative History of the Federal Antitrust Laws and Related Statutes*, part 1, *The Antitrust Laws*, vol. 1, ed. Earl W. Kintner (New York: Chelsea House, 1978), 563; Butcher, *Fundamentals of Retailing*, 37.

53. The passage of the McGuire Act had no effect on the price wars, as they were already over when the law was enacted in mid-July 1952. Cassady, "The New York Department Store Price War of 1951," 10; McCraw, "Competition and 'Fair Trade,'" "wages" quote, 212–13; Karl Rannells, "Washington Alert!" *DSE* (November 1951), 5.

54. Bean, *Beyond the Broker State*, 81, 86; Miller, "Saving Books from the Market," 222.

55. Bean, *Beyond the Broker State*, 81–83, 86. *United States v. McKesson & Robbin* (1956) declared wholesale price maintenance unconstitutional. See Bean, 82; Butcher, *Fundamentals of Retailing*, 37; Fisher, "Ohio Fair Trade: Fair or Foul," 569; "Washington Alert," *DSE* (April 1963), 5; Drew-Bear, *Mass Merchandising*, 126; McCraw, "Competition and 'Fair Trade,'" 211, 214; Washington Alert," *DSE* (November 1962), 5.

56. *Discount House Operations: Report of the Select Committee on Small Business*, 85th Cong., 2nd Sess., Senate Report 2504 (Washington, D.C.: U.S. Government Printing Office, 1958), 9, 11.

57. Barmash, *More Than They Bargained For*, 24, 40; Bean, *Beyond the Broker State*, 86; Drew-Bear, *Mass Merchandising*, 178; the discount chain Zayres had more than $1.2 billion in sales in 1977. Hendrickson, *The Grand Emporiums*, 458.

58. McCraw, "Competition and 'Fair Trade,'" 214; Phillips-Fein, *Invisible Hands*, 155–56. Nixon policy makers quoted in Jacobs, *Pocketbook Politics*, 263. On Nixon, inflation, and price controls, see Daniel Yergin and Joseph Stanislaw, *The Commanding Heights: The Battle for the World Economy* (New York: Simon & Schuster, 1998), 60–64; "Remarks of Sen. Edward W. Brooke Introducing S. 4203," 93rd Cong., 2nd Sess., December 3, 1974, in *The Legislative History of the Federal Antitrust Laws and Related Statutes*, part 1, *The Antitrust Laws*, vol. 1, 949–50.

59. Bean, *Beyond the Broker State*, 84; "Remarks of Sen. Edward W. Brooke Introducing S. 4203," 93rd Cong., 2nd Sess., December 3, 1974, in *The Legislative History of the Federal Antitrust Laws and Related Statutes*, part 1, *The Antitrust Laws*, vol. 1, "enemy" quote, 948; Gerald Ford, "Statement on the Consumer Goods Pricing Act of 1975," December 12, 1975, *American Presidency Project*, http://www.presidency.ucsb.edu/ws/?pid=5432.

60. Bluestone et al., *The Retail Revolution*, 20, 127, 131; Bean, *Beyond the Broker State*, 84.

CHAPTER 8. THE DEATH OF THE DEPARTMENT STORE

1. *Retailing in the 1970s: A Collection of Papers Presented to the National Retail Merchants Association's Annual Convention at the New York Hilton, January 1966* (New York: Retail Research Institute, 1966), n.p.

2. "The Retailing Outlook—1972, Remarks by Howard N. Feist, Chairman of the Board, Gladding's, Inc. and the Shepard Company before the Greater Providence Chamber of Commerce," 7–8, box 1, OC. On the 1970s economic transformations, see Beth Bailey and David Farber, eds., *America in the Seventies* (Lawrence: University Press of Kansas, 2004), 2–4.

3. Eleanor G. May and Malcolm P. McNair, "Department Stores Face Stiff Challenge in Next Decade," *JOR* 53 (Fall 1977), 47, 50–51, 53.

4. According to census data, the department store industry saw its total share of retail decline in the early postwar period to a low of 6.21 percent in 1954. It then experienced a rising market share during this period of consolidation, reaching a high of 11.41 percent in 1972 before starting to drop again into the early 1980s. However, as Stanley Hollander points out, these census figures are misleading about the true status of the conventional department store field as they included discount and low-price merchandisers in their count. In the early postwar period, Sears and Ward pushed these sales up, and in the 1970s, Kmart and Wal-Mart did. Traditional department stores comprised nearly 100 percent of their category in the 1929 census but only 40 percent in 1982. Hollander, "Chain Store Developments," 299 n. 2, 302. The industry's command of total retail sales fell further to 2.8 percent by 2004. "Attention Shoppers: Great Deals in Retail Mergers," *Knowledge @ Wharton*, March 30, 2005, http://knowledge.wharton.upenn.edu/article.cfm?articleid=1158.

5. Johnson and Kim, "When Strategy Pales," 587; "Robert Campeau's Special Genius," *NYT* (January 17, 1990), http://www.nytimes.com/1990/01/17/opinion/robert-campeau-s-special-genius.html; In 2003, Wal-Mart had $256.3 billion in sales, which was nearly 2.5 percent of the United States' GNP. Spector, *Category Killers*, xv.

6. Walton, *Made in America*, 125; Lichtenstein, *The Retail Revolution*, 30. Wal-Mart cut middlemen in its overseas purchasing in the mid-1970s, buying directly from East Asia.

It set up a Hong Kong office in 1981 and a Taipei office in 1983. By 1989, it had ninety staffers in Asia (ibid., 152). "Rewriting the Rules of Retailing," *NYT* (October 15, 1989), F1. At the same time, Kmart's market share dropped from 65 percent in 1980 to 40 percent by 1989; Johnson and Kim, "When Strategy Pales," 587; Bucklin, *Competition and Evolution*, 37, 113–34; "Chains Absorbing the Big Store Too," *NYT* (July 28, 1956), 24.

7. Hollander and Omura, "Chain Store Developments," table 2, 306; Bluestone et al., *The Retail Revolution*, 15.

8. Hollander and Omura, "Chain Store Developments," 306; There has long been disagreement on the definition of chains. See Jessie Vee Coles, *The Consumer-Buyer and the Market* (1938; , reprint, Arno Press, 1978), 193–94; Spector, *Category Killers*, 103–4.

9. Johnson and Kim, "When Strategy Pales," 587–78; Edward A. Filene, December 27, 1927, Address delivered before the American Economic Association, "The Present Status and Future Prospects of Chains of Department Stores," "dissimilarity" quote, 5–7, in *Prosperity and Thrift: The Coolidge Era and the Consumer Economy*, http://memory.loc.gov/cgi-bin/ampage; *The 1985 Directory of Department Stores* (Business Guides, Inc., 1984), iv, 461.

10. The summer fireworks shows began in 1958, were discontinued in 1964 after a barge exploded, and returned in 1976. Grippo, *Macy's: The Store, the Star, the Story*, 159–60; Mark D. Bauer, "Department Stores On Sale: An Antitrust Quandary," *Georgia State University Law Review* 26 (Winter 2009), 309–10; Spector, *Category Killers*, 87; For characterizations of shopping malls as "bland," see David W. Chen, "An Old River Town Debates Modern Change," *NYT* (August 2, 2001) , http://www.nytimes.com/2001/08/02/nyregion/an-old-river-town-debates-modern-change.html?pagewanted = all&src = pm. See also the first and fourth online comments for A.G. Sulzberger, "Demolition of Most of Admirals' Row is Approved," *NYT* (May 28, 2009), http://cityroom.blogs.nytimes.com/2009/05/28/demolition-of-most-of-admirals-row-is-approved/; "Slant," *Eugene Weekly*, http://www.eugeneweekly.com/2007/09/06/news.html February 12, 2012).

11. Bluestone et al., *The Retail Revolution*, 26–27; *1985 Directory of Department Stores*, iv.

12. Johnson and Kim, "When Strategy Pales" 585; Bluestone et al., *The Retail Revolution*, quotes 26–27.

13. Figures calculated from the Kwik-Index-Leading Stores listing, *1985 Directory of Department Stores* (New York: Business Guides, 1985), viii–xi, 419. According to this source, Bresee's clocked up $6 million in annual sales before it ended its department store operation in 1994.

14. Another example was the Denver Dry Goods Co. with sales of $135 million, part of Associated Dry Goods. Figures calculated from the Kwik-Index-Leading Stores listing, *1985 Directory of Department Stores*, viii–xi.

15. Wilsons, http://wilsonsdepartmentstore.com/ (accessed December 17, 2012); Anne Brockhoff, "The Gift of Downtown," *Lawrence Business Magazine* (2012 Fourth Quarter), http://www.lawrencebusinessmagazine.com/2012/12/weavers-the-gift-of-downtown/

16. On the 1950s mergers, see Johnson and Kim, "When Strategy Pales," 587; James R. Williamson, *Federal Antitrust Policy during the Kennedy-Johnson Years* (Westport, Conn.: Greenwood Press, 1995), 36. For an overview of why retailers became conglomerates, see Hollander and Omura, "Chain Store Developments," 317–18; Bill Luchansky and Jurg

Gerber, "Constructing State Autonomy: The Federal Trade Commission and the Celler-Kefauver Act," *Sociological Perspectives* 36 (Autumn, 1993), "forbidding" quote, 218, 209–10; Milton Handler and Stanley D. Robinson, "A Decade of Administration of the Celler-Kefauver Anti-merger Act," *Columbia Law Review* 61 (April 1961), 629; Bucklin, *Competition and Evolution*, 137–38; Jon Didrichsen, "The Development of Diversified and Conglomerate Firms in the United States, 1920–1970," *Business History Review* 46 (July 1, 1972), 209–10.

17. In 1967, Miller & Rhoads made its first merger with Julius Garfinckel & Co. and Brooks Brothers. Earle Dunford and George Bryson, *Under the Clock: The Story of Miller & Rhoads* (Charleston, S.C.: History Press, 2008), 97, 100; Didrichsen, "The Development of Diversified and Conglomerate Firms," 216; Robert Sobel, *The Rise and Fall of the Conglomerate Kings* (New York: Stein & Day, 1984); Bucklin, *Competition and Evolution in the Distributive Trade*, 37, 138; "Korvette Maps Purchase Of Hill's Supermarkets, Inc.," *NYT* (September 29, 1964), 62. Some slightly different figures are given in the Gamble-Skogmo entry in Hendrickson, *The Grand Emporiums*, 450–51.

18. Bauer, "Department Stores on Sale," "transaction" quote, 294; Jeff Clemons, *Rich's: A Southern Institution* (Charleston, S.C.: History Press, 2012), 169–70.

19. Spector, *Category Killers*, "retail-merger mania" quote, 89; Lichtenstein, *The Retail Revolution*, 7.

20. "The Man Who Bought Bloomingdale's," *NYT* (July 17, 1988). For a discussion of Campeau's weakness and the leveraged buyout of Allied Stores in 1986, see Bauer, "Department Stores on Sale," 277–80; Spector, *Category Killers*, 89–90.

21. Isadore Barmash, "Retail Layoffs Start to Rise as Merger Wave Subsides," *NYT* (May 23, 1998); "Robert Campeau's Special Genius," *NYT* (January 17, 1990); Spector, *Category Killers*, 89–90; Dale A. Oesterle, "The Rise and Fall of Street Sweep Takeovers," "takeover" quote, 202, 203, 228. See also Patrick A. Gaughan, *Mergers, Acquisitions, and Corporate Restructurings*, 4th ed. (Hoboken, N.J.: John Wiley & Sons, 2007), 259–60.

22. Bauer, "Department Stores on Sale," 278–82; Earle Dunford and George Bryson, *Under the Clock*, 110.

23. Bauer, "Department Stores on Sale," 278–82. Unlike Dayton-Hudson, which had Target, Federated lost the ability to be a diversified retailer in multiple retail formats. Johnson and Kim, "When Strategy Pales," 588.

24. Sanger-Harris Collection, Texas/Dallas History & Archives, Dallas Public Library, http://www.lib.utexas.edu/taro/dalpub/08318/dpub-08318p1.html#bioghist (accessed December 20, 2012); Bauer, "Department Stores on Sale," 284, 318; Johnson and Kim, "When Strategy Pales," 588.

25. "The May Department Stores Company Business Information, Profile, and History," *Company History*, http://companies.jrank.org/pages/4260/May-Department-Stores -Company.html (accessed December 20, 2012). Historic nameplates did not mean independent ownership, however. For example, Sibley, Lindsay and Curr in Rochester had been bought up by Associated Dry Goods in 1957. Elvins, *Sales and Celebrations*, 169.

26. Hollander and Omura, "Chain Store Developments," 313; Doubman and Whitaker, *The Organization and Operation of Department Stores*, 211, 155. In 1996, May acquired another Philadelphia institution, the family-owned Strawbridge & Clothier. It

renamed the store Macy's (and shuttered the historic downtown Philadelphia Strawbridge & Clothier store on Market Street). Bauer, "Department Stores on Sale," 317–18.
Description based on the author's visit to the Market Street Macy's in Philadelphia, 2012.

27. "The Golden Rule, the City's Oldest Department Store Closes after 102 Years,"
Pharos-Tribune, Logansport, Indiana (May 30, 1984), 10; "McCurdy's Department Store
Closes in Downtown Ithaca," *Syracuse Herald-Journal* (December 30, 1991), 32; "Customers Lament Loss of Store," *Syracuse Herald-Journal* (October 19, 1994), A8. In Watertown,
New York, Empsall's department store closed after losing its line of credit. "Landmark
Department Store Closes," *Syracuse Herald-Journal* (July 12, 1993), B2; Bresee's stopped
operating as a department store in 1994, though kept its appliance operation going for
years after ; "Department Store Closes after 30 Years," *Syracuse Herald American*, July
21, 1991, D4. The Jerry Cox department store closure is documented in "127-Year-Old
Department Store Closes," *Aiken (S.C.) Standard* (November 7, 1992), 8B. As of August
2012, Wilson's department store in Greenfield, Massachusetts, remains.

28. Spector, *Category Killers*, 90–91.

29. Macy's problems followed the turmoil created by its bidding war with Campeau
for Federated. Barmash, "Retail Layoffs Start to Rise as Merger Wave Subsides," NYT (May
23, 1998); Stephanie Strom, "Company News: Macy's Executives Agree to Merger with
Federated," NYT (July 14, 1994); Bauer, "Department Stores on Sale," 267–77.

30. Strom, "Company News: Macy's Executives Agree to Merger with Federated." Ste-
phanie Strom, "Federated to Close Six Stores in Merger with Macy's," NYT (September 20,
1994); "Merger Plan Set For Stores," NYT (September 21, 1994); Kenneth Gilpin,
"Federated-Macy Marriage Advanced," NYT (September 9, 1994); "FTC Ends Inquiry into
Macy Deal," NYT (August 20, 1994); "Store Closings in Merger Seen as an Unwelcome
Change," NYT (September 21, 1994), "open competition" and "virtual lock" quotes;
"Hendrickson, *The Grand Emporiums*, 386–91; Leslie Kaufman, "Federated to Close Sterns
and Rename or Shut Stores," NYT (February 9, 2001).

31. "Federated Department Stores, Inc., History," *Funding Universe*, http://www.fund
inguniverse.com/company-histories/federated-department-stores-inc-history/ (accessed
August 24, 2012).

32. Stephanie Strom," Company News: Macy's Executives Agree to Merger with
Federated."

33. Bauer, "Department Stores on Sale," 255–56; "Attention Shoppers: Great Deals
in Retail Mergers," Knowledge@Wharton, March 30, 2005, "size matters" quote, http://
knowledge.wharton.upenn.edu/article.cfm?articleid = 1158; Lichtenstein, *The Retail Revolution*, 8.

34. Howard, "Department Store Advertising in Newspapers, Radio, and Television,"
61–85; "Attention Shoppers: Great Deals in Retail Mergers," Knowledge@Wharton (March
30, 2005).

35. McNair and May, *The American Department Store*, 8; Hendrickson, *The Grand
Emporiums*, 257–58; Bluestone et al., *The Retail Revolution*, 23; Leach, *Land of Desire*, 283.

36. "FTC Issues Statement on Closure of Federated/May Investigation," August 30,
2005, Federal Trade Commission website, http://www.ftc.gov/news-events/press-releases/
2005/08/ftc-issues-statement-closure-federatedmay-investigation. See also File No. 0510111,
"Proposed Acquisition by Federated Department Stores, Inc. of The May Department

Stores Company," Federal Trade Commission website, http://www.ftc.gov/enforcement/cases-proceedings/closing-letters/proposed-acquisition-federated-department-stores-inc; Grippo, *Macy's: The Store, the Star, the Story*, quote, 180; "Executive Management Team Bios," *Macy's Inc.* website, https://www.macysinc.com/press-room/executive-management-team/default.aspx (accessed June 23, 2014).

37. "NRF Turns 100," *Stores* (February 2011); Bob Verdiseo, "Thanks for the Memories," *DSN Retailing Today* (December 16, 2002), "mix with a discounter" quote, 4; Bara Vaida, "Retail Marriage Thwarted at the Altar," *National Journal* (August 7, 2009). For a list of RILA members, see "In Case You Missed It: RILA Members Listed among Top EPA Green Power Purchasers" (February 8, 2011) http://www.rila.org/news/topnews/Pages/InCaseYouMissedItRILAMembersListedAmongEPATop50GreenPowerPurchasers.aspx. For Target's membership, see "Press Release" (June 13, 2012) http://www.nationalcenter.org/PR-Target_061312.html. Nelson Lichtenstein describes RILA as representing "the low-wage, nonunion big-box wing of the retail trade," with unionized supermarket chains being "conspicuously absent." Lichtenstein, *The Retail Revolution*, 242. Yet Safeway, which he gives as an example, was in fact a RILA member. Costco became a member in 2007. See "RILA Members Are America's Most Successful Retailers" (December 12, 2007), http://www.rila.org/news/topnews/Pages/RILAMembersAreAmerica%27sMostSuccessfulRetailers.aspx. Moreover, unionized supermarket chains like Costco, Safeway, and Kroger attended RILA conferences. See "Past Attendees," Retail Supply Chain Conference 2013, http://www.rila.org/events/conferences/logistics/Pages/PastAttendees.aspx (accessed August 21, 2012). My point is not to deflect criticism away from RILA, but rather to reveal the even greater influence of this trade group.

38. Editors to Jo A. Hartsoe, Library, Georgia State University, *Retail Directions* 127 (April/May 1973), 8; Donna Lipson, Account Executive, Lang, Fisher & Stashower Advertising to Editor and Editor response to Donna Lipson, Account Executive, *Retail Directions* 127 (April/May 1973), "big mistake" and "important factors" quotes, 8.

39. F. P. Warner, Fal Warner Associates, Cleveland, Ohio to editors, *Retail Directions* (February/March 1973), 6; Similarly, San Francisco's Magnin's (distinct from the same city's I. Magnin's) had been sold to the conglomerate Ampac, Inc., in 1969, though its fifty-one stores continued to operate under the original nameplate. And of course, even before their big mergers, Macy's and Federated were among the top department store chains, with $4.9 and $1.6 billion in sales respectively by the end of the 1970s. For snapshot histories of individual department store companies, see Hendrickson, *The Grand Emporiums*, 166–67, 259–60, 423, 443–45.

40. See *Operating Results of Self-Service Discount Department Stores* (Cornell University). The reports began in 1963, before the incorporation of the mass retailing institute in 1969.

41. "What's Ahead for NMRI," *Discount Merchandiser* 27 (1987), 38, 40, 46.

42. *1985 Directory of Department Stores*, "behalf of large chains" and "government representation" quotes, vi; "Paid Memorial: James Rennick Williams," *NYT* (April 7, 2002), 35; "ARF, NRMA Merger Gets Final Approval," *Footwear News* (March 12, 1990), http://www.highbeam.com/doc/1G1-8808991.html; Sparks, "Locally Owned and Operated," 211; "Retailers Voice," *Time* (April 29, 1935), 72; "Our Mission," *National Retail Federation*, https://nrf.com/who-we-are/our-mission (Accessed October 11, 2014); "National Retail

Federation CEO Tracy Mullin Retires," *USA Today* (May 7, 2010), http://www.usatoday .com/money/industries/retail/2010-05-07-retailretire07_ST_N.htm; Kevin Bogardus, "Coup for Retail lobby as Wal-Mart Joins National Retail Federation," *The Hill* (April 10, 2013), http://thehill.com/business-a-lobbying/292847-wal-mart-joins-national-retail-federation; Tom Gara, "Finally, a United Front for Retail in Washington Battles," *Wall Street Journal* (April 10, 2013), http://blogs.wsj.com/corporate-intelligence/2013/04/10/finally-a-united -front-for-retail-in-washingtons-battles/

43. Lichtenstein, *The Retail Revolution*, 236, 242, 248–49; "Retail Groups Plan Merger to Boost Lobbying Efforts," *Washington Post* (April 22, 2009), http://www.washingtonpost .com/wp-dyn/content/article/2009/04/21/AR2009042103986.html.

44. "NRF 2009 Keynote," http://www.youtube.com/watch?v = eVdIxn-AHE8 (accessed October 11,2014); Andrew Joseph, "Wal-Mart's Thorne Named SVP at NRF," *National Journal* (April 24, 2012) http://influencealley.nationaljournal.com/2012/04/ thorne-named-svp-at-nrf.php; "National Retail Federation CEO Tracy Mullin Retires," *USA Today*; Wal-Mart supported President Obama's push to require large employers to provide health insurance for employees, while the NRF attacked it. "NRF Asks Members to Oppose Wal-Mart on Healthcare," Reuters.com (July 13, 2009), http://www.reuters.com/ article/2009/07/13/us-mf-walmart-idU3TRE56C4GP20090713; Kevin Bogardus, "Coup for Retail lobby as Wal-Mart Joins National Retail Federation," *The Hill* (April 10, 2013), http://thehill.com/business-a-lobbying/292847-wal-mart-joins-national-retail-federation; "Retail Groups Plan Merger to Boost Lobbying Efforts,"; Paul Demery, "Trade Groups NRF And RILA Call Off Planned Merger," *Internet Retailer* (June 25, 2009), http://www.in ternetretailer.com/2009/06/25/trade-groups-nrf-and-rila-call-off-planned-merger; "National Retail Groups Decide to Nix Merger," *Washington Post* (June 25, 2009).

EPILOGUE

1. Mark Bauer, "Department Stores on Sale: An Antitrust Quandary," *Georgia State Law Review* 26 (Winter 2009), 273.

2. Bluestone et al., *Retail Revolution*, 1; "A Story of Forty Years," MDSC; on Bresee's department store's use of nostalgia in the late 1940s, see Howard, "'The Biggest Small-Town Store in America'"; "Big Business Comes to Small Towns," circa 1945, news clipping, Case 13, RC; for a broader discussion of nostalgia, see Peter Fritzsche, "Specters of History: On Nostalgia, Exile, and Modernity," *American Historical Review* 106, no. 5 (2001), 1587–618.

3. Isenberg rightly ties this cultural response to store closings to the civic meanings attached to downtown. Isenberg, *Downtown America*, 4–5. She documents the uses of nostalgia in the 1970s in urban development. This is distinct from nostalgic accounts of store closures, however, which for the most part do not emerge until the 1980s with the massive loss of local store nameplates.

4. Adam Tschorn,"Shopping Malls Greatest Movie Moments," *Los Angeles Times* (November 20, 2011), http://articles.latimes.com/2011/nov/20/image/la-ig-malls-in -movies-20111120.

5. "Higbee's," A Christmas Story House & Museum website, http://www.achristmas storyhouse.com/index.php/filming-locations/higbees/ (accessed January 3, 2013).

6. *A Christmas Story* (1983, directed by Bob Clark); Jean Shepherd, *In God We Trust, All Others Pay Cash* (1966; New York: Broadway Books, 2000). Interestingly, the 1947 Christmas classic *Miracle on 34th Street* was remade in 1994, but without Macy's and Gimbels at its center. Macy's, which has milked the promotional aspects of the original film, refused permission to use its name in the remake. And Gimbels, the historical archrival of Macy's, was out of business by then.

7. Bob Cox, "Memories of King's Department Store in Johnson City," *Johnson City Press* (October 31, 2011), http://www.johnsoncitypress.com/News/article.php?id = 95410.

8. "127 Year Old Department Store Closes," *Aiken (S.C.) Standard* (November 7, 1992), 8B, http://newspaperarchive.com/us/south-carolina/aiken/aiken-standard/1992/11 -07/page-17.

9. Peter Drucker, "Trading Places," *National Interest* (March 1, 2005); "Zahn department store, Racine,Wisconsin," *Stores Forever: A Tribute to Stores Past and Present* (August 23, 2008), http://storesforever.blogspot.com/2008/08/zahns-department-store-racine-wi -update.html; On "oldtimers," see "Pieces of the Past: Nostalgia Bubbles Up as a New Year Begins," *Ithacajournal.com* (January 1, 2010); "Death of Shepard's Department Store," *Granite in My Blood* (August 12, 2008), http://granite-in-my-blood.blogspot.com/2008/08/ shepards-department-store-providence-ri.html.

10. "Petula Clark—Downtown (1965)" YouTube June 27, 2009, Post by log05mus http://www.youtube.com/watch?v = f-oQ5KwRSMU (accessed November 16, 2011), now defunct; "Ohio Firm Wants to Buy L. S. Good," *Owosso (Mich.) Argus-Press* (September 27, 1980), 15.

11. For example, see Web site of Richard Layman, an urban/commercial district revitalization and transportation/mobility advocate and consultant based in Washington, D.C. http://urbanplacesandspaces.blogspot.com/ (accessed November 5, 2010), now defunct; Dan Reed, "How to Save a Dying Mall," *Just Up the Pike* (November 2, 2006), http:// www.justupthepike.com/search?q = department + store.

12. "Field's is Chicago" quote in "Marshall Field's fans in Chicago Launch Macy's boycott," September 9, 2006, http://www.youtube.com/watch?v = Fw16mZPP3So (accessed November 5, 2010), now defunct. YouTube has dozens of uploaded videos on the store, many receiving thousands of hits; Post 1 and 3 by BeckyPOC, Post 2 by tpot, "Marshall Field's Commercial-White Christmas," YouTube, http://www.youtube.com/watch?v = 1 NORB7KOiqU (accessed January 5, 2011). See also the Marshall Field's dedicated Web site, http://www.fieldsfanschicago.org/blog/ (Accessed October 13, 2014).

13. William Severini Kowinski, *The Malling of America: An Inside Look at the Great Consumer Paradise* (New York: William Morrow, 1985); for an example of nostalgia that celebrates the aesthetics of lost local department stores, see Paula Marantz Cohen, "Department Store Elegy," *The Smart Set* (November 20, 2007), http://www.thesmartset.com/article/article11200701.aspx. On the department store's relationship to the middle class, see Lee Siegel, "The Department Store's Magic, Dispelled by Online Shopping," *NYT* (November 23, 2012). Popular Web sites documenting shopping center history and the decline of old malls have also emerged. For example, see deadmalls.com and labelscar.com. See also lileks.com.

14. Larry Henderson, 2004, "corporate blandness" quote, I. Magnin thread, http:// www.greenspun.com/bboard/q-and-a-fetch-msg.tcl?msg_id = 00BOCc (accessed October

25, 2010); a typical critique of the 2006 merger was that it led to "homogenization and commodification." For example, see "Brands, the Honeymoon's Over," posting (December 24, 2006), http://www.truetalkblog.com/truetalk/brands/. For a "fan site" for Marshall Field's, see http://www.darrid.com/ (accessed November 5, 2010), now defunct. Also, see "Chicagoans Love Marshall Field's," *Kizer and Bender's Retail Adventures* (November 2, 2007), http://www.retailadventuresblog.com/2007/11/photos-of-fields-rally-c-timothy-state .html; "Customers Lament Loss of Store," *Syracuse Herald-Journal* (October 19, 1994), A8.

15. Crescent quote, Dave: September 4, 2010, "Remembering Great American Department Stores," http://www.dshistory.com/comments.html (Accessed September 14, 1010); "127-Year-Old Department Store Closes," *Aiken (S.C.) Standard* (November 7, 1992), 8B. Competition, overstoring, the homogenization of the department store, and service, were four reasons given for the decline in department store performance during this period. See M. Dotson and Wesley E. Patton, "Consumer Perceptions of Department Store Service: A Lesson for Retailers," *Journal of Services Marketing* 6 (1992), 15–28; "Chicago Christmas: Marshall Field's Original Frango Mints: A Holiday Tradition Missed by Many," *Huffington Post* (December 23, 2012), http://www.huffingtonpost.com/2012/12/23/chicago-christmas -marshal_n_2356295.html.

16. A Marshall Field's fan site included a YouTube video clip of a news program on ABC titled "End of an Era" from the 2006 renaming of Marshall Field's and other stores as Macy's. The broadcaster ended the program with the words: "Marshall Field's, Filene's, Strawbridge, rest in peace." The Web site also included gravestone imagery, with the dates of Marshall Field's given as 1852–2006. See http://www.darrid.com/ (accessed Nov. 5, 2010.), now defunct; "Department Store Closes," *Ottawa (Kan.) Herald* (December 26, 1998), 1; "Customers Lament Loss of Store." Newman's department store, founded in 1868, closed when it lost the lease on its building in Emporia, Kansas. "Department Store Closes," 1; Lannis Waters, Jennifer Podis, Mark Edelson,"A Last Look at the Palm Beach Mall," *Palm Beach Post* (January 17, 2013), http://clikhear.palmbeachpost.com/2013/south -florida/palm-beach-county/the-palm-beach-mall-a-last-look-at-what-remains-before-the -fall/.

17. "Customers Lament Loss of Store"; "FTC Issues Statement on Closure of Federated/May Investigation," August 30, 2005, Federal Trade Commission website, http:// www.ftc.gov/news-events/press-releases/2005/08/ftc-issues-statement-closure-federated may-investigation; Realguy440, YouTube post, "Elevator at Old Higbee's Dept. Store Cleveland," http://www.youtube.com/watch?v=MiMYc9Ixgc8 (accessed January 5, 2011).

18. "Instead of Boycotting, Buy Locally," *Oneonta Daily Star* (November 26, 2013); "Front-Door Farmers Market Hits the Web," *Oneonta Daily Star* (May 4, 2013); Amy Cortese, "A Town Creates Its Own Department Store," *NYT* (November 12, 2011); Hess, *Localist Movements in a Global Economy*; Jake Palmateer, "Meeting Looks at Future of Ex-Bresee's Complex," *Oneonta Daily Star* (January 17, 2008); "Local Nostalgia Fans, Unite! Hess's Makes Return," *Morning Call* (November 24, 2008); *Wal-Mart: The High Cost of Low Prices* (2005, directed by Robert Greenwald).

INDEX

ACKNOWLEDGMENTS

I N the mid-1980s, I worked at the Hudson's Bay department store in downtown Vancouver, British Columbia. The salesclerk position—in their estate wine department and right next to the candy counter—was quite enjoyable. Several years later, a job in women's fashions in San Francisco's downtown Emporium department store—without wine—was not so pleasant. In this now defunct department store, I learned a lot about the competitive pressures of sales and the challenges of customer relations. However, it was not until I read the late Susan Porter Benson's wonderful social and cultural history of the department store, *Counter Cultures*, in graduate school that retail became a scholarly interest. I would like to acknowledge the influence of Professor Porter Benson's book, and though she did not know me, she responded graciously to my e-mails and offered generous advice and early encouragement of this book.

My approach to the subject of department stores took me beyond the social and cultural history of my academic training. To help me understand the piles of ledgers, profit and loss statements, and operating results I gathered in archives around the country I turned to others who had talents in those areas. Thanks go to my colleagues in our Business Administration Department at Hartwick, Penny Wightman and Steve Kolenda. I would also like to thank economics professor Carlena Cochi Ficano, sociologist Cecelia Walsh-Russo, and my colleagues in the History Department: Sean Kelley, Cherilyn Lacy, Mieko Nishida, Edythe Ann Quinn, and Peter Wallace. I have been lucky to have the assistance of several excellent librarians and library staff. Special thanks to Rebekah Ambrose-Dalton, Dawn Baker, and Peter Rieseler.

Funding for this research came from my institution. Generous Hartwick College Faculty Research Grants between 2007 and 2010 supported research travel for this project. Funding for student research assistance was also provided. In that capacity, I would like to thank Anna Thompson, now a museum professional, for her excellent work for me while a history major at Hartwick College. A Winifred Wandersee Scholar-in-Residence Award from Hartwick for 2009–2010 provided additional funding as well as a much needed teaching load reduction that enabled me to write. Thanks also to the Nebraska State Historical Society in Lincoln for a 2007–2008 travel grant. I also thank the journal *Enterprise & Society* and its editors for permission to reprint portions of "'The Biggest Small-Town Store in America': A Case Study of the Independent Retailer, 1900–1990s" (September 2008).

In Oneonta, I am grateful to have had the opportunity to meet Marc and Phil Bresee of Bresee's Department Store. Marc Bresee provided the seed of primary research that began this book. He generously opened his home archive in his basement, allowing me to peruse his family store's records and photos, which he also graciously allowed me to reproduce in this volume. I also benefited from an early interview with him and his father, Phil Bresee, as well as from e-mail correspondence in which he shared information about his family store and about the profession of merchandising in general. As I presented my research on their Oneonta department store to historical societies in the area, I benefited from the shared memories of people in the community who had worked and shopped there. Thanks to the Greater Oneonta Historical Society, the Davenport Historical Society, and the Meredith Historical Society in New York State for hosting these talks. Thanks also to the late Muriel Ross and the late Georgia Blakeslee of Oneonta, who allowed me to interview them about their experiences working at Bresee's Department Store. I have also benefited from my association with historians at SUNY-Oneonta. In particular, I am grateful for the suggestions and support offered there by my friend historian Matthew Hendley. Thanks also to reference librarian Michelle Hendley for her support and friendship. And thanks to Beth Ashbaugh for investigating department stores in Japan for me and to Erin Kelley for doing the same in France. And thank you to all the people who shared stories about the department stores they knew and loved, most of which are now defunct.

I have benefited from comments and critiques by several excellent scholars, including Sarah Elvins, Andrew Godley, Jennifer Goloboy, and

Michael Zakim. Compatriots from the Business History Conference over the years have also contributed in different ways. I would like to thank Regina Blaszczyk, Stephanie Dyer, Roger Horowitz, and Howard Stanger for their suggestions and advice. In addition, I would like to thank Dan Horowitz and Helen Lefkowitz Horowitz, who shared their knowledge and experiences generously.

Special gratitude goes to Pamela Walker Laird and Mark Rose, who have supported my career development in significant ways over the years. Thanks to Professor Rose for his work on my behalf over the years. Thanks to Professor Laird especially for her editorial direction and encouragement. I value their friendship and warm collegiality as much as I am thankful for the intellectual direction they have provided for this book. And I would like to express my appreciation of editor Bob Lockhart at the University of Pennsylvania Press, who pushed me to do more. His editorial advice, as with my first book on the wedding industry, was invaluable. At Penn Press I would also like to thank the two anonymous reviewers for their contribution.

My deepest gratitude goes to my family. I would like to thank my parents, Barbara Howard and the late David Howard, for their contributions to this book. Over the years my mother has provided me with newspaper clippings on department store mergers and closures, keeping me abreast of retailing in Canada. My father and mother both traveled to an archive in Washington State where they photocopied material for me. Thanks also to my sisters, Valerie and Laurie, and their families. In terms of family support, I am also lucky to have a historian for a husband. Sean Kelley helped gather material from distant archives, read several drafts, and talked over the subject with me, for many years now. He has made this a better book than it would have been without him. And finally, I would like to acknowledge my daughter, Kathleen, who shares my love of department stores and at one time, when she was six, hoped to work at Macy's.